REMEMBERING DIXIE

REMEMBERING DIXIE

THE BATTLE TO CONTROL HISTORICAL
MEMORY IN NATCHEZ, MISSISSIPPI,
1865–1941

SUSAN T. FALCK

UNIVERSITY PRESS OF MISSISSIPPI / JACKSON

The University Press of Mississippi is the scholarly publishing agency of
the Mississippi Institutions of Higher Learning: Alcorn State University,
Delta State University, Jackson State University, Mississippi State University,
Mississippi University for Women, Mississippi Valley State University,
University of Mississippi, and University of Southern Mississippi.

www.upress.state.ms.us

Designed by Peter D. Halverson

The University Press of Mississippi is a member of
the Association of University Presses.

Copyright © 2019 by University Press of Mississippi
All rights reserved

First printing 2019
∞

Library of Congress Cataloging-in-Publication Data

Names: Falck, Susan T., author.
Title: Remembering Dixie : the battle to control historical memory in
Natchez, Mississippi, 1865–1941 / Susan T. Falck.
Description: Jackson : University Press of Mississippi, [2019] | "First
printing 2019." | Includes bibliographical references and index.
Identifiers: LCCN 2019012208 (print) | LCCN 2019022331 (ebook) | ISBN
9781496824400 (hardcover : alk. paper) | ISBN 9781496824417 (pbk. : alk.
paper)
Subjects: LCSH: African Americans—Mississippi—Natchez—History. | Natchez
(Miss.)—History. | Natchez (Miss.)—History—Civil War, 1861–1865. |
Natchez (Miss.)—Social life and customs. | Natchez (Miss.)—Social
conditions. | Natchez (Miss.)—Economic conditions. | Natchez
(Miss.)—Race relations.
Classification: LCC F349.N2 F35 2019 (print) | LCC F349.N2 (ebook) | DDC
976.2/26—dc23
LC record available at https://lccn.loc.gov/2019012208
LC ebook record available at https://lccn.loc.gov/2019022331

British Library Cataloging-in-Publication Data available

To Barry, Ryan, and Molly, with love

CONTENTS

ACKNOWLEDGMENTS - IX -

INTRODUCTION
Natchez Pilgrimages - 3 -

CHAPTER ONE
Forging New Identities in a World Gone Mad - 17 -

CHAPTER TWO
Memory Making on Parade
African American Historical Identity in Reconstruction-Era Natchez - 48 -

CHAPTER THREE
"A Taste for Associations"
Reconstructing White Identities in Postwar Natchez - 73 -

CHAPTER FOUR
"Picture Makers"
Black and White Historical Memory in Postbellum Natchez - 105 -

CHAPTER FIVE
Selling Historic Natchez to Depression-Era Pilgrims - 153 -

CHAPTER SIX
The Battle of the Hoopskirts
The Ladies Go to Court - 211 -

EPILOGUE
Natchez Today
Where More Than the Old South Still Lives - 225 -

Contents

GUIDE TO HISTORIC NATCHEZ HOMES - 253 -

NOTES - 284 -

BIBLIOGRAPHY - 325 -

INDEX - 349 -

ACKNOWLEDGMENTS

I HAVE ACCUMULATED MANY DEBTS OF GRATITUDE IN THE RESEARCH AND writing of this book. It is a pleasure to have the opportunity to formally thank those who intellectually mentored and befriended me on my pilgrimage to research and write about the captivating history of Natchez, Mississippi. Much of the credit for this book goes to historian Ronald L. F. Davis, whom I met more than twenty years ago at California State University, Northridge. Sitting in Ron's wonderfully cluttered office, I listened as he told me about a place called Natchez and his Natchez Courthouse Records Project (NCRP), which was dedicated to rescuing, preserving, and processing the town's exceptional collection of historical legal records. During my first trip to Natchez as a NCRP archival volunteer, I became intrigued with the Natchez Garden Club, founded in the early 1930s by a group of history-loving matrons determined to save their town's eroding collection of antebellum mansions. As my research interests developed first as a conference paper and eventually a book manuscript, Ron coached me every step of the way. I am deeply grateful for his many suggestions, historical insights, wicked sense of humor, and warm friendship.

Along my pilgrimage through Natchez history, I met many wonderful and extraordinary people who made my journey intellectually and spiritually fulfilling, fun, and the adventure of a lifetime. Through the Natchez Courthouse Records Project, I worked alongside a talented band of scholars affiliated with Cal State University, Northridge, who were as eager to make sense of Natchez's past as I was and knew how to have a good time while doing so. As we poured over courthouse records and shared our research finds, friendships blossomed as we connected the dots of Natchez's past and encouraged each other's research passions. I am indebted to the following individuals, many of whose scholarly works are cited in this book: Aaron Anderson, Justin Behrend, Darcy Bieber, Joyce Broussard, Janet Bruce, Rebecca Dresser, Cai Hamilton, Wendy Machlovitz, Sheryl Nomelli, Cynthia Parker,

Michael Ward, and Rosanne Welch. The friendships that developed among my gal pals were one of the best perks of my Natchez experience. You all are amazing, wise women, and your humor, wit, and insights kept me going with this project. I owe special gratitude to Cynthia Parker for allowing me to spend several weeks in her Natchez home one summer. While we sipped cold ice teas on those hot, muggy evenings, Cindy shared her fabulous collection of letters written by the Quitman sisters of Monmouth, which she used for her study of the estate's black residents in the Reconstruction era. These same letters gave me a clearer image of how the war and its aftermath impacted the once privileged and pampered world of elite white Natchez women. I am equally grateful to Dan and Jan Shiells for generously opening their beautifully restored Victorian Natchez home to me on my final research trip to wrap up this project. Enjoying the home's library and luxurious soaks in a claw-foot tub after long days of research and interviews, I too came to know the pleasures of feeling pampered.

I am extremely appreciative of the intellectual guidance I received from the University of California, Santa Barbara, and Cal State University, Northridge. UCSB cultural historian Lisa Jacobson pushed me to discover additional historical actors who helped shape the cultural image of Natchez during the postwar period as well as those who challenged it. Historians Anne Plane and Randy Bergstrom helped me to more fully appreciate how my research fit within the realm of public history. I am deeply appreciative of the many excellent suggestions these individuals and other UCSB colleagues made on this book. Merri Ovnick of Cal State University, Northridge, was especially kind and supportive throughout the duration of this project. Both CSUN and UCSB were extremely generous in providing funding that made frequent research trips to Mississippi and other archives possible. A scholarship awarded by the San Francisco chapter of the Colonial Dames during the final stage of this project was also greatly appreciated.

I am thankful to the helpful guidance and encouragement I received from the team at University Press of Mississippi, specifically Editorial Director Craig Gill, his assistant Emily Bandy, and copyeditor Anne Stascavage, whose close eye for detail and consistency notably improved the final manuscript. The critical reading provided by Ron Davis and Susan Tucker, author and retired curator of the Newcomb Archives at Tulane University, resulted in many excellent suggestions that enhanced this project. This book relied on the generous help of many archivists from various southern archives. I am particularly appreciative of Jennifer Mitchell and Mark Martin from Louisiana State University Special Collections, who patiently helped me track down many of the photos that appear in this book. Likewise, thank you to Heather Pilcher, collections coordinator of University of Louisiana, Monroe, for her quick response to my requests for photos of Natchez homes and Mary Britton Conner. Thank you to Anne Webster, retired archivist of the Mississippi Department of Archives and History, and her staff for helping me locate materials in the early stages of this research.

This project would not have been possible without the generous assistance of many Natchezians, who graciously shared their historic recollections and personally held archival materials, helping me to understand the complicated jigsaw puzzle of Natchez's past. I owe special thanks to Mimi Miller, retired director of the Historic Natchez Foundation, who assisted me with her wealth of knowledge on Natchez history and its historic homes. Mimi never hesitated to share her sources and research findings, which helped to strengthen my own research efforts. The specific contributions of Kathie Blankenstein and her daughter Chesney Blankenstein Doyle, Ser Sesh Ab Heter-Clifford Boxley as well as the late Alma Carpenter and Dr. Thomas Gandy are acknowledged in greater detail in the introduction. I want to also thank a handful of the many other Natchez history lovers and professionals who assisted and befriended me: Beth Boggess, Kathleen Bond, Diane Bunch, Marsha Colson, Debbie Cosey, Jennifer Ogden Combs, Anne MacNeil, Helen Moss Smith, and Darrell White, among others. I enjoyed every minute I spent listening to your stories, insights, and often personal memories of Natchez's past. I will always regard Natchez as my home away from home thanks to the graciousness and kindness of the Natchez folks I encountered.

Finally, I wish to acknowledge the loving support of my family as I spent far longer than I ever imagined on this project. My husband, Barry, has been an incredibly kind and nurturing partner and was always willing to listen as I worked to sort through the complexities of telling this story. I frequently relied on his wisdom and writing strengths throughout, and when the going got tough, he gently but persistently nudged me forward with his humor and love. I also am thankful for my children, Ryan and Molly, who spent a good part of their lives hearing about the people and history of Natchez. Taking my family to Natchez on a Christmas holiday road trip to see the place for themselves and later bringing my daughter along on a summer Courthouse Records archival trip are especially satisfying memories.

My love for history and particularly southern history was influenced by a group of strong, nurturing women. I owe a debt of gratitude to my late maternal grandmother Grovie Knight Baker and her sisters Maxine Knight and Lou Knight Stark who passionately loved their native South and told me our family's stories when I was young. Thanks to my parents, Joyce and Stan Thorsten, I along with my siblings, Jim and Kim, frequently were loaded into the back seat, traveling to many southern historical sites I insisted on seeing. Those visits and the stories gathered along the way planted a seed that eventually grew into this book. Thank you all for your loving support and being part of my pilgrimage through southern history. This was a transformative, rewarding journey and I am forever grateful.

MAY 2019

REMEMBERING DIXIE

INTRODUCTION

NATCHEZ PILGRIMAGES

NEARLY SEVENTY YEARS AFTER THE CIVIL WAR, NATCHEZ, MISSISSIPPI, SOLD itself to Depression-era tourists as a place "Where the Old South Still Lives." Carloads of tourists from thirty-seven states flocked to view the town's decaying antebellum mansions, hoopskirted hostesses, and a pageant saturated in sentimental Lost Cause imagery. Organized by the town's female garden club, the Natchez Pilgrimage created a popular culture experience that appealed to the tastes of 1930s tourists. All that was missing was Scarlett O'Hara herself. The Pilgrimage continues to draw audiences eager to see and experience the Old South, ringing up a substantial portion of the more than $110 million in annual tourism revenues for the oldest city on the Mississippi River.[1]

Natchez native Katherine Grafton Miller, credited with founding the Pilgrimage, spoke for many of her garden club peers when she recalled the beginnings of her devotion to the heritage tourism venture. "I at last had found that which I had been seeking all my life—a worthwhile interest, in which I could turn a seemingly fantastic imagination to good account," she wrote in a Natchez guidebook she published in 1938.[2]

The dreamy-eyed but resolute Miller was but one of many Natchezians—before and after her time—who put their interests and imaginations to work in remembering the past in ways that best served their social and cultural needs. Such work encompassed both physical and metaphorical pilgrimages and is reminiscent of a longstanding pilgrimage culture throughout much of the world. The term "pilgrim," originating in Latin and dating to the early years of the Christian Church (but practiced in all faith traditions) is defined as a foreigner, a stranger, someone on a journey to some sacred place as an act of devotion. Certainly all of us who seek to understand the past are pilgrims ourselves, foreigners on a complex journey in a strange land. In the case of Miller and her garden club cohorts, their pilgrimage was a passionate quest to remember a neatly packaged white selective telling of the past that honored the longstanding moonlight and magnolias version of the Old

South narrative, while erasing dark, troubling memories of slavery. Theirs was both a spiritual and secular journey in crafting a pilgrimage experience for Natchez tourists.[3]

In *Remembering Dixie*, I argue that the Natchez Pilgrimage was but one of many secular and spiritual pilgrimages undertaken since the Civil War by all kinds of people who resided there—newly freed slaves, elite free blacks, former slaveholders, white middle-class men and women, many of whom were too young to have personally experienced the war, yet strived to have a say in how their town's antebellum past would be remembered and commemorated. This book recounts and analyzes these pilgrimages in an effort to understand what it meant to be southern in one community in the tumultuous years following a devastating wartime defeat, and how these pilgrims fought to shape a memory of the past that advanced their personal and collective agendas. In short, how did the South's at times alluring yet troubling past continue to define and influence how the region's history would be remembered by white as well as black southerners?

This book traces the evolution and contestation of historical memory and traditions within an iconic southern community that has long prided itself on representing the romanticized values of the Old South and its Lost Cause, a myth created by staunch southern nationalists to deal with the psychological and emotional trauma of losing a long and bloody war. The cult of the Lost Cause served as the ideological underpinnings for much of the racialized popular culture that emerged above and below the Mason Dixon line in the late nineteenth and early twentieth centuries. Lost Cause ideology romanticized slavery, attributed the loss of the war to the North's greater material resources, and glorified the valor of both Confederate and Union troops, and the bravery of southern women tending the home front. Moreover, the ideology stated that slavery was not a cause of the war, nor were southerners responsible for the "peculiar institution," which was deemed a natural phenomenon beyond human control. Emphasizing that neither the North nor South was to blame for the war, the Lost Cause myth became increasingly nostalgic over time. The sentimental stories of "Plantation School" writers, such as Thomas Nelson Page and Joel Chandler Harris, helped spread the myth by promoting white supremacy in fictional tales of benevolent masters and faithful slaves. By the 1890s the Lost Cause myth transformed itself into a story of national reunion on southern terms. Aging Union and Confederate veterans regularly reunited on former battlefields toasting one another and their shared sense of national pride and reconciliation.[4]

Initially conceived to memorialize the Confederate dead shortly after the war's end, by the 1870s the Lost Cause movement had transformed itself to revitalize Confederate nationalism and pride through patriotic organizations including the United Confederate Veterans and the United Daughters of the Confederacy. By 1915, having succeeded in its efforts to restore southern honor and enjoying the fruits of reunification between North and South, the mood of the Lost Cause shifted from mournful to more triumphant, celebrating antebellum southern culture—its gardens, grand homes, and legendary hospitality—instead of war and the devastation that followed. Rather than organizing somber rituals to commemorate fallen veterans at cemeteries, Lost Cause leaders increasingly staged upbeat parades and festive evening balls.[5]

Historian David Blight in his pathbreaking work *Race and Reunion* contends that the development and expression of Lost Cause ideology that formed the basis of white southern historical memory was more or less monolithic across the South. This book shifts the scholarly conversation to how Lost Cause ideology played out at the local level and helps readers see the myriad ways in which ordinary white and black southerners fashioned a collective memory shaped by their community's distinct social needs. Moreover, this study reveals that even as Lost Cause ideology emerged in speeches, books, and popular literature shortly after the war, in smaller communities like Natchez a pro-South white supremacist tradition was not publicly articulated until several years later when Reconstruction was ending. Natchez's first postwar white historical tradition was initiated some eleven years after the war with the founding in 1876 of the Adams Light Infantry, a white male militia led by Confederate veterans and composed of young men too young to have served in the war. In addition to drilling its members and organizing public parades on national holidays, the group published texts memorializing local Confederate soldiers. A decade later, many leading infantry members organized their town's Confederate Memorial Association to build a monument honoring the town's fallen warriors. Gradually, as white Natchez men secured their mastery and increasingly turned their attention to business affairs, white women emerged as the dominant organizers of their town's collective white historical memory and traditions.[6]

Over time, white Natchez memory makers, while still clinging to the basic tenets of the Lost Cause, gradually changed the message and how these memories were expressed. The memory makers introduced in this book belonged to social clubs, militia groups, fraternal associations, Confederate memorial societies, black political clubs, and women's garden clubs. Some Natchez memory makers crafted their visions of the past in more private spaces—behind Kodak cameras and within their diaries, letters, memoirs, and scrapbook albums. As will become apparent in the pages that follow Natchez was swimming in historical memory and traditions, and more often than not they were contested.

By the early 1930s Natchez's dominant historical memory as envisioned by white elites culminated in a robust heritage tourism enterprise organized by the town's female garden club. As noted in chapter 5, the Natchez Pilgrimage home tours and pageants reinvigorated Lost Cause ideology in the form of a popular heritage tourism experience that appealed to the entertainment tastes of Depression-era audiences. While much of the message was similar to early Lost Cause rhetoric, the Pilgrimage packaged and sold it in an altogether new way that reflected contemporary performance techniques and focused more on celebrating southern heritage and culture rather than on commemorating a tragic past.

Simultaneously, this study examines the ways Natchez African Americans boldly attempted to counter a selective white memory following the war by offering nonthreatening images of themselves and their community. This study reveals how a vibrant postwar African American community battled to offset the dominant white-fabricated perspective that denigrated and demeaned all blacks as inferior people. Natchez blacks' control of public space, memory making, and politics eroded dramatically following the overthrow of Reconstruction, in part due to forces within the black community itself that largely undermined a more radical memory, preventing it from taking hold. This study argues that black memory making in Natchez differed somewhat, and perhaps significantly, from the more festive emancipation celebrations that blossomed from the end of the Civil War through the early twentieth century in towns and cities across the South.[7] In exploring why this happened, chapter 2 details the decisive role played by the city's antebellum, mixed-race, free black elites in fashioning a counter memory that largely ignored the horrors of slavery, emancipation as the celebratory foundation of black tradition making, and the cultural consequences of this failure into the twentieth century.

By the 1880s, public black emancipationist memories were all but snuffed out in Natchez as Jim Crow customs and laws took hold, and white men reclaimed dominance over public celebrations. African American wartime experiences and emancipation traditions never found their way into the dominant white collective memory of the late nineteenth century and in the decades that followed. By the time the town's garden club home tours and pageants arrived in the early 1930s, blacks were relegated to background props as silent costumed "slaves." Pilgrimage home tour scripts and pageants left out compelling black wartime memories of the several thousand Adams County blacks who had served in the Union army or lived in the wretched refugee camps where many black soldiers and their families had perished. Nor did the white-controlled historical memory machine of Natchez mention the vibrant black community that had flourished in the postwar era, sustained by a network of churches and schools catering to their social and spiritual needs. These are the memories and perspectives that historical studies like this one can begin to reclaim and weave back into the historical fabric.

Covering the period from the tumultuous era of Union occupation of Natchez during the war, followed by Reconstruction, through the economic hardships of the Great Depression, this book examines how Natchez's historical memory changed over time and who the key figures were in this process. Along the way readers will be introduced to a host of popular amusements that punctuated nineteenth- and early twentieth-century Natchez life and became the vehicles used to express historical memory. Celebratory parades and festive amusements organized by newly freed slaves, public speeches and monument building to honor Civil War casualties, white male paramilitary groups and fraternal organizations, and women's clubs all played important roles in the construction and expression of historical memory. More intimate reflections of nineteenth-century African American life are captured in the scrapbooks compiled by Mary Britton Conner (shared in chapter 4) in her attempts to hold on to the memories of an idealized antebellum past.

Although Natchez is a small town, with only a little more than six thousand residents in 1860, historians have long been drawn to the former capitol of Mississippi. Before the Civil War, Natchez ranked as one of the wealthiest communities in the antebellum South and possessed one of the highest per capita incomes in the nation. Home to the second largest slave market in the lower South, much of Adams County's wealth was derived from the large enslaved population laboring in the region. The majority of these enslaved persons toiled on some of the nation's richest cotton land situated directly across the Mississippi River from Natchez in Concordia Parish and Tensas Parish, Louisiana. Others labored as house servants or skilled laborers on the grounds of the luxurious Natchez estates built with cotton profits. The homes of the planter class bore regal sounding names like Monmouth, Dunleith, and Stanton Hall and became the icons of white memory for later generations. The planter families who lived in antebellum Natchez and the surrounding countryside formed an intricate web of kinship ties to one another, lived in luxury, and depended on enslaved laborers. The more than two hundred free

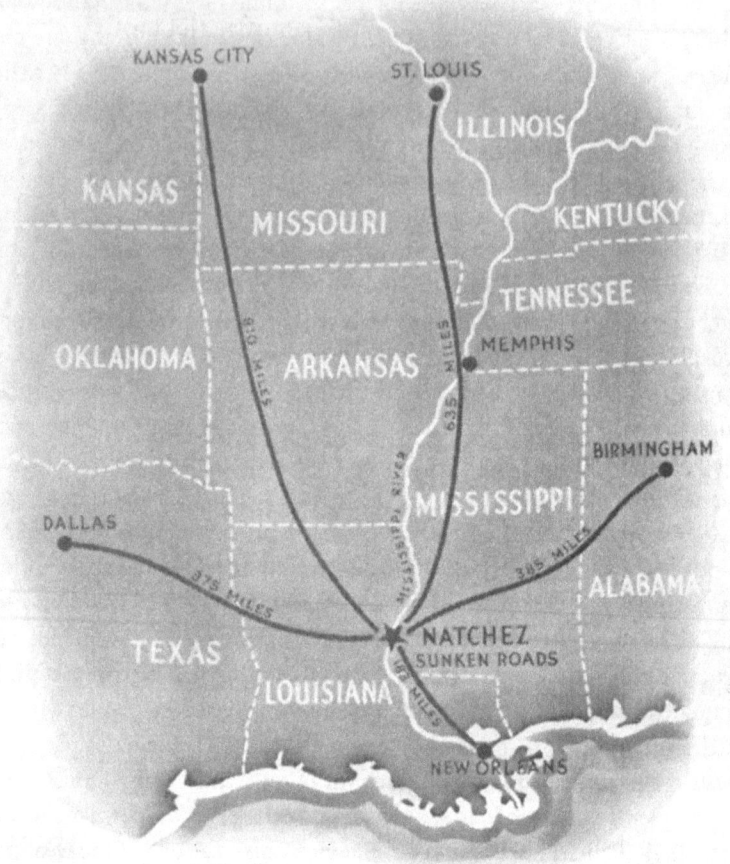

With the establishment of the annual Pilgrimage in 1932, Natchez became a mecca for tourists in search of the antebellum South. ("The Old South Still Lives," *Better Homes and Gardens*, February 1938.)

black men, women, and children—the largest community of its kind in the state—also contributed to the unique social dynamic of Natchez. Most of the free blacks were mulattos (born to white planter fathers and enslaved black mothers) who had been freed before the war. These individuals with their lighter skin tones typically were better educated and more financially secure than former slaves. Over time, elite blacks gained greater cultural authority over black memory making and took care not to offend white power brokers.

By the end of the Civil War, Mississippi's economy lay in ruins, with nearly a quarter of the white males who served in the Confederate Army killed in action or perishing from wounds or disease.[8] Agricultural strongholds like Natchez were particularly hard hit. The Natchez District consisted of a large African American population majority (over 80 percent), many of whom chose not to work for or obey their former masters.[9] Within this troubled landscape, the defeated white populace faced its own demoralizing tribulations—a humiliating military loss, Union occupation, widespread poverty, and a racial hierarchy turned upside down. As detailed in chapter 1, Adams County had all the makings for a rich and complex set of memories and counter memories: great wealth, followed by profound loss, a paternalistic planter class, a sizable free black community that did not always sympathize with former slaves, and a massive formerly enslaved labor force discovering freedom for the first time. In the process of sorting through a complex set of losses, gains, and uncertainties, white and black Natchezians faced the challenging task of fashioning new identities that would help them adjust to dramatically different circumstances in the postwar world, a story that unfolds in chapters 2, 3, and 4.

A PERSONAL PILGRIMAGE

My first encounter with Natchez came during a springtime visit in the late 1990s. It would be hard not to fall for Natchez during the spring, arguably the town's most photogenic time of year. The bounty of enormous camellia bushes laden with bold, bright fuchsia, pink and purple blossoms surrounding the verandahs of some of the South's most opulent antebellum estates was visually stunning. I was itching to get inside these icons of the South's antebellum past, and before long I did.

As a returning student (code for mature and over forty), working on a masters in history, I first traveled to Natchez as part of a ten-day graduate student field trip, organized by southern historian and California State University, Northridge, professor Ronald L. F. Davis, that included stops at the Mississippi Department of Archives and History in Jackson and Louisiana State University's Special Collections in Baton Rouge. The purpose of the trip was twofold: First, we came to explore the region's rich archives containing a treasure trove of historical documents, letters, and court records related to the Natchez District. Secondly, we were there to learn something about southern culture, society, and people, as important in Davis's mind as any book learning, what he fondly called "The Natchez Experience." For most of my fellow pilgrims, it was their first introduction to the South, and many of them came with a palpable sense of trepidation, unsure of what they would see and find.

Indeed, our venerable leader enjoyed nothing more than watching his California students squirm in their unfamiliar surroundings (what one fellow student likened to a petri dish in a creative laboratory experiment) as they made sense out of a culture very different from urban, modern southern California—home of Disneyland, Hollywood, and liberal politics, ideas, and lifestyles not always palatable in the conservative South.[10] I was a bit different from my fellow students in that I was a native southerner who still had strong ties to family living below the Mason-Dixon Line. I readily identified with grits, biscuits, and Moon Pies. The thick melodic cadences of Natchez natives and the seductive notes of blues and jazz that caressed the balmy, floral springtime air stirred up memories of my southern youth. At heart, I was still a southerner even though I had left Atlanta nearly twenty years earlier. Formally studying southern history in midlife—in southern California of all places—and reading stacks of books and articles by progressive historians transformed my ideas about race, class, and gender. The academic writings of David Blight, Fitzhugh Brundage, Jack Davis, and Ronald Davis, among others, gave me new insights into the South's past and raised new questions as well. Likewise, the fictional works of Natchez native Greg Isles, Mississippians William Faulkner, Stark Young, William Alexander Percy, Richard Wright, and Eudora Welty sparked my imagination and enhanced my understanding of the distinctive role place plays in regional identity and historical studies. These writers and others eloquently explored how the southern past was at times graceful and genteel, but simultaneously was too often marred by the unfathomable brutality of slavery and cruel racism. The books and articles I read were life changing and dramatically transformed my perspectives on the South.[11]

Immersing myself in reading about the antebellum South and postwar years under the guidance of gifted mentors profoundly touched my soul and launched a personal commitment to advocate for racial equality and a more inclusive and critically accurate rendering of the southern past. Books and discussions with others began to instill the notion that all history is contested history. In the words of Ron Davis, "it is the purpose of the outside interpretive body [historians and others] to see history as contested ground" and to tell that story. I made it my mission going forward to research and tell the Natchez story, a narrative steeped in contestation.

Despite my academic journey and leaving the South—or perhaps because of it—at heart I remain southern, proud, and protective of my kinfolk, heritage, and culture, but often disturbed by the dogged hold of racism on a region slow to embrace more progressive, inclusive, and democratic ideals. Loyalty to kin and place is a trait shared by many southerners whose Scots-Irish ancestry like my own planted those seeds centuries ago, a stance that makes it sometimes difficult to defend my ideas on racial equality and criticism of the South to my southern family, while appreciating the region's rich culture, a paradox with which I continue to wrestle. As a transplanted southerner I also believed that I understood something about the region's complicated and troubling racialized past. Over the course of my nearly two decades of research, I learned that coming to terms with southern history and race relations is no simple matter and that I still had and have much to learn.

It was no accident that I was drawn to Natchez. In between summer trips to Alabama to visit my maternal grandmother and a pair of great aunts who loved nothing better than to sit on the front porch telling tales of their Confederate ancestors over bottles of ice cold Coca Colas and warm peach pie, my parents organized family pilgrimages to southern historic sites. A visit to Biloxi, Mississippi, where Confederate President Jefferson Davis's last residence, Beauvoir, majestically stood, was followed by journeys to Mobile, New Orleans, and Charleston, perhaps the most intoxicating of all southern cities with its cobblestoned streets and historic homes painted in softly muted pastels overlooking the Battery, the ruins of Fort Sumter visible in the distance. I thought that one day I would write about Charleston, but in fact, it would be Natchez and its tantalizing and voluminous archival records that would captivate my imagination.

Ron Davis forewarned his students that Natchez was a place of mystery and secrets, and if not careful you'd fall under its spell and be forced to return again and again, seeking to unravel its tangled past. He spoke the truth. During that initial trip, most of our days were spent in the courthouse searching for records that would help us weave a story of some aspect of Natchez's past that had caught our academic fancy. While most students focused on nineteenth-century history, I was drawn to the early twentieth century, specifically the story of the determined women who organized the Natchez Pilgrimage home tours during the Great Depression. As my research unfolded, I too would dive deeper into Natchez's past, seeking to connect the dots between the ideas and events of the nineteenth-century and their impact on the decades that followed.

In between sorting through archival records, we made journeys that Davis planned for his trusting pilgrims to the rural countryside of Adams County. One day we explored decaying slave cabins at Canebrake, their walls covered in crumbling pages torn from 1930s Sears and Roebuck catalogs, probably an attempt by black sharecroppers to keep out the damp chill of Mississippi winter mornings. Another day we caravanned to Saragossa, a once elegant estate owned by one of the wealthiest slaveholders in Adams County, now decrepit and nearly hidden behind lacy Spanish moss and oak trees, their thick trunks gnarled with age. Still another day we journeyed along the lush, green Natchez Trace, once the transportation route of countless coffles of chained enslaved persons brought to the town's multiple slave markets.

Over the course of several summers spent working on the Natchez Courthouse Records Project—yet another history enterprise orchestrated by Ron Davis and supported by the National Park Service (detailed in the epilogue)—I returned to Natchez often. Processing nineteenth-century court records by day, teasing out the names of nineteenth-century litigants and their crimes—everything from violent assaults and murder, to unpaid debts, theft, and more—I used evenings and weekends to meet Natchez's homegrown history lovers. This mostly gray-haired band of talented amateur historians, passionate about sharing and preserving their town's past, gave generously of their time to share family letters, scrapbooks, photographs, and the stories and memories of Natchez. A visit with Dr. Thomas Gandy, sitting not far from his home darkroom, was an afternoon I cherished. More than thirty years earlier, Gandy had rescued thousands of photographer Henry Norman's priceless glass negatives from a leaky porch and certain ruin. In the process of creating new prints, Dr. Gandy revealed a fascinating look at nineteenth-century Natchez. Thanks to the good doctor's unwavering commitment, the faces of black and white Natchez residents—most of them long forgotten—their homes, houses of worship, businesses, and the steamboats that paddled up and down the river below were carefully restored and remain one of the town's most prized historic relics and one of the most useful vehicles to travel deeper into Natchez's past. Several of these restored images appear in chapter 4.

On another afternoon I found myself in the parlor of Alma Carpenter's antebellum home, The Elms, sipping a gin and tonic she insisted on serving even though the clock had not yet struck noon. Miss Alma, as she was affectionately known (and a teetotaler by this time in her life), was the daughter of a founding garden club member and had been married to a descendant of the wealthy and influential Carpenter family, who had made their mark on Natchez as generous benefactors following the Civil War. Miss Alma graciously shared her scrapbooks filled with newspaper clippings of the early Pilgrimage years, prompting her to recall the spirited fight between rival garden club members that nearly destroyed the town's lucrative heritage tourism business in the late 1930s. It wasn't until after Alma's passing a few years later that I learned that this beloved town matriarch had devoted countless hours transcribing the letters of the elite antebellum widow Julia Nutt and her son Prentiss, documents I would use to illustrate the hardships of the early postwar period detailed in chapter 1.

Kathie Blankenstein, whose mother in the 1930s worked as the paid secretary of the Natchez Garden Club, and who successfully negotiated a licensing deal with Gorham Silver to name a silver pattern after one of the town's most distinctive antebellum homes, became another invaluable source who gave generously of her time and shared with me the scrapbooks her mother kept of early garden club years. Kathie's daughter, talented filmmaker Chesney Blankenstein Doyle, also a garden club member and who revamped the annual pageant into a more inclusive story of Natchez's past in 2017, has been an invaluable and wise source on the current state of Natchez civic affairs.

African American Natchezians were equally generous in sharing their thoughts and memories of Natchez's past. Ser Sesh Ab Heter-Clifford Boxley, a Natchez native, remembered selling pralines and daffodils as a boy to Pilgrimage tourists in the late 1930s, and later rejecting the Pilgrimage narrative after his educational journey led him to California. Another black resident, Ralph Jennings, recalled steering clear of the Pilgrimage crowds altogether in his youth. Instead, his family's dinner table conversation focused on black ancestors. Black members of the Zion AME Baptist Church candidly shared their memories with me of growing up in early twentieth-century Natchez, often recalling painful moments of racial injustice, sometimes inflicted by members of their own families whose skin color was lighter or darker than their own. The Natchez Museum of African American History and Culture is where I first saw Henry Norman's poignant and stunning nineteenth-century portraits of black Natchezians, an encounter that led me to devote most of a chapter on the use of photography in creating black historical memories.

In between working with historical documents stored in Natchez and other southern repositories and listening to the stories of Natchez residents, black and white, I confirmed that yes, all history is contested. I committed myself to sharing those contested struggles that went beyond offering a more inclusive rendering of the past, but also sought to include perspectives that challenge the dominant perspectives of a community's historic and contemporary class, caste, and gender status quo.[12] This is what I have attempted to do in this book. And that is why the word "battle" appears in the title and is an ongoing motif throughout.

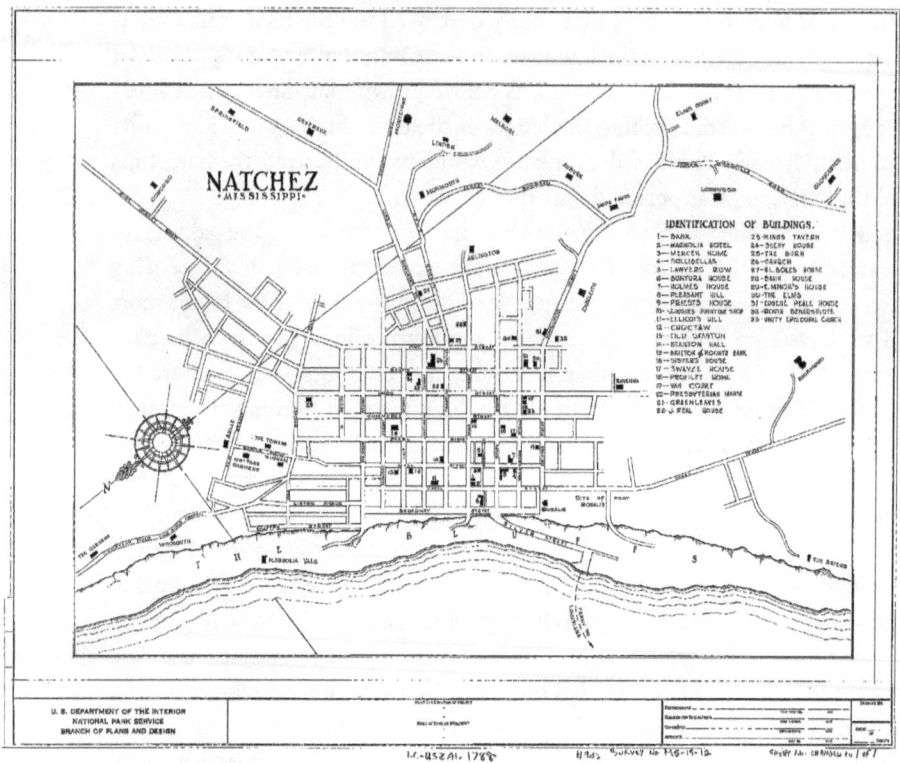

Natchez City Map, 1933. Historic American Buildings Survey, Creator. Retrieved from the Library of Congress, https://www.loc.gov/item/ms0222/. (Accessed March 6, 2018.)

Like so many white visitors who go to Natchez, I was drawn to the town's unique and astonishing array of antebellum homes. Unlike Atlanta, where I spent much of my childhood, Natchez's antebellum treasures escaped serious damage from Union troops. Natchez's most valuable real estate, while shabby by war's end, was still standing and would play a major role in my historical undertaking. Unlike some southern towns such as Charleston and Savannah, rooted in antebellum culture and memory, Natchez offers very little in the way of visible history in public civic spaces. Instead, Natchez's white antebellum memory has always been attached to its grand homes spread throughout the town and rural outskirts. This book attempts to understand why that is so.

My fascination with Natchez's antebellum homes was not unlike the passion displayed by the garden clubwomen who organized the first Natchez Pilgrimage in 1932. American women and men flocked to garden clubs in the 1920s and 1930s. And while gardening was a popular pastime in Natchez and club members dutifully gave reports on how to care for peonies, pansies, and such in the club's early years, it was the town's historic homes that captivated white Natchez women, boosting membership and making it the town's most prestigious female social club. Indeed, Natchez's home gardens were not known for being particularly lush or beautiful during the early twentieth century, having never entirely recovered from the poverty of the Civil War era. Instead, it was the town's nearly two dozen homes—and their rapid deterioration by the early 1930s—that became the primary focus of most garden club members' voluntary efforts. As Mary Louise Kendall, the last remaining founder of the Natchez Garden Club told me in 2001, just a few years shy of her 100th birthday, "It was all about the homes. We were losing so many beautiful homes. We had to do something."

I came to understand the garden club members' devotion to their town's stunning collection of antebellum homes during my first trip to Natchez. I visited several of the town's most visually impressive mansions, soaking up their stories and legends and learning something about their original owners. A visit to Stanton Hall, an icon of the town's economic golden age and now home to the Pilgrimage Garden Club and the Carriage House Restaurant was among one of my more memorable visits. Over a plate of fried chicken and the restaurant's tiny mouthwatering biscuits, I was introduced to Katherine Miller by way of her portrait hanging on the wall. It was Miller who founded the Pilgrimage and led the charge to restore Stanton Hall to its former glory. When I asked the black waitress who served me if she had known Mrs. Miller (who passed away in 1983), she deferentially nodded to Miller's portrait hanging behind her and said softly almost as if the demanding club matriarch might be standing nearby, "Yes, I worked for Mrs. Miller. She was real nice, but she could be very particular." As I would come to find out in the course of my research, Miller was not only "particular" but at times outright ornery in her headstrong determination to promote her version of the Old South tourism enterprise she founded. Each time I returned to Natchez I made a point of visiting several more of Natchez's antebellum homes, collecting family stories and impressions along the way.

The appeal of Natchez's antebellum estates remains as popular as ever among white visitors and is one of the nation's most visible expressions of southern memory and tradition. Because these homes remain such an important icon of Natchez's historic past, I have included an appendix that lists and pictures the original Pilgrimage homes still open to the public.

After completing my master's thesis on the garden clubwomen of Natchez in 2004, I sensed I had not yet completely solved the original historical riddles that had initially brought me to Natchez. Certainly, the Pilgrimage and its female founders who invited their guests to "Come to Natchez Where the Old South Still Lives" began to answer some of my questions. But like any worthy historical project, the story I had begun begged for more answers. I soon found myself pursuing these questions as a PhD student at University of California, Santa Barbara. Scouring the archives of numerous southern research libraries in Mississippi, Louisiana, North Carolina, and Washington, DC, I listened to the voices of hundreds of Natchez men and women who had much to say about how they wanted their lives and town remembered. Their letters, diaries, and editorials spoke volumes on this subject, at times contradicting one another. The commemorative booklets, convention records, and minutes of the social and fraternal organizations that Natchezians flocked to in droves in the late 1800s joined in the conversation. These kinds of documents were particularly useful in uncovering the insights, thoughts, and attitudes for the majority who left behind no personal papers, but nevertheless, had strong opinions of how they wanted themselves and their town to be represented going forward.

The legacy of Natchez's collective historical memories—black, white, male, and female—raises important questions about the impact of historical memories on a nation and its people. The purpose of this book is to reflect on the meaning of being white and black in the late nineteenth- and early twentieth-century Jim Crow South, a tumultuous period defined by economic hardship, racial tensions, and cultural shifts, issues which continue to plague the present and our memories of the southern past. Finally, and perhaps most significantly, this book seeks to recover a small portion of the memories that are most at risk of being lost, particularly the earliest postemancipation black memories that were nearly erased when white males reclaimed political power in the late 1870s. In doing so, I hope this book serves as a gentle reminder that when we seek to know and understand the past it can make us all a little more human, more accepting of one another, and kinder in our life's journey.

CHAPTER ONE

FORGING NEW IDENTITIES IN A WORLD GONE MAD

JANE DENT, A FREE WOMAN OF COLOR, WHO MADE HER HOME A FEW MILES east of Natchez at the time of the Civil War, was more fortunate than most black women of her time. Married to a successful blacksmith, who owned a modest house and several horses, and the mother of two sons, Jane, with her husband, Thomas, seemed to be successfully navigating the uncertainties of war.

But sixty-year-old Jane's life radically changed once Union troops took control of Natchez in the summer of 1863. Her once peaceful neighborhood was no longer safe as Confederate soldiers stole provisions from the Dents and others, while keeping a watchful eye on black residents and their interactions with Yankee troops. Thomas Dent was particularly hard hit by the family's change of fortune, with reports that he died or committed suicide before the war ended. Adding to her worries and personal safety, Jane's oldest son joined a local Union regiment of black soldiers.[1]

Jane's situation after her husband's death and loss of the family's blacksmith business steadily worsened during the war years. Her youngest son sold chickens and eggs to Union troops while she nursed wounded Yankee soldiers and washed their dirty clothes. Jane testified that Confederates pressured her to spy for them. When she refused, rebel troops, in retaliation, took her furniture, four horses, and blacksmith tools. She testified that when Confederates threatened to hang her and her son for working for the Yankees, she moved to Natchez. Adding insult to injury, a short time later black Union troops tore down her dwelling and husband's blacksmith house. Dent went in search of her property and discovered it at Fort Natchez, recognizing the sashes and window blinds of her former home in a Union army barrack. As historian Joyce Broussard writes, "For Jane Dent, the Civil War brought misery, terror, and impoverishment, reducing her from a once prosperous free woman of color to an impoverished laundress and nurse without a home of her own."[2] In her efforts to win compensation for her losses, she assertively told the Southern Claims Commissioner, "I think I ought to be paid by the government."³

Living less than ten miles away from Dent in an opulent antebellum estate, Margaret Conner Martin, the privileged daughter of a white Natchez planter, faced similar fearful emotions that summer when Union troops arrived in Natchez. Married to Natchez's highest-ranking Confederate officer, General William T. Martin, twenty-six-year-old Margaret (affectionately called Margarette by her husband and family) found herself alone, miserable, and terrified. She faced a series of challenges for which her elite upbringing utterly failed to prepare her. The problems the mother of five young children encountered began well before Yankee forces occupied Adams County in the summer of 1863. In October 1862 she wrote her husband that while drawing a cup of tea for her slave Melissa, who was sick with measles, she had severely scalded two of her fingers on account of "not being accustomed to the stove and boiling tea kettles." Frustrated that her painful injury made writing difficult, she added, "I suppose our enemies would be greatly rejoiced to hear of such misfortune to the delicate wives of their rebel foes." Signing her letter "Little Wife," she wrote within the same letter that her mother had discharged Thornton, a house slave, and his family due to "insolent conduct," adding that "the manners of all the negroes, with few exceptions, are intolerable."⁴

By the time five thousand Yankee troops took over much of Natchez's public spaces and commandeered numerous private homes for officer quarters and military hospitals the following summer, boiling water and managing insolent slaves would have seemed like minor trifles to the general's wife. By September of 1863 Margarette wrote of a host of new woes from Monteigne, the couple's handsome suburban Natchez estate. The Martin's slave Amelia had stolen a silver tea set, bonnets, hats, shoes, tools, medicines, and clothing belonging to Margarette and her children. Though Amelia was arrested for her crime and brought before the federal provost marshal, she was released, but not before lambasting the Martins, reporting the couple had "starved and half clothed [their] servants and worked and beat them to death." Only one day later, John, a former Martin slave, came to Margarette's door accompanied by a white Yankee soldier described as "a great, rough, red-faced brutal looking man in his shirt sleeves." John and his Union army accomplice not only took her husband's saddle, but the general's oilcloth coat and two horses, riding "out of the yard as though the place belonged to them." Declaring that she "was never more frightened in [her] life," Margarette reiterated to her husband the hardships she had endured as a single wife and mother facing the enemy alone. "Now my dear Husband, I have given you some of my experiences since the Yankees came. Do you not think my trials have been bitter and many?"[5]

Margarette's fearsome and insulting encounters with "brutal" Union soldiers and "insolent" slaves eventually got the best of her. She left Natchez, spending the last year of the war in Alabama. Jane Dent, who had far fewer options as a woman of color, lived out the duration of the war in Natchez. By the time of her death in 1900 at age ninety she held a respected place in the African American community.[6]

Jane Dent and Margarette Martin were two of countless southern women who suffered many bitter trials during and after the war. White and black Natchez individuals experienced the Civil War and Union military occupation in myriad ways, experiences that sparked the origins of a collective historical narrative in the postwar era. Natchez residents faced a variety of challenging life experiences—poverty, profound personal losses, and significant changes in the racial hierarchy and gender roles—all of which shaped Natchez's historical consciousness for decades to come. Conversely, the substantial but temporary gains achieved by blacks during this era were largely omitted from the town's collective memory as time passed. A selective white historical memory of the Civil War and its aftermath dominated Natchez and American culture, while black remembrances were nearly erased and lost. This chapter documents wartime experiences of Natchez residents in an effort to answer three primary questions: (1) How did the war and occupation impact the everyday lives of white and black Natchez residents? (2) How did people cope with life amidst the ruins of a disastrous war? (3) How did blacks and whites newly engage one another during a time of great social turmoil?

THE SOCIAL IMPACT OF WAR

Precisely measuring the degree of wartime suffering of any one person or their community compared to another is difficult. Natchez's quick surrender and few military encounters between Union and Confederate troops within Adams County suggest that the majority of Natchezians and their town endured a less extreme level of physical destruction than many other southern locales. Natchez's public spaces, its private homes, and its civilians never experienced the degree of "total war" suffered by southerners living and fighting in more strategic Confederate targets. Without question, however, Natchez families suffered grave losses; more than a third of the 1,444 Natchez white men and boys who had gone to war had died, deserted, or been disabled by the end of the fighting.[7] Many of the town's fine mansions were mere shadows of their former elegance, and some had suffered extensive damage at the hands of Union troops. Gardens were trampled and plundered by Union invaders and once well-stocked pantries were sometimes bare and their owners hungry. But as becomes notably apparent in studying the letters, diaries, and news accounts of Natchez during the war years, the conflict's greatest impact was not in the destruction of homes, public spaces, and the commercial district as experienced by other southern towns and cities.

The war in Natchez among white inhabitants was more frequently experienced as a blow to their psyches and emotional wellbeing. By contrast, formerly enslaved black refugees fleeing from rural plantations to Natchez experienced the war far differently than their white masters. Amidst the joy of tasting freedom for the first time, Natchez blacks encountered some of the harshest physical suffering of that era. But despite the suffering of both black and white Natchezians, the town and its infrastructure functioned at war's end, providing adequate shelter and sustenance for most residents. Simultaneously, Natchez remained a viable commercial center offering an abundance of entrepreneurial opportunities to those possessing capital, business acumen, and pluck.

Natchez's serving as a military garrison rather than a military target played a large role in protecting and shaping its wartime and postwar destiny. The rapid increase of new inhabitants employed by or commandeered to support the Union army, the majority of whom were African Americans, was the most noticeable marker of social and demographic change in wartime Natchez. Some 5,300 blacks lived in Natchez by 1870, more than double the African American population a decade earlier, and outnumbered the white population by nearly 50 percent. Simultaneously, large numbers of northern and foreign merchants descended upon Natchez and other small towns across the South in search of new opportunities in the two decades after the war, further increasing the population and altering the town's demographic mix. Between 1860 and 1870 Natchez's population swelled by more than 25 percent, contributing to the social turmoil that rocked the town and the white planter elites whose families had economically and politically dominated the region for decades.[8]

BLACK WARTIME EXPERIENCES

Newly freed slaves who made their way to Natchez shortly after the arrival of Union troops in the summer of 1863—most with no work and no means to purchase shelter and food—severely unsettled the town and its white residents. Many of these plantation slaves fled the countryside to avoid rebel partisan units known for killing slaves thought to be Union supporters. General T. E. G. Ransom, commander of Union Army troops stationed in Natchez, reported with frustration that slave refugees were "flocking in by the thousands (about 1 able-bodied man to 6 women and children). I am feeding about 500 and working the able-bodied men among them. I can not take care of them. They are all anxious to go; they do not know where or what for."[9] The sight of large numbers of former slaves streaming into Natchez—what General Ransom referred to as a "stampede"—was yet another humiliating reminder to war-weary white residents of their devastating defeat.

Large numbers of the able-bodied male refugees became Union soldiers; of the 5,000 soldiers stationed in Natchez during the summer of 1864—3,150 were black, many from the neighboring countryside.[10] Frequently located within close proximity to wealthy Natchez estates, crowded Army barracks housing black soldiers soon became breeding grounds for disease. A sampling of muster book reports found that among black soldiers stationed at Natchez, nearly 38 percent died in camp from diseases contracted after recruitment, a staggeringly high figure among Union soldiers.[11] Refugee camps like the one at Forks of the Road, once home of the second busiest slave market in the South, often contained the wives and children of black soldiers and were likely worse. The town's main refugee camp contained as many as four thousand blacks in the summer of 1863.

White Natchez residents took close notice of the camps, becoming increasingly alarmed by the growing number of fatalities within easy walking distance from their homes. Most of these victims were probably children infected with smallpox and measles.[12] An unpublished memoir, written by socially prominent Natchez resident Ellen Shields, recorded that "a large following of negroes, men, women and children, here died like sheep in a slaughter pen." Shields made the disturbing observation that large numbers of these refugees were hastily and only partially interred during Yankee occupation. "They were buried uncoffined, four and five in one grave; often along with dogs, cats, etc.! These grave yards were everywhere. . . . In these grave yards the dead were not sufficiently covered; in passing one could see a foot, a hand, a paw, etc.—it was awful. The stench was terrific."[13] Overwhelmed by sickness, disease, and racism, the camps offered black refugees and soldiers little hope to establish themselves, and many Natchez-based blacks perished in their first months of freedom.

Some blacks making their way to Natchez avoided the dreaded "contraband camps," but nonetheless suffered from harsh poverty. J. P. Bardwell, an American Missionary Association (AMA) superintendent, described the grim living conditions among destitute Natchez freedmen shortly before the end of the war: "Some are living in old shacks, which are in a very dilapidated condition, some with only a covering overhead exposed to the cold damp winds on every side, some in cabins without any floors, or anything to stop the spaces between the logs. Others again with only bushes stuck into the ground around them to break off the wind, without any attempt at a covering overhead. In this condition I found a number of families consisting of old and young. Most of them women and children. On a cold day, as they curl down together upon the ground, they look more like an animated mass of rags and filth than beings in the image of God." Unsanitary conditions like the ones described by missionary Bardwell coupled with oppressive heat and humidity during the summer months and a shortage of housing for a rapidly growing population seriously threatened the public health of black and white Natchezians.[14]

A shortage of affordable, nutritious food during occupation added to the misery of blacks and whites in Natchez. AMA teachers and missionaries frequently wrote of the problems they had in procuring adequate food for themselves and the poor diets of those they taught. Teacher Harriet Gaylord complained that living on army rations created great hardship for Natchez teachers. "Now that the warm weather had come one's relish for pork and beans diminishes as the heat increases. Almost the only relish that we have had on our table for the seven months we have been here is dry apple sauce and now it has become a positive disrelish."[15] Missionary Hattie Stryker reported that Natchez freedmen found it "impossible to procure the real necessaries of life. We have applicants almost daily for food or help of some kind. Starvation is staring many of the old and infirm in the face. It is not only so with the freedmen, but many of the whites are in the same condition."[16]

Natchez blacks lost far less property in monetary value than whites at the hands of Union troops, but their losses nevertheless created hardship and resentment towards their northern liberators. Forty-six blacks from Natchez and the surrounding environs of Adams County filed claims with the Southern Claims Commission (SCC) for property taken by federal troops during the war.[17] These men and women had accumulated small amounts of property usually in the form of livestock, wagons, tools, and lumber, in some cases before their enslavement officially ended in 1863.[18] Black Natchez claimants proudly attested to their Union loyalty and recalled nursing the sick, feeding the hungry, washing soldiers' dirty uniforms, and even "killing rebels" when given the opportunity. Even as SCC records attest to the profound sense of joy that accompanied liberation from enslavement, many Natchez blacks expressed anger over the valuable property they had lost in the war. Such testimony serves as a potent reminder that the Confederate defeat inflicted economic hardships on blacks living in occupied territory as well as whites.

Black Natchez claimants realized that with freedom came the responsibility to protect their property, even if they owned relatively little. Elizabeth Carr, who claimed to have two horses valued at $350 taken in July 1864 by federal soldiers, says she saw the horses frequently hitched to a cannon wagon during Union occupation. Afraid to file a complaint with the army, she told commissioners, "I think that if the government knew how bad I needed it they would pay me."[19] Although Carr failed in her attempts to collect money, black petitioner Abner Pierce succeeded in recouping losses for a "dark sorrel mule gobbled up" by federal troops.[20] Undoubtedly, a number of the blacks (and whites) who filed claims for lost property saw the SCC process both as an opportunity to collect on their legitimate wartime losses and as a welcome chance for financial gain in a topsy-turvy world. Not surprisingly, the story of Unionism in Natchez and most southern communities never became part of the region's collective historical memory. The claims of black and white Unionists and their efforts "to be paid by the government" were omitted from white Natchezian's selective telling of their past.

WHITE WARTIME EXPERIENCES

A northern teacher's observation that many Natchez whites suffered economic hardships in the postwar period resonates within numerous records of this period. While historians frequently dismiss the severity of Natchez's wartime experiences due to its early surrender and distance from major battle sites, a more nuanced reading of military and civilian accounts suggest that the white Natchez community suffered acutely from the physical and emotional turmoil of a long and costly war. Widespread plundering and destruction by federal troops, Confederate soldiers, and former slaves in the lower Mississippi Valley played havoc on white families struggling to feed themselves and their dwindling enslaved dependents. Memories of wartime suffering played a vital role in shaping a historical consciousness amidst memories of the heroism and courage necessary for survival. A letter written by a Union surgeon in May 1863 gave an eyewitness account of the ruin of personal property owned by a wealthy Natchez family at the hands of federal soldiers: "I saw the first furnished house I ever saw forsaken & part of the furniture destroyed. I believe there [were] 40 or 50 mirrors from 4 to 15 ft high and sofas, marble toped [sic] tables enough to commence a wholesale furniture store. There were over a doz. Bedsteads that cost $200.00 each. The building cost $200,000.00. Five miles from this was a building which cost $125,000.00. In this was a thousand-dollar piano. Everything was being destroyed."[21]

Monteigne, the suburban estate owned by General William T. Martin and his wife Margarette, came under particularly heavy attack likely because of its owner's high-ranking military position. In a letter written to her husband in January 1864, Margarette wrote that "our home has been completely desolated. All the wood outside buildings, stables and carriage house have been torn down and carried into the fortifications. There is not a fence on the place. The floor of the kitchen gallery has been taken up and the pantry pulled to pieces. In the house, every mantelpiece has been pulled down, the walls cut with sabers and defaced in various ways, every chandelier taken down and broken up. . . . Doors have been split and not a bolt left on a door or a window."[22]

The general's wife blamed the white Union soldiers for the behavior of former Natchez slaves who stole and destroyed planter property. Her assumption may have been correct, but likely many black recruits acted on their own volition, seeking compensation and redress for years of enslavement. Near the end of the war a white Adams County planter noted: "Negroes in town come to the places where they formerly resided & steel [sic] horses & other stock & run them to Natchez & even across the river for use or sale; Being familiar with the localities & often aided by the hired labor." No matter whether white or black, Union soldiers were taking or destroying property, and as historian Michael Wayne notes, "The results were the same." In similar fashion to other towns and cities across the war-torn South, Natchez suffered tremendous economic loss.[23]

THE FEMINIZATION OF WHITE NATCHEZ MEMORY

The accounts of Margarette Martin and other elite women attest to the fact that most white Natchezians primarily experienced the Civil War's emotional and physical hardships not on the masculine space of bloody battlefields, but on the home front. The nearly 1,500 Natchez men who served in the Confederate Army, more than half of the town's white population, would have left behind significant numbers of women—wives, mothers, sisters, and sweethearts—to face the heartaches of war and military occupation alone. Many of these women were eventually widowed or made spinsters as a result of wartime losses. According to historian Joyce Broussard, when Union troops arrived in Natchez in the summer of 1863, "754 unmarried, divorced, or widowed white women aged sixteen and older lived in and around Natchez, and of these the majority (481) were unmarried women between sixteen and twenty-nine years old." Of this group, at least 25 percent were women born into upper-class Natchez families, living in the fifty-some estate houses in town or stately suburban homes on the outskirts of Union picket lines.[24]

Much of the war unfolded for white Natchez elites inside the traditional feminine space of elegant parlors and dining rooms. At times, wartime disruptions seriously challenged racial, gender, and class norms. An abundance of historical records reveals the responses of elite whites and African Americans to military occupation. Less is known about how lower-class whites fared, but court records from this period (an excellent source for learning about social conditions) offer evidence that the chaos of the war and its aftermath left many white men and women from less privileged backgrounds equally destitute and desperate.[25] Throughout the duration of the war, economic hardships and encounters with former slaves and Union occupiers were painful reminders to white Natchezians tending the home front that the privileged world they once knew was no more. Elite Natchezians logged their experiences and deprivations in letters and journals, revealing much about the anxieties associated with war and enemy occupation.[26]

For a number of wealthy Natchez families, personal interaction with Union soldiers invited to their homes helped to pass the time and shaped their wartime experiences. Haller and Julia Nutt, known as a "Union family," frequently hosted dinner parties for federal officers, according to Matilda Gresham, wife of General Walter Gresham, the commander of federal forces in Natchez in 1863. Unionist Katharine Minor also opened her suburban home Oakland to Union officers on numerous occasions.[27] As Margarette

Martin would bitterly remark to her Confederate officer husband: "Natchez is nobly sustaining its reputation for being a good old Union Town. You remember you suggested the Federals would be entertained in Natchez? Well, they have been entertained, by some, in great style. It is surprising how many good Secessionists have become warm Unionists."[28]

Other Natchez families who remained loyal to the Confederacy found themselves forced to not only entertain their foes but at times live under the same roof with the enemy, as in the case of Ann Eliza Wilson, whose elegant home Rosalie, overlooking the Mississippi River, headquartered the federal command in Natchez. Matilda Gresham resided at Rosalie for several months while her husband was stationed in Natchez and observed that she and Mrs. Wilson "were most congenial." Though Mrs. Wilson maintained her secessionist stance, Mrs. Gresham reported that her new southern friend voiced her frustration on at least one occasion, stating, "I would like to stand by and see the first man who uttered the word secession have his tongue pulled out."[29] Matilda Gresham's wartime reminiscences, released more than half a century after the war, reflected a trend among many white Civil War memoirists who subscribed to the notion that the South was tragically victimized during the war and Reconstruction.

Housing Union officers or seeing their homes turned into military offices, mess halls, and infirmaries could not have been easy for white Natchez residents, but surely the most difficult task of all would be receiving the news of loved ones killed or wounded in service to the Confederate cause. Physical and monetary hardships paled to the emotional trauma of losing male family members and friends to the war. Many white Natchez women found this situation nearly unbearable. Unmarried Kate Foster frequently complained about her wartime hardships, but the loss of her two brothers to the war nearly drove her to despair. Upon the death of the first of her two brothers, she wrote in November 1863: "It seems as though when he left us my heart became flint. I am almost afraid to love too dearly any one now." Foster's prophecies were fulfilled; she never married and eventually channeled her melancholic memories into the memorialization of the Confederate Lost Cause.[30]

Over time, white Natchez women's traditional feminine space within the home expanded in the absence of male family members as they assumed responsibility for areas once considered masculine domains. In addition to overseeing the traditional housekeeping duties once performed by enslaved women, white females managing on their own or living with elderly men too old to fight took charge of stables, the prized horses and fine carriages that transported them about town and to neighboring estates, as well as the fields adjoining these once wealthy properties that supplied the chief source of revenues and sustenance for many Natchez planter families. White women assumed such roles to preserve the "servant ideal," a genteel lifestyle made possible by black servitude.[31] As both a crisis of class and gender, such a situation helps to explain why many southern elite white women were often inept, unnerved, and resentful when initially forced to assume cooking and cleaning tasks once routinely performed by slaves. The postwar chaos that turned the social order of southern women upside down frequently created an emotional crisis and, in their minds, physical trauma as well. As the daughter of one wealthy Natchez planter would write shortly after the war, the shortage of help "mars the flesh of my bones badly."[32] Over time many of these same women mastered and took pride in housekeeping chores, learning to make ends meet with fewer economic resources as well as assuming care of outdoor grounds and business duties once strictly part of the traditional masculine sphere.[33] Prompted by wartime demands, the expanded role of women on the home front would become grist for southern white memory making.

Severe food shortages and rampant inflation that put basic household necessities beyond their financial reach were some of the most difficult problems lower- and upper-class white Natchez women faced during and after the war. In September 1864 Natchez residents complained of "starvation prices," with butter selling as high as one dollar per pound, a cut of beef for fifty dollars, and flour at twenty dollars per barrel.[34] Given food shortages and wartime inflation, the plunder of foodstuffs from family gardens and storehouses by federal troops, Confederate raiders, and black refugees took on added significance. The journal entries of the Quitman sisters, members of one of Natchez's wealthiest planter families, resonate with the despair and anger of women left to fend for themselves as they helplessly watched federal soldiers and former slaves stealing their family's livestock and produce. "They have taken from us all our horses, even poor 'Lucy Beal,' ... the favorite animal of our dear Father," wrote Annie Rose Quitman Duncan in one entry. "The garden is constantly over run by them. The watermelon beds have been almost stripped, [even] the fruit that was not ripe enough for them to take off."[35]

The accounts of Katharine Minor, the owner of multiple plantations in Adams County, suggest that wealthy Natchezians lost far more than an occasional favorite horse or a watermelon bed. They provide additional evidence of the widespread devastation of elite-owned properties that resulted from military occupation. Despite having frequently "thrown her house open" to entertain federal officers—perhaps as a means to protect her wealth—Unionist Kate Minor failed to safeguard her substantial property, according to a claim she filed with the Southern Claims Commission in 1871. Waging one of the most hard-fought suits to win payment from the US government for lumber, 14,000 bushels of corn, 3,000 bushels of potatoes, 75 mules, and other livestock, as well as wagons and a pair of fine carriage horses, she claimed were taken by federal troops, the widowed mother of three tallied her losses at more than $53,000, one of the largest claims filed in Adams County.

Mrs. Minor's SCC deposition spoke of the hardships inflicted on all social classes and races living in Natchez and the surrounding countryside during the war. Recalling the distress of watching federal troops remove corn from her property in a long wagon train, she stated, "I remember running after them and asking them to leave it, and they told me they would pay me for it, and that was the last of it." In describing her pitiful plight and that of the former slaves remaining on her property she told the Commission: "We sold our own clothes and every thing was taken, we had nothing in the world: we lived within our own resources. We wove our own clothes for the Negroes, our people. We were very much reduced and then we were so anxious for some greenbacks, we sold our clothes to get some."[36]

The household challenges endured by fellow Union supporter Julia Nutt also bears witness to the daily struggles of newly impoverished Natchez whites. Those struggles often persisted for more than a decade after the war. Widowed during the war, Julia Nutt, the mother of eight, filed the largest SCC claim in Mississippi for $1 million in damages to her country plantations and Longwood, her suburban estate that was left unfinished when war broke out.[37] Complaints of money problems and her inability to find reliable, affordable help frequently found their way into the letters she wrote to her young adult son Prentiss, who had moved to Washington in the early 1870s to better oversee his mother's SCC claim. In March 1878 she offered Prentiss this cheerless account of life at Longwood: "I am sitting here in the nursery writing, and watching to see if there is any chance for breakfast. Little Alfred is rubbing the knives for breakfast. Old Mary is scolding in the kitchen." A few days later she informed Prentiss that "yesterday I had to borrow a little money to pay the two servants, that is the cook and the washerwoman which cost me $8. And I have to feed them and two children." Julia, who frequently worked in her garden growing peas and lettuce to feed her family, seems to have been just as inept at household chores as Margarette Martin. In one letter to her son, she noted, "On Saturday I burnt my arm very badly, while

I was ironing, and it nearly ran me crazy when ever I went near the fire."[38] Between 1866 and 1884, the US government awarded Julia Nutt $109,000 and an additional $159,884 shortly after her death in 1897 (valued at more than $7.9 million in 2019).[39] Though one of the largest sums paid by the Claims Commission, the money was insufficient to pay off the family's debts and fully restore Longwood to its former grandeur. By the time of her death Julia appears to have withered into a bitterly disappointed and impoverished woman who never fully came to grips with the postwar world.

White Natchez women bore much of the brunt of the suffering associated with wartime hardships on the home front, but the fathers, brothers, and husbands of these women contended with their own wartime traumas. The experiences of white Natchez men played an important role in forging their community's historical narrative. According to a 1903 memoir written by his daughter Ellen Shields, Gabriel Benoist Shields, kin to some of Natchez's largest slaveholders, suffered severe property and personal losses. Union troops had confiscated much of the family's livestock, leaving only a few old horses and cows. Only a handful of slaves remained on the property with most having fled when Union troops arrived. In August 1864 notorious Union cavalry officer Lieutenant Isaac N. Earl arrived at Shields' Montebello home with a band of raiders. When Shields refused them entry into his home, Earl ordered his men to take axes to Montebello's heavy oak doors and shatter the windows with gunfire. Shields and his son Surget fired back in self-defense.

According to Ellen Shield's account, written nearly forty years after the incident, the battle between her father and brother and the Union raiders lasted for close to two hours. When the federals eventually overpowered Shields and his son, they threatened to immediately execute seventeen-year-old Surget before a wounded Union soldier intervened on the boy's behalf. The elder Shields, his son, Ellen, and another sister were then transported to town where the two men were jailed and the women ordered to return home or spend the night in the women's jail. Described as a broken man by war's end, Shields spent the last of his dwindling fortune to send his wife and three sons to France to join other family members.[40] Life experiences like the ones described by Ellen Shields became both the stuff of family lore and a collective southern white historical memory that prized courage and determination in the face of danger.

BLACK AND WHITE ENCOUNTERS IN POSTWAR NATCHEZ

As white and black families coped with the consequences of wartime occupation, they daily encountered a new and often puzzling social order within the public spaces of Natchez's streets, stores, churches, and parks. The mixture of large numbers of newly freed slaves living either on their own or within overcrowded army refugee camps, coupled with 5,000 Union soldiers (more than 3,000 of whom were black, and some of whom Natchez whites knew), 100 or more northern missionaries and teachers (most of whom were women), another 5,000-plus white Natchez civilians, and the 100 or more white merchants eager to serve a diverse clientele in need of food and necessities created a volatile melting pot that at times threatened to boil over from social, racial, and class tensions. In short, occupied Natchez transformed itself into a bustling chaotic, frontier environment that was dangerous, but also filled with opportunity for those who learned how to successfully navigate a rapidly changing social and commercial space.

Natchez was not a new site of commerce. As early as the 1830s, travelers to the town described a vibrant marketplace, with much of the trade conducted by slaves on leave from the plantations where they lived and labored. Writer Joseph Holt Ingraham, a native of Maine who moved to Mississippi, wrote an 1835 account of Natchez's busy Sunday markets where slaves disposed "of their produce and lay in their own little luxuries and private stores. The various avenues to the city are consequently on that day filled with crowds of chatting, laughing negroes, arrayed in their Sunday's best, and adroitly balancing heavily loaded baskets on their heads."[41]

By 1860, Natchez had become a thriving commercial center with a well-developed municipal government providing services on par with much larger southern cities. A little more than 6,000 inhabitants lived within Natchez city limits—3,753 whites, 2,103 slaves, and 176 free blacks—amidst a large slave population of 14,292 in the surrounding countryside.[42] Natchez operated a busy port, shipping close to 50,000 bales of cotton annually, worth well over $2 million. More than 100 retail firms offered a wide variety of consumer goods, including clothing, candies, pharmaceuticals, groceries, jewelry, as well as dry goods, plantation supplies, wines, and liquors. In 1860 the owners of these local mercantile firms, 61 percent of whom were born outside the US, generated close to $2 million in revenues.[43]

Union-occupied Natchez would have astonished rural blacks and African American soldiers with a little spending money in their pockets for the first time. The numerous Union soldiers milling about streets clogged with wagons hauling lumber, cotton, provisions, and people transformed wartime Natchez into a loud and frenzied place, far more chaotic than in antebellum days. For most of the black newcomers, conditioned to onerous field work and the constant threat of punishment on the plantation, the sights, sounds, and smells of noisy, crowded streets lined with stores, stables, and rowdy saloons would have been both intoxicating and overwhelming.

The city streets of Natchez—both the seedy waterfront area, known as Under-the-Hill, as well as the more genteel shopping and business district above—were where black and white Natchez residents of all classes would have commonly encountered one another in search of food, agricultural supplies, clothing, household provisions, and business services. As consumers intent on acquiring the goods and services needed for daily life, they would have flocked to the flourishing retail establishments of Isaac Lowenburg, Henry Frank's dry goods store, or fine groceries from Wolfe Geisenberger, all Jewish immigrants, several of whom who had followed on the coattails of Union troops as peddlers who catered to the needs of soldiers and remained in Natchez to open storefront dry retail businesses. These men as well as other foreigners, northerners, and a handful of locally born men saw wartime Natchez and its large population of newly freed slaves as a vast and promising market.

Within the shops of Natchez, many black men and women would have experienced the delight of making simple purchases. The cashbook of John C. Schwartz, a Bavarian immigrant who had established his Natchez business before the war, reveals the wide variety of both practical and whimsical goods his store sold to a diverse range of customers. Consumers included planters, white merchants, white Union soldiers and authorities as well as numerous freed blacks and African American soldiers. A sampling of Schwartz's records for May 1864 indicates that his "colored" customers bought everything from coffee pots, brooms, fishing tackle, mouse traps, and spectacles to a looking glass and a flat iron for hair. All told, Schwartz recorded sales of more than $1,600 that May, his best month for 1864. By the end of that year his total receipts had tripled with sales of $8,913 conducted in Union currency.[44]

Blacks and others could likely purchase small, inexpensive goods with cash, but they increasingly came to rely on merchants for credit to buy larger items and agricultural supplies. During occupation and for the next three decades, Schwartz and other Natchez merchants made enormous profits by offering highly marked-up goods on credit at hefty premiums. Local white conservative newspaper editors took notice of these transactions and on more than one occasion cautioned that recently discharged African

American soldiers "are being cheated out of their money and time." While newspaper editors and other whites may have been genuinely concerned that black consumers were being taken advantage of, it is even more likely that they disapproved of whites and black shoppers mingling with one another. Moreover, whites criticized black shoppers for spending time away from their domestic and agricultural labors. The same newspaper article blamed merchants for enticing blacks "to loaf about the city, and almost compelling them to purchase their goods at stores, the owners of which are parties in this nefarious business."[45] Such sharp words suggest that long-time residents of Natchez were as unsettled by the sight of African Americans strolling the streets of Natchez as they were by the entrepreneurial merchants, who appeared eager to serve their darker-skinned clientele. The fine Victorian homes built in late nineteenth-century Natchez came to symbolize the increasing wealth of the town's merchants, whose upward mobility challenged the old planter class. Meanwhile, merchants' financial gains often came at the expense of black sharecroppers, who became increasingly mired in debt.

THE RISE OF A BLACK WORKING AND MIDDLE CLASS

The increasing visibility of Natchez African Americans moving about city streets as free citizens and consumers with money to spend signals the upward mobility of many blacks in postwar Natchez. Some of these men and women were members of Natchez's elite free black community who had either been born free or were freed during the war, while others gained their freedom in 1863. A strong network of churches and schools, bolstered by the right of men to vote, empowered many newly freed Natchez blacks—no matter their status—to climb the economic ladder. These social, economic, and psychic gains fueled a sense of communal optimism among Natchez freedmen during the early Reconstruction years.

The emergence of a black middle class took shape with steady numbers of black laborers joining the city payroll as carpenters, building contractors, and providers of other municipal services. For example, Anthony Hoggatt, a mulatto carpenter, was hired to repair city buildings, while other local blacks were paid for providing transportation to registrars, repairing bridges, boarding paupers, and manufacturing soap for the county. Still others earned wages as schoolboard members, teachers, justices of the peace, policemen, and jurors. In one newspaper account listing the names of ninety-six jurors, fifty-nine were black.[46]

Not to overstate the economic mobility of Natchez African Americans during Reconstruction, the majority held low-paying manual-labor jobs. In a random sample of the 1870 census, among seventy occupations held by blacks the majority were employed as draymen, hack men, and valets, jobs that both free blacks and slaves had held before the war. A handful of blacks were employed in the more prestigious middle-class positions of teachers, ministers, policemen, barbers, and municipal officials. As one historian notes, "few skilled African Americans worked in Natchez in 1860 or in 1870. Most blacks in the town were unskilled laborers both before and after the war."[47]

Blacks living outside of Natchez city limits were far less likely to enjoy any sort of economic mobility in the postwar period. By 1880 nearly three-quarters of all blacks living in the hinterlands of Adams County belonged to a family dependent on sharecropping. The new economic system protected black agricultural laborers from gang labor and gave them some say in when and where they would work in exchange for about one-third of their employer's crop; however, the system failed to help rural blacks move out of poverty and gain land. As Ronald Davis notes, "High interest rates, low cotton prices, the added expenses of chemical fertilizers, and a judicial and legislative system that generally supported creditors over debtors placed freedmen within an economic box from which, like slavery, there was no easy escape."[48]

Testimony found in Southern Claims Commission records significantly broadens our understanding of the daily life of working and middle-class black Natchez residents. Claimant and witness depositions suggests that African American Natchezians possessed a keen entrepreneurial spirit, enabling some of these men and women to build small nest eggs, acquire property, own businesses, and stay afloat during the chaos of war and its aftermath. Some Natchez blacks prospered before and throughout the war years, a status they sought to maintain during Reconstruction. Black claimant Jeanett Carter told commissioners that she and her husband "earned a good deal of money and always lived well" and were never bankrupt before the war. Richard Dorsey, another black claimant, noted that his house was "chuck full of provisions between $200 and $300 in gold and silver." While difficult to verify these claims of economic stability that were meant to buttress SCC claimants' credibility as property owners and help them win their claim, some claimants offered tangible proof of their financial status. Jane Dent, whose house was used to construct barracks for Union troops, proudly showed the deed for the property purchased by her husband in 1842.[49] The testimony of black claimants reveals that despite the dangers they faced in the social upheaval of the war, some members of the African American community not only survived but seized newfound opportunities and thrived.

Within a climate of uncertainty and opportunity, filing a claim with the SCC was only one of several ways for recently freed blacks and free persons of color across the South to gain a foothold on the economic ladder in the early years of Reconstruction. Even before the Civil War was over, some rural Adams County freedmen filed claims over wage disputes with the Treasury Department.[50] The establishment of the Freedman's Bureau in 1865 offered countless Natchez blacks yet another means to interact with a government bureau designed to give them a fair shake in the labor market and political arena. Newly freed blacks and those emancipated before the war came to rely on the bureau for food and clothing rations, medical care, and refugee camps. Additionally, the bureau supervised labor contracts between planters and freedmen and helped to arbitrate when blacks complained over terms they perceived to be unjust.

Legalized marriage was yet another way to achieve greater respect and social stability within a white-dominated society. The marriages of more than four thousand freedmen from Natchez, Davis Bend, and Vicksburg are documented in Mississippi Freedmen's Bureau registers. Many of the bridegrooms were soldiers. More than half of the troops who registered marriages in Natchez served with the Sixth Mississippi Heavy Artillery of the US Colored Troops.[51] Other black civilian couples who had longstanding unions married as well. Fifty-four-year-old Nelson Fitzhugh, a grocer and prominent member of the free black community, married his wife, Agnes, fifty-one, in September of 1864. The Fitzhugh's racial profile as noted in the Freedmen's Bureau register is representative of the complex racial mixing that had long been present in Natchez. Nelson Fitzhugh was listed as one-half white, with a one-half white father and a white mother. Agnes Fitzhugh's father was listed as white and her mother yellow, making her a "half blood."[52] Opening a bank account with the Natchez branch of the Freedmen's Savings Bank was yet another way to create a greater sense of financial security. Shortly before the Freedmen's thirty-four banks closed in 1874, the Natchez branch reported a little more than $22,000 in deposits.[53] Stories of Natchez blacks achieving moderate economic success, entering into legalized marriages, and saving their hard-earned pay—all markers of middle-class respectability—never found their way into the town's white-controlled historical narrative, although it is likely that descendants within the black community were aware of these accomplishments.

FREE BLACK DOMINANCE

Natchez blacks who had been born free or were emancipated prior to 1863 reaped the greatest gains in political and economic empowerment during the Reconstruction era. The free black community had been a highly visible segment within Natchez society for decades. By the early 1860s there were more than two hundred free blacks living in Natchez and Adams County—half of Mississippi's total.[54] As noted by one Natchez historian, "Although vastly outnumbered by slaves, free blacks would play a large role in the postemancipation era as their wealth, educational attainments, and interpersonal relationships with whites gave them disproportionate influence in political social struggles."[55] Known as "blue veins" among local whites for their light-colored skin, which served as a marker of their kinship connections to influential white family members, free blacks were accepted as a "better" class of African Americans among white Natchez elites. In the early postwar years their skin color frequently afforded greater respect as well as better employment and educational opportunities than darker-skinned persons of color. The "blue veins" laid the foundation for an elite, upper-class community of blacks who lived in a world separate from both lower-class blacks and whites. Dependent on their ties to elite whites to maintain their success, upper middle-class Natchez blacks failed to fully embrace the enslavement narrative of lower-class African Americans nor challenged whites' version of the past, a topic that will be explored in the next chapter.

The life and extraordinary career of Louis J. Winston offers a poignant example of the social mobility within reach of some members of Natchez's thriving postwar free black community. The son of a white Adams County planter and a slave mother, Winston achieved great success and recognition during his lifetime before falling victim to Jim Crow discrimination in the early twentieth century. Trained as a lawyer by his white father's close business associate, former Confederate general William T. Martin, Winston played an active role in Natchez civic affairs first as a policeman and then as a circuit court clerk, a position he held for twenty consecutive terms, beginning in 1876. Winston owned a fine house in Natchez, married, and raised a family, while also establishing a building and loan association to assist local blacks in acquiring property of their own.[56]

Winston's success, while somewhat unique, was surpassed by that of John R. Lynch, who spent much of his youth working as a slave at Dunleith, a prominent Natchez estate, before serving in the Mississippi legislature and later as a US congressman. Lynch's brother, William H. Lynch, served as a state legislator for brief periods in the 1870s and 1880s. Robert Wood, born into a free black Natchez family, was elected the first black mayor of Natchez, and served in a number of other municipal positions. Wood and prominent free black Robert Fitzhugh managed the successful congressional campaign of John Lynch.[57]

Elite, free black Natchez women, somewhat harder to trace than men, played an important role in sustaining upper-class African American culture in the late 1800s. Anna Johnson, the matriarch of a prominent, free black Natchez family, taught at the Union School for many years along with a group of other prominent black women.[58] Light-skinned Agnes Fitzhugh, enslaved before her husband Nelson purchased the couple's freedom in 1834, played a prominent role in the black community and the Zion AME Church after the Civil War. As cofounder of the Daughters of Zion, a benevolent society, Mrs. Fitzhugh helped to organize fairs, bazaars, and elegant suppers to raise one-third of the monies required for a down payment on a new church sanctuary in 1868.[59]

AFRICAN AMERICAN CHURCHES

Black churches provided a social space free from white interference where members could openly express their hopes and dreams for a better future, while fulfilling cultural, recreational, and spiritual needs. As early twentieth-century civil rights leader W. E. B. Du Bois claimed, the church became the freedmen's sanctuary and "represented both the institutionalization" of black "community life and defiance to white authority." Churches also offered newly freed black men and women training in management, finance, and organizational skills, fulfilling the various social needs of their members. Within the safe haven of a church sanctuary, black ministers across the South helped their flocks navigate the uncertainties of freedom in the postwar period.[60]

The growth of Adams County black churches and the prosperity of some of their members bear witness to the power and influence of religious institutions within the Natchez African American community. Natchez was home to a large black Catholic congregation as well as numerous Baptist and African Methodist Episcopalian (AME) houses of worship. From 1865 to 1870 the number of black churches in the county grew from seven to eighteen. Holy Family Parish, whose congregation originated within the white St. Mary's Cathedral in 1869, attracted some of the most elite members of Natchez's black community before creating a separate African American parish and church building in 1894. Nearly 70 percent of Holy Family's members were light-skinned mulattos, who believed themselves to belong to a higher caste than darker-skinned individuals. Members included a number of upper-class blacks like county clerk Louis J. Winston, constable and later bakery owner William Minor Davis, Mayor Robert H. Wood, county jailor W. W. Bowie, and state assemblyman G. F. Bowles. All of these men were recognized as being among the "better" black citizens. Other members of the church worked as skilled craftsmen, owned shops as well as their own homes. The membership of Holy Family Parish was also relatively well educated and controlled the local Republican Party. As historian Richard Tristano, who conducted in-depth research on the congregation, notes, "Founding families of Holy Family Church were exceptional. The mere fact that they were urban dwellers when the vast majority of African-Americans lived and worked on farms made them unusual."[61]

Black Protestant churches boasted a prominent but somewhat less elite membership than Holy Family Church, while maintaining social connections with black Catholics. Some of the city's most respected and financially secure Natchez blacks were members of the Zion AME Chapel. Trustees for the AME church included high-ranking members of the Natchez black community such as grocer Nelson Fitzhugh, whose net worth included $3,000 in real estate and $9,000 in personal property (equivalent to $227,000 in 2019 dollars), and drayman Charles Harris, who reported $2,000 in personal property. Zion Chapel, boasting 350 members and 200 students attending its school, played a "central role" in black Natchez life and as part of a Christian mission that radiated from Natchez "in a circumference of 60 miles in every direction." The nine satellite AME churches that grew out of the Zion Chapel included nearly 1,000 members, nine schools, 470 students, and church property valued at a little over $10,000.[62] Like their peers at Holy Family, the members of Zion AME Chapel also played a leading role in civic affairs in the early postwar years. The church hosted organizational meetings for the Union League, three AME trustees held positions within the local Republican Party, and at least four AME ministers held political office in the Natchez District.[63]

Letters from Natchez religious leaders and visitors to the town's African American churches during the early postwar years depict a vibrant, prosperous, and growing church membership that played an integral role in the lives of many black Natchezians. A correspondent for the *Christian Recorder*, the official organ of the AME church distributed across the South, reported that "there is a large Society in this place, all the leading Christian denominations are represented here, with a community strongly imbued with the principles of Christianity, in both white and colored persons. We [AME Zion Chapel] have a membership of about seven or eight hundred and a splendid church property. With the enterprising spirit of the people of this place ... we have no doubts of complete success."[64]

Correspondents were particularly impressed with black Natchez churches' resiliency in times of trouble. When Zion Chapel's uninsured church was destroyed by fire in May 1868, church trustees took on a seven-year nine-thousand-dollar mortgage for property purchased from the white First Presbyterian Church, an indication of church members' commitment and resources. As noted by Zion Chapel pastor James C. Waters, "never did a people labor more earnestly for an object than these people have.... All that pluck and courage can accomplish under God, shall be done to come out this side up with care."[65]

Visiting missionaries and ministers in the early postwar years also documented the prosperity and success of some black church members. After preaching to a large and enthusiastic crowd at the Rose Hill Baptist Church, one black correspondent noted: "The condition of the colored people in and around Natchez is very good indeed, considering the trials and hardships they have had to contend with. Some of them are quite wealthy, and the majority of them are in comfortable circumstances."[66] Two years later, another reporter observed that "there are a great many colored men in Natchez and vicinity, whose families present a considerable degree of refinement,... there are some very successful colored cotton planters in the vicinity of this place, who are comparing favorably with the whites.... In fact they are a thriving and a go-ahead people, and are determined to be something more than the mudsills of society."[67]

As the political and financial situation significantly worsened for Natchez blacks in the 1870s, the church played an increasingly important source of support within the black community. Pastor Waters noted in December 1873 that "politically the outlook is dark" but found sustenance in his faithful flock, writing: "Zion Chapel A.M.E. Church was never perhaps in a better condition, spiritually, than at present.... Much of this success is due to ... energetic working men, backed up ... by as fine a band of Christian women as are to be found anywhere."[68]

BLACK SCHOOLS

The steadfast commitment of black churches to literacy and education played an integral role in the development of a strong network of schools for adult freedmen and their children in Natchez, another important site of black community building in the postwar era. Between 1862, when the first Northern missionaries arrived in the South, and the early 1870s, when most of these teachers returned North, hundreds of mostly female, white teachers instructed newly freed slaves. Paid small salaries and often living in extreme hardship, these "Yankee schoolmarms," worked hard to provide their black students with a basic education.[69] The American Missionary Association (AMA) played the largest role of the many benevolent societies assisting blacks during the Civil War and Reconstruction and had a significant presence in Natchez. Up until the Civil War, Mississippi, like all southern states, outlawed teaching blacks how to read or write. Black pastors and their churches in Natchez labored tirelessly to reverse this trend, working closely with the AMA and other philanthropic organizations to find housing for classrooms and teachers and later to build schools.

The first AMA teachers and missionaries who arrived in Natchez in January 1864 faced a daunting task. The association's teachers were infrequently paid and often struggled to secure adequate room and board, all while trying to teach the poorest of Natchez's black students. Nevertheless, AMA teachers and missionaries proved resourceful in educating their charges. The first AMA school in Natchez was conducted under a large magnolia tree by Lizzie Welsh. In a letter written to Reverend George Whipple, the corresponding secretary of the association's New York City headquarters, Welsh explained her method of teaching the large crowd that gathered: "I take a primer with large letters and holding it as high as I can conveniently gather around me as many as can see and drill them a few minutes then take another group... . I anticipate a larger attendance tomorrow. Were it not that we expect a reinforcement of teachers soon I should feel wholly crushed." Welsh found her students to be "very degraded and in great destitution" but added that "they are very anxious to learn and very ready to receive any thing we offer them by way of bettering their physical condition."[70]

Despite a shortage of classrooms and supplies, within two months after its arrival the AMA had organized six day-schools and three night-schools with nearly thirty teachers serving six hundred students.[71] As AMA missionaries and teachers in Natchez tended to poor, illiterate freedmen of all ages, black elites paid to send their children to private schools. By late 1865 six private, black-run schools taught by black teachers were in operation, reflecting the growing wealth of members of the urban, upper-class black community and their desire to separate themselves and their families from lower-class blacks.[72]

Letters written from Natchez by AMA missionaries and the mostly female teaching staff record the exuberant gratitude of their black students, most attending school for the first time. Missionary S. G. Wright, who supervised AMA teachers in Natchez during and after the war, recorded one such prayer of thanksgiving offered by a "very intelligent woman lately from bondage" whose prayer "was enough to melt all hearts:" "'We prayed and agonized that these teachers and preachers might come to teach us and our children. Glory to God, they have come. Our eyes see them; our ears hear the sweet words which fall from their lips. Our children are taught by them. We are happy we are blessed. Lord bless these precious friends, O bless them.'"[73]

In the early days of their association, AMA workers frequently complimented the efforts of their black Natchez students. Missionary Palmer Litts reported that "I believe that there is a thirst after knowledge among the blacks unparalleled in the history of any people or nation. . . . I had some in my school who were better scholars than any with whom it has been my fortune to teach in schools for white children."[74] Teachers like Ann Keen praised elderly students who were learning to read and write alongside younger pupils. In one letter she told of an elderly Baptist minister, who was "anxious to learn, and reads a chapter from his Testament every night. The other, an old Aunty who does not know her letters yet; she says if she could only read and write she would ask for nothing more in this world."[75] Such statements attested to the sense of fulfillment missionaries and teachers found in working with freedmen, and the transformative impact education had on former slaves.

Over time, though, the relationship and sentiments between AMA officials and the black Natchez community soured as white missionaries sought to exert greater control over black institutions. Tensions flared between members of the black community and the AMA over determining who should control and teach in Natchez schools. When blacks learned that a new schoolhouse under construction for African American students would not offer employment to black teachers, many expressed anger with AMA officials. Responding to a comment purportedly made by AMA supervisor S. G. Wright that black teachers "could not compare" with white teachers, a black Baptist minister wryly questioned if northern black teachers "had lost [their] knowledge coming down here."[76] Black leaders acted upon their outrage by taking control of schools whenever possible. After refusing white missionaries' attempts to open a school at Wall Street Baptist Church, missionary Palmer Litts was dismayed to learn that blacks had "opened a school there under 'black colors.'" Adding that the freedmen seemed "determined to have the rule in regard to teachers and preachers and their favorite is Black," Litts, like many in his position, never fully came to terms with Natchez blacks' desire for autonomy and control over their schools and churches.[77] As Heather Williams notes in her study of African American education in the postwar period, male missionaries "could be concerned, committed antislavery men and, at the same time, self-promoting competitors for black people's souls and the applause for working among them. They could be simultaneously selfless in their dedication and obsessed with their own heroic allure."[78]

Growing numbers of blacks challenged the AMA over issues of racial prejudice and white interference in managing African American schools and churches. Five months after her arrival in the summer of 1865, Blanche Harris, one of the few black AMA teachers working in Natchez, reported that "the distinction between the two classes of teachers (white and colored) is so marked that it is the topic of conversation among the better class of colored people." Harris, trained at Oberlin College like many of her AMA white peers, reported that her male supervisors had requested that black teachers board with the domestics in the house where white AMA teachers lived. She also complained that she was told that "she must not expect to eat" with the white AMA teachers. Harris refused to room at the white AMA boarding house under such conditions, and instead found separate rooms for her sister and herself with a black family. According to Harris, Natchez AMA supervisors S. G. Wright and Palmer Litts pressed the two women to move to the countryside, "or any place but Natchez." With the support of the black community Harris stayed put, noting "the colored people seemed equally determined to have us remain and they would support us."[79]

Though sometimes challenged as to who would ultimately control black Natchez institutions, the strong sense of community derived from a tightly knit network of churches and schools bolstered black political agency. Churches and schools prepared and inspired African American men to vote and become active in local political organizations. Under Republican rule, for a brief time in the early 1870s, a number of Natchez blacks served in elected governmental posts, including as mayor, aldermen, justices of the peace, grand jurors, policemen, and legislators in the State House of Representatives. These gains were made possible by the large numbers of black males who registered to vote and headed to the polls. Black male voters cast nearly 60 percent of the votes cast in the January city election in 1871, resulting in a Republican victory.[80] More than 4,100 black males in Adams County were registered to vote in 1869, a figure that would drop to 3,249 by 1876.[81] The proud legacy of Natchez's African American schools, churches, and vibrant political activism during the Reconstruction era gradually faded from public view as their political agency diminished, and their stories were never incorporated into the town's dominant historical narrative.

"NO FORGETTING THE PAST"

As black Natchez residents traversed city streets on their way to schools, churches, shops, political meetings, and work places, white Natchezians took notice. Numerous letters, diaries, newspaper stories, and oral reminiscences of the postwar era reveal the immense psychological shock, fear, and sometimes rage that gripped whites as they witnessed black men and women exercising their freedom in public spaces. The struggle to cope is evident in the reminiscences of Mary Conway Dunbar, who several decades afterward recalled seeing her father taken prisoner during Union occupation "by a regiment, which had been increased by negroes. Those black men in their bright blue uniforms were a fearful sight to a southerner. I shall never forget the scene with my father in the midst of them." Nor could she accept the idea of seeing black soldiers carrying firearms, empowered to arrest whites, noting, "The arming of the negroes was a terrible thing and difficult to bear patiently."[82]

The daughters of the late Mississippi Governor John Quitman, a fierce supporter of secession before his death in 1858, shared Mary Dunbar's despair and outrage over changing racial boundaries. Annie Rose Quitman Duncan's journal records her trepidation in seeing armed black Union pickets stationed near Monmouth, the home she shared with her sisters. "For some days they were on the hills first opposite us, we could hear their gruff laugh ... & see their blue coats moving about from tree to tree." Antonia Quitman Lovell, Annie Rose's sister, so outraged by challenges to white supremacy by black enemy occupiers, for a time considered abandoning her home for England. In a letter written to a friend six months after the end of the war, she stated: "I fear you will not again return to our once lovely South—such a desolated country as it now is. Our hearts are broken with the ruin of our beloved Country, alas we have now no Country & very my great longing now is to go far away where I can never see again the face of one of our oppressors."

Although she never left her homeland for "a sweet embowered cottage in Old England," she longed for in one letter, Antonia never fully came to terms with enemy occupation either.[83] In a letter written in February 1866, Antonia expressed her deep hatred toward Union soldiers that was intensified by the African American troops stationed in Nachez, stating: "Much as I hated the race before, I feel a ten-fold bitterness to them now. I cannot grow familiar with the sight of them, the glimpse of that uniform fills one with loathing and horror, and I feel as I ever shall do that they are our bitter foes forever. With me there is no forgetting the past, indeed the present keeps it continually in remembrance. This galling yoke is more than we can bear, and now the brightest hope we have is to get away from this downtrodden country."[84]

Witnessing free black women leisurely strolling the streets of the city while dressing and acting the part of southern "ladies," a status once reserved exclusively for white women, was particularly unnerving to Antonia Quitman Lovell. Voicing the frustrations shared by many privileged white southern women, Lovell fumed with sarcastic racist venom that "the delicate constitutions of our great American Ladies of African descent," refused to "retire from the gaieties of town" and walk the distance to her home to perform domestic work. The shortage of reliable servants presented not only a labor problem for former slave mistresses but was yet another stinging reminder that the social hierarchy they had once enjoyed had radically changed.

White Natchez men were as vocal as women in their contempt for African Americans and their newly acquired civil rights and claims on public spaces. From Washington, DC, Prentiss Nutt frequently voiced his anxieties about the South's changing racial hierarchy to his mother Julia, who struggled to maintain her Natchez estate after the war. "The negro element is a curse to the whole South and unless the gentlemen of the country act their part bravely and properly it will be no fit place to live in for people of respectability," he railed in one letter.[85] But even Prentiss, who may have harbored hard feelings towards blacks because he failed to oust Natchez's black postmaster, a position which he coveted, could not totally ignore the realities of the new hierarchy. Prentiss found himself in the unusual position of a once wealthy white southerner seeking political assistance from his district's black congressman in resolving his mother's claim with the Southern Claims Commission, a process which required approval from the House of Representatives. In the letter he wrote to his mother about approaching black Natchez congressman John Lynch for help he remarked: "I met the Honorable Mr. John R. Lynch the other day coming out of the Senate Chambers.... I was glad to see him ... and he appeared glad to see me.... John Lynch is ready to help me all he can in whatever I wish."[86] The tone of Prentiss Nutt's letter indicates he accepted the idea that he had no choice but to deal with his black congressman, but as a white male he intended to maintain the upper hand in the relationship, casting Lynch in the role of an eager servant ready to carry out the Nutt family's wishes.[87]

GROWING RACIAL TENSIONS

Relations back home in Natchez between white men and blacks were often far less cordial. Natchez newspapers frequently expressed the animosity and frustration of whites toward blacks intent on taking advantage of their newly gained civic freedoms. News of the formation of five black militia companies in May 1866 carried with it an ominous warning to white citizens, reporting that " ... nearly every colored man and many colored boys in this city and county are armed and equipped with arms and ammunition.... That whilst there are many of the race peaceable, quiet, orderly, well-disposed and willing to work there are many others who are ambitious, discontented, restless, idle and reckless, who would do mischief if they could."[88]

The "mischief" male editors alluded to was the refusal of blacks to work as needed to restore the region's agricultural economy, an anxiety not unfounded, according to numerous documents. As one Mississippi judge noted in a letter to President Andrew Johnson, "[the] country Negroes lived in idleness and utter demoralization. The freedmen generally refused to work in the fields on any terms.... If not allowed to do as they pleased in every respect, [they ran] to town to make complaint to the Freedmen's Bureau or to the provost marshal."[89] Equally troubling were worries that black males lusted after white women, a prevalent fear among white southern men. By 1867 newspaper editors voiced concerns that many blacks were joining the Union League, a Republican-sponsored political organization designed to gain the African American vote. In May of that year "not less than two hundred members (colored) were admitted to the League," one Natchez newspaper reported. Editors of the *Tri-Weekly Democrat* encouraged "all sensible negroes" to "attend to their work until the proper time comes to register."[90]

White anxieties about the newly acquired freedoms of the recently emancipated sometimes spilled over into the public spaces of postwar Natchez. Acts of violence and the threat of danger served as a constant reminder to Natchez blacks that freedom from slavery offered few guarantees of safety, even under military occupation. The frontier-like atmosphere of the town comes into sharper focus with the knowledge that the town lacked an organized police force until 1870, yet another impediment to maintaining law and order in the early postwar period. A letter published in a black newspaper shortly after the Civil War noted the perils Natchez blacks faced from defeated rebel troops making their way home. "The returned rebels have commenced to actually re-enact the crimes, the barbarous, fiendish, deeds they have always been guilty of, but with increased force of savageness.... They are actually murdering colored people." Within the same article, the Natchez correspondent reported an incident where an elderly "colored lady of means and respectability was knocked down and brutally assaulted by a notorious rebel deserter." The writer concluded that "slavery is not dead," adding that the "ordinary privileges" of citizenship without suffrage "are as baseless as a shadow."[91]

Natchez blacks had just reason to fear death by hanging or other forms of violence. Recent scholarship reveals that several hundred enslaved people were murdered in Adams County by white vigilantes prior to federal occupation. Laura Haviland, a white, northern school teacher who came to Natchez during federal occupation to teach the children of the formerly enslaved, documented 209 enslaved people who were murdered either by hanging or being whipped to death by white vigilantes, many of whom were among the county's leading slaveholders. Other sources indicate that a large number of additional blacks were killed at the fairgrounds near the city as vigilante acts continued to mount right up until the arrival of federal troops in the summer of 1863. In all, historian Justin Behrend believes from 200 to 300 enslaved persons in Natchez and surrounding Adams County were lynched, tortured, and executed based on questionable charges of insurrection during the war years.[92] Not only were these crimes against humanity never investigated or prosecuted after the war, but the perpetrators returned to power in the postwar era and became part of the machine that began to spin a distorted memory that covered up such atrocities for more than a century.

Not all public encounters between blacks and whites in the postwar years were violent or contentious. Relations between the races could be amiable, even when tinged with shades of paternalism. Take, for example, the November 1866 afternoon when "an old negro accosted" white elite Joseph Shields in downtown Natchez. After the black man confirmed he was speaking to Lawyer Shields, he showered the white planter with a bouquet of compliments, according to Shields. In a letter written by Shields describing the incident to his wife, the unidentified man told Shields: "Master since I has been hanging around the Court House I just like to hear you talk, sir. You does talk so pretty. And make me understand and explain things so well sir and everybody can hear you, sir." After walking with the man for a time, Shields noted "the humble praise of this unlettered old man really was very pleasant to listen to."[93] Perhaps the black man was seeking a favor from Shields, but Shields, who relished the opportunity to speak at public events, obviously appreciated being fawned over by an African American who recognized the lawyer's place in the social hierarchy. For Shields, the encounter also served as a welcome reminder of an earlier era when blacks routinely treated whites with deference and subservience, attitudes that were in flux in the postwar period.

The failed attempts of Julia Nutt to gain the necessary signatures for her son Prentiss to file a petition for a choice civil service position in Natchez offers a second example of murky and unpredictable race relations. Prior to embarking on a law career, Prentiss Nutt served as a tutor for a Washington widow's children—a position he loathed. He hoped to gain appointment as Natchez postmaster, a position held in the 1870s by Robert Fitzhugh, son of prominent free black Nelson Fitzhugh. In numerous letters Prentiss nagged his mother to gather the necessary signatures to apply for the job, which paid an annual salary of $3,400 (equivalent to $64,000 today). "Try and send me other petitions, one from lawyers, one from the merchants and an omnibus petition with as many signatures as can be got to it, even every nigger on the highways," he wrote in one letter to his mother. A day later he brought up the matter again, writing, "It must be the policy of the people now to combine on my [petition] unless they want to see a negro continue to hand out the letters to the proud and aristocratic citizens of Adams County." Julia reported a few days later that the petition campaign was going poorly and in the process she found herself humiliated when white friends and neighbors refused to endorse Prentiss for the job. "I have done what you have asked me to do," Julia wrote her son, "and now if you don't succeed I will bear the odium of trying to put Fitzhugh out. I have had my feelings hurt several times yesterday, by persons, who I would ask to sign the petition, for the reason they had no fault to find with Fitzhugh, and that the office was conducted better than it had been since the war."[94] Fitzhugh retained his position, evidence that race did not always dictate the outcome of plum patronage appointments and that white Natchezians in some instances were willing to entrust and reward a handful of elite blacks with well-paying civic jobs.

The profound reconfiguration of Natchez social life and racial hierarchies during the turbulent postwar period became the foundation for the town's historical narrative and memory that emerged in the 1880s. Natchez whites who had survived the traumas of a stunning military defeat—poverty and loss of family members, property, and slave labor—used these life experiences to mold a historical memory dedicated to paying tribute to a destroyed way of life and those who had given their lives to defend it. In crafting their historical consciousness whites emphasized the gentility of southern civilization, the valor of Confederate soldiers, and the courage of female and elderly male civilians who heroically protected the home front. The memory crafted, however, was selective, with little room for black experiences told from a black perspective. Stories of wartime hardships among African Americans, black community building, and the exercise of civil rights were literally whitewashed from the dominant collective memory.

Even as Natchez's dominant white historical memory of the Old South resonated at home and across the nation, the African American community refused to remain silent. Shortly after the war and well before white historical consciousness took hold, Natchez blacks began to build their own traditions based on shared enslavement and emancipation experiences that bore no resemblance to the narratives of their white masters. New research makes it possible to reclaim these nearly forgotten postwar black historical memories, and it is to these stories that we now turn.

CHAPTER TWO

MEMORY MAKING ON PARADE

African American Historical Identity in Reconstruction-Era Natchez

THE MORNING OF JULY 4TH, 1867, IN NATCHEZ, MISSISSIPPI, WAS HOT AND muggy, the air thick with humidity as thunderclouds loomed on the horizon. Despite the threat of a storm, thousands of black men, women, and children converged on the city like never before. A flotilla of tiny skiffs, flatboats, and ferries carried many hundreds of holiday revelers across the murky Mississippi River from nearby Concordia Parish, Louisiana. Others traveled along the dusty roads leading from the countryside, where only a decade earlier coffles of enslaved men and women had trudged, making their way to the slave markets of Natchez. Today, the crowds came with a different purpose as they eagerly merged in a massive throng through the downtown streets.

Natchez was no stranger to festive public commemorations and celebrations. Long before the Civil War, the town's white residents had hosted parades, picnics, and orations celebrating national independence, George Washington's birthday, May Day, local firemen's associations, and the arrival of circus troupes and minstrel shows.[1] Of these public celebrations, the Fourth of July holiday was one of the most festive and cherished occasions. With the outbreak of the Civil War, however, Natchez whites like most white southerners, dispensed with Independence Day festivities, referring to it in one local newspaper editorial as "the day which brings them no brighter hopes for the future."[2] Two years after the Civil War, Natchez African Americans laid claim to public space once dominated by local whites, organizing one of the largest black celebrations not only in Adams County, but the entire South. On July 4, 1867, some 8,000 to 10,000 African Americans claimed the holiday in downtown Natchez as their own. The men wore ribbons, many carrying American flags, the women dressed in their Sunday best, shepherding their children through the crowds gathered on Main Street—all excitedly awaiting the parade organized by the Republican Union League to begin. A festive picnic followed featuring music, singing, and a stirring speech delivered by a gifted black orator on the grounds of Longwood, the suburban Natchez villa owned by proclaimed Unionist Julia Nutt, a prominent white widow who now struggled to keep a roof over her family's head.

The magnitude of the Independence Day celebration organized by black leaders in 1867 fits squarely within the context of the many nineteenth-century public parades and celebrations staged by marginalized groups in the North. Parades frequently empowered former slaves and immigrants to express what one historian refers to as the "stories a people tell about themselves."[3] Public parades and celebrations offer useful insights about urban social culture, order, and the construction of collective historical consciousness. Within the post–Civil War South, such celebrations served as "crucibles" in which blacks performed important social and political acts and roles that had long been denied to them. As historian Genevieve Fabre writes: "While performing during their celebrations, African Americans were training themselves and shaping their anticipated roles as full-fledged citizens, capable of participating in public affairs. Feasts were not only a 'big time' to enjoy; they held out a promise to refashion a better world and wield new power."[4]

Such promises also became the foundation on which to construct the beginnings of a viable postemancipation identity. Within this new mindset, former slaves began to re-envision themselves as "proud members of a heroic race and a revitalized nation."[5] Emancipation celebrations encapsulated more than expressions of thanksgiving and joy. They also symbolized the immense suffering that had accompanied the end of slavery. Embodied in the black traditions on display were remembrances of deadly refugee camps, the African American soldiers who had lost their lives in battle, and the threats of violence from Confederate vigilantes. As David Blight writes, "For many freedpeople, emancipation meant the struggle to survive in the new, chaotic social order, and it provided few if any occasions for celebration in the short term."[6] Coupled with memories of enslavement and the battle for freedom, the formerly enslaved infused their postemancipation identity with a sense of hope and new beginnings. Collectively there emerged a belief that the Emancipation Proclamation guaranteed blacks the same rights enjoyed by other free men and women. Such rights included economic independence, political rights, and social equality, such as the right to marry and raise families free of white interference.[7] A postemancipation identity gave birth to a vibrant set of traditions during and after the Civil War that included parades, commemorations, public speeches, and school exhibitions. Such traditions helped to articulate a new black historical consciousness based on the promises of freedom rather than the world of slavery that reverberated in black communities across the South.

Unlike some black communities that sustained a strong black emancipation tradition for several decades, Natchez did not. In less than a decade Natchez witnessed one of the largest emancipation celebrations in the region, quickly followed by the nearly total obliteration of black public tradition making. Several studies have documented numerous commemorations organized across the South by black communities beginning shortly after the Civil War, offering a valuable overview of tradition building within the African American community. Much of this scholarship, however, only scratches the surface of the unique characteristics and struggles of the individual black communities that forged these traditions and how they changed over time.[8] Community studies like this one help to illuminate the many subtle dynamics and differences within African American memory making. New research challenges the widely held assumption that white cultural leaders in Natchez initiated their town's collective memory making and traditions in the postwar period. New evidence reveals that it was in fact Natchez's African American community that originated efforts to establish a post–Civil War memory long before Natchez whites launched their own memorialization efforts in the 1880s.

Two large public Natchez commemorations staged in 1867 and twenty years later in 1887 reveal that social and political conditions played an enormous role in shaping the nature and content of black identity and historical tradition building in the postemancipation era. Moreover, the traditions examined here underscore the notion that historical memory is not only segregated by race and gender, but by class divides as well. In the case of Natchez, black historical memory was never monolithic and was all too often shaped by class tensions within the black community that became increasingly more evident over time. Additionally, recent findings illuminate the fluidity of racial relations during the early postwar years, suggesting that a black emancipationist identity had not yet crystallized but was very much in flux. That being said, it is important to acknowledge that tracing African American commemorations and those who crafted these traditions is often problematic due to a scarcity of primary sources. With no extant black Natchez newspapers and few available memoirs or letters written by African American Natchezians in the late nineteenth century, other sources must be used to tease out this narrative. Black church and fraternal association records, biographical accounts of black politicos, city ordinances, regional black newspapers, white newspapers, photographs, and the *Christian Recorder*, published weekly by the African Methodist Episcopal (AME) church, are also useful in constructing an account of those who shaped early post–Civil War black historical traditions in Natchez.

BLACK CITIZENSHIP ON PARADE

The festive Independence Day events of July 1867 marked the emergence of a black historical consciousness infused with optimism and hope. Southern African Americans had begun organizing public emancipation celebrations on New Year's Day in cities and towns across the South as early as 1863; however, in Natchez, blacks did not take to the streets in large numbers until the summer of 1867. Not that the significance of emancipation was lost on the black Natchez community. A church celebration sponsored by the Rose Hill Baptist Church and AME Zion Chapel in January 1865, with assistance from white AMA missionaries, attracted scores of participants. The children of congregants played the leading role in a festive celebration that included prayer, recitations, songs, and a reading of the Emancipation Proclamation.[9]

The July 4, 1867, celebration represented a culmination of several pivotal events that had unfolded in the preceding months. During the late 1860s, and the year 1867 in particular, African Americans from Natchez and the surrounding countryside began to exercise their newly won freedom in a variety of ways, a reminder that freedom was not fully realized by a specific moment like the passage of the Emancipation Proclamation in 1863, the arrival of Union occupiers, or even the end of the war.[10] In a variety of public spaces—downtown streets, churches, schoolhouses, and commercial venues—as detailed in the previous chapter, Natchez blacks gained confidence and the necessary skills to exercise the rights of citizenship while simultaneously shaping a distinctive post–Civil War collective identity.

The passage of the Military Reconstruction Acts in the spring of 1867 mobilized Natchez freedmen and blacks across the South to exercise the rights of American citizenship for the first time. These statues nullified the Black Codes passed shortly after the Civil War, which had severely limited the civic freedoms of African Americans across the South. Mississippi was the first southern state to pass Black Codes in 1865, with some of the harshest statutes. Black male minors without proof of parental support could be indentured to a "suitable" person until they were twenty-one years old. Other Black Codes prohibited African Americans from carrying firearms and charged stiff fines for vagrancy.[11] The Reconstruction Acts empowered black men and women to freely move about, gather with one another, and organize social, political, and religious associations.[12] The crowning achievement of the federal legislation established black male suffrage. In cities and towns throughout the South, including Natchez, grassroots political machines began to take shape, further empowering freedmen, and reflected the radical changes underway. The presence of federal troops bolstered the security and optimism of Natchez blacks, who quickly organized an expansive network of churches, benevolent associations like the Good Samaritans, and political organizations, such as the powerful Republican Union League. The memberships and meeting sites of these groups often overlapped with one another. These organizations became the foundation of a strong, protective, and politicized community network. By late 1867 nearly all black males in the Natchez District belonged to the Union League or a Republican club.

Natchez's branch of the Union League, organized in May 1867, attracted the largest number of members among local Republican groups—four thousand according to one regional newspaper.[13] Although the Union League's presence in Mississippi was short lived, the organization initially played a tremendous role in organizing, registering, and instructing freedmen on political issues and how to participate in the political process. In their efforts to promote the Republican Party in the South, the league sponsored speakers, distributed literature, and organized large processions like the 1867 Independence Day procession hosted in Natchez.[14] The grassroots support of local freedmen successfully elected Republican Party candidates; however, the Natchez Union League's leadership was dominated by a group of white men. President E. J. Castello, a former Union Army officer, was assisted by George St. Clair Hussey, L. D. Allen, and Frederick Parsons. The only two black members serving on the executive board were Baptist minister H. P. Jacobs and Wilson Wood, a mulatto storekeeper.

None of the men leading Natchez's First Union Republican Club were native to the area, and nearly all were somewhat shady in their personal business dealings. Both Castello and George St. Clair Hussey were implicated in a scheme to cheat black soldiers out of their military bounties. A Freedman's Bureau agent accused the pair of "using every means to secure self advancement, and wholly regardless of the welfare of the freedmen."[15] L. D. Allen, who had represented at least nine black Natchez claimants before the Southern Claim Commission a decade earlier and was now a member of the board of trustees of the State Hospital, was alleged to have defrauded one of his female clients of a six-hundred-dollar pension to which she was entitled. Additionally, a newspaper report claimed that Allen and his family were living in a local medical facility that had been designated to house yellow fever victims "while poor sick men were being carted about the streets or suffered to die from neglect in the pest house, for want of a better place to put them."[16] Union League secretary and freedman Wilson Wood came under fire for embezzling county school funds while serving as treasurer of Adams County. A local newspaper railed against black minister H. P. Jacobs as a "frothy negro preacher" because he lacked experience in "the science of jurisprudence."[17] Although the Republican leaders' conduct may have been less than virtuous and perhaps even criminal, Natchez whites found them particularly untrustworthy because they were outsiders. In a community that valued longstanding kinship ties and familiarity with a person's social background, the Natchez press vilified top Republicans as "scoundrels."[18]

L. D. Allen, the white secretary of the local Union League, used his political skills and familiarity with local blacks to tap into the strong community network within Natchez black churches. Allen effectively blended political rhetoric with religious fervor. In a speech delivered at Union Street Church, Allen praised God's divine intervention in the struggle for freedom and citizenship, noting, "He has ... given to you the civil rights bill, the amendatory bill, and lastly the military or reconstruction bill, to secure the completion of this work of regeneration from a state of servitude to that of freedom."[19]

The optimism of Allen and other Republican club leaders, coupled with a rapid growth in Union League membership, mobilized growing numbers of ordinary black Natchezians to gather, rally, and pronounce their political beliefs in public venues once controlled by whites. In early June 1867 on the steps of the Natchez courthouse, where only a decade earlier black men, women, and children had been sold to the highest bidder, large crowds of freedmen now gathered to hear radical Republican speakers discuss voting and other civil rights, issues that the *Natchez Democrat* claimed would have made "even the Arch Radical [Thaddeus] Stevens blush."[20] These public politicized events created a platform from which to construct a collective cultural identity and historical tradition within the black community.

Judging from the "at least 8,000" Natchez freedmen who gathered and marched to celebrate the ninety-first anniversary of Independence Day in 1867—the largest demonstration of black or white community solidarity in Natchez history—the Republican party won the first round in the battle for political loyalty in a remarkably transformative year. Reported as an orderly procession, the 1867 July 4 parade in Natchez demonstrated social order in a time when urban disorder was all too often the norm, as evidenced by a town known for the gamblers, petty criminals, and prostitutes who frequented the bawdy saloons of its "Under-the-Hill" riverfront district. The well-mannered procession on display in Natchez served to bring what historian Mary Ryan refers to as a "reassuring" order to "the disorder and cacophony that reigned most of the year" in many nineteenth-century American communities.[21] The orderly behavior of the Natchez freedmen marchers and spectators demonstrated the organizers' and the crowd's intent to present themselves as self-disciplined, law abiding citizens, cognizant of the standards and expectations of "respectability" within public urban space.

Union Club organizers, no doubt aware of Natchez's reputation for rowdiness and disorderly conduct, worked diligently to present a dignified impression. Organizers carefully staged the procession, ranking participants according to social and cultural importance. In what the *New Orleans Republican*, a newspaper owned and operated by African Americans, described as "A Great Jubilee," Grand Marshall L. D. Allen, the white secretary of the First Union Republican club, led the procession, followed by a brass band and glee club. Next came several horse-drawn carriages carrying the day's orator, rising national black politico John Langston, black chaplain H. P. Jacobs, and white club member Frederick Parsons, assigned to read the Declaration of Independence. A series of color bearers and color guards followed on foot with members of two Republican clubs led by their presidents close behind. Citizens traveling by foot, in carriages, and finally on horseback brought up the rear of the orderly parade.

The logistics of planning such a large event would have required the approval of town officials, including Natchez's white mayor and the local commissioner of the Freedman's Bureau, an indication that the gathering was sanctioned by at least some white civil authorities. The Union League procession, though dominated by blacks, "was of many shades of color," including white grand marshal L. D. Allen, according to newspaper coverage.[22] Following the parade, festivities were hosted on the grounds of Longwood, the suburban estate owned by white matron Julia Nutt, yet another indication that parade organizers were in good standing with some white elites. New Orleans press coverage referred to Nutt as "that liberal-minded lady" who "kindly tendered the place for the occasion."[23]

In the estimation of a correspondent reporting for the *New Orleans Republican*, Union League organizers created a memorable day, with black behavior above reproach. In contrast to the numerous white and black Natchez men and women charged with drunkenness, robbery, assault and murder each year, the parade marked a refreshing change in public behavior. The reporter's enthusiastic praise of the event, describing the procession "as the most beautiful sight imaginable, as it wound along for several miles over hill and dale, with flags and banners, fluttering in the breeze," suggests that the journalist and those he observed were emulating refined genteel behavior, a common practice among the lower classes and marginalized groups striving to make a good impression. As historian Richard Bushman writes, "Refinement had the double purpose for blacks of elevating them into the pleasure of beauty and taste and also of breaking down the racial prejudices that closed avenues of growth and economic improvement."[24] The *New Orleans Republican* reporter added with a note of pride that "not a drunken man was seen nor a ghost of a quarrel or even of ill humor exhibited throughout the day."[25]

The league's choice of dynamic orator John Mercer Langston enhanced the prestige of the event, while encouraging party loyalty and political activism among the freedmen. John Langston's career was remarkable prior to and after his speech in Natchez. The mulatto son of a white Virginia planter, Langston was one of the first two black students admitted to Oberlin College. After graduating, he became a successful lawyer in Ohio, was a leading abolitionist in the 1850s, assisted runaway slaves making their way through Ohio, and was president of the Ohio Anti-Slavery Society. He later served as the first black elected to Congress by Virginia. President Lincoln appointed Langston to recruit African Americans to the Union Army during the Civil War. During Reconstruction, he served as inspector general for the Freedman's Bureau, a Federal agency charged with assisting former slaves in their transition to freedom, which is what brought him to Natchez for the Fourth of July celebration. The speech delivered by the thirty-eight-year-old Langston was a highlight of the July 4 festivities and an important milestone in the forging of an emancipationist memory in the Natchez African American community.[26] Delivering his oration from the grandstand erected for the special occasion, Langston was lauded by the *Natchez Democrat* for encouraging his audience to "put away from them the delusive hope of obtaining land by any other means" than "by the proceeds of honest toil and economy."[27]

Langston's full remarks, as published by the black-owned *New Orleans Republican*, however, were more complex and at times directly challenged white supremacy.[28] Much of Langston's address echoed the rhetoric of other black leaders on the speaking circuit as well as the freedmen's texts and newspapers published by white missionary organizations. Urging his audience to refrain from idleness, he prescribed three requirements to fully enjoy the fruits of freedom: sobriety, property ownership, and education. But even as he instructed his listeners to follow a course of racial uplift and respectability, Langston also encouraged the crowd before him to remain steadfast in opposing white supremacy. Langston argued that blacks, by bettering themselves, would ably "meet the duties devolving upon us as men and citizens" and that "no longer can the white man, our enemy, say, 'This is a white man's government, and this a white man's country.'" Speaking from a site within a few miles of the notorious racetrack where vigilante white planters had tortured and executed at least forty male slaves found guilty of conspiracy in 1861, and just a few miles northeast of Second Creek, the plantation neighborhood believed to have been infested with dangerous slave rebels, Langston's remarks would have rekindled the wartime memories of the spirited crowd standing before him. Langston's remarks only went so far, however. Mindful of Natchez's tenuous political and racial climate, the skilled politician measured his words and refrained from calling for outright violence to secure racial, social, and economic equality. Instead, he urged his audience to "show ourselves worthy of the gift brought us, in the providence of God, and equal to the burdens of our new life...."[29]

Langston's instructive remarks, while intended for the large number of lower-class freedmen at the holiday gathering, are reflective of the rhetoric frequently sounded by Natchez black elites, many of whom were the sons and daughters of white fathers and black mothers. Many among this elite group embraced values that closely paralleled Langston's own. Like many of his class, Langston rejected white supremacy in principal but also expected freedmen to toe the line by conducting themselves with an attitude of respectful gratitude and a proper sense of decorum. Langston's remarks must have struck a responsive chord among those in attendance. The following day in the Adams County courthouse, he spoke to an overflow crowd of whites and blacks on the "Status of the American Colored Man," urging his audience to "forget the past" and bury "every prejudice and predilection ... to give our lives, our property, and our honor ... to the preservation and support of the majesty of American law."[30]

A reading of the media coverage generated by local white papers as well as the black *New Orleans Republican* reveals contradictory observations and impressions. White editorial coverage reassured its readers that the day's events posed no threat to social order, reporting soothingly that "we have never seen a celebration so numerously attended and yet more quiet and well-behaved than this was."[31] The black New Orleans reporter covering the event presented a more nuanced perspective on the festivities. Providing a richly detailed account of the day's activities, the *Republican* correspondent characterized the event as an important milestone in African Americans' quest for a postemancipation historical identity. Those on parade and those who celebrated as spectators exhibited a variety of performance techniques heavily reliant on nationalistic and gendered symbolism. Reinforcing the patriotic message of the American flags they carried, the marchers, comprised primarily of men, also marked their bodies with distinctive masculine badges of unity and agency. According to one newspaper account, nearly all of the 2,500 men in the parade came decorated with ribbons, most likely gained from service as Union Army soldiers or as members of one or more of the several black fraternal or political organizations active in Natchez. Although no mention is made in newspaper coverage of the marchers carrying weapons, it is highly probable that Union veterans marching that day would have dressed in their military uniforms and displayed their arms as was the tradition in black parades across the South at the time.[32] The marchers on parade boldly signaled to Natchez whites that as military veterans they were able-bodied men, fully capable of providing for their families and unafraid to defend themselves and their loved ones if necessary. In short, the thousands of participants and the spectators parading through the downtown streets of Natchez—space once dominated by white citizens—sent a memorable visual message of blacks' arrival on the social and political stage and simultaneously challenged white Natchezians' notions of racial supremacy.

Freedwomen exercised equal care in distinguishing the day as memorable. Domestic laborer Keziah Mably, a freedwoman who lived across the river from Natchez in Concordia Parish, Louisiana, took the afternoon of July 3 off to do "some washing for herself" in order that "she might have clean clothing to wear" to the Natchez celebration.[33] The *Republican* correspondent described in great detail the women and children who came "dressed in their very best," with "peasant girls in their white and bright crimson dresses," many sporting "fine ribbons and plumage."[34] The fine apparel worn to such events suggests that African Americans used clothing to mark themselves and their children as refined and respectable, important components in creating a postemancipation identity that distinguished freedmen and women from the slavery era.

The several thousand African American women who lined the streets of Natchez to watch the procession reflected a gendered hierarchy that was becoming increasingly more common among postwar southern black commemorations. Black male militia groups and tradesmen dominated many such occasions by the 1860s. By casting men in leading public roles such events helped to bolster black claims to citizenship.[35] Unlike a growing number of northern and a handful of southern black women in the postwar period who took on increasingly public roles as orators, Natchez African American women maintained more traditional gender roles. Black women in Natchez typically worked behind the scenes, helping with committee work and fundraising.[36] They also played a vital role in community building as teachers and members of female auxiliary groups affiliated with black churches. Watching the uniformed men on parade would have called forth a host of memories among black female spectators of their labors in the recent war, nursing the sick, feeding the hungry, and washing the clothes of black and white Union as well as Confederate soldiers. Remarking on the influence and power of black women in cultural affairs, one planter noted in a newspaper report that freedwomen were "all-powerful" in leading "the colored man."[37] The freedwomen who supported the black men who marched in public processions conformed to a postemancipation cultural identity manifested in African American communities across the South that emphasized traditional gendered notions of respectability, moral uplift, and martial valor.

A WORLD OF SOUND

While the 1867 Fourth of July celebration was reported as orderly, it no doubt produced a symphony of sounds given the large, jubilant crowd in attendance, complementing the strong visual symbols at the parade. White Natchez newspapers made no mention of parade music or songs, but the *New Orleans Republican*'s elaborate coverage confirmed that music played a pivotal role in the day's events. Nineteenth-century parades prided themselves on upbeat, spirited music, and the Natchez Union League parade featured its own brass band and a glee club, playing a medley of patriotic and popular tunes, including several favored by black Union veterans. What cultural historian Lawrence Levine refers to as a "world of sound" was an important component of African American traditions and daily life. Music, chants, and the spoken word had long served as the primary form of communication among both African communities and American slaves. During the Civil War, these musical traditions continued behind military lines as evidenced in the journals and memoirs of Union army officers who frequently wrote of African American bands and impromptu singing among black troops.[38]

During the postwar years, freedom songs and work songs—many adapted from much older antebellum slave spirituals—infused an evolving Natchez African American collective memory.[39]

The music performed that 1867 Independence Day in concert with the cheering crowds and uplifting oratory became an audible memory indelibly inscribed on the Natchez black historical consciousness. While white Natchez newspapers failed to record the music performed, the *New Orleans Republican* noted traditional holiday favorites like "Yankee Doodle," as well as the rousing military song "We'll Rally Round the Flag," also known as "The Battle Cry of Freedom." The verses of the latter tune spoke not only of the valor of Union troops but also urged blacks to join the Union cause:

> We are springing to the call for Three Hundred Thousand More,
> Shouting the battle-cry of Freedom,
> And we'll fill the vacant ranks of our brothers gone before,
> Shouting the battle-cry of Freedom.
>
> We will welcome to our numbers the loyal true and brave,
> Shouting the battle-cry of Freedom,
> And altho' he may be poor he shall never be a slave,
> Shouting the battle-cry of Freedom.[40]

The inspirational music continued on the grounds of Longwood as the glee club sang such songs as "The Fourth of July," that both celebrated national independence and emancipation. Perhaps no song better captured the rich combination of emotions that unfolded on the picnic grounds than the joyful and thankful "Thrice Hail, Happy Day!" which urged freedmen to "cherish long" the memory of "freedom's day."[41]

We have no way to precisely document the impact of the sounds and music of such processions, however, using the reminiscences of a twentieth-century African American musician from the region, we can imagine how such a spectacle of aural impressions affected the crowd. Acclaimed jazz saxophonist Sidney Bechet captured the empowering experience of musical processions for newly liberated freedmen in an autobiographical remembrance passed down from his father that described early postwar New Orleans. "Seems like there was always music around New Orleans in those days," Bechet wrote. "All those people who had been slaves, they needed the music more than ever now; it was like they were trying to find out in this music what they were supposed to do with this freedom...."[42]

In reflecting on black emancipation music, what he refers to as "joy songs," Bechet describes the intense emotional messages such music unleashed for those who performed and heard it: "They heard the music, and the music told them about it [emancipation]. They heard that music from bands marching up and down the streets and they knew what music it was. It was laughing out loud up and down all the streets, laughing like two people just finding out about each other . . . like something that had found a short-cut after travelling through all the distance there was. That music, it wasn't spirituals or blues or ragtime, but everything all at once, each one putting something over on the other. . . ."[43] Bechet saw emancipation music as having a power all its own that rested both in the often brutal memories of the past, while simultaneously empowering the newly freed to begin making the transition from slavery to freedom and finding a new cultural identity. Newly freed Natchez blacks likely found similar solace from freedom music.

Later, as the crowd gathered to picnic, music and leisure evoked a sense of refinement among the holiday celebrants. The *New Orleans Republican* noted the sweet sounds of a harp and violin prompted some people to "dance on the green," as others stretched out on the grass, "while all the old trees were covered with the young boys, delighted at the opportunity to climb." In looking back upon the memorable day, the blacks participating in their first Independence Day holiday would have agreed with the *New Orleans Republican* reporter who crowed, "Never was experienced so happy a day in Natchez."[44] Such sights and sounds marked the occasion as an important milestone in African American tradition in the early postwar era.

CLASS DIVIDES AND CONTESTATIONS OF MEMORY

As Union League revelers picnicked, sang, danced, played, and listened to uplifting speeches on the grounds of the Longwood estate, a smaller group of freedmen and black elites hosted their own July 4 procession through the downtown streets of Natchez. Like the larger parade, the Good Samaritans, a fraternal organization committed to benevolent causes, also "turned out in full regalia, with a very handsome banner, and attracted many compliments from the citizens on account of their fine appearance and good deportment. . . ."[45] In a barb aimed at the larger Union League gathering that holiday, the journalist covering the Good Samaritans applauded the group for being "entirely independent of politics, its procession was separate from that of the political organization." Capping off their parade and picnic, the Good

Samaritans returned to the city in "admirable order," and as they passed the white newspaper office they paid it a compliment of three hearty cheers."[46]

The small story that ran in the *Natchez Democrat* about the Good Samaritans is noteworthy because it dispels the notion that a single black historical tradition resided in postwar Natchez. The Good Samaritan Fourth of July procession brings into bold relief a class-based society that divided lighter-skinned blacks, many of whom were the mulatto sons and daughters of white planters, from darker-skinned persons, the majority of whom had been enslaved until 1863. Similar to those in other southern cities, lighter-skinned blacks in Natchez, who were the farthest removed from bondage, either as a result of having been born free or emancipated before the war, were part of a caste system that created a tightly knit culture based on kinship ties, separating them from lower-class, less educated freedmen.[47] The daughters and sons of the more elite black and mulatto families typically married one another, with children from these prominent families attending private schools for free blacks rather than the public schools established by benevolent groups for poor students.[48] Elite blacks socialized together at benevolent association meetings, such as the Good Samaritans, joined the same churches and fire companies, and attended the same social events.

The racial attitudes and actions of the more than two hundred free blacks who inhabited Natchez on the eve of the war—the largest free black community in Mississippi—played an instrumental role in defining the town's postbellum black cultural identity. Natchez free blacks often enjoyed significant economic and social advantages over the formerly enslaved but also lived in a highly complex world that positioned them somewhere between slavery and freedom. Within this marginalized world, according to historian Ronald Davis, free blacks carefully conformed to rules of acceptable behavior established by whites that emphasized humble deportment and an attitude of servitude in one's work and demeanor around whites. Accepting a racial hierarchy "in which everything and everybody had its place," free blacks forged a black cultural identity designed to protect their elite status and preserve social stability.[49]

The Natchez Good Samaritan association and its politically moderate members offer but one example of how members of the free black community separated themselves from lower-class blacks, including the more radical Union League. For example, freeborn elite mulatto Robert H. Wood, who served as secretary of the Good Samaritans, founded his own political group, the Robert H. Wood Republican Club. One of the most successful black politicians in Adams County, Wood quickly climbed the political ladder, first serving as justice of the peace in 1870 at age twenty-eight, mayor from 1870 to 1872, and then a host of other plum political positions until well into the 1890s.[50] As a moderate Republican who worked closely with white politicians, Wood and his lieutenants were aware of the animosity of white planters like former Confederate general William T. Martin toward the Union League and wisely steered clear of the larger First Union Republican Club. Seen from this perspective, the rousing cheer the Good Samaritans lifted to the *Natchez Democrat* editors is not surprising. Many of the Good Samaritans considered the newspaper and its readers their protectors in a time of political uncertainty and went out of their way to safeguard longstanding relationships vital to their personal success and security.

As elite blacks strived to separate themselves from lower-class freedmen, many among this privileged group maintained close ties with the old white planter class, upon whom they were dependent for their livelihood and political standing. For example, the light-skinned Louis J. Winston used his white father's connections to advance his legal and professional career by initially apprenticing with former Confederate general and attorney William T. Martin. Winston's ability to navigate a complex racial terrain while remaining humble and deferential to whites, served him well professionally and personally. In a speech delivered before the 1891 annual meeting of the Mississippi Co-operative and Benefit Association, a home loan association he founded, Winston announced to his biracial audience: "In Natchez you find the white citizens every ready and willing to assist the colored citizens in every honorable and laudable undertaking that elevates them morally, educationally and financially." In proclaiming the benevolent nature of Natchez's white citizens, Winston at the same time exhorted blacks to "strive earnestly, persistently and unceasingly to advance ourselves morally, intellectually and financially."[51] Winston's paternalistic remarks, sounding much like the accommodationist words of Booker T. Washington, reflected a keen understanding that black success in a white man's world depended on subscribing to notions of "racial uplift." Winston, like many of his cohorts, conducted himself as a humble public servant dependent on the beneficence of white men. Winston judged the sacrifice worthwhile given the results he ultimately achieved. By the late 1880s his efforts enabled more than seventy African American families to secure loans and build homes, an admirable feat.[52] For at least two decades after the Civil War, the mutual respect between black men like Robert H. Wood and Louis J. Winston and white community leaders afforded black Natchez elites more class privileges and a greater degree of political power than that of lower-class blacks.

As the Union League's political influence waned by 1869 so did the frequency and size of political and commemorative processions within the Natchez African American community. Few references to public black commemorations and celebrations appeared in local newspapers; however, the ones noted were relatively small in comparison to the 1867 Fourth of July procession, and most of these were sponsored by black elites. A masked ball was hosted at Institute Hall on January 1, 1872, to celebrate emancipation, preceded by a parade featuring the town's two black fire companies, Good Will No. 2 and Deluge No. 1. Later that year, both voluntary fire associations hosted a "grand picnic" as part of the community's Fourth of July festivities. Although the white newspaper provides no additional information, the role of the fire companies is significant to understanding the growing influence of black elites over public commemorations within the black Natchez community.[53] Of the forty-one leaders of the two fire companies, half were involved in local politics with the majority native to the area and of mulatto descent, suggesting strong ties to the elite free black community. Members of the Good Will Fire Company No. 2 were closely linked to both the free black community and political officeholders. Several of its members—William McCary, Robert W. Fitzhugh, William H. Lynch, and Robert H. Wood—served in political posts and belonged to the town's leading free black families.[54] Although the historical record is silent as to the exact content of these black elite commemorations, Natchez press coverage reveals that the town's upper-class free black community controlled black commemorations by the early 1870s.

DECORATION DAY, 1871

By the spring of 1871, major shifts in Natchez's political and cultural climate marked a significant change in African American commemorative events. Unlike the numerous black southern communities that maintained a vibrant historical tradition for nearly half a century or more, the emancipationist tradition in Natchez eroded in less than a decade. The May 1871 Decoration Day, hosted at the Natchez National Cemetery, a burial ground established by the federal government between 1863 and 1864, reflected a strikingly lower key commemoration than earlier events. Of the more than three thousand Union troops buried in the cemetery, many had belonged to the 58th US Colored Troops, a local regiment, whose members' remains had been reinterred from the bluffs, the Forks of the Roads refugee camp, and other burial sites in Adams County.[55] Union decoration days officially began in

1868, when General John A. Logan, commander in chief of the Grand Army of the Republic (GAR), a Union veteran's organization, ordered members to decorate the graves of the Union dead on May 30. The legislation offered no specifics on how such observances or ceremonies were to be conducted but instructed military posts and veterans to arrange appropriate "services and testimonials of respect."[56] Following the lead of decoration days staged across the North, Natchez attendees, primarily African Americans, decorated the graves of fallen Union soldiers with fresh flowers on May 30, 1871, followed by patriotic speeches memorializing the dead.

In contrast to earlier public black commemorations in Natchez, the 1871 Decoration Day struck a far more conservative political tone. Unlike the optimistic and impassioned address given by black politico John M. Langston in July 1867, the remarks delivered in Natchez in May 1871 by white Republican state senator William H. Gibbs avoided "all inappropriate allusions" to politics, war, or slavery, according to a newspaper report. Instead, Gibbs's remarks closely paralleled Decoration Day speeches delivered across the country that year, privileging the cause of national reunification over remembrances of slavery and emancipation.[57] Sounding a tone of reconciliation, Gibbs called for "a deserving tribute to those other dead [Confederate soldiers] sleeping not far away" who were also "brave, chivalrous and true to the cause they had conscientiously espoused."[58] Gibbs's remarks may have referred to some of the National Cemetery's two thousand unmarked graves. More likely, he was referring to fifty Confederate "strangers" buried at the city cemetery a few miles away, or the many more soldiers interred in private lots scattered across Adams County.[59]

Although several of the black Natchez Decoration Day committee members held more senior political posts than white organizers, only one black orator, Reverend Randall Pollard, is reported to have spoken during the ceremonies according to a local newspaper. An illiterate but influential member of the black community, Pollard delivered the benediction at the close of the program. Did Pollard, who had a reputation for speaking out against segregation in public facilities challenge the reunification sentiments that dominated the Decoration Day event?[60] Perhaps the minister followed a different course on that particular day. Pollard, like many black Natchez politicos, may well have chosen a more measured approach, carefully choosing his words to ensure racial harmony at a time when white Democrats were becoming increasingly more outspoken in challenging black political power and cultural authority. Unfortunately, these questions remain unanswered as Pollard's remarks were not published.

In stark contrast to the July 1867 Independence Day celebrations where masses of rank-and-file black male laborers played a pivotal role, African Americans in the 1871 Decoration Day commemoration served in a far more subservient role. Black male veterans, many wearing evidence of their military service, dominated urban space in July 1867 in a highly charged masculine-dominated event. In May 1871 a far more feminized scene emerged of male and female attendees quietly decorating the graves of Union soldiers with flowers "under the direction of a Committee suitably appointed."[61] The anonymous committee was likely a group of African American women similar to the white Natchez women who devoted their memorialization efforts to Confederate graves. Moreover, it was white men who took center stage to deliver the speeches commemorating Natchez's 1871 Decoration Day. Senator Gibbs told the largely African American audience on a day intended to honor the Union dead that the fallen Confederates were as "brave, chivalrous and true" to their cause as the war's victors.

No record remains of the crowd's response to Gibbs's message, words that former slave and civil rights spokesman Frederick Douglass would have abhorred as "destitute of political memory."[62] Coincidentally, on the same spring day in May 1871 as Natchez blacks gathered to honor their Union dead, Douglass, speaking at Virginia's Arlington Cemetery, urged the nation not to forget its troubling Civil War past. Douglass voiced a far different message than the one black men and women heard in Natchez: "We are sometimes asked in the name of patriotism to . . . remember with equal admiration those who struck at the nation's life, and those who struck to save it—those who fought for slavery and those who fought for liberty and justice. I am no minister of malice . . . I would not repel the repentant, but . . . may my tongue cleave to the roof of my mouth if I forget the difference between the parties to that . . . bloody conflict. . . . I may say if this war is to be forgotten, I ask in the name of all things sacred what shall men remember?"[63]

The marked shift in the commemorative tone from the July 1867 Independence Day celebrations to Decoration Day in May 1871 can be attributed to the growing alliance between influential black elites and white local Republicans holding public office in Natchez. By 1871 numerous prominent black Natchez men held local, state, and national political office, and it was this group of rising black politicos who planned and coordinated the Decoration Day festivities alongside white civic officials. Of the twenty men serving on the planning committee, at least eight were distinguished leaders in the black community. Hiram Revels, a prominent Natchez minister, was the first African American member of the United States Senate, serving from February 1870 to March 1871 in the seat formerly held by Confederate president Jefferson Davis. Revels had recently been appointed president of Alcorn University, a black college outside of Natchez. Simultaneously, John R. Lynch was a rising political star who became the first black elected state speaker of the Mississippi legislature in 1872 before serving his first term in the US House of Representatives the following year at the age of twenty-five. Robert W. Fitzhugh sat on the town's board of aldermen; H. P. Jacobs, who a few years prior had helped to organize the local branch of the Union League, served as a representative in the state legislature. Jeremiah M. P. Williams was a state senator. All but Lynch and Fitzhugh had been born outside of Mississippi, and four members of the group were ministers. Several among this group were officers of the Goodwill Fire Company, a voluntary organization of upper-middle-class black men referenced earlier. These black elites worked alongside local white Republican Party leaders E. J. Castello, the principal organizer of the defunct Union League, and several elected officials to orchestrate the 1871 Decoration Day event, including white county clerk A. H. Foster, who officiated as the master of ceremonies.[64]

The white and black politicos on the dais that day had forged an alliance during the early years of Reconstruction, both from their allegiance to the Republican Party and as coworkers in city government. They also bonded as leaders in local "fusion" politics. In what historian Neil McMillen labels a "peculiar arrangement," white Democrats and black Republicans joined forces to select biracial and bipartisan slates of candidates. The fusion system enabled a small group of elite blacks to hold elective office in counties where blacks held a majority.[65] Three years after the Decoration Day event, moderate Republicans and Democrats in Natchez united to create a nonpartisan fusion slate of candidates to run on the People's ticket in city elections.[66] People's Party candidates pledged to reduce taxes and to favor a "non-partisan municipal government." In November 1874, the People's candidates won all the major offices—mayor, aldermen, and school trustees—and carried about a third of the black vote. A remark made by a local newspaper that the People's ticket attracted "most of the really intelligent colored people in Natchez"—code words for black elites—suggests that numerous prominent mulattos endorsed the fusion arrangement. Indeed, several black Decoration Day organizers were beneficiaries of the fusion system: John R. Lynch, Hiram Revels, George Morris, and John Peck.[67] These leaders within the Natchez free black community saw fusion as a means to ensure political stability and advance their own political ambitions.

Based on a fragile political situation that was frequently challenged by white Democrats, Natchez black elites who served on the Decoration Day committee may have believed they had little to gain personally or politically by cutting their ties completely to the white planter class. From their perspective, advocating too vocally for the interests of lower-class blacks, who had few connections to white powerbrokers, could threaten promising political careers and jeopardize political stability. Black elites may also have reasoned that fusion offered the only viable strategy to achieve some form of economic and social gain for the black masses.

A handful of black Natchez politicians relied on fusion tactics when politically expedient, but also continued to speak out for the needs of black freedmen when feasible, acts that indirectly challenged white cultural authority. Such was the case with Congressman John Lynch, who took a strong stand on civil rights in the face of growing opposition from whites in his district. When the Civil Rights Bill was before the House of Representatives in June 1874, Lynch argued for its passage "because it is an act of simple justice ...; because it will be instrumental in placing the colored people in a position where their identification with any party will be a matter of choice and not of necessity."[68]

Decoration Day committee member Jeremiah M. P. Williams was even more outspoken than Lynch in his opposition to the fusion system and white control. Williams, a Baptist minister and state senator, in a fiery speech delivered just two months before the 1871 May Decoration Day ceremony, warned his audience that "the Democratic party is on the track like bloodhounds; it assumes the clothing of sheep.... This party, made infamous by its devotion to slavery; ... by its efforts to cheat the colored people out of freedom ... by its opposition to the Reconstruction Acts, now seeks to get the votes of colored people in the State of Mississippi."[69]

During 1870, while running against white Republican E. J. Castello, a former Union League leader who held the plum job of Natchez postmaster, Senator Williams proclaimed that "the blacks who did the voting should also hold the offices," adding that "the time had come for the blacks to rely upon themselves more and upon their hitherto white leaders less."[70] Even as growing numbers of black Republicans cut deals with white Democrats to maintain some semblance of political power, at least a handful of black politicians like Williams courageously voiced their dissent in an attempt to maintain a measure of black participation in local civic affairs.

Though occasionally speaking out on behalf of their economically struggling constituents, most Natchez black elites continued to distance themselves from lower-class freedmen, a pattern that became entrenched in the town's social structure by the end of the century. The byproduct of racial and political fusion left a lasting impression on the state, where according to Neil

McMillan, "leading black Mississippians after 1890 were characteristically men of public caution who soft-peddled black grievances, advocated alliance with the 'better class' of southerners, and counseled patient black acceptance of what they thought to be the best white terms then available." Black leaders who embraced this arrangement believed "more could be gained from maneuvering powerful whites into acting out their self-assigned paternalistic roles within the aristocratic tradition than in the open agitation for full social and political rights."[71] Elite Natchez blacks by the mid-1870s actively engaged in such maneuvers, a practice that persisted for decades in Mississippi. Although such an arrangement enabled a handful of elite blacks to maintain a political presence until the end of the nineteenth century, most blacks in Natchez and throughout the state lost political ground. By the late 1880s only a fraction of Adams County black men voted.

For nearly twenty-five years after the 1871 Decoration Day ceremonies no accounts of a public black celebration appeared in a white Natchez newspaper. (Unfortunately, no extant African American Natchez newspapers have survived to determine if the black press covered such events.) In September 1896 a local paper reported that an Emancipation Day celebration in Natchez was expected to draw large numbers of blacks from southwest Mississippi and northern Louisiana, including a reunion of black Grand Army posts and veterans. White newspaper coverage portrayed the event in far less positive terms than the coverage of 1870s Emancipation Day festivities or the huge July 4 celebration staged in 1867. No speakers were identified at the 1896 event, nor was there mention of the content of the messages delivered to the crowd nor details about the participants, their dress, or behavior. Instead, the *Democrat* editors smugly noted that they hoped the blacks visiting their city would spend money in Natchez, observing, "This is perhaps about the best purpose the celebration could serve as far as the city of Natchez is concerned."[72] Similar to the willingness of Reconstruction-era merchants to attract black shoppers, shopkeepers in the late 1890s still sold their wares to anyone who could pay, no matter their color.

Despite the sparse coverage of freedmen's Decoration Days, Fourth of July celebrations, and emancipation commemorations for much of the 1870s and 1880s, glimmers of black historical memory can be found in the oral and present-day traditions of contemporary black Natchezians. Black Union veterans and their descendants from Natchez and nearby Concordia Parish staged marches long after the last soldiers of the United States Colored Troops were mustered out of service in the summer of 1866, an annual tradition that continues. Local blacks relate stories of veteran ancestors and their families from the Vidalia (Louisiana) Parson Brownlow Chapter No. 23 of the GAR crossing the Mississippi River by ferry to join their comrades from the John Logan GAR lodge in Natchez. The groups then made the four-mile trek to the National Cemetery in Natchez. The tradition began in the late 1860s or early 1870s to commemorate a February 1864 Civil War skirmish in Vidalia in which three hundred local black troops helped to turn back an estimated 1,500 Confederate soldiers. According to Clarence Randall Jr., who annually walked in the parade from the 1920s until his death at age ninety-four in January 2010, the event was known as "the May 30 parade. And we felt it was our patriotic duty to participate every year." Noting that the parade once attracted large numbers of Boy and Girl Scouts, Randall told a newspaper reporter in 2003 that the "parade still has a nice size, but not big like it was before."[73] Local whites also carry strong memories of the Decoration Day tradition, an event white Natchez native Kathie Blankenstein remembers vividly as "Yankee Memorial Day" in the 1930s when she was a child. "Although I didn't really understand the significance of it, I found it beautiful and moving, even then. The women always wore white and carried red 'Memorial Day Lilies.'"[74]

Substantiating nineteenth- and twentieth-century memories of "Yankee Memorial Day," "the May 30 parade," or "Decoration Day" is a photograph of a black veterans' group from Natchez likely shot sometime during the 1880s, perhaps in preparation for the event. The cherished stories and the photograph passed down through several generations offer testament to a proud memory and tradition that remained vibrant within the black community of Natchez long after the Union veterans had died. Collective memory making within the black community endured despite the diligent efforts of Natchez's white press to snuff out traditions and memories of black military service to the Union.

Several conclusions can be drawn about the historical consciousness constructed by Natchez blacks in the contentious postwar period. In the first few promising years after the war Natchez blacks found a variety of creative ways to build emancipationist traditions and memories. In these years events hosted in city streets and on public grounds were as much about praising community and emancipation as they were about communicating to the white populace that blacks perceived themselves as full participants in local political life and national political culture. Events like the July 4, 1867, Union League parade and picnic, which attracted a massive crowd, sent a bold message to white residents that the social order had radically changed. A remarkable summer day filled with an array of summer amusements—food,

Grand Army of the Republic, photographed in Natchez, ca. 1880. Robert Livingston Stewart, photographer. (Courtesy of the Archives and Records Services Division, Mississippi Department of Archives and History.)

music, and oratory—created a rich landscape on which to build a new postemancipation identity and historical tradition. If nothing else, the experience of that day marked a turning point that empowered the formerly enslaved to give notice to themselves as well as the white community that "we can do this too." The spirited 1867 Fourth of July parade, which filled the downtown streets of Natchez with black celebrants followed by festivities on the grounds of a white planter family's Natchez estate, symbolized the enormous political, social, and cultural strides freedmen and their families had made since the war. Moreover, these advances signaled the beginnings of a postemancipation identity that hinted of promising future possibilities.

Changing social and cultural conditions played an enormous role in shaping postwar Natchez black historic tradition and memory, particularly those practiced in public venues that required the approval and cooperation of white civic authorities. The radical differences witnessed in the 1867 Independence Day celebration and the 1871 Decoration Day observances represented both the promise and disappointment of Reconstruction, a scenario that repeated itself in countless communities across the South.

In less than five years, the publicly celebrated emancipation memory, controlled and orchestrated almost entirely by Natchez African Americans in the summer of 1867, had nearly evaporated, replaced by a selective memory of reunification dictated by southern and northern whites and endorsed by black elites intent on clinging to political office no matter the cost. In notable contrast to the longstanding emancipation traditions in Virginia, Georgia, and the Carolinas that gradually eroded over time, Natchez experienced a far shorter burst of postwar tradition-building zeal that just as quickly faded. Natchez's Decoration Day commemoration organized in 1871 by black and white Republican leaders signaled a change in the political terrain.

The development of postwar black historical traditions increasingly reflected the growing class divides within Natchez's black community. The declining number of large black public celebrations *not* reported in white newspapers in the last two decades of the nineteenth century is perhaps an indication of the growing dominance and elitist attitudes of Natchez's free black community. Elite black powerbroker families, such as the Winstons, Fitzhughs, and Lynches, likely discouraged organizing large public black commemorations to curry the favor of their white benefactors, protect their own social position, and prevent white violence against blacks. Unlike most celebrants in early postwar affairs who were primarily black Union Army veterans, their recently enslaved families, and poor, illiterate sharecroppers, the more economically advantaged and better-educated free blacks sought to distance themselves from the lower classes. Avoiding crowded spectacles was a means for "better" blacks to protect their standing among a dominant white society that overwhelmingly disapproved of and feared large public gatherings of African Americans. By the time of the 1871 Decoration Day the vibrant historical identity introduced in the late 1860s had faded. A more restrained, moderate tradition had taken its place, controlled largely by cautious black politicos unwilling to risk their political futures. Ordinary black men and women played only a minor, passive role, charged with decorating the graves of fallen Union soldiers. Although a handful of black elites were seated on the dais that day, they served in a secondary capacity, with white officials assuming the leading role. Gambling that fusion politics and taking a stance of reconciliation were the only ways to maintain some semblance of power and upward mobility, black elites' calculation may have been the only viable alternative, given the increasingly strained racial climate. Sadly, it was a move with tremendously damaging consequences. By the late 1890s nearly all Adams County blacks—from the lower class to elites—had been disfranchised and lost their political positions.

Despite these disturbing setbacks, a postslavery, emancipationist identity pressed forward. Some blacks like former slave Reverend Jeremiah M. P. Williams courageously urged blacks to steer clear of fusion politics and a Democratic party, "made infamous by its devotion to slavery."[75] Others marched faithfully every May 30 in remembrance of the black Union soldiers who had fought for freedom. Groups of blacks continued to gather across the river from Natchez intent on commemorating their nation's day of independence long after white men reclaimed control of public space in the 1880s. Over baskets of tasty picnic fare with a band playing some of the same jubilant emancipation tunes sounded two decades earlier, freedpeople and their children used such events to recall the memories of a time when the future seemed full of great promise, while attempting to blot out more recent memories of strife and the rapid loss of suffrage, political agency, and civil liberties. Meanwhile, Natchez whites were once again hosting their own festive July 4 celebrations. It was here that large groups of uniformed white men primped, paraded, and took aim with their firearms as part of a larger mission to craft a postwar white historical identity for their city.

CHAPTER THREE

"A TASTE FOR ASSOCIATIONS"

Reconstructing White Identities in Postwar Natchez

ALL EYES WATCHED THE MISSISSIPPI. THE UNIFORMED MEN, THEIR POLISHED boots, brass buttons, and sabers gleaming in the midday sun, waited patiently on the bluff, their gaze focused intently on the Mississippi River below. As the *Natchez* approached, the Adams Light Infantry saluted the steamer's arrival with a burst of cannon fire before marching down to the wharf. There, the military company joined by future Mayor William G. Benbrook, eminent commander of Natchez's highest ranking Masonic order, greeted their honored guests, delegates from across the state on hand to attend the 1877 Mississippi Knights Templar Grand Commandery's annual conference.[1]

As the town's newest local militia escorted the Knights, dressed in their own smart dark woolen military-style uniforms set off by jaunty white-plumed hats, to Natchez's Masonic hall, the procession of white men saw few if any traces of Reconstruction. Gone were the black Union soldiers and other despised "blue devils" who once patrolled Natchez streets under federal occupation. Nor were there any posted handbills announcing meetings of the Union League, a radical Republican organization that had rallied African American men to vote in the late 1860s. Only a few years earlier, newly freed slaves exercised a host of civil liberties—voting, organizing political rallies, and marching in lively parades. By 1877 the freedoms of early Reconstruction had all but vanished, leaving in its place a dim memory of an era that had once seemed promising for black residents but had tragically failed to achieve its potential. For most black men and women on hand to witness the arrival of the elite Masonic visitors, the day eerily resembled the festive parades of white militia and male fraternal societies that had routinely strutted through city streets during the antebellum era.

The gathering of Knights Templars and the Adams Light Infantry in the spring of 1877 symbolized an end to Reconstruction. The federal government's failed efforts to reconstruct the defeated Confederate states into a free labor economy and protect black civil rights had officially ended with the presidential contest of 1876, when a backroom deal awarded the election to Republican candidate Rutherford B. Hayes in exchange for removing troops from occupied southern states. However, Mississippi state elections one year earlier had settled the matter for all practical purposes. The disfranchisement of black men swept nearly all elected African American officials from office and replaced them with white Democrats who had mounted a campaign to return city and state political power to what Natchez newspaper editor Paul Botto called the "honest, capable and intelligent citizens."[2] When Reconstruction ended, white Natchez men quickly reclaimed dominance of public space.

Militia companies and fraternal associations like the Masons were but two of a host of leisure activities available to white Natchez men in the last decades of the nineteenth century. Research in newspapers of the time and the collection of photographs made by local photographer Henry Norman in the late nineteenth century reveal an array of popular amusements that vied for white Natchezians' leisure hours. These included bicycling, baseball games, horse racing at the Pharsalia fairgrounds, and the popular circus acts and "freak" sideshows taking the country by storm housed in tents adjacent to the racetrack. Lansdowne Park, located close to the antebellum estate of the same name was a public park (for whites only) with pavilions, cabins, boardwalks, and spacious grounds ideal for picnics, hot air balloon launches, and large social gatherings organized by churches, volunteer firemen's associations, and militia groups. Another favorite gathering place for white Natchezians was strolling along the bluff overlooking the Mississippi River.

For a small town, Natchez enjoyed a vibrant theatrical calendar dating back to well before the Civil War. In 1851 showman P. T. Barnum organized a concert for singing sensation Jenny Lind, branded the "Swedish Nightingale," to a sell-out crowd in a small church in Natchez. Lind's performance and ongoing theatrical performances by a variety of entertainers helped to establish Natchez as a cultural beacon within Mississippi. The town's Institute Hall hosted numerous public events and performances and featured an indoor roller skating rink. In 1887 the extravagant *Kirmess* featured 150 local amateur male and female actors clad in elaborate costumes, performing in tableaux to represent the nations of the world. A short time later the popular operetta *The Mikado* was performed for local white audiences. The all black and nationally renowned Bud Scott orchestra performed their ragtime hits for white balls and other galas when not performing on the Mississippi steamboat circuit. For those seeking quieter pursuits, Natchez's library, also located in Institute Hall, offered more than 3,200 volumes, according to a March 1886 newspaper report.[3]

When not attending musical or theater performances, enjoying picnics, parades, and other outdoor social gatherings, many white Natchezians made time to attend one of at least five downtown houses of worship (which had their own whirl of social activities), including the Temple B'Nai Israel, opened in 1872 on the corner of Washington and Commerce Streets for Jewish congregants. The detailed diary of popular minister Dr. Joseph B. Stratton, who served the First Presbyterian Church for fifty years, is filled with descriptions of the town's bustling social calendar and those who enjoyed a steady stream of public amusements, including his own frequent participation in local events.[4]

White Natchez men in the late 1800s devoted an enormous amount of leisure time to male fraternal associations, where members developed new post–Civil War self-identities, while also memorializing a local version of the Lost Cause. Two such organizations played a leading role in crafting white male identity in postwar Natchez and in reimagining a heroic white southern past. These associations—the Adams Light Infantry (ALI) and Freemasonry—empowered white men in different ways to reclaim their sense of mastery shattered by the South's Civil War defeat. The infantry manifested a longstanding southern male militia tradition that prized rough and manly adventure and athleticism. By contrast Freemasonry expressed masculine identity through secretive rituals and behavior that was at times both refined and somewhat effeminate. Both fraternal groups, while unique in their expressions of masculine identity, helped to forge a collective historical memory loyal to the Lost Cause myth, particularly Adams Light Infantry members. Many Natchez men belonged to both groups, suggesting that militias and Masonry held wide appeal, and that postwar male southern identity had many facets.

Soldier reunions and the publication of personal memoirs of battle accounts published in mass-market national magazines such as *Century* and *Confederate Veteran* have been credited by historians as the principal means of expressing southern white male war memories in the decades following the Civil War.[5] Fraternal associations were another important vehicle for formulating southern memory that have been largely overlooked. These organizations played a vital role in expressing allegiance to the Lost Cause and its emphasis on white supremacy. Moreover, these organizations dispute the prevalent notion that voluntary associations and the memorialization work that grew out of such groups were the strict dominion of white women. A more gender-balanced account of the role of fraternal associations in shaping collective memory reveals a clearer trajectory of how white southern narratives evolved at the local level. Only after successfully reclaiming white supremacy and the actual empowerment that came with it, were Natchez men willing to pass the torch of memorialization leadership to white women.

A "CRISIS OF GENDER"

In the aftermath of military defeat and the widespread economic ruin that followed, anxieties associated with southern masculinity were particularly acute, resulting in what historians have labeled as a "crisis in gender" among shattered southern white men.[6] Such anxieties played a direct role in the formation of paramilitary groups like the Adams Light Infantry. Much of the "crisis" revolved around the profound changes war had brought to southern planter households. As Nancy Bercaw writes, "Emancipation undercut white men's mastery" and destroyed the plantation household, where patriarchal authority was grounded.[7] Moreover, the war had pushed many white women to expand their traditional domestic duties beyond the private sphere of hearth and home, upsetting traditional gendered boundaries. Despite—or because of—a decisive military defeat, the loss of their slave labor, and a marked shift in gender roles, southern white males endeavored to reclaim familiar antebellum masculine roles built around paternalistic notions of honor, mastery, and militancy.[8] Valuing above all others these three traits, which emphasized independence, the ability to command and control others, and a willingness to defend one's honor against insult, the badly beaten warriors of the South were forced to find new ways to incorporate masculine ideals into their reconstructed lives. White Natchez men, like many southern males, fell back on familiar traditions—including violence and intimidation—to restore white control and male mastery over their households and African Americans.

Two distinctive forms of manhood closely tied to the southern masculine ideals of mastery and honor flourished in the postbellum period. The masculine identities of the "Christian gentleman" and the "martial ideal" were prevalent and frequently on display—often within the same individual—in the post-Reconstruction-era South and clearly visible within the rhetoric and actions of Natchez fraternal organizations. The "Christian gentleman," modeled after revered Confederate military leader Robert E. Lee, was touted as "honorable, master of his household, humble, self-restrained, and above all, pious and faithful."[9] Martial manliness, a longstanding tradition associated with a region characterized as a dangerous rural frontier, was at times closely aligned with, and sometimes at odds with, the Christian gentleman. Southern men from an early age vied to be perceived as honorable as well as skilled fighters, adept at hunting, dueling, and waging war.[10]

A CULTURE OF VIOLENCE

Natchez's long history of violence contributed to the town's militia culture and the popularity of paramilitary groups. From its inception, the rough and tumble riverside town of Natchez had encouraged the embrace of violence by white men. Murder, assault, duels, and drunkenness were common throughout much of the town's antebellum history, particularly in the seedy Under-the-Hill saloons and brothels that greeted steamboat traffic. William Johnson, a free black barber in Natchez, recorded more than one hundred fights in the informative diary he kept from 1835 to 1851.[11]

According to Johnson, himself an avid hunter, whips, canes, swords, bowie knives, pistols, sticks, chairs, sharp teeth, and gouging fingers frequently served violent purposes in antebellum Natchez. In such a climate where danger frequently lurked in broad daylight and the wee hours of the night, Natchez men learned from a young age the value of a trustworthy weapon for bolstering their physical safety as well as their manly reputation.[12] The ritualized violence that white southern men experienced in the form of hunting, duels, slave patrols, and the like was imbedded in the ideals of militia performances and discipline.

Mississippi's militia tradition originated with a federal law passed in 1803 calling for states to organize volunteer militias. Mississippi enthusiastically embraced a vibrant militia culture as young and older men joined volunteer companies across the state. Prior to the War of 1812, Natchez organized two local militia companies that served under General Andrew Jackson at New Orleans. Long after the war had ended, the Natchez Rifle Corps and the Adams County Dragoons continued to muster, drill, and sponsor elaborate celebrations and banquets.[13] The creation of the Adams Light Infantry in the 1870s helped to educate a new generation of young men on the virtues of martial manhood, while also marking a return to Natchez's longstanding tradition of civilian soldiery.

Throughout the 1830s and 1840s diarist William Johnson's more than two dozen mentions of Natchez militia groups parading, mustering, drilling, attending funerals, drunkenly carousing, breaking up fights, or sometimes fighting among themselves are telling of the significant role military life played in daily affairs. In one such entry from October 1842 he wrote, "This has been a real Military Day. All the Companies turned out and the Fencibles Gave a Dinner Out in Capt. William Minors Pasture. It went of[f] well, very well indeed. Some of the Party was Drunk of Course."[14]

The several white militia groups in operation at the time of the Civil War were products of a longstanding tradition of paramilitary groups who policed black behavior. As sectional tensions over slavery mounted, these groups assumed even greater importance in the minds of white Natchez planters. Natchez militia companies frequently took part in regular patrols to crack down on real or imagined threats of slave insubordination. In the spring of 1860, at a time when Adams County whites were particularly fearful of "uneasiness showing itself among the negroes," a group of county elites formed the Vigilance Committee. In September of 1861 the group tried, convicted, and executed more than thirty male slaves found guilty of conspiring to kill their white masters, ravage white women, and destroy planter property in what became known as the Second Creek uprising.[15] Newly discovered evidence reveals the violence towards slaves during the war years was far more extensive in Adams County than has been previously documented. According to historian Justin Behrend, as many as three hundred slaves were executed in the Natchez District during the war.[16]

Despite evidence to the contrary, between the mid-1860s and the 1880s, federal investigators concluded that Natchez experienced fewer racially motivated hate crimes toward blacks than other Mississippi counties and southern communities. The close relationship between Natchez's elite black community and white powerbrokers may have helped to reduce awareness of simmering racial tensions in the early postwar era. Even so, there were still episodes of sporadic racial intimidation and violence in Natchez and Adams County. For example, when the Natchez community feared another black plot in the fall of 1865 (several months after the end of the war), the Adams Troop's former commander General William T. Martin recalled his men into service. After the Freedman's Bureau refused the white community's demand to disarm blacks, Martin and his militia troops took matters into their own hands. Two days after Christmas, the group conducted raids under the cover of darkness, confiscating shotguns, money, food, and whiskey from blacks suspected of potential insurrection. Eleven years later during the last year of Reconstruction, Martin and his band of citizen soldiers remained alert to squashing black behavior they deemed unruly or threatening. Such behavior might include political activism, refusal to work, or addressing a white man or woman in a way not considered adequately submissive. When in the spring of 1876 reports of racial unrest in neighboring Wilkinson County reached Natchez, Martin volunteered to organize his militia company to put down the threat.[17] Thus, at the first sign of trouble Natchez civic officials did what they had always done: They turned to their community's reliable corps of citizen soldiers to protect social and racial order.

As in other parts of the South, Natchez's white Democrats, many of whom were militia members, increasingly threatened local blacks during the waning days of Reconstruction. A. M. Hardy, the white editor of Natchez's lone Republican newspaper, *The New South*, testified before a Senate hearing in December 1876 that "the colored people were very much alarmed" by the Adams Light Infantry (among other paramilitary groups) that was ostensibly organized to celebrate the Fourth of July, but whose true purpose was to "menace the colored people of the county." In addition to their frequent parades and downtown drills, Hardy reported that ALI members, all of whom were members of the Democratic Party, made threatening remarks at Republican meetings. According to the journalist, "the democrats used to boast that, upon the first trouble that occurred, they had twenty thousand rounds of ammunition, and they could soon put a stop to it." Hardy noted that although members of the militia group showed up at Republican meetings in civilian clothes, they were disruptive and on at least one occasion shouted down a political opponent, and accused him of telling "a damned lie."[18]

A Canadian native who had lived in Natchez for three years before testifying before the Senate committee, Hardy had good reason to feel personally threatened by angry Democrats and militia members. The night before the 1876 election, while attending a Republican rally at the Adams County courthouse, Hardy was mobbed by "a crowd of fifty or sixty men and boys" who followed him to his newspaper office, "hallooing, 'Hang the carpet-bagger,' 'Shoot the radical,' and 'Rail-ride the son of a bitch.'" Hardy survived the frightening incident with no physical harm, thanks to some of the more senior militia members who helped to calm the unruly mob.[19]

Hardy's anxiety-ridden testimony, coupled with the frequent public militaristic performances of Adams Light Infantry members in the form of parades, drill maneuvers, and spirited target shooting matches, leaves no doubt that white men—young and old—who embraced the martial ideal dominated Natchez in the early days of post-Reconstruction and on occasion resorted to violent measures to achieve their objectives.

THE ALI AND THE REASSERTION OF WHITE RULE

In response to racial unrest in Mississippi, Natchez lawyer Thomas Otis Baker, a twice-wounded Confederate veteran, took matters into his own hands. He and a group of thirteen others, each representing one of the local units that had served the Confederate Army, assembled the voluntary Adams Light Infantry in June 1876, stating that "many Confederate survivors" and "a number of patriotic young men who had arrived at maturity since the close of the late Civil War" became "convinced that the formation of a military company was necessary in order to overawe seditious persons and secure the perpetuity of that domestic tranquility which had so signally marked the relations of the two races in this community but which had been so seriously threatened in other localities of the South."[20] The infantry's leadership saw white Republican leaders as "seditious persons" who threatened to destroy the old racial hierarchy, euphemistically labeled as "that domestic tranquility which had ... marked the relations of the two races," by encouraging organizations like the Union League. Such statements reflected the ALI's commitment to defending white supremacy, the principal tenet of Lost Cause ideology. The timing of the unit's organization proved fortuitous for the volunteers. Military occupation was over, and the nation's commitment to Reconstruction was evaporating quickly, giving Adams Light Infantry leaders unrestricted reign to organize their band of citizen soldiers. Within six months, the infamous Compromise of 1876, marking the death of radical Republican rule and the removal of occupying forces, made it possible for southern towns like Natchez to freely resume their passion for militia culture.[21] Mississippi legislators formally authorized the formation of such groups by passing a law organizing militia companies statewide in 1877.[22] Legitimizing these militia groups reflected both an end of Reconstruction policy and a determination among former Confederate lawmakers to reassert traditional white male mastery.

By the late 1880s, the Adams Light Infantry was comprised of nearly two hundred active members and an additional ninety honorary members. While nearly all of the group's nineteen officers had served in the Confederate Army, far fewer of the privates under their command fought in the war, most because they would have been too young for military duty. When the ALI organized in 1876, the average age of the sixty-six privates who can be identified was sixteen. As one of the town's premier militia organizations during the late 1870s and 1880s, the group no doubt helped to inculcate adolescent males and young men into a martial culture and a reverence for a war they had not actually experienced. Wearing the uniforms of military men and drilling alongside the veterans and survivors of Vicksburg, Gettysburg, and Chickamauga both served as a rite of masculine passage for the young militia privates and marked their initiation as the future caretakers of precious wartime memories.

Many, if not most, of the men who joined the Adams Light Infantry in the 1870s and 1880s were descended from an ancestor who had belonged to one of the town's earlier militia organizations. The demographic particulars of the men and youth who joined the infantry are suggestive of the group's widespread influence over community affairs. The infantry's membership was quite diverse, including middling men as well as those born to a more elite status. Twenty-five active or honorary members of the ALI belonged to the planter class, with a handful playing a prominent role in civic affairs. Chief among this elite group was William T. Martin, the esteemed Confederate general and lawyer who served as president of the Adams County Democratic Executive Committee in the early 1870s and later was elected to the state Senate. Martin's membership is also significant because he was an integral character in Natchez's militia narrative, having organized local volunteer militia companies during much of his life, before and after the war. Indeed, Martin credited himself as having played a principal role in organizing the Vigilance Committee, the same group responsible for interrogating, torturing, and murdering dozens of slaves accused of participating in the famed Second Creek uprising.[23]

Other elite Natchez men, several whom may have been members of or cooperated with the Vigilance Committee, also belonged to the Adams Light Infantry. For example, minutes kept by Martin's brother-in-law, Lemuel P. Conner, place future ALI member and wealthy planter George M. Marshall at the site of the racetrack examinations. Infantry member James Surget, a member of one of the county's wealthiest planter families, executed a number of enslaved men at Cherry Grove plantation, according to his descendants.[24] Richard Ellis Conner, younger brother of racetrack scribe Lemuel, also joined the militia group. Other prominent Natchez Infantry members included A. C. Britton and George W. Koontz, proprietors of Britton and Koontz Bank; cotton broker and industrialist J. N. Carpenter; wealthy merchant C. T. Schwartz; along with Fred and Aaron Stanton, and George M. Brown, all descendants of elite planter families whose fortunes had been severely diminished by the recent war.

Most infantry members belonged to the middle class. Of these, twenty-four were merchants, sixteen worked as clerks, and eight were elected city officials, including the town's sheriff and deputy sheriff. Others were tradesmen, including a gunsmith, a tinsmith, three blacksmiths, four carpenters, and two steamboat pilots. The roster also included William G. Benbrook, a future mayor of Natchez and one of the town's most active participants in male associations. No matter their occupation or class standing, all ALI members shared two common traits that cemented their bond as white southerners: They all belonged to Adams County's Democratic Party, and all were fervent participants in their town's martial culture.[25]

Adams Light Infantry leaders and members wasted no time in making their presence known in Natchez and surrounding Adams County in the summer and fall of 1876. Twelve days after the ALI organized, Natchez alderman John A. Dicks, an ALI officer and Confederate veteran, proposed a unanimously accepted resolution calling for a citywide celebration to commemorate the nation's centennial anniversary that would feature addresses from state senators and a "suitable demonstration" led by the Adams Light Infantry. For the remainder of the nineteenth century, the ALI controlled and organized the city's July 4 celebrations, showering white spectators with a spectacle of masculine amusements. Dressed in "blue coats with white trimmings, white trousers and fatigue caps," militia members took center stage on Independence Day, parading, playing baseball, firing cannons, and orchestrating evening fireworks before crowds of female and youthful spectators. A highlight of the day's activities was the target shooting matches reminiscent of those described by William Johnson decades earlier. Members of the Adams Light Infantry, Natchez Rifles, and Natchez Fencibles competed against one another for an assortment of household prizes that included silver butter dishes, pickle stands, spoon holders, and card receivers. Such refined prizes—seemingly more suitable for wives, mothers, and sweethearts than rugged marksmen—were not uncommon for target competitions hosted across the country. Their genteel trophies offer evidence that ALI members represented a perfect blend of the Christian gentleman and martial ideals, while persuasively confirming white men's return to social dominance. Not only were they parading themselves as virile, manly men, but also, as an ALI souvenir booklet published in 1890 proclaimed, members saw themselves as caretakers to protect "domestic tranquility," ready and able to "overawe seditious" African Americans and white Republicans when necessary.[26]

Natchez's militia culture and passion for target shooting are consistent with the nationwide appeal of shooting companies and rifle competitions in the late nineteenth century, particularly to men of higher social rank. As thousands of American men joined target shooting associations, one

Harvard geologist wrote, Americans excelled in the three "leading diversions of the open air, yachting, horsemanship and 'sharpshooting.'"[27] Significantly, competitive sports—target shooting, later surpassed by baseball and football—integrated southern men into a national sports culture. Whether hitting the bull's eye on the target range or scoring runs on the baseball diamond, Natchez militia men eagerly worked to demonstrate their athletic prowess, impulses passionately shared by American men nationwide in the late 1800s.[28] As Patrick Miller argues, the development of college sports in the South—particularly football and baseball—created a much-needed opportunity for young men to experience "exhilarating contest and conflict in battle," not unlike the martial valor romanticized in the Lost Cause.[29] Thus, even though militias continued to spend much of their time practicing military drills (a requirement of their state charter), patriotic celebrations like the Fourth of July and sporting events organized by nearby Jefferson College increasingly featured a variety of rugged, masculine athletic competitions reflective of traditional notions of southern white male honor. Militia groups like the Adams Light Infantry provided Natchez men an acceptable way to perform as strong, virile warriors, far different from the defeated southern men of 1865 who had come home emotionally and physically battered, their sense of honor in tatters. No wonder then that the *Natchez Democrat* celebrated the infantry competitions with great fanfare, devoting lengthy coverage to the names and scores of the young and old men waging bloodless battle on the playing field.[30]

Such celebrations of the athleticism and playful antics of the ALI "soldier boys," as they were affectionately referred to by the editors of the *Natchez Democrat* (who were ALI members themselves) were in keeping with the ideals of boyhood and boyishness that attracted growing numbers of American men, North and South, in the late 1800s. Theodore Roosevelt proclaimed similar rhetoric when he urged American men to denounce "the soft spirit of the cloistered life" and to "boldly face the life of strife."[31] The establishment of paramilitary groups such as the Adams Light Infantry exemplified a transformation in southern masculine gender roles in the late nineteenth century in which men found pleasure and meaning in passions associated with boyhood. Late nineteenth-century educational experts like G. Stanley Hall encouraged teachers to allow boys to act out their "primitive savage" impulses, such as fighting and rough housing, so that they would grow up "strong and virile, immune from civilization's effeminizing tendencies."[32] ALI officers adopted a similar philosophy when they organized outdoor target shooting matches, marching drills, and baseball games for their young recruits. Senior ALI members melded their organization's emphasis on boyish athleticism and "savagery" by serving as manly role models to their sons and other youthful male kin. Virile men and the physical masculine amusements that occupied their time would not only help develop more "manly boys," but also distance young men from the dangers of a feminized upbringing, a worry expressed by a growing number of male social commentators.

Additionally, Adams Light Infantry leaders frequently sought to influence a younger generation of boys through their involvement in Jefferson College, the region's oldest secondary school and military academy for adolescent boys, located a few miles outside of Natchez. Faced with growing economic insecurity, Jefferson College received much-needed funding and moral support from the militia group. Numerous infantry members served on the school's board of trustees in the 1870s and 1880s, including ALI commanding officer T. Otis Baker and William T. Martin, and were often called upon to deliver speeches at the school's annual summer commencement ceremony. The 1875 remarks of Reverend Joseph Stratton, minister of Natchez's First Presbyterian Church and a militia member himself, reflect the importance some members of the community attached to grooming "manly boys," a term that in the late 1800s connoted honor, morality, and self-mastery.[33] Quoting Juvenal, the ancient Roman satirist, Stratton told his audience: "'*Maxima debetur puero reverentia*'—the highest degree of reverence is due to the boy." Stratton went on to charge the leaders and male teachers of the school with the duty of grooming self-reliant, honorable, inventive, and moral young men. This was no job for women, according to Stratton, who declared, "Of such men may this college be the nursing mother!" To the young adolescents sitting before him, Stratton counseled, "Be as much of a man at twelve or fifteen as you expect to be at forty-five or fifty. Be in all things and at all times a manly boy."[34]

As the Adams Light Infantry's "soldier boys"—many well beyond middle age by the 1880s—paraded, pursued their boyish fun, and urged the younger generation to grow into "manly boys," politicized speechmaking was strangely absent in extant newspaper reports of the Independence Day celebrations organized by the ALI. The significance, however, of these events was not lost on the town's white leadership and citizens, however. An 1887 editorial published in the *Natchez Democrat* reached beyond regional mythmaking to reclaim a principal role for white southerners in national traditions. The newspaper's proprietor remarked that "one of the greatest errors the South made in its attempt at secession was in surrendering to the North the memories of the nation." He reminded his readers that since much of the "work of the first revolution largely belonged to the South," the "Fourth of July as well as the stars and stripes were as much the property of the South as of the North." In short, the editorial matched the militant spirit of the annual July Fourth street processions and displays of physical might, serving notice that whites had reappropriated the national narrative, thanks in large part to groups like the Adams Light Infantry. Mirroring reunification rhetoric voiced in both the South and the North during this period, the *Democrat* editor found no room in his Independence Day editorial for recently emancipated Natchez blacks. "With a restored Union, with the softening of all sectional asperities, with fraternal feelings fast becoming stronger and stronger, the people of the South should remember that the fourth of July is the birthday of the proud nation of which they form a part, and that the declaration of independence is the charter of their liberties."[35] By implication, the editor suggested civil liberties solely were the provenance of the white "people of the South," whose role it was to paternalistically manage and police a subservient black populace.

It comes as no surprise that Natchez blacks played no visible role in Adams Light Infantry patriotic events of the post-Reconstruction era. It was no accident that press coverage of black celebrations declined as coverage of the Adams Light Infantry increased. African Americans steered clear of white infantry-sponsored events as acts of paramilitary violence escalated against politically active blacks. Instead, some local blacks chose to create their own celebration, far from the shooting matches and holiday celebrations staged in suburban Natchez. A tiny eleven-line announcement that ran alongside the extensive coverage devoted to the white commemoration of the 1887 holiday offers but a few sparse details of the nature of black Independence Day celebrations that summer. Here we learn that there were several well-attended July Fourth excursions "amongst the colored persons." The two mentioned were both across the river in Concordia and Tensas Parish, Louisiana, safely removed from the suburban ALI park grounds. No details are given of the day's festivities. Instead, the article concluded with the terse summary: "We suppose all who participated had a real good time, as the necessary arrangements therefore had all been made."[36]

MILITIA-STYLED MEMORIES

Over time the leadership within the Adams Light Infantry increasingly took a dominant role in shaping the community's memory of the recent past, particularly the sacrifices of Confederate veterans living and dead. Determining that significant historical events "were fast passing into forgetfulness and that even the names and fate of many of their comrades were fading from memory and would be lost," ALI officers worked "to rescue from oblivion the historical annals of the late war."[37]

Crafting the community's first postwar collective memory, the Adams Light Infantry's remembrance of dead comrades came in the form of a forty-five-page souvenir booklet listing the thirteen Confederate military companies formed in Adams County, the battles they fought, and the names and ranks of members, noting those who were wounded or suffered mortal injuries. Both the passion and the challenge to create a lasting document to the cause more than a decade after the war can be found in the words of a former first sergeant of the Tom Weldon Rebels, who wrote to a member of the ALI Souvenir Committee of his efforts to recall faithfully the service of his military company: "Enclosed with this you find a Roll of the "Tom Weldon Rebels" made up as well as I can from memory for all the Company papers were lost during the war. I also send a sketch of the Company's history and operations in the Army that perhaps it may contribute somewhat to the laudable object you have in view."[38] Dedicated to the memory of the Confederate dead of Natchez and Adams County and of "that host of other heroes of the Lost Cause," the memento was "piously inscribed" by the Adams Light Infantry. The dedication page featured an excerpt from a popular poem honoring Scottish heroes William Wallace and Robert Bruce, serving notice that the cause Natchez's citizen soldiers had served was epic, honorable, and memorable. The closing pages of the publication listed all those who had joined the Adams Light Infantry since its inception in 1876. These two hundred men in the latter years of the nineteenth century pledged themselves to a martial ideal dedicated to rekindling the "flame" of the Lost Cause, borrowing language from the poem printed on the dedication page. Armed with "their burning spirit" these warriors scorned death and promised to emerge victorious and "immortal from the tomb." Natchez's Lost Cause soldiers—much like those who revered the bravery of Bruce and Wallace from centuries past—fervently believed their sacred cause would enable them to reclaim their honor and mastery temporarily lost to an unworthy foe.

THE APPEALS OF FREEMASONRY

Popular militia groups like the Adams Light Infantry were only one of many male organizations white Natchez men joined in the late nineteenth century.

Militia members and other men also flocked to the more sequestered, peaceful venues of Freemasonry. In keeping with a national trend that saw 40 percent of American men over twenty years of age belonging to at least one secret fraternal society by the 1890s, nearly three hundred white Natchez men joined such groups.[39] In 1860 Mississippi enjoyed the highest per capita rate of Freemasonry membership in the nation, with nearly 14 percent of white men taking a Masonic oath. A promotional pamphlet reporting on the civic and economic status of Natchez in 1881 noted that "nearly all of the secret orders of the U.S. are represented by flourishing lodges in Natchez, and with one or other of these a majority of the male citizens are identified." By the late 1800s Natchez was home to seven white male secret societies, several religious male organizations, and three volunteer fire companies.[40] It was not uncommon for a man to belong to multiple groups simultaneously, and many took pride in their numerous affiliations, whether business, political, or social, as evident from a letter written earlier in the century by John Quitman, a prominent antebellum Natchez planter, politician, and Masonic leader. "I am President of a states rights association, of an anti-Abolition society, of an anti-Gambling society, of a Mississippi cotton company, of an anti-Dueling society, of a railroad company, director of the Planters bank, grand master Mason, Captain of the Natchez Fencibles, trustee of Jefferson College and Natchez Academy besides having charge of a cotton and sugar plantation and 150 negroes."[41] Southern white men like Quitman used their fraternal ties to propel their business, military, and political aspirations, objectives that remained consistent with later generations of white Natchez fraternal men.[42]

By the 1860s Freemasonry membership in Mississippi surged, most likely as a result of the Civil War when both northern and southern soldiers found spiritual and physical sustenance in their fraternal ties.[43] Freemasonry appealed to southern and northern men for many of the same reasons. The opportunity for a man to enhance his social status and to build valuable business and credit connections are the two most common reasons for Freemasonry's widespread appeal. Some men, no doubt, were also attracted to Freemasonry and other male societies because their monthly dues helped to provide sickness and death benefits in an era when governmental welfare services were lacking. But it was the social aspects of male secret societies that likely had the greatest appeal for most nineteenth-century men. The opportunity to join other men in a "sacred asylum" that provided a sense of stability and harmony in stark contrast to the increasingly unstable world of commerce and society was welcomed by late nineteenth-century American men. Historian Michael S. Kimmel argues that in Masonry men also found a sanctioned place away from the family home in an age when men were frequently warned that they were becoming soft, frail, and emasculated in a feminized world.[44] Moreover, with the demise of slavery, the households of white southern males no longer afforded them the same sense of mastery and empowerment they had enjoyed in the antebellum years. In short, the Masonic lodge served as a much-needed sanctuary for men whose military defeat forced them to seek new identities in a world that had changed radically since the outbreak of war in 1861.

White Freemason lodges in Natchez drew the majority of their members from the middle and upper classes, in part because of the fraternal order's historic and elevated ties to the town since territorial days. In 1801 Natchez organized Mississippi's first Masonic lodge, enhancing Freemasonry's status and helping the group to wield significant influence in city affairs and attract the largest membership among fraternal societies. Freemasonry in Natchez subscribed to the York (or American) Rite, one of two complex Masonic hierarchies. While the organization proclaimed itself nondenominational, Masonic ideology and rituals reflected Protestant and Biblical influences. Masons were expected to believe in a supreme being, use a holy text appropriate to the religion of lodge members, and maintain a vow of secrecy concerning the order's ceremonies.[45]

Within the handsome state grand lodge built in Natchez in 1827 at a cost of $10,000 (the equivalent of nearly $250,000 in 2019), the town's four Masonic orders met weekly, usually for several hours at a time. Elaborate initiation rites incorporated the instruments of the stonemason—the plumb, the square, and compass—with pledges to maintain the ideals of fraternity, charity, and moral behavior. Specifically, men who took the Masonic oath dedicated themselves to charitable works, self-improvement, and temperance, meaning self-restraint in the consumption of alcohol and avoidance of other worldly vices such as gambling. In short, Masonry offered men a means to achieve respectability by identifying with late nineteenth-century middle-class values.[46]

Freemasonry across the region—both before and after the war—remained committed to its original charter: personal morality and providing aid to local charities like Natchez's Protestant orphanage. By the latter decades of the nineteenth century Natchez Freemasons continued the traditions forged by earlier generations of southern fraternal men. Pledging their allegiance to likeminded Christian brothers, they remained loyal first and foremost to southern codes of masculine honor and mastery. Although Freemasonry rituals remained secretive, a contemporary description of the Natchez

Unidentified photo of a Natchez Mason, ca. 1880. Photographer believed to be Henry C. Norman. (Courtesy of the Thomas H. and Joan W. Gandy Photograph Collection, Louisiana Lower Mississippi Valley Collections, Special Collections, Hill Memorial Library, Louisiana State University Libraries, Baton Rouge.)

Freemason's main lodge room described it as "an elegantly furnished and capacious room. Upon its walls are hung many objects of interest, noticeable among which are excellently executed photographs, by Norman of Natchez of the members of the Masonic bodies and ancient receipts to both Lodges, for subscriptions to the great national ... Washington Monument, upon which are the autographs of Presidents Zachary Taylor and Fillmore."[47] Throughout the nineteenth century, Natchez and its handsome temple frequently hosted state Masonic conventions.

Another Masonic order, The Knights Templar, strongly appealed to postwar white Natchez men because the order's pageantry and rhetoric drew upon familiar militaristic rituals similar to those favored by the popular Adams Light Infantry. Seventeen of the forty-eight Rosalie Commandery Knights Templar members in 1877 were also active in the Adams Light Infantry.[48] A vivid 1890 newspaper account of a Chicago Knights Templar procession described a scene that would have resonated comfortably within the martial cultural landscape of Natchez: "Then came the horses, prancing with military spirit, while the air was filled with the brilliant fanfare of martial music. Men bearing glittering swords came by, their snowy plumes shining against the black background of the Knight's dress. There were red crosses, black crosses, and double-barred crosses, and every uniform as neat as wax, each uniformed man wearing spotless gloves. Magnificently embroidered banners with Knightly crests on them floated on the breeze."[49]

Like the members of most American Masonic lodges, Natchez Freemasons were solidly rooted in the middle class. A demographic analysis of Natchez's most elite Masonic group, the Rosalie Commandery Knights Templars, is reflective of the membership of other Masonic lodges. In 1877 the group's membership included merchants, a banker, bookkeeper, insurance agent, newspaper editor, and several city officials, including the mayor, no doubt a means to stay connected to their male constituents. Apart from banker George W. Koontz and planter Alfred V. Davis, none of the men was particularly wealthy or part of the old planter elite. The average age of members of the Rosalie Commandery in 1877 was thirty-five, with no members older than forty-five. By the 1880s several Natchez Jewish merchants belonged to the Royal Arch Masons, a lower degree of Freemasons than the Knights Templars. The acceptance of Jewish men as Masons reflected not only a willingness of the order to accept men outside the Christian faith but is also suggestive of the growing influence and assimilation of the town's Jewish merchant class, who frequently joined men's and women's social and benevolent institutions.[50]

Freemasonry appealed to postwar southern white men for economic as well as social reasons. The opportunity to bolster one's financial standing while nurturing fraternal bonds among likeminded men who shared similar life experiences and political and social concerns would have heightened the popularity of Masonic membership. Simultaneously, the chance to rekindle friendships with former Confederate comrades also helps to explain the popularity of Masonry and other fraternal societies in postwar Natchez. More than one-third of the forty-seven members of the Rosalie Commandery served in the Confederate Army, suggesting that postwar bonding was a significant part of the Natchez Masonic experience. The comfortable masculine retreat of a Masonic lodge provided aging rebels a social space in which to reminisce over the hardships and heroics of military service and the friends made and lost. Freemasonry also enabled its southern members to position themselves as the eternal victors in the bloodless battles for self-improvement and morality, while charitably providing for widows, orphans, and brothers in need. In contrast to the militant perspective and activities of local militia groups that sanctioned violence towards blacks before, during, and after the war, Freemasonry put a more respectable gloss on white male voluntary associations. Thus, belonging to one or more fraternal groups offered a means of gaining respectability, demonstrating that at least some of a man's memberships were peaceful, noble, and far removed from the sometimes unsavory behavior of local militia companies.

MASONS AND MASTERY

Freemasonry solidarity provided white men in Natchez and across the postwar South a means to perceive themselves once again as masters of the racial order, in ways similar and different from militia groups. Late nineteenth-century Mississippi Masonic convention reports rarely touched upon matters of race, as political discussions were disallowed; however, the discourse found in convention minutes reveals that southern Freemasons did not shy away entirely from such conversations. Southern Masons endorsed Lost Cause ideology when given the opportunity. Unlike militia men who showed their commitment to notions of southern honor physically on public parade grounds and in target shooting matches, Masons relied on their minds and voices to communicate their dedication to the southern cause in the more private recesses of Masonic temples and convention halls. For example, Enoch George DeLap, a member of the Natchez Rosalie Grand Commandery, rallied to defend his adopted state's position on race, noting that "in common with thousands of others in the North, men of intelligence ... are evidently ignorant of the amount and nature of the political trials and sufferings of the people of the South.... But let any of them endure what we have endured, suffer what we have suffered, and they will naturally, and at once, arrive at the conviction that it is no ordinary ghost that is after them, but the very devil himself."[51] DeLap's comments reflected a defensive posture not unlike others who spoke out in support of the Lost Cause. Equating recently freed slaves and perhaps white Republicans to "devils" in hot pursuit of southern whites, DeLap and his Natchez brethren found within Masonic rituals a means to regain their sense of mastery over a new racial order that threatened white male supremacy. DeLap's vague references do not spell out the "sufferings" endured by southerners, but it is not hard to imagine his fellow Masons nodding in agreement over the real or imagined tribulations they had endured during Reconstruction. Masonic rituals, publications, and national and regional conventions became convenient vehicles for southern fraternal members to proclaim Lost Cause sentiments in their efforts to reclaim their sense of honor and mastery.

In promoting Lost Cause ideals, some Mississippi Masons pushed for a more muscular Christianity, particularly within the Knights Templar order. In a lengthy 1884 address to Mississippi Knights, J. M. Boon used numerous New Testament scriptural references to remind his audience of their moral responsibility. Armed with the powerful martial words of the apostle Paul, the speaker urged his listeners to "be strong in the Lord and in the power of his might," "put on the whole armor of God," "girt your loins about with truth," "put on the breast-plate of righteousness," and "take the helmet of salvation."[52] Such martial metaphors suggest that Mississippi Masons in the post-Reconstruction era saw themselves as committed muscular Christian men ready to serve as honorable "soldiers of the Cross." The Masonic Knights Templar order offered southern white men a way not only to exemplify a more virile masculine character prepared to face boldly a "life of strife," but to renew their sense of mastery and honor, attributes that had been badly damaged by military defeat.

Within the ranks of Natchez Freemasonry, men born outside the South found a means to gain entrée into postwar southern culture and frequently came to champion southern ideals as passionately as native-born members. For example, Wisconsin-born Enoch George DeLap, who served in the Union Army at Vicksburg, used his fraternal connections to become a successful insurance agent, yet another indication that some men joined fraternal associations seeking the necessary connections to achieve professional success. Perhaps assigned to Natchez as a member of the occupying Union Army or making his way there at war's end, DeLap decided to make Natchez his permanent home, marrying a Natchez woman in 1875. Soon after his arrival, DeLap was invited to join three Masonic orders and was later named honorary secretary of the Adams Light Infantry, joining the ranks of the many Confederate veterans who belonged to both organizations. Even more surprising, DeLap served on the executive committee of the Confederate Memorial Association, a group of southern patriots charged with the responsibility of raising funds for the town's monument honoring the Confederate dead. Widely accepted by his peers, DeLap was no ordinary Mason. Not only did he advance to the rank of Knight Templar, one of the preeminent degrees of Masonry, he presided over the Grand Council of Mississippi in 1873, served as an eminent commander of the local Rosalie Commandery, and was appointed the group's fraternal correspondent for many years.

DeLap was likely accepted because he wholeheartedly embraced southern whites' ideas on race and their perception of the deplorable nature of

Reconstruction. DeLap reflected the views of most white southerners, writing in a report in 1877, one year after the official end of Reconstruction: "We thank God most devoutly that the winter of our discontent has become a glorious summer of joy and prosperity, by the triumph of intelligence over ignorance, honesty over dishonesty and political rottenness, and that peace and quiet prevail in all our borders. The government of this State is in the hands of her sons, where it properly belongs; the good people of all classes, conditions, colors, and politics are contented and happy."[53]

To DeLap's way of thinking—and that of most southern white men—the return of white supremacy and the withdrawal of federal interference in southern affairs were much-welcomed turns of events. DeLap's remarks also speak to the significant role class played in Natchez race relations. The "good people of all ... colors" could be a reference to Natchez elite, light-skinned blacks who were better educated and more affluent than most local African Americans and who worked closely with white political leaders to maintain the status quo. Read slightly differently, DeLap's words also indicate an effort by whites to perpetuate a myth of contented slaves or freedmen happy with their subordinate status. Masonic membership provided white Natchez men like DeLap a way to participate in a nationally respected organization at a time when reconciliation between North and South was championed, while still maintaining allegiance to southern racial and class ideals. The role of Masonry in bridging sectional divides was not lost on the editors of the *Natchez Democrat* who wrote in an obituary following DeLap's death in December 1911, "His Masonic life was an exemplification of the fact that not only does Masonry wipe out all lines of sectionalism, but that the native sons of Mississippi who wore the grey extended the hand of good fellowship and brotherly love to the men who wore the blue."[54]

Northern-born Union veteran Captain Allison Foster also profited from his fraternal memberships. An Adams County chancery clerk and owner of a successful funeral home business, Foster was an honorary member of the Adams Light Infantry, the member of two Masonic lodges as well as a leader within a local Knights of Pythias order. Not unlike his fraternal brother Enoch DeLap, Foster clearly envisioned himself as a man of the New South, a place where in his words, "Sectionalism here, is buried in the dark gloom of the past, and its phantom, is not permitted to cross or shadow our pathway."[55]

SEPARATE GENDERED SPACES

Within the men-only environment of a Masonic lodge, Natchez Freemasons could also segregate themselves from the women in their lives, many of whom symbolized the profoundly altered and unsettling change in gender relations that accompanied military defeat. Many Natchez women, widowed during or shortly after the war, or those who never married due to a shortage of young men or for other reasons, exemplified a trend prevalent across the South that found women taking on new responsibilities, far different from traditional antebellum roles. Numerous elite white Natchez women who found themselves alone at war's end and facing severe financial difficulties successfully managed to keep their dwindling fortunes intact through their own perseverance and by aligning themselves with influential men outside of their families. Serving in the role of trusted advisors, these male surrogates transacted the necessary business and legal dealings that would have been nearly impossible for a woman of this era to handle independently.[56] Notwithstanding their continuing dependence on men in a postwar world that was still very much a patriarchal one, the lives of such southern women testify to the radical changes in antebellum gender relations that transpired from 1861 to 1865 and were never completely restored. Women like Julia Nutt and Katherine Minor (introduced in chapter 1) were elite, independent-minded Natchez matrons left with the responsibility of managing extensive properties and overwhelming debts, who challenged the gendered notions of most nineteenth-century southern men. More research is needed to determine exactly how the men of Natchez perceived headstrong women they encountered, but we do know that Katherine Minor, one of the wealthiest matrons of Adams County, was sometimes referred to as "Yankee Kate," a pejorative nickname that likely referenced both her Unionist stance during the war and her business acumen.[57]

As postwar white Natchez women, both single and married, gradually played a more active role in managing their own affairs and participating in the public sphere, their men folk increasingly spent their leisure time outside of the home. Middle-class American men and women living in the Victorian era typically engaged in gender segregated leisure activities, with men choosing between male clubs, saloons, brothels, or lodges. Natchez men clearly reflected this social trend in the latter decades of the nineteenth century, often belonging to three or more fraternal groups simultaneously. William G. Benbrook, whose political ambitions made fraternal associations essential in his thirty-three-year career as Natchez mayor from 1889 to 1922, belonged to at least eight male fraternal organizations, the Adams Light Infantry, and a volunteer fire company. Whether men like Benbrook joined for political, business, or purely social reasons, their exuberance for devoting so much of their leisure time to fraternal associations is indicative of a passion to seek out the company of likeminded men, while at the same time removing themselves from the company of women and the feminized domesticity of home.

"WE ARE ALL YANKEES NOW"

By 1890 Masonic membership in Mississippi had declined by nearly 24 percent from two decades earlier, with a loss of more than 2,600 members.[58] Although Freemasonry no longer held the same level of appeal for Natchez men as it had in earlier decades, some white Natchezians continued to devote substantial amounts of their leisure time to secret societies. In a newspaper article published in January 1895 noting newly elected officers for Natchez's four Masonic lodges, thirteen of the twenty-one men listed served as officers in more than one lodge, five served in three different lodges, and one man served in all four.[59]

Nevertheless, there was an overall decline in fraternal membership among Natchez men, which can be attributed to several factors that competed for men's time in the last two decades of the nineteenth century: rapid commercial growth, organized efforts to commemorate the Civil War, and an abundance of appealing new heterosocial amusements. Chief among these developments was the spirit of enterprise and entrepreneurship that captivated the attention of male civic and business leaders beginning in the late 1870s. Natchez, like many big and small towns and cities across the South, quickly adopted the ideals of New South boosterism, which promoted industrial growth to revitalize the war-torn southern economy. The Mississippi bluff town was a beehive of entrepreneurial activity in the late 1800s, what Mark Twain declared as a "manufacturing stronghold."[60]

Leading Natchez merchants, industrialists, and financiers enthusiastically endorsed the business philosophy espoused by Atlanta spokesperson Henry W. Grady: "There is a New South, not through protest against the old, but because of new conditions, new adjustments and, if you please, new ideas and aspirations."[61] Business and civic leaders eager to capitalize on the wealth Grady predicted poured their energies and capital into a profusion of new ventures, including six railroad lines, two cotton mills, two cotton gins, iron foundries, lumber mills, brickyards, a street railway, waterworks, gasworks, and a modern hotel featuring electricity and indoor plumbing. In a promotional booklet published in 1892 to attract northern investors to the city, the enthusiastic editor gushed, "The manufacturing spirit of the people of Natchez, together with its facilities for carrying on industries of all kinds, points to the conclusion that it will become one of the most important of southern manufacturing cities." Lest his booster message fall on deaf ears, the publisher reminded readers that southerners' negative sentiments toward northerners had "long since passed," adding "WE ARE ALL YANKEES NOW."[62]

Joining the nation's thirst for railroad development helped to propel Natchez into a center for cotton processing and trading by the late nineteenth century. By 1882 the town's first rail enterprise led by its president, William T. Martin, connected Natchez to the state capital and much of the nation. Other leading Natchez businessmen and merchants—Henry Frank, Isaac Lowenburg, Audley C. Britton, George W. Koontz, Rufus F. Learned, and Thomas Reber—jumped on board, hatching their own railroad schemes. These railroad ventures not only improved personal travel and made it easier and faster to ship cotton and other commercial goods, but also increased the fortunes of investors.[63]

Many of the same men involved in railroad development were instrumental in harnessing Gilded Age technological innovations to fuel Natchez's industrial and economic growth. Building the facilities necessary to make the new technology available to themselves and other local customers, they led the way in introducing telephone service (1881), manufactured ice (1882), municipal streetcars (1887), municipal water and sewer service (1889), electricity (1889), and indoor plumbing (1891).[64] Banker Audley Britton could barely manage to contain his enthusiasm for the town's industrial growth spurt in a letter he wrote to his daughter Mary, who was attending boarding school in Connecticut. "The two factories are in full operation now, furnishing employment to a great many persons, and giving a busy appearance to that part of the town. Then they are building the two Rail Roads.... An elevator is being constructed from the steamboat landing up the bluff.... [W]e are going to have an ice factory ... turning out 15 tons per day. The machine alone cost $21,000.... So you see we are doing something."[65] Even the town's daily newspaper promoted itself as an industrial concern and the beneficiary of new technology, assuring their readers that as a member of the Associated Press, they could deliver the "latest telegraphic news in time for breakfast."[66]

Rising with the cotton mills that occupied nearly entire city blocks, the town's Gilded Age entrepreneurs built male-exclusive and business-oriented social clubs such as the Natchez Club, which opened its doors in 1883. Here, business leaders found "agreeable relaxation from the cares and toils of business" with "innocent amusement" as well as "an extensive collection" of American and English business publications.[67] Further solidifying the town's commitment to commercial growth, leading members of the Natchez Club established the Natchez Cotton and Merchants Exchange, proclaimed as "one of the solidest organizations in the city," and a key supporter of the town's important cotton trade.[68] By the early 1890s, Natchez business elites established newer and grander men's social clubs, such as the Standard Literary and Social Club for Jewish men, followed by the interfaith Prentiss Club in 1903, which featured handsomely appointed rooms for dining, dancing, and mixed gender socializing.[69]

By the last decade of the nineteenth century, white Natchez men increasingly set aside secretive Masonic rituals, fancy uniforms, and the organization's symbolic plumb, square, and compass, for the fashionable white men's business clubs and mercantile exchanges where they could foster important business relationships. Among the thirty-six prominent business leaders who played a key role in building the new social clubs and business associations, only twelve were Masons. Twenty-two men from this group continued as members of the Adams Light Infantry. Thus, by the late 1800s an increasing array of new public spaces were available to white Natchez men in addition to the traditional religious, fraternal, and military associations they had long supported. By the latter decades of the nineteenth century investing one's time and financial resources into modern business endeavors probably held greater appeal for many southern men than spending long evenings at the Masonic temple performing dated rituals. Natchez was not the only southern city to see a decline in Freemasonry. Masonic memberships had substantially declined in much of the South at a time when white men in places like Birmingham, Atlanta, and Memphis eagerly heeded the call for New South business development.[70] The fact that more than half of the town's prominent business men had once belonged to the Adams Light Infantry offers another intriguing clue, suggesting that as the "soldier boys" matured and grew more prominent in the business community, they sought new forms of entertainment that better fit their social and professional needs. While difficult to precisely document, by the 1890s, aging Natchez militia men likely chose to wage battle in the competitive world of commerce rather than on the parade grounds and athletic fields they had frequented in earlier days.

FEMINIZATION OF THE LOST CAUSE

Coinciding with marked changes in male social bonding by the late 1880s and 1890s, large numbers of middle- and upper-class white Natchez men and women, no longer restricting themselves to their separate spheres as in earlier decades, joined one another in a variety of benevolent and leisure pursuits. Chief among these was the formation of the town's Confederate Memorial Association (CMA) in March 1887 to memorialize those who had died serving the Confederate cause. A number of the male organizers, including association president Charles Chamberlain, were officers or members of the Adams Light Infantry as well as veterans. At the organization's first meeting thirty-five "ladies" were elected as honorary members. Female members of the CMA initially worked behind the scenes, primarily decorating Confederate graves; however, within a few years they ranked as leaders in the town's memorialization movement. By 1890, with Melanie Frank serving as the organization's vice president, and assisted by Laura Montieth, Ellen Henderson, and Livie J. Baker (all married to Adams Light Infantry members), Natchez women took the lead in growing the group's membership.[71]

The women had no trouble attracting female members. Within a few months' time women dominated the organization with 160 female members while male membership remained stagnant with about forty members. Analysis of the CMA's female membership helps to characterize the group. Of the eighty-five female members who appear in census or other archival records, the average age was thirty-five. At least fifteen among this group were still in their teens, meaning that a substantial number of these women had not experienced the war personally. Thirty-three percent were born during or after the war, and another 12 percent were children during the conflict. Thus, a substantial number of the organization's female membership based their knowledge of the Civil War on memories passed down through family members. It comes as no surprise that a sizable number of the women were related to Confederate veterans or a male family members active in the Adams Light Infantry. Forty-one percent of the women were affiliated with a militia member, and at least 30 percent had a familial connection with a veteran.

Natchez women joined the Confederate Memorial Association for any number of reasons. Some may have wanted to alleviate grudges held against them during the war. For instance, it is somewhat surprising to see Katherine Minor's name listed on the membership roll. In the early 1870s "Yankee Kate" had presented herself as a staunch Unionist before the Southern Claims

Commission, where she eventually won her hefty claim of more than fifty thousand dollars. The savvy widow and mother of three may have joined the association to restore her family's reputation in Natchez society as a loyal southerner, suggesting that both Unionists and Confederates put aside their differences in the postwar period to produce a myth of unity that had never existed before or during the war. Most women who joined the CMA, however, did so because the organization offered a purposeful way to grieve or commemorate a family member who had served the cause. The tragic deaths of the Foster sisters' two brothers resonated with many members who were mourning their own losses. None of the three sisters married, and Kate Foster spent much of her life devoted to Confederate memorialization, first as a leader in the CMA and later as a founder of the Natchez chapter of the United Daughters of the Confederacy.[72]

Many of the female CMA members eventually married, but nearly 40 percent of the group was either single or widowed at the time they joined the organization. This finding, coupled with the knowledge that nearly half were related to Adams Light Infantry members and most related to Confederate veterans, suggests that Natchez's memorial association served as a kind of female auxiliary to the town's highly esteemed militia groups and offered a means for women to indirectly participate in Natchez's martial culture within traditional gendered boundaries. Not content to serve merely as idle honorary members, the group's female members quickly assumed a prominent, useful role in the organization. Indeed, the female members were responsible for raising the remaining funds needed to purchase the three-thousand-dollar monument erected to honor the town's Confederate dead.[73] Thus, the memorial association served as an acceptable way for women many of whom had never experienced the war firsthand—to publicly proclaim their dedication to Lost Cause ideology and take an active role in their town's reverence for martial culture.

In keeping with southern social norms that precluded women from speaking at public gatherings, men served as the orators when the monument was unveiled on April 25, 1890, at Memorial Park, a cemetery adjacent to Saint Mary's Basilica. The town's annual spring Memorial Day ceremonies continuously showcased male orators, parading veterans, and militia companies; however, as the decade progressed the feminization of the Lost Cause became increasingly more evident. On the day of the monument unveiling ceremony the *Natchez Democrat* published a letter written by a male CMA leader complimenting the women who had raised the remaining funds needed to pay for the statue, after "the gentlemen had exhausted their persuasive powers."[74]

Numerous Memorial Day speakers frequently credited Natchez women as worthy comrades in the battle to honor the dead and perpetuate the memory of the war. In his remarks at the monument's unveiling, K. Palmer Lanneau, son-in-law of Confederate General William Martin, invoked classical martial imagery for the special occasion, comparing the mothers of the Confederacy to the "Spartan mothers of old," citing the legendary Greek city-state known for its military prowess and a social structure in which women enjoyed a level of power and status unique within the ancient world. Two years later, Reverend Vernon H. Cowsert, "the son of an old Confederate soldier" also relied on classical lore in paying homage to local women who had supported the war effort. "Wives and mothers, who with more than Spartan heroism bore your part in the fatal struggle, to the admiration of the world have you exemplified the graces of Christian widowhood. To you in many instances is still entrusted the perpetuation of the memory of those we mourn. Continue in the future as in the past to depict the virtues of their glorified ancestors into the ears of children's children, until that memory shall become the very mirror in which they shall dress themselves—the model of all that is best in human character."[75]

Reverend Cowsert in his tribute to heroic Natchez wives and mothers, whom he portrayed as staunch supporters of the Confederacy, conveniently overlooked the fact that this simply was not the case. "Yankee Kate" Minor, Julia Nutt, and even Margarette Martin, a Confederate general's wife, among others, had questioned, resented, and spoke out against the war. The embellishment of the Lost Cause myth with such ebullient sentiments, whether true or not, suggests that white Natchez women held a special place within their community's postwar memory. Like the Spartan women of old, southern women were expected to dutifully mourn and honor their fallen soldiers and, equally important, perpetuate their memory among the generations that followed.

By the end of the decade, F. J. V. LeCand, veteran, ALI officer, and Memorial Association member, urged the women of Natchez to join the recently established United Daughters of the Confederacy (UDC) to continue their good works, describing the group as "fresh troops to a line of battle which is well nigh exhausted."[76] LeCand's remarks proved prescient; as aging veterans and Adams Light Infantry founders began to die, new "troops" were needed to carry the torch forward. By the end of the century the UDC played the dominant role in memorializing the Civil War in Natchez and in communities across the South. After the Confederate monument had been erected and Natchez's Memorial Association faded from public view, many of Natchez's most active female Memorial Association members—Kate Foster, Melanie Frank, Emmie Martin Lanneau, and Laura Montieth—became founding members of their town's local UDC chapter, which will be discussed in greater detail in chapter 5.

By Memorial Day 1912, Natchez UDC members had appropriated for themselves the role of perpetuating their town's Lost Cause legacy as suggested by a letter published in the *Democrat*, signed by "A Daughter of the Confederacy." "The Memorial Association, faithful and loving, teaching us to remember! ... teaching the generation year by year by their loyal example, 'Lest they forget.' To this little band of true-hearted women with tender memories we are indebted ... the Sons and Daughters of the Confederacy are standing reverently, waiting and willing to take up the work so nobly, so bravely begun."77

Statements like this one served two purposes. First, Natchezians were urged to guard their precious memories of those who had served the Confederacy in battle and on the home front and of the losses incurred for a worthy cause. The Confederate daughter's words also marked a significant turning point in the gendered development of the town's cultural institutions and in how white women perceived their role in crafting their community's historical narrative. As one historian noted, the feminization of the Lost Cause "enabled women non-combatants to lay claim to the most important event in southern history."78

Even as Natchez women played an increasingly more dominant role in public commemorations honoring the cause, local men never entirely exited the stage. As evidenced by a joint resolution drafted by the local chapters of the United Confederate Veterans and the United Daughters of the Confederacy, the sons and daughters of the Lost Cause continued to work hand in hand to preserve such memories well into the twentieth century. In September 1923 the two organizations joined forces in Natchez to request county officials to preserve the souvenir publication memorializing the Confederate dead published by the Adams Light Infantry more than thirty years earlier. Noting that few copies of the document remained and that the pamphlet was "exceedingly frail and perishable," the men and women asked that the memorial be recorded in a deed record book and that a copy be deposited in the city vault, with an assurance that future custodians "never, never permit its removal therefrom."79

THE RETURN OF WHITE MALE DOMINANCE

By the end of the nineteenth century, Natchez white men were far less worried about dominating social space and maintaining racial supremacy than in earlier decades. They had good reason to feel this way. The martial-minded Natchez men who had proudly paraded through Natchez streets as members of the Adams Light Infantry or a Masonic lodge in the late 1870s had succeeded in their mission to regain social and racial control. The nagging uncertainties associated with profound economic decline inflicted by military loss, the emancipation of large numbers of slaves eager to attain civil and social rights, and the sobering, soul-searching questions related to their identities as men who had lost the war were quietly retreating. Participation in male organizations such as the Adams Light Infantry and the Freemasons had enabled southern white men like those in Natchez to construct a confident new identity and in the process reclaim a sense of honor and mastery that on the surface was not so very different from the antebellum era. True, southern white men's notions of masculine honor and mastery, primarily expressed through slaveholding and a paternalistic mindset, were swept away at war's end. By the 1880s, however, remnants of these antebellum ideals were very much alive in postbellum Natchez, in large part because the rhetoric of male fraternal and martial associations proudly promoting their allegiance to Lost Cause ideology made it possible for white men to reclaim their dominance of social and public space.

Of course, parades, dashing military uniforms, and at times threatening racist behavior are only part of the story in white men's return to power in postwar Natchez. Equally important in the downward spiral of African American political and social decline was the constitutional statute in 1890 that disfranchised black men, accompanied by a sharp drop in black political appointments during the same decade. Moreover, the state's dozen or more Jim Crow laws passed from 1878 to 1930—some of the most stringently enforced in the South—governing public accommodations, schools, transportation, marriage, and nearly all aspects of life, confirmed blacks' status as second-class citizens. Passionate white Mississippians determined to reestablish their manhood and restore the antebellum social order, backed by laws that disfranchised black men and segregated social space, had little trouble snuffing out the advances made by southern African Americans during Reconstruction. As historian Neil McMillen writes, "Reviled as inherently dull, servile and vicious, set apart by habits of mind and social convention that made skin color the mark of human worth, black Mississippians were

Jim Crowed early, well before a rising tide of extreme racism swept across the state after 1890."[80] In addition to separate schools for black and white children (one of the most common Jim Crow laws across the South), Mississippi governed nearly every aspect of life. It was a crime for a white person to marry a black with one-eighth or more "negro blood." Hospitals were required to create separate entrances for white and colored patients and visitors. Prison wardens were ordered to provide separate eating and sleeping quarters for white and black prisoners. As one black Natchezian wrote, "White supremacy was based on oral or traditional discrimination without legal sanction. Negroes accepted these traditions as a way of life and as a method of survival."[81]

THE DECLINE OF MASONRY

The photograph of a large crowd of mostly white men—many wearing their Masonic aprons and Knights Templar sashes—on hand to witness the laying of the cornerstone for a new Masonic temple in 1890 is symbolic of social changes underway in late nineteenth-century Natchez. Many in the crowd are elderly, bearded, white-headed, and leaning on canes—comforted, no doubt, in the knowledge that upon death they would receive an honorary Masonic funeral.

By 1890, Masonry was no longer the force it once had been in Natchez cultural life. Although fewer men joined the organization, Freemasonry and its members continued to command respect, their activities drawing small crowds of spectators. Addressing the group that day was Douglas Walworth, a prominent Natchez lawyer who spoke of the role of Masonry in civic life. "Surely there is a lesson for us all here today whether we be Masons or not; a lesson of change, of change which is written upon humanity as it is upon martial structure, whether of wood or stone; a lesson of decay; a lesson of the limit of human effort; a lesson of the advancing tide of events as time rolls on in its irresistible march, sweeping away life, monuments and edifices—all things but the essence of good."[82]

Walworth and the other Masons who had assembled for an important and sacred moment in the life of their fraternal order saw themselves as forces of good in the life of their community, whether in the building of a fine new Masonic temple, providing financial aid to needy orphans and widows, or preserving white southern honor and traditions. Walworth's speech also suggests that he and his audience realized the cultural role of male

Natchez Masons, city officials, and other whites and blacks gather to raise the cornerstone of the city's Masonic temple after it was demolished in 1890. Norman Studios. (Courtesy of the Thomas H. and Joan W. Gandy Photograph Collection, Louisiana Lower Mississippi Valley Collections, Special Collections, Hill Memorial Library, Louisiana State University Libraries, Baton Rouge.)

associations in the Natchez community was changing. The cultural heyday of Freemasonry, other fraternal associations, and militia groups like the Adams Light Infantry was ending, in part because such groups had fulfilled their purpose. Additionally, female patriotic associations such as the United Daughters of the Confederacy and the Daughters of the American Revolution had claimed for themselves a more prominent role in community cultural affairs. Meanwhile, many men sought out each other's company in one of several new social clubs where business deals could be hammered out in the comfort of a male retreat. Moreover, a younger generation of men, often in the company of female friends, pursued an array of new leisure activities: Mardi Gras celebrations, Kodak camera outings, bicycle rides, and amateur theater productions starring local residents. On the eve of a new century it would be left up to this new generation of Natchezians, often following the lead of women, to shape their community's collective historical memory.

CHAPTER FOUR

"PICTURE MAKERS"

Black and White Historical Memory in Postbellum Natchez

WE HAVE NO WAY OF KNOWING EXACTLY WHAT PROMPTED CHARLES SMITH, a well-groomed African American man in his early twenties, to visit the studio of white Natchez photographer Henry C. Norman for a portrait sitting sometime in the 1880s. Perhaps he had just joined the Superb Cornet Band, one of the town's popular musical ensembles, and wanted to impress family and friends with his handsome uniform and shiny musical instrument. Indeed, nineteenth-century Americans often posed with pianos, violins, and other musical instruments to demonstrate their cultivation and respectability.[1] Or, he may have been preparing for an upcoming concert and wanted a memento to document the special occasion.

Whatever his reasons, the evidence of Smith's hiring the town's best professional photographer to capture his "likeness" is found in the finely crafted portrait Norman created for his client. Smith stands erect in front of a decorative Victorian-era façade that Norman frequently used in his portraits of both his black and white clientele. Dressed in a richly brocaded wool uniform, set off by a starched white collar, polished buttons, and a cap bearing the band's insignia—the young musician held his prized cornet close to his heart. Smith gazed squarely and confidently into the camera lens, an image that continues to command attention more than a century after the young man posed.

Smith was only one of the hundreds of black and white Natchez residents who flocked to Henry Norman's studio on Main Street in the heart of downtown Natchez and later to his home studio on nearby Washington Street between 1870 and the early twentieth century, leaving a rich collective visual memory of the community's racial hierarchy, social landscape, popular amusements, and the individuals who populated the town.[2] The

Charles Smith. Norman Studios. (Courtesy of the Thomas H. and Joan W. Gandy Photograph Collection, Louisiana Lower Mississippi Valley Collections, Special Collections, Hill Memorial Library, Louisiana State University Libraries, Baton Rouge.)

large collection of Norman negatives and photographs—some 75,000 in all, of which 60,000 were salvageable—rescued in 1960 and restored over the course of several decades by physician Thomas Gandy speaks to the sumptuous sense of place projected by Natchez and surrounding Adams County in the late nineteenth century.[3] Norman's images and those left by numerous amateur photographers from the late 1870s to early 1900s reveal a town still attached to its antebellum moorings, evidenced by photographs of the many dilapidated pre–Civil War estates still standing. Simultaneously, striking visuals of black and white Natchez residents often wearing fashionable ornately beaded gowns, velvet-trimmed suit coats, and flamboyant hats, posed with bicycles, cameras, toys, and other contemporary amusements are all symbolic of a town and populace that reveled in a new era of consumer culture and the pleasurable sense of modernity that accompanied it. But upon deeper investigation, there are multiple, complex, and often conflicting layers of meaning imbedded in what often appear as the simplest of photographs. Like many Americans of their time, the late nineteenth-century Natchezians whose likenesses have been preserved, eyed the approaching new century with a mixed sense of optimism and uncertainty.

This chapter explores the connections between visual images of Natchez blacks crafted by white photographers in the postbellum era—primarily studio portraits, postcards, and candid photos—and the construction of collective historical memories. The photographs taken of Natchez blacks first by the skilled professional Henry Norman and later by amateur camera enthusiast Mary Britton Conner reveal as much about the individuals behind the lens as they do about how whites and blacks perceived southern African American identity and the status of black citizens in the racial hierarchy. On the one hand, photographs and postcards empowered blacks to play a more assertive role as paying customers in the process of memory making. On the other hand, black consumers lacked full control over how photographers composed the images and distributed them commercially.

The photographic images of Natchez's leading professional photographer and the album of Mary Conner, a planter-class white female amateur, shed light on a new set of postemancipation identities adopted by black residents. Henry Norman's black portraits shot in the late 1870s and 1880s revealed a community imbued with a sense of pride and optimism in the future, far different from the white community's fixation on the past. Simultaneously, the portraits offer a record of those who could afford a trip to Henry Norman's studio, a small luxury for most portrait clients. Over time, photographs shot in Natchez revealed changes to the black identity. Only two decades later, the pictures Mary Conner produced in the 1890s and early 1900s reflected some of the adverse impacts of Jim Crow on Natchez blacks. Many of the blacks she photographed appeared subservient and closely tied to a white household, in some ways similar to the antebellum slave era. Despite the strictures of Jim Crow, however, many of those photographed by Conner reflected a sense of agency and strength. By contrast photographs taken of whites in the postwar era reflected a very different kind of identity from black subjects. Some, like Mary Britton Conner, appear mired in the antebellum era decades after the end of the Civil War. These striking and diverse visual images are an expression of the region's collective social memory.[4]

The creators and subjects of the majority of these photographs belonged to a generation who by and large were either too young to have experienced the war personally or had escaped the conflict's direst consequences—poverty, physical suffering, and loss of family members and property. These individuals were nevertheless shaped by the war and its outcome, and the visual memoirs they left shaped southern culture for decades. Most of these photographs never achieved fame or a wide audience, but nevertheless are important sites of history and memory making.

A host of intriguing questions are raised in analyzing the subject matter, style, and tone of the photographs taken by both professional and amateur Natchez camera buffs. What do post-Reconstruction-era photographs of Natchez African Americans reveal about black social and economic life in the latter decades of the nineteenth century? What kinds of social and cultural messages were Natchez African Americans sending to themselves, their social network, and the dominant white community through the photographs they posed for? How did whites perceive such images? As cultural historian Alan Trachtenburg writes, "Like miniature replicas, [photographs] give us worlds to ponder and amaze ourselves with."[5]

Those who study historic photographs customarily look for agency in works produced by the group under investigation. Unfortunately, archival records with which to document the work of amateur and professional black Natchez photographers are thin. Nevertheless, we can still discern agency in the photographs blacks commissioned. As Trachtenburg argues, individuals who pose within photographs are not passive bystanders but serve as essential "maker[s] and manipulator[s] of a picture." Photographs taken by white photographers of local African Americans in late nineteenth- and early twentieth-century Natchez reveal something of how black men, women, and children saw themselves and their place in the social strata. Many of these images displayed a sense of agency, an aspect common to portrait photography regardless of race. Moreover, these images sustained a collective memory long after the shutter snapped and have the power to document an important piece of the historical narrative.

A PASSION FOR "LIKENESSES"

Well before the Civil War, photographic imagery captured the fancy of Americans nationwide. By the 1850s nearly every town in America had at least one commercial photographer as Americans eagerly sat for their "likenesses." Natchez was no exception. A March 1851 Natchez newspaper advertisement proclaimed that Henry Gurney's Sky-Light Daguerrean Portrait Gallery rendered "the most beautiful shading, softness and strength of tone to their pictures." Another article described Gurney and his partner as "elegant artists" whose studio was "crowded day by day with throngs of beauty and fashion."[6] Gurney, like most photographers of his era, catered to an elite and upper-middle-class clientele that had the time and financial means to sit for a portrait. A number of photographers established themselves in wartime

Natchez, but Henry Gurney remained the leading photographer of the city. In the years immediately following the war Gurney strived to beat out his competition by offering bargain prices. In one 1867 ad he informed his customers that "by request of the ladies, Gurney will continue to take cheap pictures for two weeks longer. Gem pictures, 25 cents each; $3 pictures for only $.50 cents each."[7]

By the time Henry C. Norman, a twenty-year-old Georgia native, moved to Natchez in 1870 and joined Gurney's studio as a camera operator, growing numbers of Americans of all social classes eagerly purchased commercial photographs as inexpensive, novel keepsakes. The burgeoning demand for photographic services within Natchez enabled Norman to open his own studio over a downtown bookstore in 1877. Within his well-appointed studio featuring a large polished mahogany Century camera with lacquered brass fixtures, Norman earned a reputation as both an "operator" and "artist."[8] A booklet published in 1881 enthusiastically promoted Norman's skills, noting: "His productions are not merely likenesses, but in every sense, pictures. . . . He can produce pictures from the ordinary album card, to elaborately finished life-size portraits." Like many fine portrait artists of his day, Norman's studio reflected an attention to creating a refined, genteel space for his customers, much like a comfortable parlor. The same promotional literature boasted that "his suite of rooms are elegantly furnished, upon the walls of which are hung portraits, groups, and pictures architectural of landscape; an inspection of which will convince the connoisseur, that they are the productions, not only of an experienced operator, but of an artist."[9] Women, men, and children would have found such a space hospitable and inviting.

For the remainder of the nineteenth century Norman's business grew and prospered, ranking him as the town's most successful and gifted photographer. Best known for his portrait work, Henry Norman's talents were not limited to his indoor studio. He frequently took his camera into the streets of Natchez, capturing storefronts, merchants and their employees, shoppers, and festive parades. On other days he ventured into residential neighborhoods just beyond the business district, frequently photographing families on their porches, dressed in their Sunday best. As well he took his camera beyond Natchez city limits into the rural countryside, catching black sharecroppers at work in the cotton fields or white families relaxing on their porches and the spacious lawns of their estates, often with their black servants positioned behind family members or on the outer edges of the photo.[10]

A lack of written or visual narratives created by Natchez blacks from the late nineteenth and early twentieth centuries suggests there is little way of knowing how blacks perceived themselves in the town's highly stratified racial hierarchy. Photographer Henry C. Norman's exquisite portraits of the African American men, women, and children who purchased his services in the 1880s and 1890s, however, help to fill in the gap and provides a rich body of evidence about African American life. Moreover, Norman's visually stunning photographs offer a distinctive black visual aesthetic and an important counter memory to the highly visible and, at times, violent ways in which white Natchez militia groups, fraternal associations, and the town's Confederate Memorial Association controlled the town's cultural and social landscape. The portraits counter the multitude of racist cartoons, articles, and jokes littered across the pages of national and local publications that, at best, depicted blacks as ignorant and childlike "Sambos," and, at worst, as dishonest sexual deviants. As photo historian Deborah Willis writes, African Americans in late nineteenth- and early twentieth-century America "believed that defining their own identity and beauty through photography was a significant step in the fight against negative representations."[11] Read from this perspective, Norman's African American portraits suggest that the elite and middle-class blacks he photographed saw themselves very differently from demeaning stereotypes and rejected the white community's attempts to erase blacks from public commemorations and southern culture.

Of the close to two hundred black portraits that have survived from Norman's collection, the most noticeable trait is the profound sense of dignity embedded in the faces and postures of his subjects.[12] Whether in photographs of a working-class laundry woman or laborer, a middle-class railroad conductor, or the elite black members of the community—politicians, ministers, and the better off and educated—Norman's African American patrons reflect both the photographer's respect towards his subjects and self-respect of his black clientele. Racial stereotyping is absent; Norman's studio portraits of Natchez blacks are nearly identical to the poses and settings that appear in his portraits of whites. As photographic historian John Stauffer asserts, the black subjects in Norman's portraits appear respectable "and not only comfortable, but empowered by posing for a white man."[13] True, Norman depicted his black subjects as respected members of the community. But more was at stake here. No doubt, black portrait sitters gained a sense of agency from posing for the town's leading white photographer, but at the same time these individuals posed for themselves, seizing the initiative to express visual messages of dignity, hope, and optimism—an act of empowerment unto itself. Borrowing from African American essayist bell hooks, "The camera was the central instrument by which blacks could disprove representations of us created by white folks."[14] Very likely, the blacks who posed for Norman came with a similar purpose in mind.

A THRIVING SENSE OF COMMUNITY

For whatever reasons Norman's black patrons chose to come to his studio, their decisions reflected the robust black community and consumer culture that thrived in postwar Natchez and in cities and towns across the South. By the 1880s having lost the battle for the ballot as well as the use of public space to stage large scale commemorations, Natchez African Americans turned increasingly inward, following a trend within black communities nationwide. In Natchez, Saint Catherine Street, one block north of the town's main commercial district, flourished as the heart of an intricately networked and vibrant black community. Here, churches, schools, black-owned businesses, and fraternal organizations thrived, providing African Americans the necessary resources and public spaces to build a strong community and sense of identity in late nineteenth-century Natchez.

By the latter decades of the nineteenth century, the development of Saint Catherine Street as a hub of black social life marked a significant shift in the town's spatial and racial relationships. Natchez had never been rigidly segregated along racial lines. For a number of years, blacks and whites had lived alongside one another. Prior to the 1890s, the homes of Natchez black elites were scattered among those occupied by white residents on neighboring downtown streets. For example, mulatto policemen Minor Davis and Wynant Bowie lived on State Street integrated among white households. The black Hoggatt brothers, William and Anthony, made their homes on Canal Street, and former black mayor Robert H. Wood owned a home on Market Street in 1880, both neighborhoods that were well populated by whites.[15]

By the late 1880s and early 1890s increasing numbers of elite and working-class blacks had formed a new and racially separate community on Saint Catherine Street. Of the more than 560 black households noted in the 1892 city directory, more than 10 percent were located here.[16] For example, the families of lawyer George F. Bowles, carpenter Anthony Hoggatt, and former policeman turned bakery owner Minor Davis lived in homes adjacent to the household of black circuit court clerk Louis J. Winston, owner of one of the neighborhood's most prosperous homes, known as "Winston Hill." Not far from this cluster of handsome residences on the same street were the homes of Louis Kastor, a prosperous saddler and harness maker, policeman

J. Stevenson, physician Dr. John B. Banks, and Charles Russell, the owner of a confectionary and ice shop.

Many of these black men were not only neighbors with longstanding personal ties, but most also had offices and shops in close proximity to one another. Busy Franklin Street, one block south of the Saint Catherine neighborhood, was home to Louis Kastor's saddle and harness making shop, Charles Russell's ice depot and sweet shop, and Dr. John Banks' medical office, along with a number of other black-owned barber, butcher, and grocery establishments. Additional black businesses were found on nearby Main and State Streets, such as the bakery of Minor Davis and law offices of George Bowles and Louis J. Winston.

Spatial connections between the elite men and women living on Saint Catherine Street extended beyond residential and business ties. Some had grown up together in the same household or married into one another's families. Louis Kastor, the son of a white German immigrant and one of the neighborhood's most prosperous mulatto residents, shared the same black mother with Charles Russell, and lived with his white stepfather, Sidney Russell, and other family members in the early 1880s.[17] Charles Russell would eventually marry one of the daughters of well-respected carpenter Anthony Hoggatt, another resident of Saint Catherine Street. Prominent lawyer George Bowles married Laura Davis, the sister of Minor and Thomas Davis. Thomas would later work as a clerk in Bowles' law office.[18]

Church membership within Holy Family and Zion Chapel, the two most prominent black Natchez churches, further strengthened communal ties among many Saint Catherine Street residents. Several of Holy Family's most prominent members resided on Saint Catherine Street, including Louis J. Winston, Minor Davis, and brothers Anthony and William Hoggatt. The building of a separate Catholic sanctuary in 1894 on the corner of Saint Catherine and Orange Avenue for black parishioners who had formerly belonged to and worshipped in the large and lovely St. Mary's Cathedral, located several blocks away, was no doubt a factor in the rapid growth of the neighborhood. Louis Winston persuaded fellow parishioners to support the construction of a new parish church that was in close proximity to St. Catherine Street, a neighborhood that he had developed through his building and loan enterprise, the Mississippi Cooperative Benefit Association. Both Minor Davis and Wynant Bowie were beneficiaries of home loans financed by Winston's organization.

Many of the neighborhood's black Protestant residents worshipped at the Zion AME Chapel located on the corner of St. Catherine Street and

Pine Street. Several of Zion Chapel's members had achieved financial success and were firmly entrenched among elite blacks, including Dr. John B. Banks, Charles Russell, and Louis Kastor. The majority of this congregation, however, found themselves among the working class, laboring as draymen, porters, domestic servants, seamstresses, and cooks. Many among this group rented rather than owned their homes on Saint Catherine Street within an easy walk of Zion Chapel, and some boarded with fellow church members.[19]

Prosperous African Americans as well as those of more moderate means living on Saint Catherine Street or elsewhere in Natchez had a wide array of businesses eager to fulfill their consumer needs and desires. Black-owned grocery markets, meat shops, barber shops, saddle and harness makers, hack drivers, blacksmiths, carpenters, brickmasons, painters, shoemakers, seamstresses, milliners, bakers, lawyers, doctors, and a dentist catered to a black as well as white clientele in 1880s Natchez.

Several of the town's most successful black entrepreneurs were lauded in contemporary publications. A photograph of light-skinned Louis Kastor accompanied a biographical sketch that touted his business acumen as "a first-class harness-maker" with "one of the largest and best-equipped stores" in the country. The report noted that Kastor began his operation with sixty-five dollars and was presently "doing a business of some $22,000."[20] Milliner Ella Henderson was recognized for enlarging her shop and for being treated by travelling salesmen with the respect due "white ladies in the same business."[21]

Turn-of-the-century Natchez had its own chroniclers of black business success, offering additional evidence of a flourishing consumer economy within the postwar African American community. A 1902 publication that recorded the history of AME churches in the state also included a detailed account of black prosperity and business success. The author, Reverend Revel A. Adams, pastor of Natchez's Zion Chapel, devoted particular attention to his hometown flock, noting the names of the nearly seventy founding church members along with some twenty biographical profiles. In addition to paying tribute to members' loyalty and service to the church, Adams frequently noted the professional and financial achievements of his church members. Mrs. Lydia Beemis, cited as "loyal to every interest of the church," was also heralded as "a school teacher of considerable ability and a professional dressmaker." Professor George W. Brumfield, a church officer and principal of the black Natchez Public School "with fourteen teachers and more than one thousand pupils under his supervision," was applauded for his ownership of "a palatial residence, and property valued at more than $3,000." Mrs. A. Jane Taylor, while earning no praise for her spiritual life, was recognized for such secular accomplishments as having "traveled through every section of the U.S. . . . and extensively through the principal countries of Europe . . . South America and the West Indies." Not only a "good conversationalist," the affluent and sociable Mrs. Taylor was complimented for owning "a beautiful home and other valuable property."[22] Reverend Adams's publication offered evidence that despite the economic and social restrictions of Jim Crow, some members of the black Natchez community continued to thrive as consumers and proprietors well after Reconstruction ended.

The vast majority of black Natchez residents, however, including those residing on bustling Saint Catherine Street, were not business or property owners. Most barely eked out a living from low-paying manual labor. Indeed, nearly all of the retail establishments in downtown Natchez were white owned. With few if any black-owned stores selling dry goods—textiles, clothing, toiletries, and a vast assortment of other commonly used household merchandise—black consumers would have had no choice but to shop at white-owned Natchez stores, such as Chamberlain & Patterson, F. A. Dicks, and Henry Frank Dry Goods.[23]

VISIONS OF BLACK AGENCY

While there is no evidence telling us exactly how white retail establishments treated black consumers in late nineteenth-century Natchez, it would have been no small matter for Natchez African Americans to make their way into Norman's downtown Main Street studio, one of a handful of photography businesses in Natchez, all white owned. At a time when African Americans' worth as wage earners and citizens was frequently denigrated, sitting for a Norman portrait asserted their worth and pride as black consumers. As paying clientele, the black men and women who sat for a portrait hired Norman, chose what they wore, likely had a say in the props used, paid for the image, and determined how their photographs would ultimately be used. The sheer number of black portraits produced by Norman and their exquisite quality suggests that his African American patrons enjoyed a hospitable experience during a time when many southern photographic studios limited service to blacks on certain days of the week or posted signs reading "For White People Only" or "No Coons Allowed."

The portrait of an unidentified mother and her daughter, approximately five years of age, gives us a sense of the experience of sitting for a studio portrait. The mother, who looks to be of middle- or working-class status

Unidentified woman and child. Norman Studios. (Courtesy of the Thomas H. and Joan W. Gandy Photograph Collection, Louisiana Lower Mississippi Valley Collections, Special Collections, Hill Memorial Library, Louisiana State University Libraries, Baton Rouge.)

based on her rather neat but plain black skirt, shirtwaist, simple hat, and small purse resting in her lap, appears in sharp contrast to her young daughter. The girl's elegant white party dress, stockings, dress shoes, and white bow in her hair were probably worn for a school exhibition, graduation, or May Day celebration, a popular social event among Natchez children, white and black. Dressing her daughter in fancy clothing suggests that the mother was making a statement to bolster her family's respectability and refinement in a world where many blacks were denied basic courtesies.[24] The mother sits in a small chair with no fancy props or background scenery appearing in the photo, befitting her modest social status. Unlike upper-class women, the woman sits with her knees spread apart, hardly a refined pose. Drawing the child close, the woman's fingers gently clasp her daughter's arm as the child's other hand rests securely in her mother's lap. The mother gazes confidently but solemnly into Norman's lens, while her daughter poses more casually, her back arched and her hip extended. Appearing somewhat playful, the young girl shyly casts her eyes downward. The viewer senses this was an important moment for a proud young black mother who found the time and money to visit her town's best photography studio to create a treasured visual memory of herself and her daughter.

Alex Mazique, ca. 1880. Henry Norman, photographer. (Courtesy of the Thomas H. and Joan W. Gandy Photograph Collection, Louisiana Lower Mississippi Valley Collections, Special Collections, Hill Memorial Library, Louisiana State University Libraries, Baton Rouge.)

We do not know exactly how this image was used or displayed, but such photos played an important role in demonstrating middle-class respectability within black households and as such would have found a prominent place on a household wall or in a cherished family album. As bell hooks writes, photographs took on particular significance for African Americans. "The walls and walls of images in southern black homes were sites of resistance.... These walls were a space where, in the midst of segregation, the hardship of apartheid, dehumanization could be countered. Images could be critically considered, subjects positioned according to individual desire." Hooks spoke from personal experience. She recalled her illiterate grandmother's wall of photographs, artistically arranged much like one of her beautiful quilts. "Her walls were essential to our sense of self-identity as a family. They provided a necessary narrative, a way for us to enter history without words.... The images were crucial documentation, there to sustain and affirm oral memory."[25] Norman's black portraits—both the studio experience and the finished product—would have claimed a similar purpose and place of reverence in the memories and homes of Natchez African Americans.[26]

In contrast to the unidentified mother and daughter photograph, a number of Norman's portraits reveal that many of his black clientele were prosperous and enjoyed a more elevated social status. The portrait of family

Two boys believed to be the sons of "Janitor John," ca. 1880. Henry Norman, photographer. (Courtesy of the Thomas H. and Joan W. Gandy Photograph Collection, Louisiana Lower Mississippi Valley Collections, Special Collections, Hill Memorial Library, Louisiana State University Libraries, Baton Rouge.)

patriarch Alexander Mazique projects a sense of masculine dominance. His handsome dress clothes and stylish mutton chop whiskers reflect the rapid rise in the Mazique family's fortunes following the Civil War. Alex Mazique's family became one of the most prosperous in Adams County during Reconstruction, beginning with the acquisition of Oakland, the plantation home where he was born into slavery. By 1900 the family had acquired nearly a dozen plantation properties.[27] Mazique's penetrating gaze and the vitality rippling beneath his dignified attire reveal that here was no lowly sharecropper or laborer, but a prosperous man who commanded respect and fair treatment in his business dealings.

Similarly, a portrait of two school-age boys identified as "Janitor John's boys," further exhibits the middle-class status of some Natchez blacks. Dressed in suits for school boys stocked by most dry goods stores in the 1880s, the boys' outfits with black lace-up boots reflected their status. The brothers' stylish clothing is complemented by the tapestry-covered and fringed ottoman one of the boys sits on and the ornate Victorian façade in the background. Such props frequently were used in Norman's portraits of white and black subjects, creating the effect of a handsome parlor, another marker of cultural refinement. Despite their young age, the handsome brothers project poise and gentility as they gazed confidently into the camera.[28]

Unidentified woman in formal gown and headpiece. Henry Norman, photographer. (Courtesy of the Thomas H. and Joan W. Gandy Photograph Collection, Louisiana Lower Mississippi Valley Collections, Special Collections, Hill Memorial Library, Louisiana State University Libraries, Baton Rouge.)

The portrait of a young unidentified woman offers additional visual evidence of how some within Natchez's postwar black community had achieved high-ranking status. The photogenic model's elegant formal white gown with an eye-catching feather fan hat and floral bedecked bodice showcases her personal style and perhaps her own dressmaking skills. Her gaze, like so many of the portraits Norman shot of sophisticated black men and women in the last decades of the nineteenth century, is self-assured and confident.

The poses struck by black Natchez men, women, and children who sat for their likeness in Norman's studio bear a striking resemblance in style and tone to the famous and broadly circulated 1850s photograph of Frederick Douglass.[29] Disregarding portrait conventions of the time where subjects nearly always looked beyond the camera lens, Douglass's piercing eyes glared directly into the camera, striking a dramatic, even somewhat intimidating facial expression. His powerful physical traits—strong mouth, furrowed brows, rough beard, and folded arms—convey defiance, intensity, and an underlying strength. Few understood the impact of photography better than the civil rights activist. When photography was still in its infancy, Douglass skillfully blended his portraits, writing, and public speaking to promote himself as a national leader on issues of race and as a man of dignity and intelligence. Noting that photography was a democratizing experience, one that allowed former slaves to create pictures of themselves as easily as the wealthy, Douglass also recognized the unique impact of photography as a powerful political tool for the masses.[30] The confident postures and gazes struck by Alex Mazique and other black Norman subjects suggest that they modeled their personal portraits after that of the revered Douglass and that Norman as a skilled camera operator worked as their accomplice in creating photographic images that resonated with a similar sense of strength, gentility, and respectability—and perhaps to whites at least—unexpected wealth within the black community.

Whether or not African Americans carried visions of the aging Douglass in their minds when they sat for a portrait in Norman's Natchez studio, photography enabled them to fashion a new self-identity during a time of great social change and racial anxiety. As one historian writes of the nineteenth century, "The question 'Who am I?' loomed large on a national scale, and Americans often answered that question with pictures."[31] Like Frederick Douglass, Henry Norman's black clientele found in photographs a way to distance themselves from slavery and to imagine a strikingly different and more promising future for themselves and their offspring. Enraptured with the imaginative qualities of photography, Douglass once wrote: "Poets, prophets, and reformers are all picture makers—and this ability is the secret of their power and of their achievements. They see what ought to be by the reflection of what is, and endeavor to remove the contradiction."[32]

No matter their economic or social status, the African American individuals photographed by Norman likewise envisioned themselves as "picture makers," even as all American blacks faced setbacks with the 1883 repeal of the Civil Rights Act, which had prohibited racial discrimination in public accommodations. Having one's picture made and acquiring that image enabled the black Natchez community to reconstruct for themselves a proud new identity far removed from enslavement and the humiliations of Jim Crow racism. Such acts of agency and consumption foreshadowed the concept of the "New Negro," a late nineteenth-century cultural movement that heralded a rebirth of black culture, literature, art, and music.[33]

Norman's memorable photographic images etched on delicate glass negatives miraculously survived for nearly eighty years before their discovery and rescue in 1960. The spirit of hope, optimism, and promise recorded in the gazes of Norman's black subjects, however, would prove far more fragile and fleeting. Less than a decade after Charles Smith and the Mazique family posed for Norman's camera, Lost Cause ideology and the increasingly hostile dictates of Jim Crow severely tested the gains of emancipation and Reconstruction.[34]

A NATCHEZ KODAK GIRL

While he was the best known and most skillful professional photographer within Natchez, Henry Norman was not the only one to record visual memories of his town. Thanks to a flurry of technological advances in late nineteenth-century photography—most notably dry-plate negatives and George Eastman's inexpensive and lightweight handheld Kodak cameras—the popular hobby became more accessible and affordable to amateur photographers who eagerly set to work capturing the people and places around them. Among the nearly 100,000 Americans who owned a Kodak camera by the late 1800s, numerous Natchez men and women eagerly purchased camera outfits and quickly took to the streets and countryside in search of subjects. For example, Natchez merchant brothers Robert and William Stewart photographed families gathered on front porches and numerous city scenes, leaving a large collection of mostly unidentified images, while Agnes Carpenter, the daughter of one of the town's wealthiest business magnates, trained her camera lens on friends and family members as well as the black servants in her household.

No one, however, was more smitten by the popular amusement than Mary Britton Conner, who devoted much of her lifetime to shooting, printing, collecting, selling, and identifying countless photographic images. Tracing the evolution and scope of Conner's photographic gaze offers a unique perspective on how southern female amateur camera enthusiasts embraced the popular pastime. Mary Conner's photographs reveal the social climate of post-Reconstruction Natchez as seen through the eyes of a prominent white woman raised in an environment suffused in Lost Cause romanticism and Jim Crow racism. In stark contrast to the modernizing, progressive narrative visible in portraits commissioned by black consumers in Henry Norman's studio, Conner's photographs reflect the depth of white southerners' nostalgia for antebellum notions of race, dependency, and paternalism in the waning years of the nineteenth century.

The youngest of four daughters, Mary Britton Conner was born in 1863 to wealthy banker Audley C. Britton and Eliza Macrery Britton. Marrying into one of antebellum Natchez's most elite families, Mary Britton Conner demonstrated a lifelong flair for creativity that she expressed through the visual arts and local theatrical productions. Mary's early passion for artistic pursuits blossomed while studying at the West End Institute Boarding and Day School for young ladies in New Haven, Connecticut, in the early 1880s. Her father, who was extremely close and affectionate with his children as evidenced in family letters, expressed pride in his youngest daughter's talents but also worried that Mary's fondness for art might adversely impact her health. In a letter praising a painting he had received from Mary, Audley Britton cautioned his daughter to not "confine" herself too closely to her art projects lest it cause her a "crooked figure" and to become "stoop shouldered."[35]

Whether Mary followed her father's advice is unknown, but the Britton family's interest in the visual arts and in photography in particular is evident in their correspondence, revealing that photographs coupled with letters helped nineteenth-century Americans weather long absences and distances from loved ones. In one letter Britton informs his daughter that he has not forgotten his promise to have his photo taken. "I intend going at once to attend to it, and will send it to you," he writes.[36] In another letter, Britton thanks his daughter for sending along a photo of a young man, perhaps a suitor of Mary's. "I was very much gratified yesterday to receive a photo of Mr. Smith. I like his looks exceedingly and am so sorry that I have never met him."[37]

Mary coupled her interest in art with a strong passion for local and regional history and preservation. Like many southern women of her day, she actively honored and fixated on the South's Civil War past. Along with her mother, Mary joined the town's Confederate Memorial Association in the late 1880s, helping to raise funds to build a monument honoring the service of local soldiers and affirming her loyalty to Lost Cause ideology. Later in life, she fought to save from the wrecking ball her town's old city hall and the marketplace where slaves once traded produce and foodstuffs. The words she wrote on the back of a photograph of the site with demolition near completion are telling of her nostalgic sympathies and worldview: "Tearing down of our most attractive, quaint and picturesque old market!"[38] Conner, like most white Natchez residents, mourned the passing of the site that over time was romanticized as a treasured town landmark.

Given her enthusiasm for the visual arts and photography, it is not surprising that Mary Britton Conner left few written records of her life; her pictures and the albums she created speak for her.[39] One exception is an essay she wrote at the age of nineteen entitled "A Southern Character Sketch," printed in 1882.[40] The essay bears strong similarity to the countless fictional accounts and memoirs crafted at this time by both amateur and professional writers across the South. The narrative traces the life of Conner's childhood nurse, "Aunt" Susy Banks, born in the early 1800s and whose parents had been favorite slaves of her maternal grandparents. Closely adhering to prevalent racist stereotypes used by popular plantation school writers like Thomas Nelson Page and Joel Chandler Harris, Conner's black characters are portrayed as happy, faithful, and childlike. According to Conner, "Susy passed a happy child-hood, receiving the best of care, kindly treated, carefully trained and surrounded by nothing but comforts." As Conner writes, these comforts included training as a maid from the age of six, playing alongside the master's young daughter in a "beautiful old forest," and learning "the arts of sewing patchwork quilts, darning and other feminine accomplishments." At the age of eighteen, Susy married Gilford, who "excelled in thrumming on the banjo and dancing," as his "long feet encased in shoes of unpolished calf-skin would shuffle and back-step, until one would think he had not a bone in his supple feet." According to the essay, Susy lost her husband to a tragic drowning accident, and later two of her three sons who "joined" the Confederate army were killed, one while serving Conner's uncle. The war, according to Conner, "brought no relief" to Susy, who now worked for Conner's parents and their family of four children. According to Conner, Susy did not care that slavery had ended, "for she had known nothing but kindness all her life." Such comments depicting faithful slaves who served their masters during the war, who were well taken care of during and after slavery, and who preferred enslavement over freedom were assumptions shared by many elite white Americans by the late nineteenth century, and closely adhered to Lost Cause ideology.[41]

By the time Conner wrote her sketch, Susy was white-haired, toothless, and could be found most hours of the day "smoking a large pipe, doubtless dreaming of the olden time." Despite the demeaning racist commentary sprinkled throughout the narrative, Conner's genuine affection for her elderly nurse is palpable when she writes in the closing paragraph, "When the heavenly messenger comes, may he bear her gently to that city where 'there shall be no more death, neither sorrow nor crying.'" Conner would later train her camera on the descendants of Susy Banks, with the visual poses and captions she recorded mirroring the nostalgic, sentimental notions woven throughout the character sketch she wrote years earlier.[42]

As Mary matured, her devotion to creative leisure pursuits intensified. Shortly before her marriage to Lemuel P. Conner Jr. in 1888, she played the leading role of Cleopatra in the "Kirmess," an ornate historical pageant staged by local residents to benefit the town's library and orchestral club. White audiences experienced a night of spectacle as they watched a series of tableaux vivants, illuminated by the first electric lights seen by many Mississippians, at Thomas Reber's Casino at Forks of the Road (site of one the city's former slave markets).[43] The production opened with a march of nations led by Britton and her entourage of "Egyptian" attendants, followed by 150 local

Black and White Historical Memory in Postbellum Natchez   123

Mary Britton Conner in the role of Cleopatra, Queen of the Kirmess, 1888. Henry Norman, photographer. (Courtesy of the Thomas H. and Joan W. Gandy Photograph Collection, Louisiana Lower Mississippi Valley Collections, Special Collections, Hill Memorial Library, Louisiana State University Libraries, Baton Rouge.)

actors representing Japan, Italy, France, Russia, Germany, Spain, Sweden, the Goddess of Liberty, and America.

It was during the preparations for the "Kirmess" that Mary Britton likely became infatuated with the notion of not only posing for but creating her own photographic images. Once again Mary made her way to Norman's studio at age twenty-four to record her role as Cleopatra, resulting in one of Henry Norman's most mesmerizing images, which conveys both the spirit of a Victorian era amusement and the romanticized notions of the production's leading heroine. Reclining in a chair, her body tilted to one side as her arms cradle her head, Britton strikes a seductive pose that shows off her glittering costume and gladiator-style sandals to full effect. A soft dreamy smile floats on her lips and in her eyes. Britton's reign as queen of the Kirmess would be the first of many leading roles she would play in shaping her community's cultural heritage and historical memory. During much of her adult life, often accompanied by her husband and children, Conner acted, sang, directed, and designed sets and costumes for numerous local theater productions.[44]

"AN ART WITHIN THE REACH OF WOMEN"

Mary Britton Conner's enthusiasm for photography both as a subject and later as a photographer and collector reflects the enormous popularity of cameras and photographs among Americans in the late nineteenth century. Even as men fully embraced the popular amusement with more than 150 camera clubs and photographic societies organized in towns and cities nationwide by 1896—some of which opened their doors to women—consumer magazines and the Kodak ads in them urged both boys and "Kodak Girls" to take up the hobby. Dozens of magazine articles advised female amateurs that photography led to improved physical and mental health. An 1896 article targeted to female readers claimed that "many a ruddy cheek there is whose hue has been won on long camera tramps, many an elastic step which would have been slow and halting, many a spirit dull and languid, but for the leading of the lens."[45] Photography also appealed to women because it gave them an acceptable way to escape the confines of domestic life. A female writer for an 1890 *Outing* magazine article noted: "Photography makes a strong appeal to women for the reason that she [sic] may study and practice it in her own home ... yet it does not interfere with daily duties and pleasures ... it is an art within the reach of women of modest means; no expenses are entailed beyond the purchase of a good outfit, always to be had for a modest sum."[46]

Frances Benjamin Johnston, one of the earliest and best-known female photographers, offered a rather daunting list of requirements to women who wanted to succeed in the field both as amateurs and paid professionals. In "What a Woman Can Do with a Camera," published in an 1897 issue of the *Ladies Home Journal*, Johnston noted:

> Photography as a profession should appeal particularly to women, and in it there are great opportunities for a good-paying business—but only under very well-defined conditions. The prime requisites—as summed up in my mind after long experience and thought—are these: The woman who makes photography profitable must have, as to personal qualities, good common sense, unlimited patience to carry her through endless failures, equally unlimited tact, good taste, a quick eye, a talent for detail, and a genius for hard work. In addition, she needs training, experience, some capital, and a field to exploit.[47]

Johnston was likely basing her advice on her own experiences and perspective on succeeding in a profession that was dominated by men. Throughout

A Natchez camera enthusiast shoots a playful scene of her companions with a box camera in the late 1800s. (Courtesy of the Thomas H. and Joan W. Gandy Photograph Collection, Louisiana Lower Mississippi Valley Collections, Special Collections, Hill Memorial Library, Louisiana State University Libraries, Baton Rouge.)

her sixty-year career, Johnston showed great versatility in adapting to the marketplace, first as a successful celebrity portrait photographer in the early days of her career, as a garden photographer in the 1920s hired by wealthy garden club patrons, and later, while in her early seventies, photographing noteworthy antebellum homes across the South, work that eventually led her to Natchez in the late 1930s.[48]

Even as articles written by Johnston and other photographers encouraged women to pursue photography, magazine advertisements for cameras assured women that photography was an appropriate past time for respectable women of all ages. Eastman Kodak Company was particularly adept at targeting female consumers. Images of elegant, fashionably dressed "Kodak Girls" ran alongside advertising copy touting the features of a Kodak camera much like a fashion accessory, such as this one that ran in the *Ladies Home Journal*: "Made of aluminum and covered with the finest seal grain leather, the Folding Pocket Kodaks are as rich and dainty as a lady's purse, yet they withstand the rough usage of travel and changes of climate far better than any heavy camera. Carried in the hand, in a case, or in a shopping bag, they are convenient and inconspicuous."[49]

Kodak advertisement published in women's magazines in the early 1900s. The ad promotes Kodak cameras as a fashion accessory to female photography enthusiasts.

When not touting the appeal of owning one's own camera kit priced at twenty-five dollars or less, consumer publications frequently featured the work of professional photographers, including Johnston, whose frequently published work claimed a number of awards at exhibitions in the United States and Europe. In all likelihood Mary Britton Conner and her fellow Natchez camera enthusiasts were familiar with and inspired by the work of Johnston and other celebrated photographers, male and female. A collection of photographs of Conner's family and exterior shots of her Clover Nook home reveal that Mary's camera was never far from her side in the 1890s and early 1900s. The smudges and imperfections that appear in a series of duplicate prints suggest that Mary, along with taking pictures, was also experimenting in the darkroom as she diligently worked to perfect her technique. It is quite possible that Conner set up a darkroom in her large two-story home, or she may have had access to a local camera club darkroom. Conner's early photographs bear similarities to the work of published images and reveals a keen photographic eye. Additionally, her work suggests that she followed the

Unidentified child (probably a Conner child). Mary Britton Conner, photographer. (Courtesy of Louisiana Lower Mississippi Valley Collections, Special Collections, Hill Memorial Library, Louisiana State University Libraries, Baton Rouge.)

advice of photography enthusiasts urging women to focus their cameras on domestic scenes: children, pets, and gardens. The candid images she made of her young children are particularly compelling, capturing their innocence and pleasure while at play on the gallery or gardens surrounding her home.

Clearly captivated with photography like so many of her era, Conner remained an avid amateur until shortly before her death in 1936. She filled her home with photography albums, a large postcard collection, heirlooms, curios, and a collection of daguerreotypes, leading one local newspaper writer to declare: "Clover Nook probably has more in it of a museum character than any other place in Natchez."[50]

"HER BOOK" AND BURDEN

Like many upper-middle-class women at the turn of the twentieth century, Conner organized her photographs, the newspaper and magazine articles she collected, as well as invitations and theatrical programs that punctuated her daily life in the form of scrapbook albums. One of her albums in particular sheds light on the time and place she lived as well as the complex racial relationships that governed her life. The red cloth scrapbook's treasure trove of photographs, postcards, newspaper clippings, and miscellaneous ephemera—most of which focus on Natchez blacks who had been closely associated with the Britton family for decades—offer a rare snapshot of the racialized world of a turn-of-the-century upper-class white Natchez woman who diligently worked to compile what she titled "Her Book: The White Man's Burden and Other Things."[51]

The title of Conner's album is significant and framed the contents of her collection. Referencing Rudyard Kipling's poem written amid contentious debates over the American colonization of the Philippines after the Spanish-American War, Kipling's words evoked a tremendous outpouring of response. First published in *McClure's* magazine in February 1899, Kipling's poem, "The White Man's Burden," was reprinted in thousands of newspapers and magazines nationwide and was estimated to have reached over one million American readers. The poem's title and stanzas quickly found their way into sermons, editorials, jokes, cartoons, parodies, and Congressional speeches, contributing to a culture of empire both at home and abroad. The British writer's poem resonated with Conner as she worked diligently on her album of photographs and miscellaneous ephemera of the African Americans she encountered daily.

While many readers believed Kipling's message was meant to encourage Americans to join European nations in taking on the "burden" of "civilizing" what they perceived as their inferior colonial and colored subjects, the poem suggested alternative meanings as well. One historian asserts that the meaning of the poem often confused American readers and "channeled anxieties about what it meant to be white."[52] When the poem was published in early 1899 such anxieties ran rampant among American whites who expressed worries about "the negro problem," black migration from the Deep South, racial unrest, and the potential for labor unrest among blacks as well as the growing numbers of "undesirable" Irish and Eastern European immigrants rapidly settling in American cities. Indeed, Conner's photographs, captions, and the newspaper clippings she so carefully preserved suggest that in her mind Kipling's poem meshed easily with notions of southern paternalism and a determination by whites to maintain their racial advantage.

Such sentiments resonated strongly with South Carolina Senator "Pitchfork" Ben Tillman's interpretation of the poem, which he shared on the floor of Congress the day after Congress ratified US control over the Philippines in February 1899. Tillman sought to reverse the vote and offered Kipling's poem as a "prophecy" of "our danger and our duty." In explaining why he and most other southern senators voted against the treaty, he stated: "It was not because we are Democrats, but because we understand and realize what it is to have two races side by side that cannot mix without deterioration and injury to both and the ultimate destruction of the civilization of the higher. We of the South have borne this white man's burden of a colored race in our midst since the emancipation and before."[53] Conner penned the words "Her Book: The White Man's Burden and Other Things" on the album cover, implying that the paternalistic "burden" of being white and maintaining racial control rested with white women of the South as much as it did with men.

As revealed in her album, Conner considered the individuals she photographed as "her" people, a notion shared by many of her southern elite white female contemporaries. Louisa Poppenheim, a prominent United Daughter of the Confederacy member, wrote in one of her contributions to the UDC's official scrapbooks, that it was "to the patient teachings and personal training of the southern woman [that were] due to the civilization and Christianizing of the Negro in America."[54] Notions of racial uplift and paternalistic fervor in an imperial age were not limited to southern white women. During the time when Mary Britton Conner aimed her camera at Natchez African Americans, numerous northern suffragists were demanding that the "backward races" of the Philippines and Hawaii, both recently acquired territories, be civilized and morally uplifted before they were given political rights.[55] While there is no evidence to suggest Mary Britton Conner and those of her social circle embraced women's suffrage, a similar sense of imperialistic maternalism guided Mary as she turned her gaze on the blacks within her midst. On the opening spread of her album Conner wrote: "Some of my most faithful friends are within these very pages." Pasted below is a newspaper clipping of Kipling's poem.

VISIONS OF THE OLD SOUTH

Over a span of roughly two decades Mary Britton Conner, a daughter of the Old South who came of age in the New South, collected, arranged, and commented on nearly 150 images dating from the late 1890s through the first decade or so of the 1900s, expressing a strong desire to preserve a dominant white social order rooted in Lost Cause romanticism. What becomes evident in analyzing the photographs and the captions she scrawled on the margins of these images is her desire to regenerate the region's antebellum past. Her ideas about race, memory, and southern identity as expressed in her album photographs and captions are consistent with the notions found throughout

Mary Britton Conner and her daughter, Eliza, 1898. Henry Norman, photographer. (Courtesy of McMurran/Conner/Martin Collection, #74, University of Louisiana, Monroe, Special Collections Department.)

turn-of-the-century white southern texts that romanticized and sentimentalized the past at the expense of forgetting emancipation. Taking pictures that paid reverence to antebellum southern culture, including African American enslavement, became a means to endorse and maintain the status quo.[56] The portrait Conner commissioned Henry Norman to take of her and her young daughter Eliza in 1898 is a case in point.

For her portrait sitting, Conner wore an ornately embroidered antebellum-styled hoopskirt gown that had belonged to an antebellum ancestor, a bonnet tied primly under her chin, and a matronly shawl draped around her shoulders. In one hand she displays a colorful fan, a possession marking her as a lady of leisure, while on her left side her daughter Eliza stands wearing her own finery—a flower bedecked hat, black patent shoes, a short dress, and pantalets trimmed in eyelet lace. Eliza clutches what appears to be a small dark-skinned doll. In all likelihood Conner and her daughter wore the costumes for a local theater production, and the gown may have belonged to Mary's mother and the child's grandmother, also named Eliza. In any case a portrait sitting furnished an opportunity to create a valued keepsake. The fact remains, however, that in having the portrait made, Conner saw value in regenerating an image representative of an earlier era. Rather than choosing a contemporary sleek-fitting gown that many Natchez women wore for their portraits in the 1890s (as evidenced by surviving Norman portraits), Conner chose instead to dress herself as a mistress of the Old South, indicative of her passion to pay homage to the spirit and visual memories of an earlier, lost decade.

"Her Book" is further proof of Mary Britton Conner's strong emotional ties to a specific imagined past, a past linked to the African Americans whose lives had intersected with her own or her ancestors. The date inscribed on Conner's album—1907—is also telling. Her mother Eliza—her last parental tie to the antebellum and slave era—died that year. Shooting, collecting, and organizing her photographs for an album that focused on a nostalgic past likely offered a source of comfort to Conner. Recognizing that slavery was a relic of a bygone era and that notions of devoted faithful slaves were giving way to a less predictable and more unstable racial order, such an album offered Conner and other southern white women like her a means to try to hold on to and re-create an imagined idyllic past. Furthermore, the culture of empire so pervasive in early twentieth-century American political and cultural rhetoric likely inspired Conner to document the southern blacks within her midst. Imperialism exerted a strong appeal for many white Americans fascinated with what were considered "backward" cultures. This sort of attraction is witnessed in the more than a dozen images of black baptisms Mary collected on the banks of the Mississippi River. According to one newspaper clipping in Conner's album, more than 2,000 African Americans and 250 whites gathered to attend one such event.[57]

In studying the details of one of these photos it becomes apparent why such spectacles captivated Conner and the many other white residents on hand to witness the event. Dated 1897, the image was taken by a photographer who stood close by to record an intimate moment between the blindfolded baptismal candidate and his minister just seconds before the young man was immersed below the murky water. Several skiffs filled with black women wearing white Sunday dresses and straw hats were close by to witness the sacred occasion. Behind the boats can be seen a crowded hillside dotted by a field of umbrellas to ward off the penetrating rays of a hot summer sun.

The scene conveys a sense of liveliness and noisy festivity, far different from the more sedate religious rituals of the town's Episcopal church where Conner's family and other white Natchez elites worshipped. By contrast Episcopal baptism was a quiet, quick, formal affair accomplished by sprinkling a few drops of holy water on an infant child's forehead. Black baptisms, like the one recorded in Conner's album, were loud, crowded, spirited affairs,

African American baptism, 1897. Photographer unknown. (Courtesy of Louisiana Lower Mississippi Valley Collections, Special Collections, Hill Memorial Library, Louisiana State University Libraries, Baton Rouge.)

captivating southern whites who witnessed a charismatic religious spectacle, where black ministers washed away the sins of their repentant flock and the music of emotional African American spirituals filled the humid air.

Whatever drew Mary Conner to attend these gatherings, she used photographs—her own or those of others—to capture these moments of a distinctive black cultural rite of passage. Whether strolling through the crowds of a black baptismal service, or the grounds of her Natchez home and surrounding neighborhood, Conner, armed with her trusty camera, joined America's imperialist project, using photography to hold on to a remnant of the past that was slowly yet doggedly fading away.

Conner's passion for Old South visual imagery and her focus on African Americans reflects the turn-of-the-twentieth-century preoccupation of whites worldwide in gazing at, documenting, and cataloguing the culture of nonwhites. The human exhibits of African, Middle Eastern, Chinese, and Native American peoples living in stereotyped ethnologic villages on display at the 1893 World's Columbian Exposition in Chicago and at numerous other large fairs in Western cities at home and abroad during this era mesmerized visitors, promoters, and social scientists alike. Public enthusiasm for "Aunt Jemima," a fictionalized black female character, whose delicious hotcakes and stories of slavery enticed large crowds of fairgoers to purchase pancake flour, is the most memorable example of advertisers who used images of happy former slaves to hawk a variety of new products to American consumers. As Micki McElya writes, "With every sweet and buttery bite, fairgoers were transported to the Old South of popular imagination as they marveled at their own modern good fortune."[58]

Closer to home, Mary Conner and many of her contemporaries were attracted to similar images of black servitude to affirm their sense of white identity and mastery. In addition to buying the fictionalized characters sitting on a grocer's shelf, elite white southerners like Conner drew upon real people they had known and loved since childhood and who had served their families for a generation or more.

Reflecting the nation's rapid growth in tourism and interest in foreign cultures, Mary Conner turned literally to her own backyard to capture and eventually commodify the "other" within her midst. This trend, what historian Robert W. Rydell characterizes as part of an "exhibitionary complex" at work during the second half of the nineteenth century and the early decades of the twentieth, enabled both European and American whites to spread imperialistic ideals far beyond the grounds of the fairs hosted within the United States and Western European nations.[59] Postcards and other visual mementoes sold at the fairs were instrumental in spreading a key tenet of imperialism: Nonwhites were inferior and needed to be governed and controlled by racially superior whites. Similar racist, paternalistic notions of imperialism prevailed in former Confederate locales like Natchez, keeping antebellum attitudes intact long after the end of slavery. Within such an environment white rule dominated a second-class black citizenry, most of whom remained poor and uneducated and faced a political and economic system impervious to change. Similar to the visual imagery produced by world fairs, exhibitions, and advertisers of a wide array of goods, photographs and postcards found in personal albums, at souvenir stands, and in the local drugstore played an integral role in spreading Old South ideals across the region, nation, and the world at large.

Mary Britton Conner took advantage of the international craze for postcard collecting and the rapid growth of tourism at the turn of the century to boost her family's income at a time when many formerly wealthy Natchezians, including her lawyer husband, were hard-pressed for cash. The fortunes of Lemuel Conner Jr. improved for a short time after marrying Mary, the daughter of a wealthy banker in the late 1880s, but within a decade Lemuel's legal career faltered. In fact, like many southern white men, the career and finances of both Conner Jr. and his father Lemuel P. Conner Sr. never fully recovered after the Civil War.[60]

Like many upper-class southern white women of her generation, Mary Conner looked for opportunities to augment her family's income in ways that would neither tarnish her elite status nor challenge traditional gendered boundaries. Mary dutifully followed the advice of Frances B. Johnston to use photography to create "a good-paying business." Indeed, the process of turning photographs into income-producing postcards was not difficult. "Anyone, from the owner of the corner drugstore to a lady looking to supplement her income, could be a postcard publisher," according to one historian. "One had only to submit photographs or art work to the many agents kept in countries all over the world by German printers who in turn saw that the postcards were printed and delivered."[61]

Conner had all the credentials for the job: a passion for camera work, a creative mind, and familiarity with her town and its people. The enormous popularity of postcards at the turn of the twentieth century and her business relationship with the town's most successful photography studio explains why Conner penciled in the margins alongside many of her album photographs the letters "pc" or "postcard," suggesting she planned to pursue publishing and selling these images as picture postcards or had already done so. By the 1920s Conner expanded to include the work of others, advertising and selling photographs shot by Henry Norman, his son Earl, and Henry Gurney, the senior Norman's first employer, and perhaps some of her own photographs as well. Although it is unclear how this business arrangement worked, or if it was successful, the penny postcard advertisement Mary used to promote her services is both persuasive and enthusiastic: "Having a collection of Negatives from the Gurney and Norman Studios, dating from candle-light days to 1920. I shall be glad to receive orders for copies of you and yours. Wee folk, grown-ups, belles and beaux, brides and grooms, real grandmothers and grandfathers, negatives from portraits, daguerreotypes, and silhouettes, Natchez scenes, homes, schools, bluffs, Brown's Garden and 'Natchez-Under-the-Hill.' I have them all! Gift albums to order. Orders taken for photos enlarged or colored, and for miniatures." Prospective customers were encouraged to telephone Conner at her Clover Nook home between the hours of nine and eleven a.m.[62]

HER "MOST FAITHFUL FRIENDS"

Mary felt a strong, genuine affection—what she likely perceived as love—for in her words the "faithful friends" whose faces peer out at us from the fragile pages of her album. Many of those pictured likely regarded their employer with varying degrees of affection, for the ties between the black servants and their white employer extended for a generation or more. Living side by side, Mary Britton Conner and "her" people had bonded over both the joys and tragedies of life: births, marriages, prosperity, sickness, poverty, and death. They had also shared in the more ordinary, mundane moments of life—everything from the cooking of meals to fretting over a feverish child to washing and mending clothes and houses to laughing over a funny prank—all incidents that gave texture and meaning to daily existence. Many of these relationships had been forged several decades earlier by Mary's parents and grandparents under the terms of slavery. By the late nineteenth century Mary, like many of her generation, sought to continue these bonds of servitude between white employers and their African American help. The sentiments in Conner's "Her Book" speak to the enormous complexities of southern race relations, both the mutual, genuine affection that bonded blacks and whites, as well as the ways in which whites used nostalgic narratives of black servitude to clarify their identity and to characterize the South's past and present as a benevolent interracial order with whites on top.[63] As novelist Howell Raines notes, "There is no trickier subject" for a southerner "than that of affection between a black person and a white one in the unequal world of segregation." He goes on to write: "For the dishonesty upon which a society is founded makes every emotion suspect, makes it impossible to know whether what flowed between two people was honest feeling or pity or pragmatism."[64] No doubt, all of these emotions and more flowed between Conner and the blacks who shaped and colored her life for more than seven decades. Conner's scrapbook of photos and clippings revealed an abiding affection for people whose family ties to her own stretched back for more than a generation, but simultaneously projected her perceived racial and class superiority over her album subjects.

At the root of the connection between Conner and most of the people she captured on film was a domestic relationship built on the ideologies of a traditional elite southern family and household. White southern elites during the antebellum era thought of their family as more than just blood relations. Family members included all who lived on their property: immediate kin, miscellaneous relatives, and enslaved blacks. The households comprising these various "family" members were much more than physical structures, but more importantly were deeply imbedded reminders of the past and present hierarchy that governed relationships and nearly every facet of everyday life. In short, the antebellum household, run with slave labor, was the primary source of mastery for upper-class white males and their wives. As evidenced in the Britton and Conner households, the ideologies and practices of the elite southern household remained present and shaped life long after the war.[65] Conner's "Her Book" showcases one such southern household at the turn of the twentieth century. Slavery was gone, but the sense of mastery and dependency between whites and blacks in a world no longer antebellum, but not yet modern, is apparent and intriguing.

The majority of photographic images in Conner's "Her Book" album are those of the people who worked on the grounds of Clover Nook, the Natchez home she occupied with her husband and four children. She shot similar types of photographs at her parents' nearby home and those of friends and neighbors. Of these photographs, most are of elderly, middle-aged, and youthful black women, suggesting that either the majority of Natchez white households' domestic staffs by this time were female or that Mary felt more comfortable photographing women.

The content of the images and the captions that accompany them indicate that Conner perceived a warm, personal, if not familial connection with those she photographed. In several captions she affectionately refers to a person as "the great and only," calling out a person whom she held in high regard. Others are identified as "Aunt" or "Uncle," both monikers of slavery, but also a token of fictive kinship and respect for black elders who had served a white household for many years. The black men photographed on the grounds of Clover Nook are nearly all elderly or middle aged, reinforcing the idea that domestic work was gendered space primarily dominated by women, and an indication perhaps that younger black men sought work elsewhere. The handful of photographs Mary took or appropriated from other photographers of black men working on steamboats, standing behind large ginned bales of cotton, or posed beside their horses and wagons indicates that southern urban work space among male and female black laborers in the late 1800s was divided along traditional gender lines. As one of Conner's album photographs reveals, the gendered boundaries of household space remained fluid. In the yard Richard Butler, identified as an employee of Britton and Koontz Bank, poses next to "Aunt Lucy," an older apron-clad woman, holding a small dog. In contrast to nearly all of the other black men Mary photographed, Butler is dressed in professional attire, wearing a white dress shirt, vest, dress pants, and shoes. We have no way of knowing what brought Butler to the Britton or Conner home that day. Perhaps he was visiting kin and friends, or he was there on business for the bank, or had been sent by his employer to take care of a task at his home. In any event Mary found him

"Aunt" Lucy and Richard Butler. Mary Britton Conner, photographer. (Courtesy of Louisiana Lower Mississippi Valley Collections, Special Collections, Hill Memorial Library, Louisiana State University Libraries, Baton Rouge.)

to be a willing photographic subject whose longstanding ties to her family continued to identify him as a member of the Britton/Conner household despite—or even because of—his recent upward mobility.

In nearly all cases, the persons photographed are named, often with both a forename and surname.[66] Page one of the album sets the tone for the nearly forty pages that follow. At the center of the page is a small oval portrait of "Aunt Fanny Ramsey," a spry elderly woman who is noted as "Our Ole Time Stork," suggesting she was a midwife to the Britton family and possibly other women within the Natchez community. On the same page is an image of an elderly black man with the caption: "A faithful slave whose hands were shot to pieces on the battlefield while rescuing his wounded master. He was given a medal by the Confederate veterans." While some African Americans may have volunteered to aid the Confederate army, most did so in hopes of gaining their freedom or receiving better treatment from their white masters. Others were forced to build fortifications and entrenchments and sometimes given weapons in emergency situations. Many of these soldiers fled to Union lines at the earliest opportunity.[67] Conner, like many of her class and race, chose to regard black males who sustained wounds while serving the Confederacy as faithful, heroic slaves.

Page from Mary Britton Conner's album, "The White Man's Burden and Other Things," ca. 1907. (Courtesy of Louisiana Lower Mississippi Valley Collections, Special Collections, Hill Memorial Library, Louisiana State University Libraries, Baton Rouge.)

A succession of outdoor images follows of African Americans posing with family members, friends, pets, and livestock on the grounds surrounding Clover Nook and other white-owned Natchez homes. What is striking about the majority of these photographs is the way they elide time and evoke memories and images of slavery in the Old South. Many of Conner's servants perform work tasks very much like the ones conducted for their white masters under slavery. Most of the women pictured wear aprons, their hair covered with a bandana and sturdy work shoes on their feet—garments indicating their labors were not yet finished when Mary's camera found them. In many of the photographs her subjects pose with the tools of their trade: men stand next to wagons and livestock; buckets are within reach of the women. The candid nature of the images suggest that Mary's photographic subjects were called away from their indoor chores for a picture taking session staged on the better lit outdoor grounds.

Judging from the relaxed, pleasant expressions of most of Mary's subjects, the white mistress and her camera were a welcome diversion from the drudgery of tedious household chores. Late nineteenth-century white women like Conner depended on black servants to execute most household tasks, labors for which the white mistresses were held accountable. The work of most domestic servants had changed little from the slavery era by the time Conner assumed responsibility for her own household in the late 1880s. These labors included kitchen work, meal preparation, serving food, ironing and laundry, sweeping floors, dusting furniture, weeding gardens, collecting eggs from the poultry, as well as caring for white children.

An autobiographical sketch written by Natchez civic leader Roane Fleming Byrnes of her 1890s childhood reveals southern white households' dependence on blacks who had served them before and after emancipation, and the litany of chores they performed: "Judy who fed the chickens, Aunt Tildy who milked the cows, Uncle Bernie who mended fences and outhouses, Hardeen who more or less kept the house, Uncle Cato, the gardener, and cooks, nurses, washerwomen, and the children of all of them, too numerous to name separately."[68] Such remembrances give us a sense of what life was like for an upper-middle-class white family in a small southern town and suggest how the domestic work of her servants made it possible for Mary Britton Conner to pursue her passion for photography.

Conner's photographs provide visual evidence of the importance of outdoor yards and porches of white homes as sites of work as well as community for black domestic servants, not unlike the role these areas played during slavery.[69] Such spaces offered a place of welcome, if only temporary, respite from tedious and physically tiring housework. Here was a place to catch a breath of fresh air, relax for a few moments and reconnect with friends and relatives, hear local news, and as in slavery times, exchange juicy tidbits of household gossip. This sense of enjoyable community can be found in the many photographs Mary took of small groups of blacks gathered on her family's grounds. The image of Lucy, Bud [Scott], "Mammy," and Ed Shaw is but one example. Scott, the leader of a popular ragtime band in Natchez, is the focal point of the picture. A strapping man, his posture is relaxed, one

Famed musician Bud Scott, second to right, is pictured with servants at Clover Nook. Mary Britton Conner album. (Courtesy of Louisiana Lower Mississippi Valley Collections, Special Collections, Hill Memorial Library, Louisiana State University Libraries, Baton Rouge.)

leg crossed in front, standing next to Lucy, who is nearly as big as Scott. The musician dwarfs the elderly, petite "Mammy" (believed to be Lucinda Sharpe). Completing the foursome is Ed Shaw, wearing a hat perched jauntily on his head, his hands shoved casually in his pockets. Scott was likely visiting relatives and friends who worked on the property. Such photos suggest that those in front of the camera were quite comfortable having their images made, enjoyed the attention they received, and felt at home in the white-owned spaces where they both worked and amused themselves.

Other photos reveal that Mary connected black servitude with a nostalgic past. Take for example the photograph, which was one of four, shot of "Aunt" Cornelia Dobbins posing beside a large spinning wheel. Dressed in clothing similar to what she would have worn as a slave, Dobbins appears to be spinning yarn, a common and indispensable form of household production that occupied many slave women's time in the antebellum era. Conner's caption accompanying the images is revealing, noting that Dobbins "spins, weaves, and knits as they did long years ago and who made some mittens and socks for me of yarn made by herself." In an age when manufactured garments were becoming increasingly available, Conner and her family would no longer have relied on Dobbins' spinning skills to produce their household's clothing. Positioning Dobbins next to the antiquated household device, however, created a sentimental, nostalgic image for Conner that preserved a warm and treasured memory from her youth.

Cornelia Dobbins demonstrates the use of a household spinning wheel. Mary Britton Conner album. (Courtesy of Louisiana Lower Mississippi Valley Collections, Special Collections, Hill Memorial Library, Louisiana State University Libraries, Baton Rouge.)

Mary Britton Conner's amateur photographs, while lacking the technical proficiency, artistry, and formality of Henry Norman's portraits of black Natchezians taken roughly two decades earlier, nevertheless document an important segment of Natchez's social and racial hierarchy not typically found in Norman's work. The visual memories captured by Conner are in many ways strikingly different from those of Norman, whose black clientele in most instances projected middle- or upper-class prosperity and respectability. In contrast, Conner photographed working-class blacks who were less financially secure than those who ventured into Norman's studio to pay for their likeness. The majority of those featured in Conner's images worked for her as nursemaids, cooks, washerwomen, gardeners, and handymen, whose occupations reflected the lower-class economic station held by the majority of Natchez African Americans at the turn of the twentieth century.

The fortunes of and opportunities available to most blacks had significantly altered between the time Norman created his memorable black portraits in the late 1870s and early 1880s and when Conner took up photography in the 1890s. One of the most telling examples is John Lynch, Natchez's best known and most successful black politico introduced in chapter 2. In 1901 Lynch quit Mississippi for good when he accepted a position as paymaster for the army during the Spanish American War. After having made numerous real estate purchases in Natchez and Adams County from 1870 to 1898, including four plantation properties, Lynch began selling off his land, with the final transaction completed in 1902. Traveling the world for the US Army, serving in Haiti, the Philippines, Cuba, and Hawaii, Lynch upon retirement from the military, settled in Chicago in 1912 to practice law and pursue real estate ventures. His autobiography makes no mention of him ever returning to Natchez.[70] Clearly, with the turn of the new century, the former congressman found a more hospitable environment than his native Mississippi, both abroad and in the North. Like Lynch, many Natchez blacks at the turn of the century determined that their prospects for security and comfort lay elsewhere. Those with the financial resources began leaving the state, a trend that rapidly multiplied across the South in what became known as the "Great Migration."

Even as Conner's photographs captured images of blacks who were not as economically secure as Norman's African American clientele appear to have been, the two photographers shared some similarities. Take, for example, the photo of a large black family Mary visited. Conner's image mimics the popular style of photograph that Norman created for many of his best white clients with family members and their black servants posed on the front steps of their home, including one Norman shot of his own family in the 1880s. Mary's caption notes that Pleasant and Lloyd had thirteen living children, including a recently born pair of twins. This family portrait reveals that Mary not only felt comfortable leaving the grounds of her home with her camera by her side, but that she was drawn to recording the more intimate details and spaces of black life. In similar fashion to the black baptisms that she likely photographed, a visit to Pleasant and Lloyd's modest home was a chance to document the "other" in her midst.

In yet another similarity with Norman's black portraits, the African Americans in Conner's images bore expressions of dignity and self-assurance in their body language and facial appearances. Despite their working-class

Martin and Nelie. Mary Britton Conner album. (Courtesy of Louisiana Lower Mississippi Valley Collections, Special Collections, Hill Memorial Library, Louisiana State University Libraries, Baton Rouge.)

status, the majority of Mary's black subjects appear in control of their situation and the space they occupied. Her photograph of Martin and Nelie, a couple identified as having once "belonged to Dr. Jenkins," is but one example. The couple stands erect, their shoulders pushed back, their gaze focused directly and confidently into the camera lens. If such images as these gave Conner a perception of white mastery over her servants as her written captions alluding to former ownership implies, those pictured seem to have appropriated a very different kind of meaning, judging from their confident appearance. Borrowing from historian Elizabeth Fox-Genovese, former slaves like Martin and Nelie appear to have known their worth and cherished their pride, and "refused on principle to be mastered."[71]

In contrast to her subjects' self-assured poses, many of the captions accompanying Conner's images characterize those photographed as childlike, playful, docile, and above all, faithful—paternalistic attributes reminiscent of the era's popular plantation literature. For example, in one image a woman stands next to a line of eight shoeless children. The caption reads: "playing candidate," most likely a reference to a person who will soon be baptized. The photo to its right is labeled "a sister shoutin.'" "Sister," a reference commonly used for black females, is one of several individuals caught in a lighthearted moment of merriment or dancing. Mary Conner filled the pages of her album with photos of black men and women whose photographs reflected

"A sister shoutin'" may have been taken at the time of a baptism. Mary Britton Conner album. (Courtesy of Louisiana Lower Mississippi Valley Collections, Special Collections, Hill Memorial Library, Louisiana State University Libraries, Baton Rouge.)

contentment and a relaxed sense of ease; however, these postures should not be confused with childlike, docile behavior. She may have believed that the blacks whom she captured on film, many of whom had been part of her family's household for decades, signaled continuing white mastery over black servitude and bolstered her elite white identity. Even though the African Americans captured by Conner's camera are on her turf, and their labors were not so different from the antebellum slave era, the images recorded by Conner directly challenged her notions of mastery. Photos like those of Martin and Nelie offer ample evidence that few if any of Conner's servants saw themselves as helpless, hapless, or mastered dependents.

Humorous poses of black men created yet another way for whites to project white mastery over black servants at the turn of the twentieth century. One Conner photo captures Haddie doing a handstand, while another portrays a pair of laborers pretending to use the tail and mouth of a donkey to communicate with one another. The playfulness on display in several of

Laborers at Elgin present a humorous, stereotypical image popular in early twentieth-century depictions of African Americans. Mary Britton Conner album. (Courtesy of Louisiana Lower Mississippi Valley Collections, Special Collections, Hill Memorial Library, Louisiana State University Libraries, Baton Rouge.)

Conner's photographs is similar to many turn-of-the-century snapshots of blacks and whites taken with inexpensive Kodaks and other cameras marketed to amateurs. The antics caught on camera may well have been a nod to the informal poses adopted by countless Americans who experienced a sense of liberation in having their likeness recorded outside the confines of a professional photography studio. Likewise, the comedic poses may have been an attempt to mimic racialized humor in popular silent films of the era.

On the other hand, Conner's collection of photographs suggests that many of her African American subjects may well have been performing for their white photographer and employer. The performative nature of images conveying pleasant, affable, humble demeanors may well have been a way for local blacks to maintain a positive yet subservient relationship with their white employers and former masters, a behavior civil rights activist W. E. B. Du Bois referred to as living behind "the veil." Blacks across Jim Crow America frequently resorted to using "the veil" to gain some measure of security in a white supremacist world.[72] Given that Conner hoped to convert a number of her photos into moneymaking postcards, she likely directed her subjects to pose in ways that would appeal to white buyers' stereotypes of southern blacks.

"Mammy's mad" may have indicated that some black servants did not like having their photo taken by their white mistress. Mary Britton Conner album. (Courtesy of Louisiana Lower Mississippi Valley Collections, Special Collections, Hill Memorial Library, Louisiana State University Libraries, Baton Rouge.)

Although most individuals in Conner's album photographs are seemingly cooperative in posing for their shutterbug happy employer, upon closer inspection, her album reveals that a handful of blacks subverted stereotypes implying docility and playfulness. Some even controlled how their likenesses would be made. For example, the caption beside one image of a smiling barefoot young black girl wearing a white dress reads: "This one would not dance because she was a Christian and would not have her picture taken with the dancers." Whether the girl refused to join the group photo for religious reasons or simply wanted to be the star attraction in a solo photograph of her own is unknown. Whatever the reason, the girl dictated how Conner's photograph would be staged. In another photograph one of Conner's children stands near a black woman seated on the gallery steps of Clover Nook. The child looks into the camera lens while his caretaker looks downward, a stony expression on her face. Conner's caption reads: "Mmm Mammy is mad." Clearly, not all of Conner's subjects were willing or cooperative, suggesting that blacks exercised some control in when and how their photographs would be staged, and some may have rejected her photographic advances altogether.

"WHOSE ANCESTORS BELONGED TO MINE"

The images Conner produced, selected, and captioned reveal her to be a woman who remained deeply invested in her family's slaveholding heritage. Indeed, there is a strange sense of intimacy documented in the pages of Conner's album. Particularly striking is that Conner no less than fourteen times noted who an individual or their ancestor had "belonged" to in antebellum times. One caption scrawled next to an image of several elderly black men and women reads: "Mammy belonged to John Routh. Uncle Cato to the Inges, Rose's family to Judge Turner, Lucy to the Caspers of Ft. Adams." Still another traces the lineage of persons who had once belonged to her maternal grandparents. "Some of Grandma Milberry Dickinson Macrery's colored folks." In another caption, Levi is identified with the comment "whose ancestors belonged to mine."

Conner's strong attachment to and interest in her family's ties to slavery comes as little surprise given her parents' and grandparents' significant slaveholding legacy. Her maternal grandparents, Andrew and Milberry Dickinson Macrery, transported slaves to their new home when they traveled over the Natchez Trace in 1805.[73] By 1830 Andrew reported 120 slaves, making him one of the largest slaveholders in the county.[74] Mary's paternal uncle William J. Britton and her father, both natives of New York, were also some of the region's largest slaveholders. In addition to serving as a cofounder of Britton and Koontz Bank, William Britton served as an agent for the Nautilus Insurance Company of New York, where he issued life insurance policies on slaves. By 1860 Mary's father, Audley Britton, held the largest number of slaves within Natchez city limits.[75] Additional Britton-held slaves worked on the family's Eutaw plantation in neighboring Concordia parish. Of Britton's thirty-eight slaves working at his downtown Natchez estate, twenty-three were ten years old or less, suggesting that Audley Britton preferred to train his youngest slaves as house servants, a common practice among slaveholders. Many of the black adults found in Mary Britton Conner's scrapbook were likely the formerly enslaved children within the Britton household and who by the 1880s and 1890s were employed by the Britton, Conner, or a neighboring family.[76]

The family Mary Britton married into had a profoundly disturbing slaveholding legacy. One of the largest slaveholders in Adams County, Mary's father-in-law Lemuel Conner Sr. in 1860 held 256 slaves who labored on his two plantations in Concordia Parish. Lemuel Conner played a pivotal role in the infamous racetrack "trials" and execution of a group of slaves accused of planning an uprising in 1861 (described in chapter 3).[77] The events were never recorded in a local newspaper, but white residents knew about it, including Mary Conner. Her father-in-law's notes about the proceedings, in which he referred to himself as "president," were stored in Mary and Lemuel Conner Jr.'s nightstand for years and were donated to the archives at Louisiana State University after Mary's death.[78] In addition to Mary's familial ties to slavery—by birth and marriage—her friends and neighbors were as firmly connected to slavery as she was. The pages of Mary's album are filled with the names of many of Natchez's most prominent slaveholding families alongside the images of those they had once enslaved, suggesting an attempt by Mary to recall the South's mythical benevolent slave narrative and reconfirm white mastery over local blacks. The slaveholder names found in Conner's album read like a who's who of wealthy Natchez bluebloods: Judge Edward Turner and the Chotard, Ayers, Jenkins, Chase, Winston, Inge, and Routh families. Both the Britton and Conner families had extensive kinship ties to this group. Conner's captions are a reminder that the mark of bondage lasted long after emancipation and that black identity in the eyes of many whites remained indelibly linked to those who were once empowered to buy, sell, and own human flesh.

Mary Britton Conner through her immediate family, the man she married, and the intricate kinship ties which linked her to a web of former slaveholding elites had a deep and complex connection to slaveholding. The words of writer Susan Sontag, "To photograph is to appropriate the thing photographed," distinctly resonate with Conner's lifelong mission to photograph and preserve the black faces within her midst.[79] A sense of appropriation of antebellum and contemporary connections was at work as Conner diligently collected, carefully labeled, and affiliated photographs of the black men, women, and children who remained bound to the slaveholding legacy of her family and community at large. Conner recognized that slavery was dead, but nonetheless remained attached to nostalgic notions of faithful, dutiful servants and an era that she had been born too late to experience personally. Her words found at the top of one album page: "A glimpse into days gone by" acknowledged a keen sense of longing to re-create a mythical, romanticized antebellum past accessible only through historical memory.

As with any collection of historical photographs it is difficult to fully unravel the multiple meanings found within the images in Conner's album or the exact nature of the relationship between the photographer and her subjects. Yet the numerous newspaper articles, poems, editorials, and cartoons sprinkled throughout the album confirm Conner's traditional views on race and identity. In between clippings praising the work of Booker T. Washington, poems, and local obituaries paying homage to dutiful former slaves, Conner included fourteen articles honoring faithful slaves, many of these dedicated to the "Beloved Old Black Mammy." Conner, like many white southerners of her generation, revered "mammies"—black women who cared for white children and played a key role in overseeing domestic duties of the household before and after the war. Indeed, no better way existed to prove a white southern elite woman's social status than to be surrounded by devoted, faithful servants, particularly the nurturing maternal figure of a beloved "mammy." As one historian writes, "having a mammy became a badge of having been 'raised right' as a proper southerner."[80]

Clippings found in Conner's album indicate she championed the idea of building a national monument to "mammies," a campaign that garnered enormous support in the early decades of the twentieth century. One such article headlined "A Monument to the Mammies" is typical of the articles Conner preserved. The anonymous author wrote nostalgically: "Every family in those dear old days had a black mammy. . . . My Mammy Charlotte had complete charge of everything about the house. She had been thoroughly trained by my husband's mother. She made the jellies and the pickles, the ice cream, the cakes, doing a little of everything to make our home comfortable and happy. . . . She was mammy to all the children of the house, and all the other children that floated in from other people's houses."[81]

Mary Britton Conner remembered her own "Mammy" in a similarly affectionate fashion and wished to sustain these nurturing bonds with black women for herself and her children. In a studio portrait found within the Conner's family papers, but not included in her scrapbook, is an image of a fair, plump baby boy about eight months old held securely in his black nursemaid's arms. The child, Mary's oldest son Lemuel P. Conner III, looks directly at the camera while his caretaker (most likely Lucinda Sharpe) gazes serenely at her white charge, seemingly oblivious to the camera. Identified only as "Mammy" on the back of the photo, the woman is considered an important enough member of the household to have her photograph taken with the Conner's first child, but nevertheless remains nameless. Nursemaid Lucinda Sharpe served in the Conner household well into her eighties.[82]

Numerous scrapbook photos reveal Conner's lifelong infatuation with the maternal black women who nurtured her as a child. Conner used her camera to re-create similar bonds between her four children and the black men and women who labored for her. One such photograph picturing her son is captioned "My baby Gaillard and his body guards." "Uncle" Robert holds the boy, with "Mammy" and other "fond friends" standing nearby. Conner sought to maintain her childhood ties to her family's "Mammy" long after her own youth had passed. In a letter from August 1892 Mary at the age of thirty wrote her parents: "Tell Mammy howdy for me and I'm waiting for her letter. Read this to her."[83]

THE LEGACY OF NATCHEZ PHOTOGRAPHS

The exquisite portraits of the black men, women, and children who flocked to Henry Norman's downtown Natchez studio dressed in fine suits, shirtwaists and hats, beaded bridal gowns, and neatly tailored uniforms stand in sharp contrast to the amateur photographs Mary Britton Conner created of the plainly dressed African American domestic laborers in her midst. The portraits Norman crafted for his black clientele can be read as expressions of agency, pride, and optimism—a decidedly different and more promising narrative than the ones orchestrated by whites in the public spaces of Natchez just footsteps outside the photographer's studio. Moreover, Norman's photographs empowered his black subjects to directly challenge the rampage of racist cartoons, jokes, articles, and pictures circulating in the pages of newspapers and consumer periodicals nationwide. As symbols of personal and collective empowerment, Norman's portraits contested characterizations of blacks as innately inferior, simplistic, and unworthy of respect or civil rights.

Today, many of Norman's images, painstakingly reproduced by Dr. Thomas Gandy more than a century after they were created, hang proudly in a permanent exhibit at Natchez's First Presbyterian Church, with a smaller collection of black portraits on display at the town's Museum of African American History and Culture, ensuring they will remain in public view. In the dignified faces and poses we have a record of African Americans who envisioned a very different sort of identity and life for themselves from what they had known in slavery and the postbellum era.

When "Portraits of Black Natchez," an exhibit of approximately sixty Henry Norman photographs of dignified, confident blacks, made its debut in the Old Capital Museum in Jackson, Mississippi, in February 1983, the collection bluntly challenged images of docile, subservient African Americans that had reigned supreme for decades in the minds of white southerners. The exhibit, which later traveled to cities across the South, stunned audiences and pushed Americans to rethink their ideas about southern African American history. So shocked by the images, one museum curator called the designers of the exhibit to verify that the photographs were not "fakes." Patti Black, former director of the Old Capital Museum who oversaw the exhibit, noted the significance of the portraits shortly before the exhibit's premiere, stating: "We were aware that Natchez had an exceptional middle class population of freedmen after the Civil War, but we had no documentary evidence of it until these photographs surfaced."[84] The exhibit, coupled with the publication of several books authored by the Gandys on their collection of Norman photographs, recovered a nearly forgotten visual memory that told a very different and complex story from the one familiar to most southern white Americans. Conversely, the Old South visual imagery created, sold, purchased, and collected by white southerners like Mary Britton Conner in the early years of the twentieth century infused new energy into visions of black servitude and inferiority consistent with Lost Cause ideology.

Conner's album was not so much an exhibit of her own photographic skills, but an expression of her notions about race, historical memory, and where she and other white southerners of her class fit within a shifting social landscape. The album she crafted became not only a memory book of artifacts and images of the black Natchezians who had been a part of her and her family's life for decades, but a visual manifestation of her family's identity as white elites. The last few pages of her album reveal that Conner's efforts to return to a romanticized antebellum past ultimately failed. Here Conner pasted newspaper articles addressing the increasingly uneasy racial climate in the early 1900s. An article bearing the headline "President [Wilson] Offended by Negro" tells of black spokesperson W. M. Trotter protesting segregation within federal agencies, a policy endorsed by the southern-born Woodrow Wilson. Referring to Trotter as a "burly Bostonese black," the newspaper reported that the White House interview ended when the "tone of the negro [became] offensive." Alongside the article a small clipping reported, "Negroes Say Old Songs Are an Insult to Race," yet another sign that some African Americans were becoming more resistant to living behind "the veil" and playing out roles that required them to act subservient and docile in their relationships with whites.

Directly across from the articles about Wilson's ideas on race, Mary pasted a group photograph of local white World War I soldiers and beneath it the studio portraits of two young white children. Turning away from the black servants upon whom she had depended for much of her life and who captivated her photographic gaze for many years, Conner seems to have distanced herself from the people she once regarded as "some of my most faithful friends." Or perhaps these "friends" had moved away from Clover Nook and

Natchez, far from the peering lens and world of a white matriarch who still pined for the Old South, a world where black bodies once serviced the needs of white households and white mastery ruled.

A few years before her death in 1936 at the age of seventy-three, Mary Britton Conner again returned to her passion for photographic memory and visions of the past. Laboring over the photographs left by Henry Norman to his son Earl, who would continue his father's legacy as a skilled professional photographer until his death in 1951, Mary identified hundreds of the black and white Natchez folk who paid a visit to Norman's studio to have their likenesses made.[85] Her work left a record linking faces and names from Natchez's past, arguably the most important contribution she made to her town's historical memory. Even as Mary toiled over Norman's portraits, a younger group of women were hard at work on their own version of Natchez's storied past. It is to that story we now turn.

CHAPTER FIVE

SELLING HISTORIC NATCHEZ TO DEPRESSION-ERA PILGRIMS

JOURNALIST ERNIE PYLE SPOKE FOR MANY DEPRESSION-ERA AMERICAN tourists who packed their bags for Natchez, Mississippi, when he wrote, "Today I've lived in the antebellum atmosphere until I don't know whether I'm me or Jefferson Davis."[1] Pyle was one of thousands of white, middle-class Americans who journeyed to the out-of-the-way Mississippi River town to experience the Pilgrimage, a heritage home tour organized in 1932 by the female garden club that paid homage to Natchez's opulent antebellum past.[2] Ushered inside some of the Old South's most prized estates, now bordering on genteel shabbiness, tourists entered into a spectacle that had all the makings of a Hollywood production. The tourism experience that Natchez sold its visitors was so well packaged, filled with pageantry, glamorous costumes, and vivacious belles radiating southern charm, that the only element missing from the scene was Scarlett O'Hara herself.

The widespread appeal of the Pilgrimage, Natchez, and its upper-class homeowners to Depression-era white visitors reveals how images of the Old South were memorialized and commercialized during the 1930s. The creators of the Pilgrimage repackaged the dramatization of a mix of decades-old southern racialized ideology and white historical memory initiated in the early postbellum period as a product for Depression-era consumption. As impacted by contemporary social tensions it is also the story of how one southern community's selective expression of historical memory captivated white tourists eager to immerse themselves in the world of the Old South so vividly portrayed by Margaret Mitchell, Stark Young, and other popular writers and entertainers during the 1930s. The Natchez Pilgrimage suggests the power of popular culture in shaping a tenacious collective mythic memory that remained in force for much of the twentieth century and lingers even still today.

Natchez by the 1930s was but a shadow of the once-wealthy antebellum community that boasted more per capita income than any city in the South.³ With their cotton crops plagued by the boll weevil and having never fully recovered economically from the Civil War, the region's planter class failed to produce sufficient revenues to restore prosperity. Likewise, the eager promises of late nineteenth-century New South boosters that sparked economic growth in places like Charlotte, Birmingham, and Atlanta, never materialized in Natchez even though a number of the town's civic leaders embraced the ideology. In many respects Natchez and its economic state shared more similarities with Charleston in the early twentieth century than any other southern town, where as historian Stephanie Yuhl writes, "the dominant attitude in the city was one of indifference" where most white Charlestonians "failed to embrace New South innovation," resulting in economic decline.⁴ Equally reluctant to accept change, Natchez, too, found itself in a state of steady decay. Major railroad routes bypassed Natchez, hindering development as a modern commercial hub, further ensuring the town's obscurity as a place more ensconced in the past than the present.

Even when other southern communities began to show signs of economic growth, Natchez remained depressed due to declining cotton prices and the persistent boll weevil. By 1931 cotton prices had dropped to six cents per pound, an 85 percent drop from April 1920 prices of forty-two cents per pound. A year later, in 1932, prices bottomed out at four cents a pound. Between 1928 and 1932 the state's property tax assessment declined by $80 million. Equally distressful, Mississippi's unemployment rate reached the highest in the state's history. Not surprisingly, Mississippi's state government was bankrupt and only sighed a breath of relief when federal funds began to arrive in 1932. In sum, as Mississippi resident and beloved writer Eudora Welty observed, "Mississippi—white and black—really didn't have too much to do with the Depression. It was ongoing. Mississippi was long since poor, long devastated."⁵

By the early 1930s, Natchez's antebellum real estate, though often shabby, remained an intact showcase of nineteenth-century material culture, largely because homeowners lacked the finances to remodel or build new homes. As William Allen, a former architectural historian of the US Capitol writes, "The opulence of Natchez in the nineteenth century simply could not be exceeded or matched by succeeding generations. To them fell the task of caring for and living with the taste of their ancestors even when that taste was out of fashion. Because of their careful stewardship, today Natchez can boast of the most comprehensive collection of complete and authentic interiors of

Gloucester, like many Natchez estates, appeared unkempt by the early 1930s. Within a few years after the Pilgrimage tours began, Natchez's homes were much improved in appearance as documented in the photos appearing in the Guide to Historic Natchez homes found in the appendix. "Gloucester," Natchez, Adams County, Mississippi." Ralph Clynne, photographer. Adams County Mississippi Natchez, March 29, 1934. Retrieved from the Library of Congress, http://www.loc.gov/pictures/item/ms0030.photos.092843p/. (Accessed April 15, 2018.)

any historic American city." In short, no other historic southern city could match the quantity and quality of Natchez's architecturally significant homes, giving the small Mississippi River town enormous cultural authority from the early twentieth century to the present.[6]

Natchez's collection of about fifty "great houses," presided over by descendants of formerly wealthy planter elites, showed signs of financial distress that had begun decades before the 1929 stock market crash. With the exception of the Victorian-style homes built by incoming Jewish merchants after the war, the Victorian architectural era nearly bypassed Natchez. The city fell into a somewhat comatose state, a kind of Old South version of the fictitious "Brigadoon."[7]

At first glance, neither the town, its antebellum homes, nor gardens seemed inviting in the early 1930s. A Depression-era guidebook noted that in Natchez "homes that are little more than ruins stand proudly beside mansions whose beauty and lines have been carefully cherished and preserved."[8] Journalist Ernie Pyle wrote of one estate, "The house is cold and dark. The rugs are frayed. The fantastic grillwork around the porch has crumbled in

Magnolia Vale's formal gardens were a popular destination for Natchez tourists before the Civil War. (Courtesy of Louisiana Lower Mississippi Valley Collections, Special Collections, Hill Memorial Library, Louisiana State University Libraries, Baton Rouge.)

sections. Many of the rooms are mere storehouses. In all its 1850 richness, it is not a place the average person would want to live in." *Atlantic Monthly*'s David Cohn presented an equally dismal assessment. "People live surrounded by rare furniture and the tax collector's bills; their cupboards were filled with old silver and little to eat."[9]

The town's once-celebrated and well-manicured estate gardens and grounds may have been in worse shape than the antebellum homes they were intended to embellish. During the nineteenth century, the forty nabob families (Natchez's wealthiest white citizens who controlled most of the affluence and political power during the antebellum era) began surrounding their mansions with elaborately landscaped gardens, likely hiring white master gardeners who directed crews of slaves to create English-style sculptured gardens. As Theodora Britton Marshall and Gladys Crail Evans, descendants of the town's planter elite who penned a detailed guide to Natchez in the late 1930s, write, "Great expense and care was lavished on the gardens where brick walks and walls, fanciful pavilions and summer-houses, underground drainage systems and artificial lakes were constructed by the slaves. Every garden had its hot-house where the rarest plants were tenderly nurtured even in this gentle climate."[10] The nabobs spent large sums on exotic plants, purchasing gardenias, tea roses, and crepe myrtle from China, camellias, azaleas, and boxwood from Japan.

These ornamental gardens not only provided pleasant outdoor-living spaces that were an extension of the "big house," but often became the domain of female mistresses who grew and used cut flowers to share at weddings, funerals, and other special occasions. A diary entry written by Rose Quitman, daughter of planter John Quitman and a resident of Monmouth, speaks to the importance of gardens in southern culture. In describing a particularly beautiful flower, young Rose suggests the deep sense of pleasure elite women gained from their home gardens: "a large, beautiful white camellia, each leaf was perfect and looked as if nature had taken no little pains in fringing them."[11]

Of Natchez's estate gardens, Brown's Garden, on the grounds of Magnolia Vale overlooking the Mississippi River, was perhaps best known and drew a steady stream of visitors in the nineteenth century, many of whom were steamboat passengers who hired a hack to drive them through the picturesque, formal gardens. According to Marshall and Evans, those who visited the scenic garden during the years before the Civil War "could stroll between ancient green Indians mounds, along shady walks lined with bright camellias and azaleas, fragrant with sweet jasmine, honeysuckle, intoxicating gardenias and oriental roses, and beneath lavender clouds of chinaberry or wisteria."[12] Other Natchez estate owners created elaborate, expansive park-like grounds, "shaded by giant, moss-festooned trees" that have been a hallmark of Natchez's natural beauty to the present.[13]

Although several Natchez estates during the antebellum period prided themselves on maintaining lush, colorful gardens, some historians argue that it was more likely that the grounds of most Natchez estates remained more rustic than well manicured. Most owners, in keeping with nineteenth-century landscaping trends, were satisfied with regular weeding and raking to maintain a clean yet simple appearance.[14]

By the 1930s, many of Natchez's estate gardens had fallen on hard times and were far less attractive than during the antebellum era. Limited financial resources pressed most estate owners to attend to a host of costly home repairs. Leaking roofs, crumbling foundations, and peeling paint took priority over maintaining labor intensive and expensive gardens. Even the once lovely Magnolia Vale's famous gardens fell into disrepair, with much of the landscape having sunk into the Mississippi River, leaving only a handful of the old camellias as a reminder of the once picturesque grounds. Several of the photographs shot in the 1930s of Natchez estates by professional photographer Earl Norman (son of Henry Norman) show estates overshadowed by large trees in need of pruning with few ornamental flower beds or shrubs on view. In some instances weeding work is long overdue and many homes lack grass yards, which were in vogue by this time. Indeed, of the extant Norman photos from this period, there are few photos of formal gardens. In most cases the front view of homes and some interiors are the focal point. Photographic evidence suggests that both Norman and the homes' property owners chose to place their focus on Natchez's more impressive historical architecture and interiors rather than the old gardens that had lost their bloom and were more faded than fragrant.

The town's garden club records confirm that Natchez gardens by the 1930s were not what they had once been. Pilgrimage founder Katherine Miller, recalling the spring of 1931 when Natchez hosted Mississippi Garden Club delegates, noted, "though we had flowers we did not have the landscaped gardens which delegates to a garden club convention would expect to see." Though Natchez's gardens may not have looked their best for state garden club visitors, the gathering was considered a great success after some antebellum homeowners opened their doors for a peek inside. According to Ruth Audley Britton Beltzhoover in a newspaper interview years later, when the delegates arrived at Monteigne and finished seeing the rose garden, they asked to go inside the house. "Later on in the day we went through Green Leaves and The Elms. The ladies loved going through the houses so much that next year we decided to open the houses to tourists and call it the pilgrimage."[15] Etta Mitchel Henry, state president of the Mississippi Federation of Garden Clubs, was effusive in her praise for Natchez's antebellum homes, declaring at the close of the March 1931 convention: "These fascinating, historic mansions must not remain hidden from the world any longer. A Natchez pilgrimage must be arranged so that visitors from other sections of the country may be permitted to see this living page from the nation's past."[16]

Miller and her garden club cohorts took the feedback of Henry to heart and by early fall the idea of hosting a tour of homes for the public the following spring was proposed. Initially met with skepticism by homeowners who thought their homes too dilapidated to be of interest to outsiders, Miller persisted.[17] When homeowners balked at opening for a week-long tourism event, Miller writes of leaving her sickbed to meet personally with the homeowners to convince them of her plan. She not only won their consent, but also convinced them to dress up in hoopskirt gowns.[18]

With fifty dollars in their club treasury, Miller and the garden club marched forward, launching what would become over the years a formidable public relations and marketing campaign. Carrying seven dollars in her purse to cover bus fare, Miller traveled to New Orleans in search of an advertising slogan for her Pilgrimage enterprise. George Healy Jr., formerly of Natchez and an editor of the *New Orleans Times-Picayune*, supplied the words "Come to Natchez Where the Old South Still Lives and Where Shaded Highways and Antebellum Homes Greet New and Old Friends." This slogan was eventually shortened to the more memorable "Come to Natchez Where the Old South Still Lives." Accompanying Healy's slogan was an illustration of a crowd of elegantly attired men and women gathered before the entrance to a stately plantation home. On either side of the doorway was an elderly male and female slave to welcome them. Such an image was in keeping with national advertising campaigns that used symbols of the Old South—plantations, belles in hoopskirts, cavalier southern gentlemen, and eager-to-please black servants—which historian Karen Cox notes led consumers "to see the South as the region that maintained the values of preindustrial America and continued to represent a culture of leisure, pastoral romance, and loyal servants—a lifestyle to which many middle-class consumers aspired."[19] In the original 1932 Pilgrimage illustration and increasingly so in the advertisements that followed, hoopskirts and the women who wore them became the prominent iconic image communicating a message of domestic southern femininity and suggesting a model of behavior for *all* American women. By the mid-1930s men were erased from the promotional posters, which featured a sole belle adorned in a bonnet and frilly hoopskirt gown, sending a dual and conflicting message that modern-day women were in control of an event that paid homage to a romantic past. A crew of Pilgrimage volunteers, including the older children of many garden club members, was recruited to hand tint the advertising posters, a tradition that continued for a decade or more. Miller and her volunteers distributed the posters to newspapers and magazines across the country.

Many Natchez residents not affiliated with the garden club volunteered their services to ensure the success of the first Pilgrimage. Hotelkeepers donated office space to the garden club. Stenographers wrote and typed letters that were sent to automobile clubs, tourist organizations, chambers of commerce, and newspapers promoting the Pilgrimage dates. Others compiled mailing lists of media outlets across the country. In an era well before modern publicity techniques or the internet, the club's work to launch a national publicity campaign was strenuous with no guarantee for success. But as one member said, "We did not hitch our wagon to a mere star, but reached for the moon and the sun also."[20]

While publicizing their tours of homes to the nation, other garden clubwomen rallied the town to spruce up yards, gardens, and downtown streets.

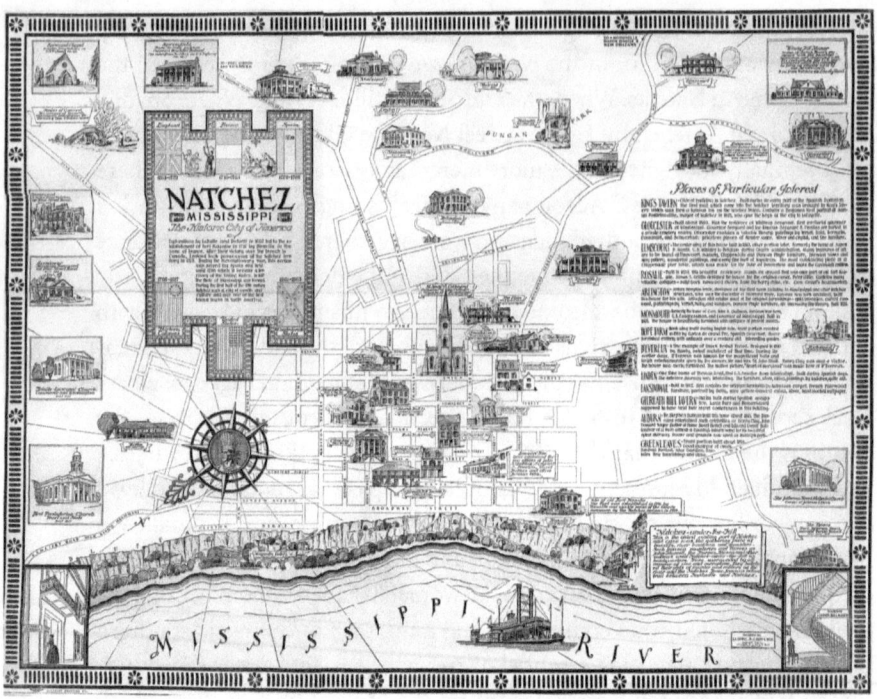

Natchez Pilgrimage map, 1934. Designed by architects J. T. Liddle Jr. and Henry E. Weir, apparently as a private venture in conjunction with their work for the Historic American Building Survey (HABS) in Natchez. (Courtesy of Preservation in Mississippi, https://misspreservation.com.)

An article that appeared in the *Natchez Democrat* issued a call to arms to residents with the headline: "Citizens urged to clean yards; only 10 days now remain." The article reported that the garden club had distributed more than five thousand plants and shrubs earlier in the month in its quest to spruce up the town. Downtown Natchez worked equally hard to put on its best face for the occasion. Flags and brightly colored ribbons hung from windows and balconies. When not cleaning up their town, some Natchezians sewed Indian, colonial, and antebellum costumes. Young women brushed up on their city's local history and its houses as they prepared to serve as tour guides. The town's premier black orchestra led by Bud Scott tuned their instruments for the parade. Members of the Zion Chapel African Methodist Episcopal Church practiced traditional spirituals to be performed for guests. Residents dug through musty old trunks to air out antique clothing, paintings, coins, firearms, and Civil War relics to exhibit.[21] One Natchez resident recalled that when her mother donned a taffeta dress worn by her mother during the late 1800s the material slowly disintegrated in the warm spring sunshine.[22]

Despite the flurry of preparations not all Natchez residents shared Katherine Miller's enthusiasm and optimism, and many remained downright skeptical of the venture. So panicked were garden club members and city leaders that their invitation would be rebuffed that a last-minute parade with floats and the Louisiana State University marching band was organized for opening day as a means to attract country folk to the town. Two sons and two daughters of prominent Natchez families were crowned as royalty for the event. William A. Adams reigned as King Japonica and Elise Brown was anointed Queen Azalea for the daytime court, while King Hartman Moritz and Queen Carolyn Davis ruled over the evening court.

The ladies need not have worried. Despite unspectacular gardens and once elegant homes that had slipped into shabby gentility, by noon on March 28 several hundred visitors were streaming into town, a total that would reach approximately 1,500 by the end of the event, prompting a decision to keep the houses open an extra day to accommodate the large crowds. Some drove themselves; others came by tour bus, while wealthier patrons came accompanied by their chauffeurs. A 1942 magazine article recounts that first Pilgrimage morning as Katherine Miller anxiously awaited the arrival of Pilgrimage guests.

> Everything had been done. Posters invited the whole nation to Natchez, "where the Old South still lives." The last letter had gone out; the last preparation reached completion. There was nothing to do but wait—and feel frightened. The Pilgrimage day came. Katherine Miller hurried out. To her surprise, she had to dodge cars in the usually quiet street. A busload of tourists entered pilgrimage headquarters as she opened the door. Another bus drew up. Then another. Private autos jammed the roads. A packed train with special cars stopped at the Natchez station. The town swarmed with pilgrims."[23]

With only a dozen cars lined up to transport Pilgrimage guests that first morning, a call went out for residents to donate more cars to the effort. Tour organizers faced more than transportation headaches. Accommodations for the unexpected numbers of visitors had to be found as the town's limited number of hotel rooms quickly sold out. Again, Natchezians came to the rescue opening their homes to strangers who were only too pleased to find themselves sleeping in once elegant villas steeped in historic lore. Some guests lodged in rooms once occupied by John Audubon who gave dancing lessons in Natchez to finance his naturalist studies, or where Jefferson

Davis courted and later wed Natchez belle Varina Howell. Journalist Lillian Merriwether, who accepted an invitation by Miller to attend the Pilgrimage in the late 1930s, writes of arriving in town after ten o'clock in the evening with no reservation. "I wondered how it would be to spend a night in the lobby! However, my dilemma was short lived. There was a committee to place visitors in the various homes of Natchez." Merriwether was escorted to the home of Harriet Laub and her daughter and was enchanted upon her arrival to find her hosts dressed in colonial attire and hoopskirts after their return from that evening's Confederate Ball. "I was a tired pilgrim that night," Merriwether writes, "and after a refreshing warm bath, I found myself between the sheets of an immense old mahogany four poster bed, canopy and all, in an enormous room with lovely antique furniture all around me." The next morning, she breakfasted with her hosts before beginning her morning tour of homes.[24]

Pilgrims in 1932 had the choice of driving their own cars on the tour route or being driven by garden club members to visit the twenty-four homes and King's Tavern, one of the oldest structures in Natchez, which had served as a stagecoach and mail stop on the Natchez Trace for many years. Homes were divided into groups that corresponded to routes marked by four different colored placards bearing an illustration of a hoopskirted belle. Each tour package was priced at two dollars per person, or about twenty-five cents per house. Guests had time to take in two tour routes per day, four houses in the morning and four in the afternoon. In subsequent years guests could stop by one of several tearooms operating in members' homes for a light lunch between the morning and afternoon tours. As described by club publicist Roane Fleming Byrnes, the club's seventy-two members—"all women," she noted—"advertised and opened to the public twenty-four Ante-bellum houses, furnished and intact, some of them built as early as the seventeen-eighties. The 'pilgrims' were conducted over moss-hung roadways—once Indian trails—to white-columned mansions where they were received as honored guests by ladies in hoopskirts and mammies in bandannas."[25] The Natchez Pilgrimage was without question a commercial enterprise, but the clubwomen's dedication to their mission offered both a unique journey for visitors seeking to experience a slice of America's past and, equally important, a way for members to make their own sacred personal journey into their town's not so distant past.

Journeying into Natchez's past proved lucrative. Home tours the spring of 1933 generated nearly $6,200 in revenues for the club (the equivalent of $118,000 in 2019), marking a considerable success. By 1935 proceeds had tripled what they were the first year, bringing in $19,000 (a value equivalent of $345,000 in 2019).[26] In 1933 club members agreed to pay homeowners one third of tour receipts for that year's Pilgrimage. A year later, the percentage paid out to homeowners increased to fifty percent.[27] By the spring of 1940, the number of tourists had swelled to 25,000 people.

Even as the garden club ladies filled their club's coffers, residents witnessed other noticeable changes. As Byrnes writes, "At the very lowest ebb of depression, immediately following the bank holidays, her usually quiet hotels, restaurants, filling-stations, shops, secluded mansions were crowded with tourists. The dreamy old town felt the thrill of renewed life." The Pilgrims who made their way to Natchez came from every state of the union and included writers, artists, editors, architects, educators, and groups of students, according to Byrnes. "Natchez suddenly awoke from threatened oblivion 'to find herself famous'—praised in magazines and papers all over the country."[28]

A series of richly detailed and sometimes humorous letters written by George Kelly, owner of Melrose, to his wife Ethel during an early Pilgrimage season when Ethel was called away to assist their daughter with the birth of the couple's first grandchild, paint a vivid picture of the demands of the chaotic Pilgrimage enterprise on the sleepy old town. What follows is a sampling of Kelly's reports on the whirlwind of activity surrounding the Pilgrimage.

Eleven days before the weeklong event kicked off, George wrote to his wife that "Zeke [Melrose servant] has cut the front lawn and the place looks like a man with a fresh haircut! I'm sorry, but though it looks as you want it to, I like the grass flowers and such." A few days later, he took another stab at the freshly manicured grounds of Melrose: "The yard is cut and the garden mowing is going on and the lawn looks like a clipped poodle!"[29]

On March 31, the first day of the Pilgrimage, George wrote to his wife breathlessly:

> The reason I'm so behind is because of the mob at Melrose. You write to keep the gates locked until 10 o'clock. What did you mean by that? We got the signs painted for 1:30 and the inner gate was locked until that time. You told me nothing about the morning, nor left any memo. about it. We moved the time up from 2:30 to 1:30 and people began to arrive at 1:00 o'clock and there must have been 150 there by 1:30.... When I left, the special men, sent by Officer Joe Serio, had just arrived, about 15 minutes after the specified time, and the five of them have all they can do to try and keep the cars in even mild disorder, the cars being parked both sides of the road from the pond to the inner

gate, extending even to Boger's fence opposite the pond! Some jamb [sic]!! There must be several hundred cars and hundreds of people. The front field will be so plowed up that we should be able to plant it!

The Ogden girls—Maria and ?—brought Lucy Jane [Melrose servant] out and they left just as the crowd was coming up the driveway, and it must have taken them five minutes to get through the mob! I waited and followed. If I hadn't been in a profuse perspiration and nearly distracted from having to smooth things over, the crowd taking my explanations at the gate very nicely, however, I would have counted the cars, but I simply did not have time to do so.

By the way, Mrs. Ballou [garden club member], when she arrived today, said "Somebody asked me 'How did George Kelly manage to survive the depression with all these fine things'?"; showing her usual "common" tactlessness!! I replied: "Tell 'em I didn't!," and passed on, with a sardonic smile![30]

The following day, crowds continued to pour in, George wrote, as he fretted over a lack of flowers on the grounds:

There are no flowers, I'm sorry to say, except the purple azaleas on the front drive and the remains of the white one outside the drawing-room windows. A few of the tall, red tulips remain, but the rest have all gone. They were beautiful, however, when in full bloom.

The pink snap-dragons, that Mary got from Blythe, matched the pink double-glass Bohemian decanters perfectly, as also the rug and the new pink drawing-room furniture covering, so that the effect caused many enthusiastic comments.

I have just telephoned Mary [garden club member] and she is all set for tomorrow and Ralph Booth says he will be on hand an hour before the set time, so we ought to be able to handle the crowds. I counted exactly 700 tickets in the box, not including several cars whose occupants paid cash just to see Melrose especially, which was pretty good for a single attraction, the total of tickets for the morning tour being about 800, but Melrose being off the afternoon route, so people had to make a special trip to see it.[31]

A day later, George mused on expanding the Pilgrimage, telling his wife that he and other Natchez men believed that "the ladies should get their heads together and do some hard thinking and run the Pilgrimage longer than a week" because "all the people who want to come to Natchez cannot be accommodated in one week." To emphasize his point, he added, "It seems as if, with the Pilgrimage growing larger each year, it must eventually come to be organized upon a money-making basis for all who take part."[32]

His enthusiastic reports to Ethel continued on April 4, noting:

> There were 277 cars at Melrose last Tuesday and I counted 767 tickets. More people coming each day! We have about 8 men on duty, not including the gatekeepers, Ralph Booth and Wade Newell.
>
> The men all look at the moose and the oilcloth, while the women all rush for the furniture. One said that the marble in the front parlor was genuine Abyssinian marble, and another immediately asked: "How did they get it over here?" It's getting so that every piece, picture, curio and furnishing has to be identified as of this, or that, material and historical data supplied, or the Pilgrims' cravings remain unsatisfied![33]
>
> Mrs. Ballou said there must have been a thousand there. The sisters [Ethel Kelly's sisters] said nearer 2,000! From the looks of the pile of tickets I think about 800 to 900 nearer the mark.[34]

By the last day of the 1935 Pilgrimage on April 6, George Kelly was expressing a sigh of relief, writing: "I'm sincerely glad that the Pilgrimage is over, for Melrose anyway. I was talking to one of the men at the outer gate, a Mr. Bullock, a carpenter out of work, who has kept a record of cars arriving at places for the last four days. At Longwood, Wednesday, 227 cars; at Melrose, Thursday, 302 cars; at Longwood, Friday, 200 cars; at Melrose, today, 307 cars. . . . Of the 307 cars at Melrose today, 181 were foreign cars from every state almost, Cal., Wash., Conn., Oregon, etc., and 126 home (i.e., Miss.) cars." By the time the last pilgrim had left his doorstep, Melrose had welcomed close to 4,300 visitors, according to Kelly's calculations. At a quarter a head, ticket sales for Melrose in 1935 were approximately $1,080, of which Melrose received $300 (the equivalent of more than $19,000 and $5,500, respectively, in 2019 dollars).[35]

A guestbook kept by the garden club hostesses of Arlington reveals a sampling of some of the guests who came to Natchez. On the opening day of the 1937 Pilgrimage season nearly half of the tourists were Natchez residents, eager for a tour of a prized town relic. Of the thirty-three out of state visitors who recorded their names that day, eight hailed from California, another eight from New York, three from the Chicago area, and two women from Yugoslavia and Czechoslovakia, respectively. Another simply wrote "Africa." Rounding out the group who toured Arlington—described in tour literature as a "veritable museum of the Old South"—was a Catholic nun from Memphis and a New York man who playfully added "The Yank" next to his signature.[36]

Natchez appealed to an eclectic group of tourists and journalists in search of a romanticized past. Garden club hostesses greeted them in faded antebellum hoopskirt gowns, many retrieved from old trunks where their mothers and grandmothers had stored them decades ago. Once ushered inside homes bearing such regal names as Monmouth, Dunleith, and The Elms, tourists listened to hostesses who wove stories of some of the South's most prominent families in thick southern drawls. Tourist brochures from early Pilgrimage years offered brief descriptions of each home and give a sense of the type of information tourists would have heard. Laced between the dates of when homes were built, some dating back to the 1700s, club publicist Roane Byrnes offered tidbits about furnishings, family members, and legends concerning the nearly two dozen homes on tour. Visitors to Melrose were told they would see a home that could "serve as a model for the luxurious surroundings and cultivated taste of its period. Its lofty double drawing-rooms with brocatelles, the courtyard at the back with its Antebellum kitchen and milkroom still in use, carry the onlooker back to an idyllic past." Monmouth visitors were warned to be on the lookout for the ghostly appearance of a "beautiful maiden who died of unrequited loved." With few direct references to the Civil War, attention was called to the home of General William T. Martin's home, Monteigne. Visitors were told that "due to prominence of the general, unusual vengeance was wreaked on his home during the Civil War, furniture destroyed, and horses stabled in drawing rooms." Colorful legends were associated with King's Tavern, considered to be the oldest house in Natchez. Brynes wrote that when repairs were made to King's Tavern, "a jeweled dagger was found in the chimney and several skeletons were discovered buried" beneath the barroom floor.[37] Such tales added to the allure of homes that had been lived in for a century or more and represented significant eras in the nation's history, stretching from the precolonial era through the federal occupation of Natchez during the Civil War, while omitting mention of the Confederacy's defeat. Ornate brass chandeliers, massive mahogany tables laden with family heirloom silver and china, and family portraits became useful props as Pilgrimage hostesses proudly shared ancestral histories that included all the makings of a bestseller: romance, premature deaths, and great wealth. A *New York Times* report in 1935 typified the stories filed by

An early Pilgrimage publicity shot promoting the warm welcome awaiting Natchez visitors during annual spring home tours. (Courtesy of the Thomas H. and Joan W. Gandy Photograph Collection, Louisiana Lower Mississippi Valley Collections, Special Collections, Hill Memorial Library, Louisiana State University Libraries, Baton Rouge.)

smitten reporters attending early Pilgrimages. Natchez, the journalist wrote, was a "romantic little town ... tinged with a nostalgia for days and manners that are gone."[38]

Amidst the chipped paint, fading tapestries, and sparse gardens, Natchez visitors found a social structure that had emerged in the early years of the twentieth century. By the early 1930s a growing middle class outnumbered planters and had assumed civic leadership. These rising middle-class men and their wives—in Natchez and across the South—identified with that which they took to be the beliefs and values of the planter elite, thereby ensuring a culture of segregation and white supremacy.[39] Southern states and towns with high percentages of blacks, such as Natchez with 52 percent, adopted some of the most stringent racial practices, commonly referred to as Jim Crow, to protect white supremacy. Separate schools, movie theaters, swimming pools, public restrooms, churches, and restaurants were a part of everyday life for black and white Natchezians. About the only place whites and blacks encountered one another in an integrated social space were the homes of middle- and upper-class whites where black female domestics cooked, cleaned, and tended their employers' children. White Natchez women not only controlled the management of their homes and the black women they hired, but also played a significant role in shaping and guarding the town's cultural heritage as members of the Natchez Garden Club.

The Pilgrimage expressed one southern community's glorification of its colonial and antebellum heritage, while simultaneously articulating Depression-era cultural values. In analyzing the appeal of a tourist attraction in a small, remotely located southern town that drew large numbers of visitors from across the nation, two important questions emerge. First, what can be learned about changing gender roles in studying the enterprising clubwomen who organized the Pilgrimage and other heritage tourism projects? Secondly, why during the 1930s did the American South, and Natchez specifically, engage tourists, readers, and filmgoers more than almost any other region of the country? The answer to these questions reveals as much about audience tastes and cultural preferences as it does about the producers of this popular entertainment attraction.

TO "GARDEN FINELY"

During the early twentieth century, women's clubs nationwide focused their voluntary efforts on improving the social welfare of their communities. By the late 1920s and early 1930s a growing number of American women began to support a new wave of clubs devoted to gardening and floral arranging, a pastime associated with a sense of refinement dating back to the early nineteenth century.[40]

Pledged to creating beautiful gardens and homes, the Natchez Women's Club gave birth to the Natchez Garden Club (NGC) in 1928, originally formed as a subcommittee one year earlier to establish a "city beautification program." Natchez club members worked to beautify their city and the curb appeal of individual homes by planting shrubs and trees and eliminating other public eyesores.

No doubt, the nation's growing enthusiasm for home gardening boosted the appeal of Natchez Garden Club membership. In the early twentieth century with the rise of industrialization resulting in a tremendous growth in cities and the arrival of large numbers of immigrants, Americans increasingly sought a nostalgic and simplified past. Many found their escape in home gardening, as writers frequently advised their readers that spending more time outdoors would lead to improved health and boost spirits. Virginia Tuttle Clayton notes that garden writers from this period promoted "an intimate, 'livable' garden designed with old-fashioned charm and simplicity, one that incorporated native plants to emulate the effects of the natural American landscape, and would provide the type of soothing domestic space that could counteract the ill effects of contemporary frenzied life and restore unnerved Americans to a wholesome, contented state of mind and body. In fact, any garden would serve—although simple, old-fashioned gardens and wild gardens, with their favored associations, might prove especially effective."[41] From the first several decades of the twentieth century to WWII, books and magazines on gardening blossomed, including *Better Homes and Gardens*, founded in 1922, producing a bounty of new gardening products, tools, and furnishings, and enormous enthusiasm for women's and men's gardening clubs.

Female garden clubs in Mississippi were hugely popular by the 1920s, following the lead of a Garden Clubs of America president who proclaimed enthusiastically, "We ... are beginning to realize that we have come together on an irresistible wave of desire for the beauty of gardens. Our object is to 'garden finely' and to induce others to join us in this neglected art."[42] Early Natchez Garden Club minutes reveal that club members worked to fine tune their home gardens and public spaces, while also learning new gardening techniques and identifying plants that would thrive in the humid Natchez climate.

By the early 1930s under Pilgrimage founder Katherine Miller's direction, clubwomen added to their agenda of beautifying Natchez's outdoor public spaces the preservation and commercialization of their town's antebellum architectural past. As the garden clubwomen increasingly shifted their focus from petunias to architectural preservation, they began to promote their town's colonial-era ties (a popular interest in 1930s America) and to articulate anew a memorialization message that closely resembled the late nineteenth-century Lost Cause ideology of the Adams Light Infantry, Adams Confederate Memorial Association, and the United Daughters of the Confederacy (UDC), organizations which all had paid tribute to Civil War veterans, vindicated the region's decision to secede from the Union, and glorified the cultural lifestyle of the Old South.

Young, middle-class white women in Natchez who had once flocked to the United Daughters of the Confederacy (UDC)—among the most popular of Lost Cause organizations across the South—by the late 1920s were seeking new social and volunteerism outlets.[43] Not surprisingly, as Confederate veterans and their survivors died, activities like the annual Natchez Memorial Day observations gradually began to lose their appeal. In keeping with this trend, UDC membership gradually declined among younger Natchez women. The Natchez UDC chapter reported sixty-five members in 1918, but only twenty-five by 1936.[44] Natchez newspapers by 1925 largely ignored the UDC—another sign that the once popular organization was losing public appeal. Its ceremonies were no longer considered newsworthy, having become a routine part of the town's cultural life. In January 1929 the *Natchez Democrat* reported that the annual celebration of Robert E. Lee's birthday, organized by members of the UDC, was canceled because many of the elderly members were ill.[45]

By the early 1930s, a younger generation of white middle- and upper-class women of Natchez turned to the thriving Natchez Garden Club to express and preserve the cultural ideals of their town and region. The garden club seized cultural authority in 1930s Natchez, embracing the traditional values of nineteenth-century reunification and memorialization, while infusing elements of Depression-era popular culture into their work that appealed to a mass audience. In the process of defining their community's cultural image, these women redefined the meaning of traditional southern womanhood. With the early success of the Pilgrimage, the Natchez Garden Club's membership roster blossomed and became the most prominent and popular social club for white women in Natchez. Over time, news of the garden club dominated the pages of the local newspaper, the *Natchez Democrat*, with fewer mentions made of the original Women's Club.

LADIES OF THE CLUB

Some background on the Natchez Garden Club's early membership is beneficial in understanding the Pilgrimage and its development as a cultural entity of the 1930s. The majority of the founding sixty-three members were married, with a handful of widows. The education level of members is unknown; however, from conversations with descendants of these members, it appears that few, if any, of the women attended college. Most of the women lived in middle-class households with husbands who worked as merchants, insurance and real estate agents, automobile dealers, or owners of small businesses. Only ten of the sixty-three original club members lived in a prized antebellum Natchez estate. By the late 1930s thirty-three clubwomen among a membership of 175 (19 percent) held paying jobs, reflective of an upward trend in employment among American women that rose to 25.8 percent during the decade.[46] Of the thirty-three club members working outside of their homes, fifteen were married, eight were widows, and the remaining ten were single. Most of the employed clubwomen held clerical jobs, also consistent with national employment trends.[47]

Although most club members did not own one of the approximate two dozen homes shown on early Pilgrimage tours, their passion for Natchez history was rooted in longstanding family traditions of memorializing southern culture. Of the sixty-three members of the NGC in 1929, at least nineteen (30%) had mothers, grandmothers, or a member of their husband's maternal family who had belonged to either the Confederate Memorial Association or the United Daughters of the Confederacy.[48] Particularly important, approximately one third of the membership had ancestral ties to elite Natchez families, yet another strong psychological link to the past and the town's noteworthy collection of antebellum homes. As was the case across the South, many of these elite planter families' fortunes had declined during the war, and their offspring were, by the 1930s, living a less affluent lifestyle. But while the incomes of these planter-class descendants may have dwindled and they no longer lived in antebellum splendor, their reverence for the traditional genteel lifestyle of the Old South never waned. Indeed, their reduced financial circumstances may have fueled a desire among club members to recapture some semblance of their aristocratic heritage, if only in the temporary annual staging of the Pilgrimage.

The findings of a team of University of Chicago sociologists who conducted an in-depth study of Natchez residents in the 1930s support the notion that numerous middle-class Natchez women used their garden club membership and interest in historic preservation as a means to elevate their social status. The acquisition of an "old plantation mansion" was the best way for "mobile upper middles to demonstrate their reverence for the past," but if this was not an option, membership in the town's "Historical Club" [garden club] was the next best alternative, according to the researchers. The scholars noted that since club membership was limited and "a hard nut for the upper-middle class woman to crack," many found other ways to show their reverence for their town's storied past, such as offering themselves as tour guides, opening their homes as rooming houses for visitors, or serving meals for a price in their homes or gardens "where guests were served by Negro servants wearing the traditional antebellum servant costumes."[49] The research team's findings attest to the sharp class boundaries still intact in 1930s Natchez.

The eighteen garden club members who had acquired Pilgrimage homes either by inheritance or through current wealth often lacked the money required to renovate their aging and decaying antebellum estates. Oakland, the home of club member Jeanne Minor McDowell, daughter of the once wealthy Katherine Minor ("Yankee Kate," chapter 1), was but one example. In 1860 the Minors had owned property valued at $555,600; by the 1930s however, the decrepit condition of their home forced its occupants to relocate their beds when it rained.[50] According to Mary Louise Kendall Goodrich, the longest surviving member of the Pilgrimage founders, "[Natchez] was losing so many beautiful homes. They were falling down and there was no money. We had to do something."[51]

AMATEUR HISTORIANS AT WORK

With a third of the early club membership descended from a member of the Natchez chapter of the United Daughters of the Confederacy or the Confederate Memorial Association, it was natural that the club would be supportive of preservation projects that focused on honoring the town's Confederate heritage. Although her ancestors were not among the upper echelon of Natchez planter families, Katherine Miller, given credit for establishing the Natchez Pilgrimage, was descended from a line of Natchez women who supported the Confederate Memorial Association in the 1880s. Building upon her family's antebellum legacy, her passionate efforts to honor her town's antebellum past played a major role in shaping public perceptions of antebellum Mississippi in the twentieth century and beyond.

Like many Natchezians, Miller was a product of Scots-Irish descent. Her paternal second great-grandfather John Grafton left Northern Ireland in about 1790, first settling in South Carolina before moving to Natchez around 1800. He purchased land and was considered reasonably successful as a planter, and his name is frequently found in Adams County court records of the late eighteenth and early nineteenth century, noting his real estate as well as slave acquisitions. John's son, Allen, Katherine Miller's paternal great-grandfather, capitalized on his father's plantation operation. He became a large landholder of property six miles north of Natchez and in 1840 held sixteen slaves, making him a sizeable property owner in Adams County. Another of Miller's paternal ancestors, Reuben Collins, achieved even greater stature as a property holder with forty-seven slaves listed in the 1840 Federal census.[52]

Like so many planter families, the Grafton's fortunes declined at the close of the Civil War. As the proprietor of a sizeable estate, Miller's paternal grandfather, Thomas Grafton, with seventy-one slaves in 1860, was unable

Katherine Grafton Miller pictured in an antebellum gown that belonged to her grandmother. Earl Norman, photographer. (Courtesy of Historic Natchez Foundation.)

to sustain his family's wealth or remain a member of the planter class following the war. The father of ten children, Grafton was respected and well known within Natchez during his lifetime. He served for a year in the State House of Representatives beginning in 1852 and later served in the Civil War as commander of a squad attached to Walsh's Company of the first Mississippi Regiment. In 1865 he was elected county treasurer. In that same year he established the *Natchez Post*, a brief one-year venture. A short time later, he joined the *Democrat* as assistant editor and later served as editor for thirteen years. By the 1890s he served as a justice of the peace and as a notary, suggesting solid middle-class status in Natchez's social hierarchy. Relying on his journalistic skills, he published numerous historical sketches about Natchez that appeared in the *Democrat*, promotional literature, and later in his granddaughter's book, *Natchez of Long Ago and the Pilgrimage*. Thomas Grafton's love for the past, as reflected in his writings, appears to have had a strong influence on Katherine and may have inspired her own passionate interest in preserving her community's history. Shortly before his death in 1894 at the age of seventy-three, Thomas Grafton described Natchez as "the garden of the South, the favorite land of the emigrant hunting a home."[53] Grafton's occupational choices and tax records suggest he was a hardworking and respected member of the middle class, and while he likely had contact with local planters after the war, he probably was not part of their inner circle, and struggled to maintain his large family's middle-class lifestyle.[54]

Katherine's own parents were of modest means. Her father, Kirby W. Grafton, worked as a clerk and her mother, Elodie Rose, was the daughter of Thomas Rose, antebellum master builder and architect, and Fannie Ward, a schoolteacher.[55] Her aunts, Molly and Jennie Grafton, worked as seamstresses after the war and were listed as honorary members of the Natchez Confederate Memorial Association. Miller's family history suggests that while her ancestors may at one time have been members of the planter aristocracy, the Civil War had irreparably damaged the family's fortunes. By the time Katherine Grafton was born in 1895 her family fit solidly within the town's middle-class social structure.[56]

At an early age, Miller claims to have been a daydreamer whose "head was in the clouds most of the time."[57] At twenty-two, Grafton, a tall dark-eyed brunette who appeared more stylish than beautiful, married J. Balfour Miller in June 1917. Her husband, whose ancestry in several published accounts linked him to an old Natchez family, was listed as a wholesale grocer in the 1920 census, and later became a real estate agent who achieved considerable success.[58] In the late 1920s, the Millers purchased Hope Farm from the Montgomery sisters, descendants of the once wealthy Davis, Clark, and Montgomery clans. The purchase of the home, built in 1775 for Don Carlos de Grandpre, one of the Natchez District's early Spanish governors, suggests a calculated quest by the Millers to enhance their social status among the Natchez elite by purchasing a historic home. While Hope Farm's past was impressive, by the early twentieth century the property was close to ruin and faced being condemned.[59]

The couple remained childless, allowing Katherine Miller to devote her time to restoring her home, taking a leadership role in the garden club, and leading an active social life. In 1931 the Natchez Garden Club elected her president. In her characteristic fashion of downplaying her abilities, perhaps in a show of false modesty, she later wrote, "I had never belonged to any organization, civic or otherwise. I was inexperienced in club work, but the Garden Club idea appealed to me strongly and soon I was putting my heart and soul into the work of beautifying Natchez. A new venue of thought and effort was thereby opened to me, and since that time it seems that my feet have trod in a garden of lovely experience."[60]

As club president, Miller's feet seem to have trod in many directions before assuming leadership of the Pilgrimage. She used her position to influence beautification efforts throughout the city. In November 1930, after seeing an oak tree on fire in a local park, she wrote a letter to the mayor and aldermen of Natchez reminding them of a city ordinance forbidding the burning of leaves and grass under the trees in Duncan Park. "Please see that your order is carried out so that no further damage will result from indifference or from carelessness with fire in that wonderful playground whose gift to the city we all enjoy."[61] When not scolding civic leaders, Miller helped to organize flower shows and plant sales at wholesale prices to Natchez residents. She also took a strong interest in promoting city beautification to black Natchezians, visiting their high schools and churches. Within her scrapbook, she records an occasion of speaking before an African American congregation on the subject of "Cleanliness is next to Godliness." Her dedication to uplift the black community of Natchez appears transparently self-serving for white property owners when she writes, "I felt our first work was with the colored people as the humblest cottage, untidy and unsightly as most of them were, either mar or make the beauty of our city—since we have no zoning laws and since our colored people live side by side with some of our loveliest homes."[62] Miller's club chose to address the issue of improving the appearance of black residents' yards through the donation of flowers and shrubs.

Miller's role as an outspoken and committed supporter of city beautification efforts throughout Natchez suggests that the growing city cleanup and improvement movement sweeping the nation influenced her actions. She and her fellow club members likely also came under the influence of Mississippi native Ellen Sullivan Woodward, a vocal supporter of city beautification who also led the civic and community development department as well as the woman's department for the Mississippi State Board of Development (MSBD), a private-sector organization that strived to bring businesses to Mississippi. Woodward, who wrote a monthly column for the *Mississippi Builder* from 1927 to 1933 and traveled throughout the state to "sell the South," was a well-known public official whose optimistic message likely resonated with Katherine Miller's booster instincts. Taking a progressively feminist position, Woodward proclaimed, "The work of upbuilding the New South is by no means confined to southern men. Women are real builders—builders of ideals, builders of progressive thought, builders of homes, communities and cultural sentiment ... builders of highways, schools, social centers, and welfare institutions." As early as 1927, Woodward had advised, "cleaning up a city has much to do with bettering business conditions."[63]

Ellen Woodward's statements fit squarely with how Miller saw her purpose as a leader in city beautification, a mission perfectly suited for her garden club peers.

While Miller in her younger years with her soft brown eyes and brunette hair bore an uncanny resemblance to the soft-spoken character of Melanie Hamilton played by Olivia de Havilland in *Gone with the Wind*, in reality her temperament was more in tune with the spirited Scarlett O'Hara. Miller possessed a vivacious personality that seems to have captivated many outsiders who met her. Author Harnett Kane described her as "a dark-eyed brunette young matron with something of the pent-up energy of a buzz-bomb . . . a combination of Miss Nelly of N'Orleans and Tallulah Bankhead, with a slight dash of P. T. Barnum."[64] Journalist Ernie Pyle seemed equally charmed by Miller's vivacity. "Mrs. Miller is dynamic and sophisticated, a natural-born-doer-of-things. They say she has fifteen ideas a minute and that thirteen of them are terrible but the other two are knockouts. She is a southerner from generations back, yet she gives you the feeling of a New Yorker, in sporty dress, doing big things in a big way."[65]

Natchez resident Virginia Morrison, whose mother, Ruth Beltzhoover, was a close friend to Miller, recalls, "Mrs. Miller had a way of charming people, a way of telling a story that drew people in."[66] The stories Miller told were spoken in quick bursts of energy that captivated her listeners' attention. A *Chicago Tribune* reporter who interviewed her in the early 1950s wrote that "Miller is one of the South's fastest talkers. Ask her a simple question and she takes off on a nonstop flight through history, legend and dramatic fancy. She is a dreamer, an enthusiast, completely charming in the best deep south tradition, and as compelling in full swing as a Kansas cyclone."[67]

Miller parlayed her verbal gifts into convincing the town's business and political leadership to adopt the idea of an annual Pilgrimage, a task that according to Miller took a fair amount of salesmanship. While the upper class relished their town's past, Natchez male business and political leaders were at first skeptical that Miller and her followers could attract tourists during a national depression. But Miller refused to take "no" for an answer. According to Natchez physician Thomas Gandy, who often met Miller and her husband for drinks at the Carriage House Restaurant on the grounds of Stanton Hall, Katherine Miller was "sweet at times, but domineering as Hell." A longtime Pilgrimage Garden Club member recalls Miller as a woman of "spunk," who was used to getting her way. She remembers Miller controlling Pilgrimage Garden Club meetings with an iron fist. "It was 'yes, Katherine,' or 'no, Katherine.'" The outcome of some of those meetings soon became public knowledge, noted Dr. Gandy. "She had some of those garden club women scared to death of her. If she liked you, there was nothing she wouldn't do, and if she didn't like you, there was nothing she wouldn't do. They were afraid of her, but she could also be very charming."[68]

Successful in her first public business venture, Miller moved quickly to cinch control over the Pilgrimage and ensure her influence by convincing fellow club members to elect her as publicity chairman, a position that earned her a cash honorarium and the opportunity to travel. From her letters and reports to the Natchez Garden Club in the 1930s, she clearly relished her trips to women's clubs across the country, and the frequent contact she had with newspaper and magazine editors nationwide. Her first speaking tour, for which she dressed in a hoopskirt gown and presented colored lantern slides of Pilgrimage homes, took her to nearby Vicksburg, Jackson, Meridian, and Laurel, Mississippi, in the fall of 1932.[69] A few months later, she was invited to speak before a convention of state garden club presidents in Des Moines, Iowa, where her speech was greeted enthusiastically. Testimonials like the one from the Atlanta president and trustee of the Tallulah Falls School vouch for her success. "Mrs. Miller has the most beautiful slides—not too many, and selected with great judgment to show the most interesting and historic houses and some splendid pictures of drawing rooms just as they were and still are. Mrs. Miller is young and very good to look at, and has one of the most beautiful speaking voices I have ever heard. She wears a lovely hoop skirt costume, very becoming, and here she carried a huge round bouquet of camellias. Everybody was entranced."[70] In early 1936, she reported that she had delivered her "Natchez, Where the Old South Still Lives" presentation to thirty-seven clubs across the South and as far north as Chicago.

When not speaking before groups, Miller took the opportunity to visit a town's local newspaper office to promote the upcoming Pilgrimage season. In the 1970s Miller reminisced about the early days of the Pilgrimage, noting, "I found out long ago that hard work and money can accomplish any goal."[71]

In 1937 Miller solidified her social rank and reputation by orchestrating the purchase and restoration of Stanton Hall, one of the first projects of the newly formed Pilgrimage Garden Club (PGC).[72] The story behind the purchase of what had been one of Natchez's grandest estates remains a favorite among PGC members and offers a glimpse of Miller's legendary determination. Longtime club member Alma Carpenter, the daughter of NGC and later PGC treasurer Alma Kellogg, noted, "We had all of eighty-seven cents in the treasury when we decided to buy Stanton Hall." In the end, Miller successfully obtained the loans to secure the property for $28,000, providing her garden club with one of the most architecturally impressive clubhouses in the nation.[73]

Miller's commitment to restoring Stanton Hall to its former glory can be attributed to more than her passion for architectural preservation. Her maternal grandfather, master builder Thomas Rose, assisted in constructing the mansion, owned by one of the town's wealthiest cotton brokers, Frederick Stanton. Her ancestor's ties to the property—not as an owner but as a skilled artisan who helped to design and build the palatial estate—appear to have instilled in her a deep sense of family pride and a desire to preserve a landmark linked with her family's past.[74]

While Katherine Miller may have been motivated to embrace her town's past as a means to elevate her social status, her passion for the past appears genuine and helped to fulfill a personal quest to find greater self-fulfillment. After launching the Natchez Garden Club's first tour of homes in 1931, Miller soon recognized a calling to memorialize the Old South's historic cultural values. With limited career options open to women that were socially acceptable for those of her class standing, Miller had struck gold. Organizing home tours found acceptance within the confines of the South's traditional conservative society where a woman's place was expected to remain close to home. As protectors of the home who better to look after Natchez's most visible and valuable relics than its women? Women like Miller who led the Pilgrimage found an absorbing and satisfying way to express their creativity and use their organizational abilities while providing a valued service to their community. It was a role Miller cherished throughout her life.

Miller, who came to symbolize New South womanhood, was but one of many garden club members who achieved success in the public sphere. Her friend and fellow club member, Ruth Audley Britton Wheeler Beltzhoover, was the co-owner and chief buyer of Famous and Price, an upscale Natchez department store. (Beltzhoover is credited as one of the few garden club members who stood up to the assertive Katherine Miller. The two remained lifelong friends despite occasional public differences.) After her husband died in 1945, Beltzhoover took over the store as a way to provide for her children and maintain her antebellum estate Green Leaves.[75] Frequently, she made buying trips to New York City, where one Natchez resident recalls, "All those Yankees loved her." Beltzhoover also put her entrepreneurial smarts to work operating a tearoom in the garden of her home to feed hungry pilgrims as the yearly crowds grew larger. Although Beltzhoover credited her husband with coming up with the idea, she and another club member who shared in the profits oversaw the operation. With seating for one hundred patrons, guests were charged seventy-five cents for lunch and a dollar and a half for dinner that included fried chicken, gumbo, rice, cornbread, and pineapple salad. When local restaurant owners tried to shut her tearoom down citing a lack of proper equipment to sterilize dishes, she fought back. "I said, 'Come look in my kitchen.' And he (the official) nearly fainted. Here in the kitchen we have a huge big washtub; in fact, we had three of them. Then he said, 'Oh. When did you do that?' And I told him, 'About 1910.'"[76]

Mary Louise Netterville Kendall Goodrich, a founding NGC member, used her clout to try to preserve the unique historic architectural character of downtown Natchez. Kendall Goodrich owned Monteigne, the former home of General William T. and Margarette Conner Martin. Kendall Goodrich recalled in a 1982 interview the difficulty in working with business leaders who were bent on modernizing the downtown business sector. "I spoke before the Chamber of Commerce several times, just begging the business people to spend—if they did spend money on their buildings—to spend it in the Natchez manner. This was my theme: 'I am not asking you to spend any money on your building, but if you do spend it, spend it so it will look like Natchez. We don't want to look like a little town in the Midwest . . . like every other town. We want to look like Natchez used to look." While Kendall Goodrich and her garden club supporters achieved some victories in historic preservation, they also lost some battles as is evident in the mixture of old and new architecture in downtown Natchez today. "The business people in Natchez said they wanted to be modern," she lamented. "They didn't want to look old-fashioned. They just didn't realize. We sold the world on Natchez, but we couldn't sell the Natchez business people on Natchez. It was a tragedy really."[77] Kendall Goodrich may have been disappointed in the outcome of her preservation efforts, but the leadership skills she gained as club president and civic activist prepared her to serve as a Democratic National Committeewoman for Mississippi for twelve years beginning in 1936, as president of her family's Coca-Cola distribution franchise, and as vice president of the Garden Club of America.

Not all garden club members enjoyed the same level of success in the public sphere or in life. A few members faced great personal hardship. The town's struggling economy worsened by a global depression created difficult circumstances for many members, and in some cases members faced homelessness and poverty, a reality that defied the stereotyped image of women's clubs as a pleasant social gathering place for affluent dowagers pouring tea. The financial struggles of Eliza Bennerscheidt, an early garden club member, represents one of the most drastic declines in wealth among the Natchez elite. Eliza's husband, Frederick was descended from the Davis family, at one time one of the wealthiest planter clans in Adams County. Frederick's grandfather, F. A. W. Davis, was part of a family who in 1860 owned more than 14,000 acres and retained 843 slaves in Louisiana, an estate valued at nearly 1.7 million dollars.[78] Bennerscheidt and her husband, a florist who was also employed as the motion picture operator by the Baker Grand Theater, were served an injunction in 1936 for falling behind on mortgage payments on their dilapidated home and fourteen acres in Natchez. Frederick Bennerscheidt lost the home to foreclosure a short time after his wife's death that same year.[79]

For other members, putting their intellect to good use provided a sense of self-satisfaction. Alma Kellogg recalled in her later years the enjoyment she found serving as treasurer for the Natchez Garden Club and later the Pilgrimage Garden Club. "I loved working with figures. I could add and subtract and really enjoyed keeping up with the club's finances."[80] The detailed records she kept note the many business transactions of each club: the 1938 purchase and maintenance of the PGC's headquarters Stanton Hall; the construction of the Carriage House Restaurant (located within Stanton Hall) in the 1950s; the purchase of King's Tavern and its restoration in 1971; and the acquisition of Longwood in the 1970s. She also managed the procurement of supplies for the Pilgrimage as well as negotiating advertising space and insurance coverage for the event.

At least one of the most prominent and dedicated garden clubwomen in Natchez was not a native southerner. Ethel Moore Kelly, a New York debutante, settled at Melrose in 1901 shortly after marrying George M. D. Kelly, another descendant of the once enormously wealthy Davis clan whose branch of the family had retained their fortunes primarily because of northern family ties. Mrs. Kelly assimilated quickly into the social life of her husband's hometown and adopted a lifelong commitment to the preservation and memorialization efforts of her new community. Her active participation in the garden club reflects the keen interest of early twentieth-century upper-class women in clubs and civic volunteerism. As one of the most enthusiastic Pilgrimage supporters, Ethel Kelly and her daughter drove to Virginia soon after the Natchez Garden Club welcomed state garden club delegates in 1931 to learn more about that state's home tours.[81] During the dispute over the division of club revenues in the late 1930s, Kelly was one of the few homeowners to remain loyal to the Natchez Garden Club and was an outspoken critic against commercializing the Pilgrimage.

A PASSION FOR LOCAL HISTORY

Natchez Garden Club members shared a keen reverence for local history that became apparent not only in their club work but also in other leisure and paid pursuits. The growing number of early twentieth-century white Natchez women who dabbled in historical pursuits—writing short sketches, magazine articles, memoirs, and fiction; selling antiques and historical photographs; or volunteering their time to restore and preserve historic homes, public buildings, and transportation routes—found a source of pleasure, purpose, and profit in these efforts.

One of the most common means to express a commitment and interest in local history was through writing. During the 1930s, more than a dozen white Natchez women, many of them garden club members, wrote and published historical sketches about Natchez's territorial and antebellum past, many of which demonstrated an impressive ability to document local history.[82] It is worth quoting a colorful passage from a press release written by garden club member Roane Fleming Byrnes, whose writing is typical in style and content to her cohorts, who were busily churning out their own sentimental prose. Byrnes urged travelers to hurry to Natchez where:

> You can still find the Dixie of song and storybook—columns and live oaks and mammies and all ... a place where the mocking birds sing as sweetly as ever in the camellia bushes and the magnolias. Barefooted little black boys play on the corners whistling dance tunes. Mulatto washerwomen in faded calicoes saunter along the sidewalks, sometimes swinging clothes baskets between them, sometimes balancing bundles carelessly on their heads. Old fashioned mule-drawn drays rattle by piled high with cotton bales; sweet olives and cape jasmine perfumes the air in the warm sunshine.[83]

The clubwoman's sensuous description of whistling black boys and sauntering laundry women conjured up Lost Cause stereotypes reminiscent of the mythical images that Mary Britton Conner attempted to capture with her camera a few decades earlier (see chapter 4). Byrnes was as eager to preserve this world of mammies, mockingbirds, and moonlit mansions as she was to share it with admiring visitors—wallets in hand.

In the process of chronicling and preserving their region's past, Natchez women forged new and satisfying self-identities. As Drew Gilpin Faust writes, telling stories is a powerful force in the formation of identity. "We all live in the stories we tell, for these tales fashion a coherent direction and identity out of the discontinuities of our past, present, and future."[84] Moreover, writing served as a way for these women to create a sense of order and meaning in a time of tremendous economic and social upheaval. Penning their thoughts about the southern past gave Natchez female writers not only a means to express themselves in the public arena but the potential to earn a much-need paycheck during the Great Depression.

Many of the sketches the women produced became part of the garden club's promotional literature that attracted journalists, celebrities, and tourists to Natchez. Club leader Katherine Grafton Miller joined the ranks of published garden clubwomen with her promotional book *Natchez of Long Ago and the Pilgrimage*. The souvenir book detailed the beginnings of the town's home tours and included a reflection on the personal impact of her heritage tourism work, noting, "I at last had found that which I had been seeking all my life—a worthwhile interest, in which I could turn a seemingly fantastic imagination to good account."[85] Accomplished author Edith Wyatt Moore, a widowed mother and writer for the WPA's Federal Writer's Project, wrote detailed historical sketches of Pilgrimage homes that appeared in special "Pink Editions" of the *Natchez Democrat* during tour season. She, like Katherine Miller, also conducted favorably received public lectures in cities across the country. As a single mother, Moore's livelihood depended on her writing. She joined the WPA slave narrative project, interviewing numerous former Mississippi slaves; contributed to the WPA American Guide series; and authored a history of Natchez's Under-the-Hill area. Moore also spent countless hours in the county courthouse researching old wills, land records, letters, and journals for her articles, book, and the WPA Historical Records project.[86]

Club member Theodora Britton Marshall was particularly adept at converting her historical interests to profit-making ventures. Marshall, who clerked in the Adams County sheriff's office and later served as city tax deputy, coauthored two guidebooks on Natchez. Her books highlighted the area's antebellum homes, a task for which she was well suited as a descendant of an elite Natchez family who made her home at Richmond, one of the town's architectural gems.[87] During the 1930s, Marshall teamed up with Catharine Dunbar Brown, another passionate local amateur historian, to launch Ye Olde Booke Shoppe from "a most attractive cozy basement room with an open wood fire" at Marshall's antebellum home. Brown, who worked as a bank teller and later as an insurance agent, prided herself on her ancestral ties to a Natchez planter family and frequently wrote and spoke about her passion for historic preservation as a leader of the local Daughters of the American Revolution (DAR) chapter.[88] Brown frequently scoured the countryside for historic relics—books, tea cups, dressing tables, chairs, shaving stands, beds, garden benches, Indian arrowheads, and tomahawks—in her quest to stock her antique store.

Brown's correspondence reveals that she took her job as a merchant of historic goods seriously. In a flurry of letters exchanged with a man from Cordelle, Georgia, intent on procuring a set of antique cup and saucers for a lady friend, Brown wrote that she went out to the "country in search of the coffee cups like the ones you bought from us recently. Could only find one cup and saucer, the other cup having been broken! Wasn't that tough? Can get another set of six. Just say the word, and they will be on their way to the young lady in question and will reach her in time for her birthday." As part of their business venture, Brown and Marshall routinely mailed historical books to interested collectors on spec. This aspect of their business did not always prove profitable as evidenced by a rejection letter from a New York bookseller who wrote that the "books received are in such bad condition owing to your climate that they are practically of no value."[89]

Other Natchez clubwomen melded their writing skills and fondness for local history to assume leadership roles in important civic projects. Club publicist Roane Fleming Byrnes is best remembered for her work to establish the Natchez Trace Parkway, a 444-mile stretch of scenic roadway that winds its way from Nashville, Tennessee, crosses through Alabama, and terminates in Natchez. Byrnes's personal and lifelong career as a clubwoman and civic volunteer offers insights on the way many southern women meshed their personal interest in history with either paid or unpaid employment. Byrnes, like most southern and American women of her time, had no formal training in administration, management, or roadway construction. When elected president of Mississippi's Natchez Trace Association in 1935 at the age of forty-five, she initially demurred from taking the post, stating that she had never even presided over a church meeting.[90]

Byrnes's qualifications to manage the complex roadway project seem questionable given her sheltered upbringing. Born into an old Natchez family in 1890, she grew up in aristocratic surroundings. Living at Ravenna, a two-storied colonial-style house built by her maternal grandparents in 1837, Roane lived among a busy and large household consisting of her grandfather, her parents, a bachelor uncle, a distant widowed cousin, and her mother's sister and husband and their two children, a not uncommon arrangement among elite white southerners of this era. In an unpublished autobiographical sketch Roane recalled her childhood in 1890s Natchez as a time of "unruffled, faintly melancholy satisfaction" with "almost all of us cousins, all of us democrats."[91] A half dozen or more black servants took care of Byrnes and her large family, cooking, cleaning, washing, and maintaining Ravenna's grounds and livestock. With nearly all her daily needs met, Byrnes never needed to drive. Ironically, though her life's work was devoted to building a roadway, Byrnes doesn't seem to have given this limitation much thought, remarking flippantly that "there were always too many other people around to do it for me."[92]

The leisurely lifestyle that allowed the young Byrnes to swim in creek holes, ride horses, and gaze at the stars with her mother also enabled her from an early age to write dozens of romantic tales. Byrnes never achieved commercial success as an author, but over time found ways to channel her creative energies into club work and her chief passion, overseeing the campaign to fund and construct the Natchez Trace Parkway. Building began on the trace project in 1937 but was not completed until May 2005. Even at a time when New Dealers enthusiastically promoted federal investment in infrastructure improvements, convincing Congress to appropriate funding for the project at the height of the Great Depression was difficult. Byrnes tenaciously hounded lawmakers to fund the parkway and pressured individuals to sell their property to make way for road construction. A journalist's account of one of the meetings she presided over is telling of her determination. "Mrs. Byrnes ... badgered congressmen, senators, the National Park Service—anyone—to carry out the dream of the rebirth of the old Natchez Trace for modern day travel."[93]

EXPANDING THEIR BOUNDARIES

The overwhelming majority of journalists (mostly male) who filed more than one hundred stories about the Pilgrimage during its first decade endorsed the work of Natchez clubwomen as practical and timely. Frequently using wisecracking prose, journalists portrayed Natchez clubwomen as a combination of strength and feminine flirtatiousness—steel magnolias on a mission. Many admired the women for their business savvy, spunk, and directness, characteristics not unlike Scarlett O'Hara, the spirited heroine of the decade's bestselling novel. Ernie Pyle described Pilgrimage founder Katherine Miller as "dynamic and sophisticated, a natural-born-doer-of-things." Male columnist Gail Borden approved of garden club members for being "almost entirely lacking in tea-pourers and blossom-snappers." In another column, Pyle lauded one of the "loveliest of the homeowners" for her candidness when she told Pyle, "I stand at the door and shake hands and say, 'We're so glad you could come' and by the time I've said it 1000 times in the afternoon I could cut their throats."[94] Natchez women's sense of humor and their friendly banter with visitors (not unlike the smart repartee of a 1930s film or radio show) won them accolades from tourists and journalists alike.

Much of the clubwomen's appeal to visitors is found in evidence that suggests Natchez clubwomen expanded the boundaries of southern womanhood without fundamentally challenging traditional gender roles. Journalists' glowing portrayals of Natchez clubwomen reveal that outsiders lauded Natchez matrons as purposeful modern women with good business instincts, who nonetheless remained southern "ladies." Taking on more prominent public roles than earlier generations of women, club members looked like demure southern belles on the outside, but in truth, they were much more formidable. As columnist Gail Borden wrote, "In spite of the name of their group, the ones who keep up the club are hard-hitting, energetic business-women whose business these last 10 years has been the saving of their city. They may be interested in magnolias, cape-jasmine, roses and azaleas as such, but their prime motivation is saving this beautiful and romantic southern town from the twin ravages of time and poverty."[95] In Borden's mind, Natchez women situated themselves in the best of both worlds—making a positive civic and economic contribution, while maintaining traditional feminine roles. As the organizers of a venture that generated $100,000 or more in revenues for their town during the late 1930s, according to some accounts, Natchez women won respect and admiration for performing a service within the traditional boundaries of middle- and upper-class white southern womanhood.

Ironically, as the garden clubwomen of 1930s Natchez expanded their tourism enterprise, gaining valuable business experience and new opportunities in public life, they promoted an ideal of southern womanhood far different from the one they lived. Antebellum southern ladies and the postwar women who helped to memorialize the Old South would have led far more sheltered lives than Natchez women of the 1930s, most likely free of business concerns and engagement with public life.[96] By contrast, the daily lives of the garden clubwomen who dressed the part of sheltered antebellum southern ladies on their home tours, were a far cry from the women they represented. When not bustling about in hoopskirts, club members were actively engaged in public life. The Pilgrimage required numerous members

Some of the principal members of the Natchez Garden Club who organized the Natchez Pilgrimage in 1932. Seated in the middle and looking behind her is Katherine Miller, the founder of the historical homes tour. The women seated, left to right, are Alma Kellogg, Ruth Audley Beltzhoover, Miller, Beck Benoist, Clara Ballou, and Lalie Adams. The women standing, left to right, are Emma Marks, Mary Lamdin, Roane Byrnes, and Edna Parker. Earl Norman, photographer. (Courtesy of Louisiana Lower Mississippi Valley Collections, Special Collections, Hill Memorial Library, Louisiana State University Libraries, Baton Rouge.)

to involve themselves in a variety of business roles. Some tried their hand as publicists, speakers, and tour guides. Others negotiated national marketing and licensing agreements and oversaw the restoration of historic properties purchased by the club. One look at the garden clubwomen in an early 1930s photo reveals that they were performing a fascinating kind of minstrelsy. During Pilgrimage season, they dressed for the past, but the rest of the year they revealed themselves as thoroughly modern with their smart bobs, stylish furs, lipstick, and rouge.

THE IDEAL HOME SOUTHERN STYLE

Heritage tourism ventures like the Pilgrimage empowered white southern women to take a more active role in public life, a transition that remained fully rooted within the traditional female domains of house, home and garden. Natchez garden club members often justified their mission by modeling what an ideal home could be in traditional feminine terms that found easy acceptance among both men and women. Quoted in a 1930s magazine article, Pilgrimage founder Katherine Miller stated: "So much is said and done today towards the material progress of our people. I feel that a few days in Natchez, wandering about our homes, will enable our visitors to carry away with them an idea of what a home really can be. Our forefathers built securely, a home, not for today, but for generations. Too few of us live in homes today; we do not realize the peace that can come from a garden, however small. We must begin to create as well as preserve for posterity."[97]

Miller's comments reflected her ongoing commitment to both the early twentieth-century national passion for gardening and the Better Homes America (BHA) movement, a nationwide government and mass media campaign, which promoted individual home ownership, the renovation of older structures, and the purchase of standardized and often scientific household appliances and commodities. The BHA campaign, promoted through displays of model homes built nationwide, magazine articles and government pamphlets, conflated "better homes" with "better communities," "better babies," "healthier families," "happier people," and "better times."[98] Originated in 1921 by Mississippi native Marie Mattingly Meloney, editor of the women's magazine the *Delineator*, the program was enthusiastically embraced by Mississippi women, several of whom won several national Better Homes awards from 1929 through 1931.[99]

Katherine Miller and her peers likely came under the influence of Ellen Woodward—the city beautification enthusiast noted earlier in this chapter—who while serving on the Mississippi State Board of Development encouraged Mississippi towns and citizens to join the annual Better Homes in America competition. Woodward led hundreds of BHA chairwomen she had appointed to promote the ideals of home ownership and improvement, and she did so with language supportive of New Deal tenets. Woodward's optimistic message to her foot soldiers across the state would have resonated with Pilgrimage leaders like Miller, who strongly promoted the sanctity of home ownership. According to Woodward, "Home ownership facilitates thrift ... makes for self-respect and wholesome living ... fosters cooperative activity on the part of all members of the family [and] gives the family an incentive for sacrifice." Her words would have made most Natchez Garden Club members in their quest to save and show off Natchez's antebellum homes feel right at home.[100]

Capitalizing on the popularity of 1930s "Ideal" modern home exhibits that touted the latest in kitchen appliances, bathroom fixtures, and furnishings to visitors hopeful of owning a home someday, Miller and her cohorts envisioned their town's antebellum home tours as another way to cater to white Americans' support of domesticity. Numerous magazine articles featuring inspirational illustrations of home life from the past also may have influenced the clubwomen. Such stories linked traditional ideals of domesticity—female homemakers, well-cared for children, and a well-managed home—to national patriotism.[101] What better way to capitalize on such ideals than to show off Natchez's antebellum homes, many of which had been within the same family for several generations?

Simultaneously, Miller's statement also implied criticism of the domestic and family values of nonsoutherners, who in her words had no "idea of what a home really can be." From Miller's perspective, the most appealing kind of home was one built not only for "today, but for generations"—a far different kind of home than many Americans lived in, if they lived in a single-family residence at all. Miller believed that domestic bliss depended upon not only a "securely" built home, but also a "garden, however small," an ideal she frequently mentioned in articles written about her. Miller advocated a home aesthetic in keeping with her own home, Hope Farm, a spacious but somewhat modest cottage, built in 1775 to house an early Spanish governor when Mississippi was under Spanish rule. When Katherine and Balfour Miller bought Hope Farm in the late 1920s the home was hardly inhabitable; the gardens were overgrown, the paint was peeling, and the upstairs gallery surrounding one wing was rickety. Over time as their finances allowed, the Millers restored the house to its former grandeur, filling the rooms with antiques and the outdoor garden with "almost every known kind of old-time flower."[102] In many ways, Miller was a model homeowner, who closely followed the Better Homes' recipe for domestic stability and contentment.

Miller showcased her home as one that lived up to the national standards prescribed by the Better Homes movement, but with a southern twist. Among several attractive photos of Hope Farm published in a 1930s magazine article about Miller and the Pilgrimage, there is a photo of her kitchen. Although Miller was childless, one of the photos showed black family servant Anna Higgs feeding Katherine's baby nephew in the bright, clean room. At a time when many home economists and civic leaders favored servant-less homes filled with modern household appliances to help wives and mothers tackle their domestic chores, the photo implied that Miller set a different ideal for the southern home. The Miller home had it all—a reliable, well-trained servant, the latest appliances, and even a well-scrubbed, adorable baby. The table is modern as are the cabinets and fixtures, nothing like how the home's original eighteenth-century kitchen would have appeared.[103] The photo suggested that contemporary appliances were not the only commodities that made a modern home sound and efficient, but that retaining black servants was another important component of a well-managed home. In short, the image communicated that black servants were not simply nostalgic emblems of yesteryear, but were just as essential as laborsaving technologies in creating an efficient home that did not overburden homemakers with excessive drudgery. While Miller worked tirelessly to preserve her town's antebellum past, she, like many white southern women, was unwilling to sacrifice modern conveniences—including domestic servants to help her maintain a comfortable home. Indeed, servants like Anna Higgs enabled Miller and her fellow club members to devote endless hours to their club work. Katherine Miller and her closest cohorts—department store owner Ruth Audley Beltzhoover, club treasurer Alma Kellogg, and Mary Louise Kendall, active in her husband's profitable Coca-Cola distribution franchise—saw the Pilgrimage as the best of two very different worlds. Not only did their heritage tourism enterprise empower them as women in the modern business world and generate needed revenues to fix up their aging homes, it also created a vehicle to promote traditional white domestic values rooted in the heritage of the Old South.

HOME TOURS

Capitalizing on the interest in antebellum southern home life and Natchez's abundance of antebellum estates, the focal point of the Pilgrimage season were the daily home tours of some of the town's most iconic—although often dilapidated—estates. Tour brochures produced by the Natchez Garden Club focused on furnishings and architectural features that emphasized wealth, status, and connections to European culture. Of Elms Court, visitors were told that the home represented "a departure from the usual type of architecture in the section, being a copy of an Italian Renaissance villa. It is especially admired for its lacy iron-work which was brought over from Belgium. House contains many treasures—portraits, busts, chandeliers, china ... and dining table over which is suspended a punkah, a relic of slave days.... Elmscourt has always been famous for the beauty of its entertainments and the number of celebrities who have visited there."[104]

The home tours, as with all aspects of the Pilgrimage experience, offered a selective rendering of Natchez's slave past. In keeping with most cultural mediums of the early twentieth century, the home tours repressed and avoided discussions about the causes of the Civil War and its consequences, slavery, and race relations. Early tour scripts rarely, if ever, mentioned slavery and usually only to bolster claims of an antebellum homeowner's massive wealth. In describing Homewood, the estate David Hunt built for his newlywed daughter, a Pilgrimage tour script noted, "one million bricks were used, all of which were made on the premises by slaves." After pointing out the many noteworthy architectural features of the home, guides noted, "David Hunt was the richest man of his day in Mississippi, and ... the largest slave holder in America, ... at one time owning 1700 slaves."[105] While tour scripts subtly acknowledged slave labor, details of antebellum slave life were largely ignored. As David Blight notes, "A segregated society required a segregated historical memory.... Slavery (and the whole black experience) had no place in the formulas by which most Americans found meanings in the Civil War."[106]

Although nearly absent from the scripts used by Pilgrimage guides, African Americans were not entirely invisible from the tour. Most blacks, usually women, remained in the background of tours and portrayed subservient roles, similar to the publicity photographs in magazines that showed black maids dressed in slave costumes adjusting their mistresses' hoopskirts or helping them into a carriage. As described in one promotional booklet, blacks took on the role of docile, faithful servants ready to assist visitors:

> Perhaps a grizzled, bent, old ex-slave stands to bow you in, or a strapping courteous young negro will direct the parking of your car and reply if you question him, that he is of Natchez or Louisiana, as the case may be, and that his people have been here since 'befo' de War' in the service of the same family. At another place as you step up onto the gallery a little colored boy stoops and wipes your shoes lest you have the embarrassment of taking in unnoticed souvenirs of park and garden.[107]

On rare occasions, African Americans took on speaking roles during home tours, as was the case with Zereeta, a black hostess serving at Melrose, one of Natchez's largest estates, now owned by the National Park Service. According to Marion Kelly Ferry, whose family owned Melrose at the time, during the early years of the Pilgrimage, Zereeta was particularly creative in the stories she performed for attentive audiences. One day Ferry overheard the black woman tell a group of tourists about a horsehair trunk that sat in the corner of the dairy building. "'That is the very trunk that old Mr. Davis [the original owner of Melrose] carried with him to the California Gold Rush in 1849. That is the very trunk that crossed this continent," she told her audience. When Ferry approached Zereeta later and reminded her that the ancestor in question had probably never heard of California let alone the Gold Rush, Zereeta remained unconvinced. According to her employer, Zereeta said, "'Aww, Miss Marion, they just loves that story.'"[108] In the minds of many Pilgrimage hostesses—black and white—the real purpose of the event was for entertainment and profit rather than strict historical accuracy.

Seldom did magazine or newspaper articles mention antebellum blacks or the modern-day African American community working behind the scenes to serve Pilgrimage tourists. Mississippi writer David Cohn proved to be the rare exception, using racialized imagery in an article published in 1940 to state: "Natchez is not, as you might imagine, all moonlight, Quality, and ante-bellum houses. It is also Negroes." Cohn tells the story of his "old friend" Green Smith, better known as Santa Claus, a "gray-haired man of about sixty, with pork-chop lips, popeyes, and an irresistible smile." Smith, who sold roasted peanuts, was a favorite among tourists and local children. Noting that Smith's business was good because of the large tourist trade, Cohn added that Sweetheart, Smith's wife, "has more washing and ironing for the white folks than she can do."[109] In the Pilgrimage's rendering of the past, as elsewhere in the South, contemporary black laborers continued to be portrayed much the way Lost Cause ideology imagined slaves: using longstanding physical stereotypes, who were loyal, contented workers performing menial labor that whites typically shunned.

SELECTIVE DRAMATIZATIONS OF THE PAST

When not organizing home tours or attending to the countless tasks to ensure a successful tourist season, garden clubwomen put their creative juices to work writing and choreographing pageants, a popular entertainment form that reached its zenith in the early years of the twentieth century. The pageants were comprised of tableaux, scenes presented by costumed actors who remained silent and appeared as if in a picture.[110] The Confederate Pageant complemented the romanticized narrative of Natchez's past conveyed by the house tours. Among the early historic pageants that reenacted Natchez's past with dance, costumes, and music was "Under Many Flags," written by Elizabeth Dunbar Murray, who was involved in creating numerous productions in the early twentieth century. Written in 1916 to commemorate the two hundredth anniversary of the founding of Natchez, the pageant had never been performed due to the outbreak of World War I. Dusted off and presented as a street play staged for the first Pilgrimage, Murray's production represented the town's Indian, English, and Spanish past.[111] When the annual pageant moved indoors in 1933, garden club members created a variety of tableaux based on Murray's original drama. White Natchez men, women, and children performed in the annual pageants, many playing various roles for years.

That these pageants so resonated with the American public in the 1930s has much to do with early pageant organizers' reliance on popular performance techniques of the 1930s, most notably those found in motion pictures. For example, organizers integrated ballet numbers that had absolutely nothing to do with the narrative, in a manner that closely paralleled film musicals of the era. The entrance of the Pilgrimage Queen and King and their royal court preceded a large group of dancers wearing contemporary ballet costumes. In a scaled back, less sophisticated version of a 1930s Busby Berkeley musical, the dance numbers offered a popular form of entertainment, but did little to advance a plot ostensibly dedicated to highlighting key moments in Natchez history. Pilgrimage organizers periodically staged some of the early pageants outdoors on the park-like grounds of the town's most elaborate estates. With the homes prominently featured in the background, framed by stately moss-covered oaks, pageant audiences reveled in Natchez's natural beauty, enhancing the "authenticity" of the narrative.

Much of the pageant content put women at the center of a romanticized genteel past. While the female organizers paid tribute to Natchez's masculine martial virtues, men seemed more like useful props than central figures in the narrative. Audiences saw no battle scenes, nor did any of the tableaux depict the outcome of military engagements. Instead, pageant viewers witnessed the more feminine social aspects of preparing for war where women organized Confederate balls to "celebrate" the impending departure of young cadets to the front, or sewed the Bonnie Blue Confederate flag that would be carried into battle. Additional tableaux created scenes of aristocratic leisure—dancing and painting lessons, tea parties, weddings, croquet games, and Maypole dances featuring young children in frilly costumes. Other tableaux dramatized more serious rituals, such as family prayers and graduation exercises.

The only scene that prominently featured men was the foxhunt tableau where the hunters toasted one another after a successful chase. Here again audiences saw a domesticated scene, far removed from sweating horses, barking hounds, and men closing in for the kill. The hunters appeared nothing like the virile, athletic sportsmen and militia members so prevalent only a few decades earlier in Natchez public traditions. Pageant organizers may have choreographed a toasting scene because it would have been impossible to stage an actual hunting scene. Moreover, raising their glasses in a toast was likely considered a male bonding ritual. Such scenes were prevalent within liquor advertisements of the era, which linked their libations with the imagined pleasures of being a white male in the Old South.[112] The Natchez hunting men, who toasted one another as their hunting dogs looked on, complemented the camaraderie found in popular advertisements, while recalling a masculine ritual of the antebellum era.

The garden clubwomen's attention to historical accuracy in costuming and design was lacking in the earliest pageants. Tight production budgets accounted for some of the inaccuracies. William Adams, who served as King of the Confederate parade and ball in 1932, remembered wearing "some make-shift kind of costume . . . a pair of gray flannel slacks and some sort of morning coat that they must have rented from somebody."[113] One year later with the introduction of the more formalized Confederate Pageant, kings began wearing Confederate uniforms, a tradition continued for many years. Mary Louise Geddes, who served as a member of Adams's royal court in 1932 recalled that she wore a "very simple dress made of tarlatan," which cost less than twelve dollars for materials and labor.[114] As the pageants drew larger crowds over the course of the decade, pageant coordinators devoted greater attention to the authenticity of the costumes worn by participants, relying on the *Godey's Ladies Book* and *Peterson's*, two popular mid-nineteenth-century magazines that featured intricately detailed drawings and descriptions of clothing worn by men, women, and children. Seamstresses frequently designed early pageant gowns as exact replicas of famous ball gowns and morning dresses worn by an antebellum ancestor. In the tradition of antebellum Natchez gentry, dressmakers often adorned Pilgrimage dresses with lace and beading imported from Austria, France, London, and Asia.[115]

The attention devoted to creating historically accurate costumes did not extend to the representation of slavery in Natchez pageants. The pageant creators ignored slavery and sectional conflict as major contributing factors to the Civil War, preferring instead to emphasize reunification. For example, the 1938 pageant told the story of a young man from New York who traveled to Natchez in the 1850s to visit his southern cousins. While in Natchez, the young man "finds the girl of his dreams" and decides to remain in Natchez. As Natchez troops are being feted on the eve of leaving for battle, the hero of the story, "now a true Southerner" enlists "to fight for his adopted country."[116]

Also ignored was the devastating outcome of the war. Rather, pageant creators preferred to glorify the martial virtues of southern soldiers. In a show of patriotism and sectional reconciliation, early programs concluded with the entrance of the American flag, demonstrating in David Blight's words how "romance triumphed over reality, [and] sentimental remembrance won over ideological memory."[117]

Although choreographers omitted the topic of slavery during early pageants, African Americans performed black spirituals at barbecues and other Pilgrimage functions around town. By 1938 Pilgrimage organizers responded to white Americans' strong interest in African American folk culture by promoting "Heaven Bound," a theatrical presentation of spirituals performed by local black churches. According to one magazine writer, the star of the show was the ninety-year-old "Aunt" Ibby Robinson, a slave before the war, who sang 'Pilgrim of Sorrow,' as she walked haltingly thru the audience, occasionally prompted by a singer in the gallery."[118] By featuring an old, enfeebled, and forgetful black woman—the ultimate nonthreatening black character—"Heaven Bound" fit comfortably within the parameters of the white-controlled Pilgrimage narrative. The question remains as to whether the garden club would have promoted a show that starred performers who were not old, enfeebled, and silent on the slave past and contemporary racial issues.

From 1940 through 1965, pageant organizers included a tableau representing slaves picking cotton while singing a black spiritual. According to one early pageant brochure, "Among the sweetest memories of the Old South is that of singing pickers, their mellow voices enlivening labor with song, and filling the evening air with laughter." Early pageant coordinators used the scene of contented slave laborers to note the paternalistic relationship between slave masters and their property, a key tenet of Lost Cause ideology. One early program text stated: "A planter looked after the welfare of his slaves and was loved by them, for they were carefree and happily sang at their work."[119]

Natchez's Confederate Pageant fit squarely within a larger national story that resonated with Americans' love of traditional, patriotic narratives in the 1930s. In many respects the town's annual pageants were strikingly nationalistic. Ironically, while many of the early programs were entitled "The Confederate Pageant," only a small portion of the program related to Civil War history. Rather, the pageants traced Natchez from its eighteenth-century colonial-era beginnings, first depicting the Natchez Indian tribe, the earliest dwellers of the region, followed by the periods of French, English, and Spanish colonial rule before the establishment of Mississippi as a US territory in 1798. Not until the close of the program did the antebellum period and the Civil War make its appearance. By depicting Natchez first as a European colony and later as the capital of a US territory, pageant organizers positioned the town within a bigger national story, emphasizing the colonial period and the early days of the republic. Early pageant narratives tapped into the popularity of historical fiction and biographical accounts of these eras, portraying them as heroic and transformative. Natchez's ties to the failed Confederacy only enhanced what was already a compelling story, adding romance, military valor, and tragedy to the town's historical narrative.

The inclusion of national heroes in pageant narratives amplified these nationalistic overtones. Early pageants paid tribute to well-known Americans who had either visited Natchez or played a role in its history. These included Senator Henry Clay, Mexican War hero Zachary Taylor, and celebrated naturalist John Audubon, who completed several paintings while residing in Natchez. Jefferson Davis, the only president of the Confederacy and a Mississippi native who wed a Natchez belle, received minor attention for his role as a Mexican War hero rather than his secessionist politics and Civil War service. Featuring early American heroes revered by 1930s school children and adults alike further enhanced Natchez's reputation as a worthy national historic site that espoused patriotic ideals.

Producers of the pageant used Natchez's ties to the Old World to enhance the town's reputation as a site of genteel culture, another means to situate Natchez within a larger, appealing national framework and legitimize the South as a standard-bearer of cultural authority. The program text for numerous scenes reminded viewers that the people of Natchez "led a cultured life." In promoting historical Natchez as a repository of genteel values, pageant organizers looked to Europe for guidance. In reenacting a ball given in honor of esteemed politician Henry Clay in the 1850s at a local estate, audiences learned that "great mansions were built and furnishings brought from the Old World that gave to these mansions a splendor equal to the best in Europe. Guests from far and near came in costly carriages and their negro drivers and footmen watched from the lawn the splendor of the scene within."[120] Early pageant audiences were invited to join in the final dance scene of a Confederate ball, further heightening the vicarious appeal of their heritage tourism experience.

THE MASS APPEAL OF THE OLD SOUTH

Natchez's successful entrée into the heritage tourism marketplace, while owing much to appealing pageantry, can be attributed to several pivotal developments, with the first being the rapid growth of modern tourism. An increasing number of Americans owned automobiles and traveled the nation's network of new and improved roads, and this mobility played an integral role in building Natchez as a successful 1930s tourist destination and in promoting the Natchez Trace, a scenic motor route. Surprisingly, vacation expenditures rose consistently during the first six years of the Depression. This unexpected development can be attributed to the expansion of paid vacations among American workers and the development of an aggressive and sophisticated professional tourism apparatus at both the state and federal levels. By the end of the 1930s "over twenty-five million workers received vacations with pay, and sixty million Americans were taking at least a week's vacation away from home."[121]

A surge in economic nationalism during the Great Depression, symbolized by the popular "Buy American" movement, also played a role in the growth of tourism. By the 1930s advocates of paid vacation and tourism executives convinced many Americans that leisure and vacations away from home were "a necessity for the social, cultural, and economic health of the nation."[122] Newspaper mogul William Randolph Hearst Jr. fervently promoted the "Buy American" campaign in editorials, headlines, and newspaper articles published in the twenty-seven newspapers he owned. Hearst bombarded readers with the claim that "cheap foreign goods" and "alien manufacturers" were at the root of the nation's economic troubles.[123] The "See America First" campaign, which grew out of the "Buy American" movement, encouraged Americans to satisfy their wanderlust with domestic travel before venturing overseas. Consumer travel, according to campaign advocates, was not only personally satisfying but nationally beneficial.

Not only did the mass media prod Americans to plan vacations to historic sites, but they also nurtured Americans' interest in the Old South. The popular success of D. W. Griffith's controversial film *Birth of a Nation*, first screened in 1915, encouraged filmmakers to develop southern-themed movies because these films made money.[124] While *Gone with the Wind*, released in 1939, stands as the most successful film of this genre, many earlier films reflected similar romanticized images of the South. During the Depression a number of musical extravaganzas were set in the Old South, such as *Hearts of Dixie*, an early talkie picture that showed former slaves remaining faithful to an old plantation after the Civil War. Movies about the antebellum South starring Shirley Temple ranked among the most popular films of the era. *The Littlest Rebel* and *The Little Colonel*, both produced in 1935, show Temple being adored by both her white and black "families" on the old plantation. Filled with banjo-playing "happy darky" stereotypes, these films helped to reinvigorate stereotypes introduced in antebellum minstrelsy and popular music, and later by plantation fiction from the 1880s.[125] Many of these same themes found their way into the Natchez Pilgrimage's narrative of life in the Old South.

Travelogue newsreels, often accompanying feature films, introduced armchair travelers to a host of American locales, including the Deep South. MGM's travelogue, *Old Natchez on the Mississippi*, was one of several newsreels shown in theaters nationwide and overseas. Produced in Technicolor and recorded in five languages, *Old Natchez* featured happy slaves at work with particular attention devoted to elderly Jane Johnson, a former slave credited with saving Melrose from destruction during the Civil War. At the close of the film, the narrator states, "Out of the more practical features of the North we may have obtained our economic status, but it is to the South that we turn for the music and romance of our yesteryears."[126]

National advertisers also capitalized on the nation's attraction to southern themes in advertisements that frequently featured stock southern characters and locales. Fueled by the ongoing success of Aunt Jemima and her pancake flour, first introduced to consumers in the 1880s, American advertisers flooded the 1930s marketplace with similar subservient black advertising spokespersons. A survey of *Time* magazine from the 1930s found both logical and absurd representations in advertisers' use of southern stereotypes. For example, Virginia's Commission of Conservation and Development promoted "Hams from Ole Virginia as good as though you went to the plantation and had Mammy cook it."[127]

Ever on the lookout for new ways to promote Natchez as a haven of the Old South to prospective tourists, early Pilgrimage organizers contracted with a variety of advertisers who placed pictures of Natchez homes on their products. Lillie Vidal Boatner, a longtime executive secretary of the Natchez Garden Club, and club president Harriet Dixon wrote letters to large corporations urging them to include Natchez imagery in their advertising. Their efforts proved enormously successful. Mobil Oil featured full color photos of Natchez home exteriors on its calendars, as did Congress Company on playing cards. Tomlinson Company developed a line of Natchez-inspired reproduction furniture. *House and Garden* designed a Natchez bedspread,

Kate Don Brandon, president of the Natchez Garden Club, working with executive secretary Lillie Vidal Boatner, who helped negotiate numerous licensing deals for the club, ca. 1936. Earl Norman, photographer. (Courtesy of Kathie Boatner Blankenstein and Chesney Blankenstein Doyle.)

while Campana Company, a manufacturer of toiletries, offered an Old South line of soaps, memory boxes, and talcum powders. Advertising their toiletries as "quaint as a hoop-skirt, gay as a parasol, colorful as a plantation garden," magazine ads for Old South not only capitalized on familiar and popular icons of the American South, but also listed the dates of upcoming Pilgrimages. Boatner's and Dixon's most prestigious licensing agreement came when they convinced Gorham Silver to create a silver pattern, designed and named after a motif found on the parlor furniture of the Melrose estate.[128]

Fueled by their negotiating success, the marketing duo began contacting celebrities who would add prestige to the Pilgrimage by their attendance. Famous guests who accepted their invitation included Henry Ford and his wife, John D. Rockefeller, Mary Pickford, and General Douglas MacArthur. Beloved ventriloquist character Charlie McCarthy expressed his regrets in not being able to come to the 1941 Pilgrimage when he wrote playfully: "[Edgar] Bergen just won't let me get away for any nice social events. He just keeps me here and makes me work all the time. The guy's jealous of me, that's why."[129] Lillie Boatner sought to influence film history when she wrote movie star Myrna Loy, suggesting she would make a wonderful Scarlett O'Hara in MGM's *Gone with the Wind*. When Vivian Leigh signed on for the part, Boatner, ever the skilled publicist, followed up with a note inviting her to Pilgrimage. To further entice the star to come to Natchez, the club named a beautiful japonica bush at Melrose for Leigh. They airmailed her dozens of the red blooms and she was photographed with the flowers. The photo was released to hundreds of papers nationwide, crediting the Natchez Garden Club and announcing upcoming tour dates. Although no record shows Leigh actually visiting Natchez, the film crew for *Gone with the Wind* used the town as the site for background shots instead of Atlanta.[130] An enormous coup came when the club and its Pilgrimage was featured on the Maxwell House Show Boat radio program, which was broadcast from coast to coast. Boatner would later write of her publicity work for the garden club: "Ideas came to us fast and furiously in those hectic days—and I mean HECTIC."[131]

The mass media exhibited an incredibly strong interest in the American South, if not perhaps an obsessive fascination. Between 1929 and 1941 the *Reader's Guide to Periodical Literature* listed approximately 4,206 magazine articles featuring the South.[132] Publications targeted to a mass audience typically featured favorable coverage of the South, celebrating the region's distinctive food, architecture, furnishings, and gardens. Further embellishing the South's reputation as an attractive tourist destination, several magazines during the 1930s published sentimental memoirs of life in the Old South, reminiscent of the plantation stories of Thomas Nelson Page and Joel Chandler Harris, in which faithful slaves were characterized as "happy darkies." Natchez tourism profited with the strong media interest in the South. A steady stream of positive feature stories with photo spreads on Natchez appeared in mass consumer publications during the first two decades of the Pilgrimage, including *Better Homes and Gardens*, *Atlantic Monthly*, *Saturday Evening Post*, *House and Gardens*, *Ladies Home Journal*, the *National Geographic Magazine*, the *Chicago Tribune* and the *New York Times*.[133] Such articles give the impression that publishers and readers could not get enough of the Old South and its antebellum homes.

Further investigation reveals that publishers and authors had more than "moonlight and magnolias" on their minds when it came to coverage of the South. Critical articles of the South appeared in such leading intellectual periodicals as *American Mercury*, *Literary Digest*, *New Republic*, and *Scribner's*. The *Yale Review* pondered the question, "Is the South Advancing?" while *Nation* reported that the South was the "No. 1 economic problem" and *New Republic* wrote on the "Plight of the South."

Increasingly, publications scrutinized the South's racist practices and problems. Several prominent African American writers voiced their concerns on the status of American blacks. *Harper's* published scholar Horace Mann Bond's thoughtful "A Negro Looks at His South" in 1931. Bond, a native southerner, complained that white southerners defined the region by the cultural attributes of the white population, where "the Negro is merely a bit of back-stage scenery used to deepen the effect of the leading silhouette. In the South, the white man is the southerner, the Negro-well, a Negro."[134]

In the spring of 1931 when nine black youths were falsely tried, convicted, and sentenced to death for the rape of two white women aboard a train outside of Scottsboro, Alabama, African Americans came to the forefront in a news story that gripped the nation for much of the decade and into the 1940s. As the case wound its way through a lengthy appeals process, national magazines and newspapers provided ample coverage. The *New York Times* devoted 766 articles to the case with sobering headlines such as "Nine Negro Youths to Start New Fight for Their Lives in Alabama Court."[135] The Scottsboro case was but one of many negative events concerning southern race troubles published during the 1930s. More than 150 magazine articles about lynching appeared, while newspapers such as the *New York Times* and *Los Angeles Times* printed more than two thousand articles on the subject.[136] Ironically, many of the same publications updating readers on the fate of the Scottsboro defendants and lynching statistics also promoted the pleasures of vacationing in the Old South. The *New York Times* published at least fifty articles on Natchez from 1932 to 1940 with the majority promoting the town as a tourist destination.

A HUNGER FOR AUTHENTICITY

The reconciliation between South and North in the early 1900s laid the groundwork to celebrate southern culture in new ways during the age of Jim Crow. Intrigued by the many highly favorable images of the South—as well as the negative portrayals—many Americans, particularly northerners, hungered to see the region for themselves. Such an experience satisfied what cultural historian Warren Susman characterizes as Americans' passionate desire to "know and feel the details of life, its styles in different places, to make oneself part of some other's experience."[137] The Great Depression motivated Americans to rediscover their nation's history. By returning to the past, Americans could find a sense of security in a time of tremendous upheaval, a way "to know what kind of firm ground other men, belonging to generations before us, have found to stand on."[138] This hunger to rediscover the American character and through it the American Dream stimulated a return to traditional values and a preoccupation with heroes from the nation's past.

Closely related to their need to document and experience the past, Americans held a strong, nostalgic longing for a national history that they perceived as simpler and more attractive than the uncertainties posed by 1930s America. Simply put, heritage tourism events like the Pilgrimage offered an antidote to the worries of life in Depression-era America. In discovering the pleasures of the Old South in 1930s Natchez, as expressed through a parade of romanticized tourist experiences—once-elegant mansions presided over by gracious hostesses, Confederate pageants bathed in romantic imagery, barbecues prepared by southern "mammies," evening balls, and programs of black spirituals—white visitors encountered what they perceived as a simpler, golden era in America's past, offering a sense of hope and inspiration for grappling with the anxieties of the present.

As Americans searched for a usable past, sales of historical fiction and biographies soared. Popular works of historical fiction both celebrated and criticized the southern way of life. These included the epic sagas *Gone with the Wind* and Stark Young's *So Red the Rose* as well as Erskine Caldwell's stories of poor whites in *Tobacco Road*. Moving beyond the pleasures of novel reading, the Pilgrimage invited 1930s audiences to step inside the world of Scarlett O'Hara and Rhett Butler and experience vicariously a carefully constructed mythical past.

Americans eager to learn firsthand about their nation's past flocked to numerous southern heritage tourism sites during the 1930s and the decades that followed, in what became an annual rite of spring. Virginia enticed tourists to experience the colonial era in several house museums, most notably Mount Vernon (the nation's oldest house museum) and Thomas Jefferson's Monticello, opened as a tourist site in 1923. Colonial Williamsburg, launched in 1934, took heritage tourism to a new level. Here, tourists could view the homes, shops, a church, and government buildings of an entire colonial town. Richmond, once the capital of the Confederacy, used the motto "Down Where the South Begins" to promote its Civil War monuments, battlefields, and Confederate Museum (now the Museum of the Confederacy). Charleston, South Carolina, captivated growing numbers of visitors after the city experienced a burst of historic preservation activism in the 1920s, a place where tourists were told they were likely to meet an "old-time negro." Atlanta, which had lost most of its antebellum mansions in General Sherman's "march to the sea," instead touted itself as the "Metropolis of the Southeast" and "Gate City of the South." Further south, Savannah described itself as a "tourist paradise." Closer to Natchez, tourists on a southern pilgrimage could travel to New Orleans, which became known as an exotic location filled with romance, history, and culture. Biloxi, Mississippi, promoted the Gulf Coast as the "American Rivera," and in Alabama, Mobile's Azalea Trail and Bellingrath Gardens became known as a springtime garden paradise.[139] As Cox writes, "States throughout the South bolstered the region's image as a place that was not only a great destination to escape northern winters but also one where northern tourists could personally engage with the Old South narrative of plantations, black servants, and rural America."[140] What distinguished Natchez from its competitors in the heritage tourism market were the large quantity of tour homes open to the public (usually about two dozen) among close to fifty in all that were easily visible to visitors on foot and from their cars. These included opulent town houses like Stanton Hall and equally stunning suburban villas like Melrose, which embraced "the town like a crown of jewels." According to Mimi Miller, director of the Historic Natchez Foundation, which has played a pivotal role in preserving the homes, "The architecture here is unique and very much Natchez, as compared to New Orleans. . . . We probably have the largest collection of nineteenth-century preserved interiors in America. We have that rare situation of houses that still have the original faux marbling, the original wallpaper. That's what Natchez has to offer more than any other community in the world."[141] In short, Natchez in the 1930s and the years that followed offered more bang for tourists' bucks than nearly any other historic destination in the Deep South.

PILGRIMAGE AUDIENCE RECEPTION

On the surface, white tourists and journalists participating in early Pilgrimages seemed to unanimously endorse the event. A closer examination, however, reveals that Natchez pilgrims responded in a variety of ways to Mississippi and Natchez that were both ambivalent and sometimes negative. Early news stories filed by journalists—many from the North—expressed a sense of uncertainty, if not trepidation, regarding their visits to Natchez. Well-traveled journalist Ernie Pyle, expected "to see almost a ghost town, with muddy streets, broken store windows and vacant shacks, and I supposed we'd have to make the best of an 1880 boarding house or something."[142]

A 1938 letter from Baltimore educator Peter Carmichael, who taught philosophy at Louisiana State University, reflected similar anxieties that plagued wary northerners as they journeyed south. "I came to Louisiana two years ago expecting, while crossing the State of Mississippi, to encounter Neanderthals living in caves and flying at one another with awful shillelehs," Carmichael wrote. "The preview which one had received in distant Baltimore aroused nothing but alarm and withdrawing. So when I reached the borders and started across the State along the edge of the Gulf of Mexico, I was much afraid." As Carmichael traveled through Mississippi, he found himself looking for evidence of lynchings, writing, "I began to look around for ropes and faggots and was careful to inspect every tree limb and the arms of telephone poles, expecting to see on all sides the incontrovertible evidence of Mississippi's principal business in life." Relieved when he found no evidence of foul play, the tone of Carmichael's article relaxed as he took pleasure in Mississippi's scenic beauty and was charmed by the gracious Natchez women he met.[143]

We would expect to find more 1930s accounts like Professor Carmichael's, or even more scathingly negative commentary on the region's shortcomings, but this is somewhat surprisingly not the case. Journalists, tourists, and scholars took comfort in Natchez's ability to distance itself from a turbulent modern world. Professor Carmichael approached Natchez as a kind of mythical experience immersed in a distant past. "The happy sense of great remoteness, not only from cities but also from today, as if one were witnessing scenes of the sixteenth century; the feel of nature in one of its gentlest and yet most exquisitely somber moods, of flowing campestral lands, of turns and descents into medieval forest, will be remembered during many an idyllic hour to come."[144]

Carmichael was not alone in seeing Natchez as a welcome retreat far from the chaos of cities and a modern, troubled world. In numerous accounts of trips to 1930s Natchez other writers were seduced by the community's pastoral charms. In writing of her first Pilgrimage, Lillian Meriwether found solace in "trees arching their branches overhead, and birds flying . . . old liveoaks with their moss hung branches and the gardens beyond. To a city dweller nothing could be more alluring." *Chicago Tribune* reporter India Moffett found in Natchez a source of inspiration for Americans. "Every young person should be brought to see these relics of the great past of this section of our country. History is a living, breathing thing here. Here is an atmosphere of true hospitality and friendliness, of gentle living far removed from the hectic life that is ours in metropolitan centers."[145]

Numerous writers likened a trip to Natchez as a kind of religious pilgrimage to a sacred shrine. *Chicago Tribune* writer Gail Borden in 1936 proclaimed that "if ever a place should be made a national shrine—which, in this case, God forbid—that place is Natchez. For it has stood almost untouched these 200 years and more." Though Borden questioned his sentimentality in wanting to preserve a town like Natchez, he argued that the Pilgrimage was a way to stand firm in the face of change. "But it is not easy to see some beautiful house, some keystone of a family's growth through centuries, torn down to make room for apartments, cheap stores, rickety bungalows and all the other things associated with 'modernity.'"[146] Another writer that same year described the appeal of southern destinations like Natchez as a place where pilgrims could "worship at deep Dixie's shrine of springtime beauty [that] has become a part of the life of thousands in every state in these United States of America."[147] Natchez clubwomen's savvy decision to use the popular term "pilgrimage" for their heritage tourism venture sparked newspaper and magazine feature writers' imaginations, who churned out copy depicting Natchez's scenic charms as a must-see national shrine.

Garden club members mirrored journalists' work, portraying the Pilgrimage and Natchez as a soothing antidote for the stresses of modern life. They beckoned travelers to hurry to Natchez so that they could relive the past. "Go now that you may enter as an invited guest, which is so large a part of that atmosphere 'of belonging,'" one guidebook urged. "It is an elusive quality and defies attempts at close analysis, but gives to a Pilgrim the delightful and strange emotion of living in another time."[148]

Club member and author Theodora Marshall noted a litany of troubles white visitors to Natchez could escape: "While the rest of the world is fretting over war threats, money fears, business booms, racial antagonisms, industrial upheavals, spiritual chaos, Natchez reclines in her garden-like seclusion, with the poise and serenity of a 'grande dame' of the old world, free to enjoy the gentle felicities of the 'peace which the world cannot take away.' It is this peace that the new age is finding in Natchez."[149] Marshall glossed over the fact that her hometown and the South as a whole were immersed in dangerous and often lethal racial antagonisms. Instead, Marshall, like other Pilgrimage publicists, focused on the appeals of Natchez's "garden-like seclusion" and "halcyon days of long ago." Natchezian Nola Nance Oliver in her 1940 guidebook wrote of black churches where visitors could still hear spirituals sung and a "pahson" [parson] "eager to greet 'our white friends.'" The author also shared her town's longstanding custom of "Penny Day" where coins were collected in downtown stores for "old darky beggars," a gesture she hailed as "thoughtful" and "good-natured" for the "needy Negro from his 'white folks.'"[150] Promoting the old ways of the Old South to white visitors, Pilgrimage organizers emphasized a simpler, more harmonious era in America's past, far removed from economic troubles, untrustworthy big businesses, and "spiritual chaos." The Natchez Pilgrimage reassured white visitors that despite the social and economic havoc wreaked by the Civil War, a people and its cultural values could survive and be revitalized through hard work and perseverance. While not all tourists accepted the narratives peddled in Natchez, many visitors fed up with the nation's high unemployment and economic troubles, found the Natchez Garden Club's messages uplifting and soothing.

The responses of professionals and civic leaders who came to Natchez during the early Pilgrimage years offers additional insights into audience reaction to the town and its popular heritage tourism venture. The University of Chicago sociologists, whose study *Deep South* focused on Natchez social and cultural life, offers one of the most fascinating examinations of the community in the early 1930s. The research of Allison Davis, Burleigh Gardner, and his wife Mary Gardner was one of several participant-observer studies conducted by sociologists in regions throughout the United States during the 1930s.[151] Allison Davis, assisted by his wife Elizabeth, and the Gardners lived among their Natchez subjects for nearly two years beginning in 1933, much longer than most sociologists who conducted similar projects. Moreover, Allison Davis, the lead investigator, was African American. As a biracial team, the researchers could integrate themselves respectively within the white and black communities of Natchez, even as they carefully followed the social mores of a segregated town so as not to create suspicion.[152]

Historians today regard *Deep South* as an important primary source that documented class and caste relationships in a southern town. Although they carefully noted and analyzed the segregated customs of the town and the enormous economic disparity between whites and blacks, the University of Chicago researchers remained objective in their observations of a heritage tourism amusement that presented the "life of the old plantation days," a familiar narrative communicated throughout the South during the 1930s. Rather than critiquing the racially biased messages that promoted Lost Cause ideology in Natchez, the Gardners, the white members of the research team, focused their observations on the Pilgrimage as a vehicle that enabled upper-middle-class women to demonstrate their reverence for the past and enhance their class status. *Deep South* does not reveal if the Gardners completely embraced the Natchez Garden Club's version of the Lost Cause. We do know that Mary Gardner (a northerner by birth) during her Natchez stay accepted an invitation to serve as a Pilgrimage hostess and dressed the part in an antebellum gown loaned by a garden club member.¹⁵³ The Gardners may have assumed the role of Pilgrimage participants to infiltrate the upper-class white community they studied. On the other hand, it could also be an indication that even educated scholars probing the inner workings of a Jim Crow society accepted to some degree the Pilgrimage narrative that enjoyed widespread appeal among many white Americans.

The comments of First Lady Eleanor Roosevelt revealed an entirely different kind of attraction from her visit to Natchez in the late 1930s. Mrs. Roosevelt, an advocate for racial and social justice, saw the Natchez Pilgrimage as an inspirational example of women's capabilities in business and city beautification. In a magazine column she penned after touring Natchez during Pilgrimage season, Mrs. Roosevelt was captivated more by antique dresses, furniture, and china than the town's racial problems, noting: "Never tell me that women are not able in business. Natchez is being built up financially by a woman's idea carried out by women. They have obtained good publicity and they have one great advantage, the houses displayed are really homes. They are lived in today and frequently the mistress of the house receives you herself. Some of the dresses worn are genuinely old and the furniture is good of its date . . . and the china and silver is extremely interesting."¹⁵⁴ The glowing statement of Eleanor Roosevelt, who was clearly taken with the feminist implications of the clubwomen's entrepreneurial venture, is yet another indication that white journalists, tourists, scholars, and even the liberal wife of the president found the commodity peddled by early Pilgrimage organizers viable for a variety of reasons, not necessarily associated with complete acceptance of Lost Cause ideology. As demonstrated in the experiences of Ernie Pyle, Professor Carmichael, the Gardners, and Eleanor Roosevelt, those who traveled to Natchez in the 1930s came for different purposes and took away a variety of impressions and remembrances that fit their personal needs. Even as the garden clubwomen of Natchez put forth their vision of their community's past, the pilgrims who purchased their tourism product invested the experience with their own unique meanings.

AFRICAN AMERICAN RESPONSE TO THE PILGRIMAGE

Many blacks living in Natchez during the early Pilgrimage years resented the pageants and home tours but simultaneously found ways to profit from the steady flow of white pilgrims who came to Natchez each spring. Throughout his adolescence, Clifford Boxley sold pralines for about two dollars a box and daffodils for ten cents a bunch to tourists on the downtown streets of Natchez during the late 1940s and 1950s. "Young black males weren't interested in the antebellum homes and the pageant; that was white folks' business," says Boxley. "We saw the Pilgrimage as a way to make a few pennies or dollars." As the eldest son of seven children whose single mother worked as a maid for about fifteen dollars a week, Boxley took responsibility "to generate any kind of income that I could in order to have something." His memories include seeing black adults selling a variety of products and services to white pilgrims. Black men frequently served as cab drivers for tourists, while black women wearing antebellum-styled servant costumes worked as greeters, standing behind white women in hoopskirts. Rachel Bell, a light-skinned black woman, remembered as a "master praline maker," dressed in a long skirt and wore a bandana as she moved about the main thoroughfares of Natchez selling her sweet treats and hot parched peanuts. A black man known as "Snowball" pushed a wheelbarrow with a block of ice selling flavored shaved ice cones. Many of the black street vendors worked year-round selling their wares but were particularly busy during the Pilgrimage season.[155] Other blacks who grew up in Natchez during the early decades of the Pilgrimage remember little being said about the event, almost as if it did not exist. Ralph Jennings recalls sitting around his family's dinner table discussing black ancestors rather than the home tours and pageants.[156]

Not until 1965 with the passage of federal civil rights legislation did African Americans organize formal protests against the Pilgrimage enterprise. Civil rights statutes ensured that anyone could purchase a pageant ticket. On the other hand, because Pilgrimage homes were privately owned, tour organizers did not have to sell tickets to African Americans.

"ON THE LEVEL" WITH NATCHEZ ELITES

Even as many white tourists sought to preserve their memories of the Pilgrimage by purchasing a diverse array of souvenir toiletries, bedspreads, playing cards, homemade pralines, and hot peanuts, most visitors found their Pilgrimage hosts the most memorable aspect of their trip. The Pilgrimage organizers and their spouses not only put a human face on southern culture but satisfied the strong desire of 1930s middle-class Americans to interact with the upper classes. Hobnobbing with the rich, or in Natchez's case, the once rich, satisfied a longstanding middle-class preoccupation with aristocratic cultural values and lifestyles that dated back to the nineteenth century. Refinement, according to historian Richard Bushman, "held out the hope of elevation from ordinary existence into an exalted society of superior beings."[157] Such hopes would certainly have entered the minds of Depression-weary Americans. At the same time; however, the Depression fueled hostility toward the wealthy, whom many saw as greedy and selfish, and lacking any interest in advancing the common good.[158] Yet, even as the Depression may have diminished Americans' admiration for the wealthy, it seemed not to have dampened their curiosity about how they lived.

Judging from the reactions of Northern journalists, visitors perceived the Natchez upper crust as both different from and more likeable than the rich stock characters ridiculed in 1930s screwball comedies and Marx Brothers films. Some journalists interpreted the hospitality and humility of tour guides as evidence that their defeat in the Civil War and their subsequent economic struggles had reformed them. Of David McKittrick, the once-wealthy owner of Elms Court, journalist Ernie Pyle noted: "He has been wealthy. But our recent depression wiped him out. He lives there amidst the grandeur that isn't. But he is no eccentric relic himself. And he doesn't flaunt that notorious dignity that declines to recognize the passing of eras. He tells you that he was rich and that now he is poor. His speech is one of culture and broad travel. His dignity is in his naturalness. You feel warm toward him."[159] Ernie Pyle's description of his drawing room visit with McKittrick and other elite Natchez men revealed likeable yet somewhat humbled men who, despite their reduced circumstances, found ways to enjoy an aristocratic life of leisure. Pyle never mentioned in these profiles how these men earned a living, allowing both employed as well as unemployed readers to feel at ease with Natchez's male elites, and a lifestyle that mysteriously did not seem to depend on employment. Of hospitable William Kendall and his family, owners of Monteigne, Pyle wrote: "They are important people in Mississippi. . . . They offer you a highball. They show you around. 'Don't ask me what any of this antique stuff is,' Kendall laughs, 'for I wouldn't know.' And I wouldn't know if he told me, so that puts us on the level."[160]

Finding himself "on the level" with his Natchez hosts, Pyle and other visitors found an appealing comfort zone with the humbled Natchez elite. Minimized class distinctions enabled Natchez visitors to relate more easily to their hosts as somewhat idolized social aristocrats, whose reduced economic circumstances created a more equitable social relationship. Such a perception created a warmth and empathy among Natchez visitors for their hosts and their financial difficulties, a situation likely shared by some tourists. At the same time, journalists and visitors may have experienced a vicarious pleasure in seeing the upper class humbled in much the same way 1930s movies portrayed the upper class's fall from grace.

How best to explain what attracted and ultimately won over nonsoutherners' support for a cultural event like the Pilgrimage that endorsed a southern past built on a racist social structure, an ideology ostensibly rejected by the North only seventy years earlier? Depression-era culture and ideas on race during this period suggest that an event like the Pilgrimage satisfied the desire of white Americans—living above and below the Mason Dixon line—for a more conservative, traditional social structure. As David Blight so aptly notes, "We reminisce not merely to render the past retrievable, but to serve present interests and needs." Southern cultural leaders who worked diligently to erase slavery and the emancipation story from the historical narrative largely shaped the nation's memory of the antebellum South and the Civil War.[161] The creators of the Natchez Pilgrimage and other likeminded enterprises were part of this process. The proud display of antebellum homes and gardens as part of a cultured, genteel lifestyle not only ignored their construction by slave labor but also presented a selective telling of the town's past consistent with Jim Crow practices. The near absence of African Americans in this staging of Natchez's history reflected a desire by female club members to stay the cultural course by glossing over a tragic aspect of the past as well as to avoid engaging contemporary racial tensions brewing beneath the surface in 1930s America.

The Pilgrimage also likely offered a comforting antidote to white middle- and upper-class travelers disturbed by the messages of social equality imbedded within the tenets of the New Deal. Although Franklin Roosevelt's plan never truly challenged America's class and racial structure as he acquiesced to the demands of conservative southern politicians, some Americans nevertheless sensed the threat of chaos that could result in a new and uncomfortable social order. The growth of Communism, particularly among rural southern blacks, also intensified the anxieties of conservative-minded whites.[162] Natchez's public entertainment offered white visitors a welcome sense of security built upon white supremacy and traditional class and gender distinctions.

By skillfully using elements of popular culture that appealed to a mass audience, female garden club members not only guided historical memory in 1930s Natchez but also assumed business responsibilities as well as civic leadership. The garden clubwomen combined their personal charm, perseverance, and pragmatism to achieve their goals, even though some in the community initially doubted their mission and others questioned whether

Pilgrimage leaders like Katherine Miller should be compensated for their work directing the heritage tourism venture. Disputes over how tour revenues would be divided eventually led many of the original homeowners to form a second club in 1936, followed by a volatile court case labeled by the press as the "battle of the hoopskirts." It is to this memorable squabble and wrangling over historical memory making and its commercialization that we now turn.

CHAPTER SIX

THE BATTLE OF THE HOOPSKIRTS

The Ladies Go to Court

IN THE SPRING OF 1941, THE TWO RIVAL WOMEN'S GARDEN CLUBS OF NATCHEZ declared war on one another in what became one of the more curious episodes in recent southern history. "The Battle of the Hoopskirts," as it was labeled by newspapers and magazines nationwide, delighted the American public. The conflict had all the makings of a juicy tabloid story—nasty insults hurled by some of Natchez's most prominent ladies, rowdy courtroom antics, clandestine late-night car rides, a befuddled mayor, not to mention laxatives, hound dogs, and snubbed local royalty.

The dispute erupted when the Pilgrimage Garden Club, formed in 1936, extended its home tours to compete with the dates of the home tours staged by the original Natchez Garden Club. But as historical records reveal, much more was at stake than a heated court battle to determine future Pilgrimage tour dates. What the club matrons of Natchez were really battling for were the control and spoils of their town's cultural image in the twentieth century. The issue was not so much a differing definition of the past as much as it was a conflict over who would control the handling the presentation of that past and, as new research reveals, marked differences in lifestyles and ideals between members of the warring factions. The opposing clubs agreed on the end product—a highly romanticized, whitewashed image of the Old South mirrored by books, movies, and other popular culture of the era. However, as historical analysis will show, each group held very different ideas of who should control the packaging and implementation of this past within popular culture.

The first signs of trouble within the Natchez Garden Club (NGC) erupted in the fall of 1935 when sixteen homeowners contested the division of Pilgrimage tour receipts. When the majority of Natchez Garden Club members vetoed the petition of the homeowners (those living in the residences open for tours) to increase their share of tour revenues to 75 percent, the unhappy homeowners seceded from the club under the leadership of Pilgrimage founder Katherine Miller. The rebels quickly formed the Association of Pilgrimage Homes, later to become the Pilgrimage Garden Club (PGC). Eight homeowners remained loyal to the original club and pledged to show their homes during the Natchez Garden Club's sixth annual Pilgrimage the following year.[1]

After numerous delays a committee representing each club agreed to meet two years later in November 1937 at the Eola Hotel in downtown Natchez. Minutes from that meeting record a tense atmosphere with members posed for conflict. Over the next four days, it became clear that neither club was willing to compromise. The Pilgrimage Garden Club refused to give ground on the matter of the Pilgrimage board being comprised exclusively of homeowners. The Natchez Garden Club refused to agree to this demand in part because their club, with only eight members who owned Pilgrimage homes, would be far outnumbered by Pilgrimage Garden Club homeowners. The Natchez Garden Club's plan called for an equal number of homes representing each club, thus ensuring equal representation in producing the annual Pilgrimage.[2]

In response to the Natchez Garden Club's proposal, Annie Barnum, the outspoken president of the Pilgrimage Garden Club, restated that her club desired an exclusive board of homeowners because the Pilgrimage was a homeowner's proposition. "They own the homes, pay the taxes and if they are willing to do the work and finance the Pilgrimage, give a certain percentage away, they ought to be allowed to run it in their own way," noted the fifty-seven-year-old Barnum in the heated negotiation session.[3] As the owner of two Pilgrimage tour homes—Arlington and Monmouth—Barnum had more at stake than most members.[4] Home ownership remained an underlying division between the two factions making it virtually impossible for the clubs to reunite. After continuous bickering, the meetings ended as acrimoniously as they had begun. Neither side was willing to reduce the number of homes they had shown during the 1937 Pilgrimage, and by the end of the meeting, the Pilgrimage Garden Club was willing to accept only seven Natchez Garden Club members' homes. The clubwomen left the Eola Hotel with no solution, paving the way for a full-fledged rebellion four years later.[5]

Failing to reach a compromise the two clubs staged independent Pilgrimages between 1937 and 1940. And while all-out war did not break out between the clubs, garden club members did spar on occasion. These skirmishes are now legendary. One of the most memorable pranks occurred during the Natchez Garden Club's Confederate Pageant. According to Natchez Garden Club members, rival mischief makers fed a laxative to the hound dogs appearing in the hunt scene tableau. A few moments later the Natchez Garden Club Pageant queen found an unpleasant surprise as she paraded across the stage in her long, elegant, white gown.[6]

In March 1941 the hoopskirted troops launched a full-scale attack. Three days before the expected conclusion of the Pilgrimage Garden Club's tours—and the launch of the NGC's tours—a notice appeared in the *Democrat*, announcing that due to "popular demand" the PGC would continue its tours.[7] The club relocated its headquarters to the Elks Lodge, conveniently situated adjacent to the town's two main hotels. With the headquarters of the two clubs only a half block apart, the battle began in earnest. Colorful banners hung outside each club's headquarters advertising themselves as the "official" Natchez Pilgrimage. Adding to the inflamed atmosphere, each club hired an African American band to play from the upstairs gallery of their headquarters. Downtown Natchez streets were filled with lively Dixieland tunes as the rival clubs hawked their tickets to visitors who were getting much more than they bargained for.[8]

Not surprisingly, more than a few hapless guests were overwhelmed and confused by the fight for tourist dollars. One newspaper article noted that when 230 troops of the thirty-seventh division from Ohio arrived in town they were "promptly engulfed in the middle of the local garden club's battle for tourists that waxed so fierce it threatened to make the ancient siege of Vicksburg seem like a snowball fight." The soldiers found themselves confronted with cut rates to see the antebellum homes. Officers took charge to explain the rivalry to their troops and sent an equal number of men to each club's home tours. Furthermore, the soldiers were confronted with an invitation from the Pilgrimage Garden Club to attend a dance which just so happened to be scheduled the same evening as the Natchez Garden Club's opening Confederate pageant and the chance to see "pretty Miss Mary Louise Enochs reign as queen." The PGC's dance was free, but the chance to see royalty would cost the soldiers one dollar.[9]

Not all Natchez tourists fared so well. One newspaper article reported that several frustrated tourists packed their bags and left. Another visitor, overexcited by the warring women, suffered a heart attack. Indeed, the blood pressure of many of the town's leading citizens was climbing during late

March 1941. More than fifty years later, club veterans of the "hoopskirt battle," found the 1941 Pilgrimage difficult, noting, "The split almost caused a nervous breakdown in town. It wasn't very pleasant."[10]

While many in Natchez publicly expressed dismay at the discord, others relished the adrenaline rush of a brouhaha that captured the attention of the nation. Years after the conflict, PGC member Ruth Beltzhoover recalled those days with delight. "I love to talk about it," she told a reporter, recalling "the time she went with some lawyers 'in the middle of the night to some place north of Jackson' to sign some papers. 'We were suing the Natchez Garden Club,' she said, 'and they were suing us. It got so tangled up nobody could remember anymore who was suing who. I was dressed like an old man, with a hat pulled down over my ears and an old coat so nobody would recognize me.'" Beltzhoover, who was in her early forties at the time of the late-night shenanigans, never explained the reason for the disguise, but apparently it worked because on the way to Jackson she passed a carload of rival NGC ladies who failed to recognize her.[11]

The thrill of the chase appealed to more than just the matrons of Natchez. Kathie Boatner Blankenstein, a Natchez resident whose mother served as the paid executive secretary of the Natchez Garden Club for many years, recalls that as a young girl she became an activist for her mother's employer. During the ruckus of 1941 she made flyers promoting the Natchez Garden Club's tour dates and placed her advertisements on cars parked on Natchez streets. The conflict became more than a series of childish pranks. "The fight became very bitter," recalls Blankenstein. "Old childhood friends stopped speaking, and even the men got involved much to their chagrin." Angry Natchez Garden Club members went so far as to boycott the department store owned by Pilgrimage Garden Club member Ruth Beltzhoover.[12]

As the days passed the conflict intensified as garden club members vied for the business of unsuspecting tourists. "In the lobby of the city's leading hotel, crinolined members of Natchez's first families alternately glared at lifelong neighbors and beamed on visitors as they vied for patronage," reported one newspaper. One clubwoman was overheard to say to a prospective sightseer, "Don't see her old home, see my old home. My old home is better than her old home."[13]

Soon, more than angry glares were being exchanged between the two feuding clubs. On March 25 members of the Natchez Garden Club met at Connelly's Tavern, the historic structure they had restored and converted into their clubhouse, to discuss their legal options with their attorneys Gerard Brandon and Wilfred Geisenberger, husbands of two active NGC members.

On March 26 an injunction was granted to the NGC against PGC homeowners, prohibiting them from showing their homes through the scheduled NGC Pilgrimage tour dates. The judge ordered PGC women to strike their banners, silence their band, and close their mansions.[14]

A day after granting the injunction, Judge A. B. Anderson rescinded his order against the Pilgrimage Garden Club. He concluded that the injunction was "hastily granted and that the defendants were entitled to a five-day notice for a hearing before the issuance of an injunction."[15] But the Natchez Garden Club refused to let the matter pass. On the following day a new temporary injunction was granted against the Pilgrimage Garden Club, ordering the club to immediately stop advertising its Pilgrimage.[16] As tenacious as their rivals, the PGC held their ground and ignored the court order much to the delight of the press covering the heated contest. The Pilgrimage Garden Club's banner was still hanging, its headquarters remained open, and tour tickets were being sold. A PGC member told one reporter, "We are going on through Sunday just as though nothing had happened." Sheriff H. R. Jenkins, charged with executing the court's mandate, refused to be quoted.[17]

Tourists witnessing the struggle often got an earful as they visited the mansions of the PGC members. One journalist reported: "Angry ladies indignantly pointed out to their visitors the posted copies of the court order firmly attached to the classic portals. 'Think of it,' they exclaimed. 'They used nails and large ones, too. That is an example of what 'they' are trying to do to us.'"[18] Another Pilgrimage Garden Club member had more to say on the matter in a magazine article published that spring. When asked if the PGC's decision to extend their Pilgrimage was in retaliation to the Natchez Garden Club's plans to open its tours with a ball, she responded in keeping with the noble image her club strived to project to guests: "We don't know anything of such tactics. The Natchez we know and love is the Natchez of ladies and gentlemen. That is the city we are trying to recreate as it was before the War between the States."[19] Several articles reported that Natchez Mayor William J. Byrne seemed to be overwhelmed by the commotion. The *Atlanta Constitution* quoted the frustrated mayor as saying, "The women can run the pilgrimages as best they can. I'm sorry that they can't get together but it looks impossible now." The story added that the frustrated mayor probably would not run for reelection when his term expired.[20]

Some newspapers took the feud more seriously and worried that the demise of the Natchez Pilgrimage could be harmful to the nation. An editorial published in an Alabama newspaper concluded, "The Pilgrimage serves to keep ever alive the customs, traditions, and spirit of the Old South."[21] Future war correspondent Ernie Pyle found himself caught up in the skirmish as well and lamented the rivalry that separated the clubs into enemy camps. "It has broken friendships, completely reorganized social groups, caused hard words to be said and little tricks to be pulled. There seems small hope of ever settling it. I've heard the stories of both sides. Each side is right, there's just no question about it. It's just one of those things."[22]

The March 29, 1941, edition of the *Natchez Democrat* spelled out details of the judge's restraining order which prohibited PGC members from further advertising, selling tickets, and maintaining their headquarters to continue tours sponsored by their club up to and including April 6, 1941. However, within the first two points of the injunction, PGC members saw a loophole and they moved quickly to take advantage. The article stated that "the injunction does not restrain owners of homes in Natchez from keeping them open to guests, whether a charge is made or not." Secondly, the judge noted, "It does not prevent any occupant of the home from continuing the operation of a tea room, or other business, and to receive patrons therein and charge therefor."[23]

The court order, whether unknowingly or not, once again gave the Pilgrimage Garden Club another battle victory. The Sunday, March 30 edition of the *Democrat* included a two-page spread of individual ads purchased by PGC homeowners announcing that their homes were open for tours that day at a price of fifty cents. Each display ad carried a tag line noting, "This advertisement is made by the owner of the above house and is not sponsored, nor inspired by the Pilgrimage Garden Club—Nor is it made for the benefit of the Pilgrimage Garden Club."

The battle paused for a four-month ceasefire when the 1941 Pilgrimage season ended in early April. But by August open warfare erupted between the two clubs as the rivalry moved into the Adams County Courthouse. Sixty-three-year-old Chancellor Richard Wiltz Cutrer of Magnolia, Mississippi, a veteran jurist who had served on the chancery bench for nearly thirty years, presided over the hearing. The idea of dismissing the case quickly and quietly, however, was abandoned when the seasoned judge's suggestion that club members coordinate their tours and reach an agreement, was rejected. The ladies would have their day in court, and no man in Natchez would stand in their way. As the *New Orleans Times-Picayune* reported, "other than attorneys and officers of the court, no men were in evidence" in Chancellor Cutrer's courtroom.[24]

The Natchez Garden Club charged that its national advertising campaign had attracted tourists to the Pilgrimage during the disputed dates of operation, and that the Pilgrimage Garden Club had "lured away" prospective

Natchez Garden Club patrons.[25] In response to these charges, the PGC stated that its listed homes were "more attractive" and had more "originality," claims reminiscent of those made during the failed negotiation sessions of November 1937. The club asserted its right to open and advertise its Pilgrimage homes anytime it wished, claiming that no contractual agreement existed between the clubs. The Natchez Garden Club asked for the recovery of total ticket sales of the Pilgrimage Garden Club after March 23. Meanwhile, the Pilgrimage Garden Club sought four thousand dollars in damages for the alleged wrongful closing of its headquarters.[26]

Former Natchez Garden Club president and publicity chairman Harriet Dixon took the stand on the opening day of the trial. At first chatting in polite whispers, the predominantly female audience frequently burst into applause during Dixon's testimony. The judge warned he would ask spectators to clear his courtroom if there were further demonstrations. Dixon noted that her club had "steadily increased" its advertising expenditures and had spent nearly $5,000 in 1941 for publicity that was sent to every state in the nation. In addition to advertising expenses Dixon reported that total costs for producing the Pilgrimage were between $8,500 and $9,000. The crowd broke into enthusiastic applause when she charged that extension of the Pilgrimage Garden Club tours constituted "unfavorable advertising" and its announcement gave the press "a free hand to renew the war."[27]

Proceedings during the second day of the trial were calmer as the fashionably dressed women listened to the testimony of fellow club members. Harriet Dixon returned to the witness stand offering testimony on the alleged solicitation of Natchez Garden Club customers, the profusion of signs placed by both clubs, past disputes over use of public buildings, and cost and content of advertising materials. Before the day's testimony ended, Virginia Stewart of the Natchez Garden Club's registration committee reported that her club had suffered nearly a 15 percent decline in 1941 revenues from the previous spring, with receipts totaling $19,756.[28] Before the hearing concluded several additional witnesses were called including NGC president Tima Sullivan and members Anna Alexander and Ethel Kelly, owner of Melrose. Photographer Earl Norman (son of Henry Norman) was called to the witness stand to identify photographs of signage he took during the "battle," while A. T. Bowie, vice president of the Britton and Koontz National Bank, testified regarding receipts from balls hosted by the Natchez Garden Club. Newspaper accounts do not mention former Pilgrimage Garden Club president Katherine Miller taking the stand during the hearing. Club treasurer Alma Kellogg appears to have been one of the few witnesses called to testify on behalf of the Pilgrimage Garden Club. Kellogg reported that her club collected a total of $35,684.45 from the 1941 Pilgrimage season, some $15,000 more than Natchez Garden Club tour receipts. Each Pilgrimage Garden Club homeowner received a check for $1,025 (the equivalent of more than $16,000 in 2019).[29]

After two and a half days of testimony, Chancellor Cutrer ruled that the injunction filed by the Natchez Garden Club in March had been wrongfully issued and that the club was not entitled to damages. Furthermore, because the Pilgrimage Garden Club had not filed a cross bill, they also were not entitled to damages. In his closing remarks Chancellor Cutrer asked the two clubs to "forget your differences and settle this matter in a friendly manner, because I fear that if you do not work out some plan by which both can carry on peacefully and satisfactorily you are going to eventually kill both, as the public will not care to take part in your family quarrel."[30]

But neither side seemed willing to mend the family quarrel as quickly as the judge would have liked. Five days after the court's ruling, the attorney for the Natchez Garden Club filed an appeal with the Mississippi Supreme Court. The appeal was eventually dropped in December of that year, most likely in response to the United States' entry into World War II. Despite the war, each club moved forward with their independent 1942 tours. From 1943 through 1945, however, each club canceled its home tours, thus putting the feud on hiatus and allowing tempers to cool after more than five years of sparring. Indeed, according to one magazine article published in the summer of 1942, "It has taken a World War to bring civic peace to the once-embattled community of Natchez. Now that the nation and the world are embroiled in a gargantuan struggle for survival, this little Southern city high above the rolling flood of the Mississippi River has quit its feudin' for the duration. By common consent, Natchez's war of petticoats and petunias is in abeyance."[31]

Although Natchez's "great houses" remained shuttered to tourist crowds for the duration of the war, tourism did not come to a complete standstill in Natchez. Thanks to a bizarre 1932 murder case, scores of tourists came to see "Goat Castle," a dilapidated mansion once known as "Glenwood." Inhabited by eccentric Richard Dana and his housekeeper Octavia Dockery, the pair were accused of orchestrating the murder of spinster Jennie Merrill at her neighboring estate. The case attracted national media attention in large part because of goats "who cavort through the stately rooms and nibble the priceless antiques." Dana's mansion, according to one magazine writer, "has proved a greater attraction than the carefully tended homes and gardens of Natchez's feudin' elite." Although clearly guilty, the pair never served prison time. Instead, an innocent black woman was sentenced to hard labor in prison. As Karen Cox writes about the case, "Natchez, too, was thrown into

This lively cartoon image portrayed the battle that erupted between rival garden club members and homeowners over how heritage tours would be conducted in Natchez during the late 1930s. Numerous newspapers and magazines across the nation covered the hoopla. (Courtesy of Multnomah County Library, "Petticoat Peace Quiets Quarreling Natchez," *American Weekly*, August 16, 1942.)

the spotlight, and what the media exposed was not flattering. Pilgrimage tours aside, this was a society in flux. Old South romance simply served as a cover for Jim Crow ugliness."[32]

The Pilgrimage Garden Club staged the city's first Pilgrimage in the postwar era in 1946. In 1947, six years after the heated courtroom battle, the two clubs paid heed to the judge's words and voted to produce a joint Pilgrimage for the first time since 1936. Each club would receive one-half of the tour monies to give as they chose to their homeowners. The money from the jointly sponsored pageant was divided evenly between the two clubs. Thus, one of the more unusual chapters in recent Natchez history ended. But was there more to the story than a lengthy, bitter feud between prominent Natchez matrons that bruised feelings and ended in a rowdy courtroom battle? In hindsight, the battle waged between rival garden clubs more than fifty years ago may seem like a humorous anecdote in Natchez's longest-running heritage tourism enterprise. Upon closer examination, however, the issues that emerged between the two clubs suggest several significant, new developments that were occurring by 1941 in southern culture. These included a new way of memorializing and marketing the South's past for public consumption and profit, the advancement of female empowerment at the community level, and substantial differences in personality and perspective that divided warring club members.

PRESERVING THE SOUTH WE LOVE

While club members of the rival factions found themselves in harmony on the message of their medium—"Natchez, Where the Old South Still Lives"—they were at odds over exactly how this message should be packaged and how the spoils would be divided. But there were other distinctive divisions as well that threatened to break up the club. The more conservative Natchez Garden Club members, most of whom belonged to the town's First Presbyterian Church, increasingly took offense to what they saw as the "commercialization" of their town's past, and particularly to some members' desire to personally profit from the event. Natchez Garden Club members identified themselves as "prohibitionists, or, at least, the temperance people," according to one irate NGC member's spouse, as opposed to their rivals, most of whom belonged to the Episcopal church and who were labeled by the same critic as "the drinking and grasping crowd."[33] Claiming the moral high ground, NGC members poised themselves as guardians of the Old South's more spiritual and noncommercial values as reflected in this club statement which described their mission to preserve "not alone the physical evidences of the past wealth and ease of living in the Old South, but above all the spirit, traditions, grace, culture, hospitality and atmosphere of the South we love."[34] Natchez Garden Club members appear to have subscribed to the civic volunteerism ideals espoused by the General Federation of Women's Clubs, an association that endorsed sacrificing personal gain for larger goals that would benefit the club and community. Furthermore, personally profiting from the Pilgrimage was not possible for the majority of Natchez Garden Club members because most did not own a tour home.[35]

Adding fuel to the fire, numerous NGC members took offense to Katherine Miller's demand to be paid for her services as Pilgrimage director. George Kelly, husband of NGC member Ethel Kelly and owner of Melrose, wrote a heated letter to his wife detailing PGC homeowners' demands in early October 1935. "Home Owners want 70% of entire net, with 5% to Catherine Miller, making 75% as before. Catherine to have entire and complete charge of pilgrimage, the 5% net estimated to pay to her $800, figured on last year's receipts. Catherine to appoint the executive committee—the secretary, the treasurer and other committees of the Garden Club and control ALL!"[36] Such demands further tarnished Miller's reputation as both brash and pretentious among her more conservative peers. In response to her critics Miller, whether as an assertive modern businesswoman or simply a woman in need of income, stated: "As Director of the Pilgrimage and feeling that I have promoted every idea for the organization since it started three years ago, and since I give all of my time all of the time, I think I should be paid for my efforts.... If I had not been so intense and so deeply interested I could never have carried the idea out with the visible opposition I had the first year."[37] Disheartened that club members did not immediately endorse her proposition, Miller concluded that "as a rule women cannot see things in a big way." After reviewing the "legality" of paying a member for her services, the club agreed to give Miller a one-time honorarium of $500. No mention was made of permanently hiring her, yet another bone of contention between Miller and NGC loyalists that eventually led to an irreparable split.

What is more, Natchez Garden Club members were outraged that Miller and her band of rebels tried to exclude nonhomeowners from the sacred business of memorializing the South's past. Club minutes suggest that Pilgrimage Garden Club members failed to understand the very personal connection that existed between Natchez Garden Club members and the town's most treasured artifacts. These sentiments were expressed in a statement read during a July 1937 executive board meeting. "The members of the Natchez Garden Club feel that they belong to Natchez and that they owe a duty of civic service to Natchez and the entire community in return for their share in the heritage of its history, culture and natural beauty. They feel that in a sense (aside from that of proprietorship) the ante-bellum homes of Natchez and the Natchez country belong to the entire community."[38]

Although only eight homeowner members remained loyal to the town's original Natchez Garden Club after the split, the NGC's rank and file membership was deeply committed to historic preservation. In a number of instances middle-class NGC members were descended from the planter class and had ancestral ties to Pilgrimage homes, thus intensifying their bonds with the cultural event. While many NGC members' devotion to historic preservation was no less passionate than the members who owned tour homes, they lacked the one commodity (a prized antebellum home) that would have given them entry into the Natchez upper class and the power to control the memorialization of their town's past.

The determined Kate Brandon, who fought valiantly for her club as Natchez Garden Club president, offers a poignant example of a member whose family's wealthy antebellum status had declined by the 1930s. Her husband, Gerard, came from a wealthy, powerful line of planters and was the great-grandson of Gerard C. Brandon, the first native-born governor of Mississippi. The governor's son, also named Gerard, held 146 slaves in 1860, ranking him as a wealthy man of considerable property. By the 1930s, however, the

Brandon family's fortunes had noticeably diminished. Although her family no longer owned an antebellum estate, Kate remained passionately devoted to the historical preservation of Natchez and valiantly defended the rights of her club's largely middle-class membership.

Natchez Garden Club members believed that their Pilgrimage Garden Club rivals had attacked the sacred character of their club's preservation mission and "Yankeefied" a once-noble civic venture. The women scorned and deeply resented this breach in ethics. The pain of this grave injustice was expressed by NGC member Harriet Dixon, whose mother was descended from the once-prominent Shields planter family and served as an honorary member of the Confederate Memorial Association and the United Daughters of the Confederacy: "Sometimes we are made to feel there is no place for us anywhere."[39] Dixon's anguish suggests that the hard feelings caused by the split were intensified by the intricately woven kinship ties that existed between members and upper-class Natchez families as discussed in earlier chapters. Cousins, aunts, nieces, and in-laws whose family ties sometimes reached back for nearly two centuries were battling one another over town landmarks that held deep personal significance. Even though some members had not lived in a family heirloom for a generation or more, they still considered these homes a cherished part of their family legacy.

From the standpoint of Pilgrimage Garden Club homeowners, it is understandable why they endorsed the idea of milking the profits out of a successful tourism business. The funds they earned each year helped them pay for the costly and numerous expenses incurred in preserving their aging homes. The descendant of one Pilgrimage homeowner, who left the Natchez Garden Club during the revolt, acknowledges that it was a matter of common sense. "These women were all thinking about saving their houses and helping each other."[40] Another longtime Pilgrimage Garden Club member recalls, "Five hundred dollars meant everything to the homeowners. Their homes were leaking like crazy, the foundations were rotting, and we were losing too many beautiful homes."[41] NGC members and their significant others also expressed concern over the costs involved in the tourism enterprise, with one husband writing, "It certainly is expensive to take part in the Pilgrimage—wages, damage, etc."[42]

Although Natchez Garden Club members criticized their PGC rivals for "commercializing" the Pilgrimage, they also applied their own marketing savvy to boost profits. As noted earlier, the club initiated a slew of creative marketing campaigns to promote their home tours, including playing cards, calendars, toiletries, furniture, and a silver pattern named after Melrose, the ancestral home of prolific letter writer George Kelly, whose wife Ethel was an active NGC member. Clearly, both clubs had discovered that heritage tourism could be good business. What appears to have differentiated the Natchez Garden Club ladies' entrepreneurial drive from their adversaries was their commitment to compensate their homeowners while also depositing substantial profits into their club treasury. In contrast, the principal aim of Pilgrimage Garden Club homeowners appears to have been to reinvest tour profits into the upkeep of individual members' personal property.

The aging homes of Natchez had come to symbolize more than just a remarkable and distinctive American architectural style. They were this community's link to a highly revered ancestry and culture that offered a source of profit—either for personal gain or for civic volunteerism. By the early 1930s only a handful of Natchez's antebellum homes remained within the original planter families who had built them. The rival garden clubs of Natchez used these stately homes as pawns in a complex, emotional battle to control the preservation of their town's cultural image. Like their grandmothers who had initiated the memorialization movement in the aftermath of the Civil War and their grandfathers who had paid homage to the Lost Cause by joining paramilitary organizations in the decades following the war, the hoopskirted warriors of 1941 were no less passionate in their cause, and both homeowners and nonhomeowners were determined to play an active role.

As Mark Twain so aptly noted, "women are the bricks of society." Despite an intense rivalry that at times bordered on pettiness and threatened to ruin a profitable business venture, the garden club ladies of Natchez were the bricks and mortar that preserved a treasured collection of antebellum artifacts that otherwise would have fallen into ruin. Seeing their efforts in this light, we can begin to understand the significance of the "petticoat rebellion," which marked a major turning point in the marketing of one town's antebellum past and another step in the empowerment of southern women.[43]

The battle over a community's cultural identity and, in the case of Natchez, the memorialization of its past can be highly volatile and polarizing. The Natchez Garden Club as the originators of the 1932 Pilgrimage symbolized a shift away, although not a complete break, from the Lost Cause to a somewhat more progressive movement. Although more modern in spirit the club's civic volunteerism ideals remained traditional in terms of gender roles. By contrast the Pilgrimage Garden Club founded in 1936 represented a new pattern within New South womanhood and civic volunteerism. Pilgrimage Garden Club members who outwardly memorialized the South's antebellum past were not so much committed to its deification on the basis of an emotional attachment as much as they were seeking an opportunity to profit from it and protect their homes from ruin. The issue that divided the two factions was not so much a differing definition of the past as much as it was a different management of that past as a marketable commodity.

While the two clubs now stage a peaceful Pilgrimage each spring and fall, the question of how to handle their community's complex past is an issue that is likely to remain very much alive and highly debatable for the garden clubwomen of Natchez in the twenty-first century. And just as Natchez women of the 1880s and 1930s took the lead in defining their community's cultural identity, this charter in all likelihood will remain firmly in the hands of future generations of Natchez women. Commemorating the ten-year anniversary of the Natchez Pilgrimage, Katherine Grafton Miller spoke of this mission to a group of garden clubwomen in 1942. "You will always keep [Natchez] a national shrine, recreating each spring the life, the customs, the wealth and culture of a section of our nation which once bordered upon a separate kingdom so great was the power of its affluent splendor. Some day we shall pass on. Others will take our place. But the flame of your torch shall never be extinguished."[44]

Recent developments in Natchez—some positive, others contentious—as chronicled in the epilogue suggest that the torch lit by Katherine Miller and the garden clubwomen of 1932 burns ever brightly in Natchez. To be sure, more work is needed to share a more comprehensive narrative of the past in Natchez, not just the "affluent splendor" Katherine Miller spoke of, but of dark, troubling human tragedies as well. In keeping with Natchez tradition, the women of Natchez will be playing a leading role in carrying the torch forward in this challenging and noble endeavor.

EPILOGUE

NATCHEZ TODAY

Where More Than the Old South Still Lives

IT IS MID-AUGUST 2017, AND I AM IN NATCHEZ FOR ONE FINAL RESEARCH trip before putting this manuscript to rest. Natchez and the nation's eyes are fixated on Charlottesville, Virginia, where only a few days ago the chaotic and tragic unrest over plans to remove the college town's enormous Robert E. Lee sculpture sparked angry protests led by white supremacists, neo-Nazis, and members of the Ku Klux Klan, resulting in the death of a young female activist. Erected a century ago, the statue was built at a time when Jim Crow customs, laws, and rhetoric governed the states from the old Confederacy while glorifying the cult of the Lost Cause. The controversy in Charlottesville is on the minds of the people of Natchez, a place that like so many southern towns has its own cherished memories and a memorial dedicated to the defeated Confederacy.[1]

I have come to listen to the people of Natchez and hear their thoughts on the current state of heritage tourism in a town dripping in historic memories and relics of the past. I am not disappointed. The people here have much to say, and so amidst the chorus of chirping cicadas and the song of the whip-poor-will in the last days of a volatile summer, I listen to the stories and perceptions of modern day Natchezians who still find themselves linked, enthralled, and sometimes troubled by their town's past.

Nearly six years have passed since my last visit, and while the primary icons of the town's history—the grand, opulent antebellum homes—remain as visually stunning as ever, much has changed. There is a newfound sense of energy, urgency, and purpose that churns beneath the surface here that becomes palpable when inquiries are made about the status of heritage tourism. What becomes refreshingly apparent is a profound civic commitment shared by many in the community—whites and blacks—to promote and tell a more inclusive and accurate historical narrative. Many have labored in this effort, some for decades, and the results are becoming increasingly visible. Yet, despite noteworthy progress, there are still signs of reluctance bubbling beneath the surface of Natchez's heritage tourism marketplace that suggest some within the community—white and black—resist letting go of historical memories whitewashed in antebellum myths.

During my last visit in 2011, Natchez, like much of the nation, still wrestled with economic recession, and tourism among other industries here struggled. Today, while the town is not exactly bustling with visitors during the heat and humidity of August, there are clear signs of tourism resurgence. Riverboat cruise ships regularly dock at Natchez Under-the-Hill, where bright cherry red "hop on hop off" buses, more typically found in larger tourism locales, pick up guests and ferry them to historic sites around town. Walking trails with handsome interpretive markers traverse the downtown streets of the city, sharing the story of Natchez's antebellum wealth enjoyed by white planter elites, but also the town's historic African American neighborhoods. A slave quarter from a Natchez plantation that burned long ago was recently rescued and restored by a woman whose grandfather was born into slavery. A younger generation of black Natchezians are also part of the change. In August 2016 African American entrepreneur Jeremy Houston founded Miss-Lou Tours, which delivers a lively and well-researched narrative while transporting visitors by van to historically significant black history sites, beginning with the Forks of the Road slave market. While most Natchez visitors come from neighboring southern states, a substantial number of foreign tourists also travel here, eager to learn what makes this storied place tick. Representative of this trend, Houston's first van load of tourists hailed from France.

In a town where only a decade or so ago antebellum house tour docents rarely if ever used the term "slave" to credit those whose labors built the great homes and made the lavish antebellum lifestyle of their masters possible, that too is changing. A growing number of homeowners whose houses are shown each fall and spring as part of the Pilgrimage tours along with National Park sites such as Melrose and the William Johnson House (both open year-round) have made significant strides in sharing the topic of slavery more transparently and in greater detail.

What accounts for the dramatic shift in how Natchez shares its past in the twenty-first century? The influence of a trio of powerful outside forces—namely the National Park Service, the Historic Natchez Foundation, and the Natchez Courthouse Records project—are the forces of change that are on the forefront of transforming the historical narrative here into one that is more inclusive, accurate, and critical in a place that has promoted itself for nearly a century as the place "Where the Old South Still Lives."

California-based historian Ronald Davis's own history in Natchez is informative and speaks to the significant cultural and social changes witnessed here. He recalls not long after Martin Luther King Jr.'s assassination in the spring of 1968, sitting in a segregated Natchez movie theater, witnessing segregated bathrooms in the local courthouse, and discovering that public swimming pools in Jackson, the capital of Mississippi, were closed to keep blacks and whites apart. There was much that caught his attention in those days as a young, inquisitive graduate student. He wrote of that time:

> I was intrigued by all those ante-bellum mansions, the town cemetery, the ridiculously-fetching Confederate Pageant that white tourists loved and outsider intellectuals smugly sneered at, and the way so many shotgun shanties and impoverished shacks were strung out amidst still grand villas north of downtown. . . . And why, given all of its history and rich material culture, did downtown Natchez seem pretty much like a sleepy ghost town in comparison to Savannah and Charleston and New Orleans? Certainly, the answer, given the town's rich history, had something to do with the "paths not taken" as well as the roads perpetually but never mindlessly traveled by the ongoing inhabitants of the town and its hinterland.[2]

The vision and leadership of the National Park Service over the past three decades has played a vital role in waking up the "sleepy ghost town" Davis witnessed as a graduate student, resulting in a far broader, more accurate and inclusive interpretation of Natchez's history. The mandate of the park service from its arrival in Natchez in 1988 was to create an inclusive history that valued the entire historic community—Native Americans, early Europeans, and the blacks who were enslaved to enrich the white planter class.[3] In 1991 the National Park Service called upon Davis to produce a study of the black experience in the Natchez area from the earliest times through Reconstruction as a starting point for interpretation.[4] Simultaneously, Natchez National Historical Park (NNHP) focused on creating a bold intrusion into the town's public space, first restoring and preserving the suburban villa Melrose and then turning to historic Fort Rosalie overlooking the Mississippi River and the William Johnson House located in downtown Natchez. According to Davis, "It was as though the National Park arrived with a phalanx of outsiders—rangers, historians, curators, and technical resource people."

Fortunately, the National Park staff did not labor alone in their efforts to create a more inclusive, meaningful, and accurate interpretation of Natchez's past. Within a few years after its arrival, the National Park staff benefited from the research efforts of dozens of eager students from California (including me) as part of the Natchez Courthouse Records project, "hungry to get in on the telling and, indeed, making Natchez history," according to Davis. Poring over 90,000 legal cases and 1,200 large volumes of legal records, dating from the 1790s to the early 1930s, rescued by Davis and his students from oblivion in the Adams County Courthouse basement in the early 1990s, the treasure trove of documents generated a wealth of new research findings on social and economic history and the complexity of life in the Natchez district. More than a hundred undergrad and graduate students completed internships in the program, carefully processing and archiving the fragile documents, with many students over the years producing seminar papers presented at a series of Historic Natchez conferences attended by scholars and local residents. Beginning in 1995 and culminating in the Second Creek Seminar in 2011, these conferences gathered scholars beholden to no local interests and represented an important example of what can be done when institutions dedicated to presenting historical memories commit to a fully inclusive and fully critical perspective as their goal. In addition to numerous conference papers, the research conducted on Natchez's valuable collection of courthouse records generated articles as well as books, adding to an impressive bounty of historic scholarship on Natchez.[5]

Saddled with the responsibility of managing the contest for the creation of new public spaces and historical narratives that challenged those who sought to preserve the traditional story of the "big house and white history" while largely omitting the story of slavery and racial injustice, the park service faced significant and difficult challenges. Fortunately, the park service found an important institutional ally in the Historic Natchez Foundation (HNF), established in 1974, with the purpose of preserving historic structures other than privately owned homes. The foundation, under the capable leadership of historic preservationists Mimi and Ron Miller (outsiders from North Carolina), had been busy developing a body of scholarship noting, preserving, and exhibiting the historic sites in the town important to both the white and black history of Natchez for more than a decade before the arrival of the National Park Service.

The HNF's primary mission was to preserve and interpret the town's architectural and material culture, but since its inception the foundation also has committed itself to sharing the full story of the Natchez scene in its published walking guides and lectures. Mimi Miller is also credited with saving many of the town's early shotgun-style houses used by former enslaved families shortly after the Civil War.[6] Working closely with the HNF, a handful of residents pledged themselves to telling the town's fuller history. The work of the late physician Thomas Gandy, assisted by his wife Joan, offers one of the best examples of this level of commitment. In the late 1980s Dr. Gandy, who had earlier rescued a remarkable collection of nineteenth-century glass-plate negatives (see chapter 4), and his wife teamed up with the park service and the HNF to offer a much-expanded visual view of an all-inclusive Natchez history. Dr. Gandy reproduced a historic goldmine of hundreds of nineteenth-century photographic portraits of black elites, working class blacks, and white residents, later exhibited from Mississippi to Los Angeles and published in numerous books edited by the Gandy team. Gandy's photo collection is now on permanent display at the town's First Presbyterian Church in downtown Natchez.

In June 2009 the Natchez National Historical Park contracted with an outside consulting firm to develop new exhibit panels for the park's visitor center, marking a major milestone in Natchez's journey to reinterpret its history more accurately and inclusively. Outsider Ron Davis was hired to provide the historic information and scripting used to design the exhibit panels, which was reviewed at every stage by park staff. Davis determined that the original panels, while informative and attractive, did not reflect the contested struggle that based on years of research he considered to be essential to the narrative. The revised exhibit panels boldly tell the story of all classes and races of Natchezians, tracing the stories of Native Americans, blacks, and whites in thoughtful reflections on colonization, slavery, the Civil War, and the civil rights movement, from the earliest days of Natchez's past to the present. Visitors can listen to numerous interviews with local residents via handsets that relate to the large timeline accompanying the exhibit. According to park supervisor Kathleen Jenkins Bond, when the exhibit opened a decade ago it was the closest fulfillment of the park service's mission statement to date. In the spring of 2018 the NNHP visitor center added a traveling exhibit detailing the history of the Forks of the Road and the names of many of the people bought and sold at the slave market, ensuring that more visitors will be exposed to Natchez's slave past.[7]

The 2009 debut of the visitor center's revised panels visibly manifested and reset the town's heritage tourism industry direction, quickly followed by the Civil War sesquicentennial in 2011 and five years later by a substantive tricentennial celebration. Each of these historic milestones nudged Natchezians to take a fresh look at how they perceived, packaged, and shared their town's past with a public audience. Comprehensive institutional shifts as well as those generated at a personal level motivated changes in Natchez's historical narrative, a story ingrained in the town's social fabric for more than a century. The following vignettes and personal stories offer a glimpse of the changing and still challenging landscape of Natchez heritage tourism and those involved in leading these efforts.

INSTITUTIONALIZING AN INCLUSIVE HISTORY

When Vicksburg native Kathleen Bond moved to Natchez in 1993, the Natchez Pilgrimage—the town's main tourism product—had been in full swing for sixty years. Bond's arrival had been preceded by the establishment of the Historic Natchez Foundation, the opening of the Natchez Indians historic site on the outskirts of town, and Historic Jefferson College under the leadership of the Mississippi Department of Archives and History. About the same time, a small group of black women organized the Natchez Association for the Preservation of Afro-American Culture (NAPAC), leading to the opening of the Natchez Museum of African American History and Culture. But it was the big antebellum houses that still dominated the attention of tourists and those controlling local tourism. Without question, the original Pilgrimage slogan "Natchez Where the Old South Still Lives" was very much alive and well.

Bond, who now serves as superintendent of Natchez National Historical Park, credits the NPS over the past twenty-five years for maintaining "a strong and growing emphasis on race, gender, age relevance, diversity, and inclusion." As a result, Natchez today shares its historical narrative with local residents and visiting tourists in ways far differently from past decades. "Now days it's more noteworthy when slavery is *not* mentioned on a house tour," she says. It was Melrose—the home that became the first historic property to come under the NNHP umbrella—that set the standard on how to address slavery here. Enslavement is addressed in a replica of a nineteenth-century slave cabin located behind the main house. Over time, the exhibits have changed and improved, and today share a narrative that includes names of some of the enslaved who worked and lived at Melrose. "It is not a faceless discussion," proudly notes Bond. Visitors can view exhibits at their own pace and also listen to an audio that shares personal and sometimes brutal stories about the enslaved men, women, and children who labored and lived at Melrose.

Removing the human tour guide from the slave exhibit at Melrose makes for a quiet and reflective experience, while ensuring that the same message is delivered to each visitor who enters the cabin. As Bond notes, even at a National Park Service site, it's not always possible to completely control the message delivered by trained guides.[8]

Bond, who began her work in Natchez as a museum curator for the park service, spends much of her time these days thinking about tourism issues and their relationship to historical sites. "In Natchez, we realize that people are looking for a variety of different tourism experiences. We have people who come here for a *Gone with the Wind* experience and don't want to think about slavery because it's too depressing a subject. More progressive visitors, particularly international visitors, expect someone to explain race relations and the civil rights movement." Millennials offer a whole different set of challenges, says Bond. "Most younger visitors don't give a flip about house tours; they want an experience. To me the most important issue is the visitor experience at a Natchez house. It's problematic and difficult. We want them to see the house, think about the story while a person is talking to them. We are doing some real head scratching to determine what will entice visitors to give us their time and money."[9]

Fortunately, Natchez's historical narrative is no longer primarily controlled and delivered by Pilgrimage house tours. While home tours remain a popular mainstay of Natchez heritage tourism, there are an array of new and imaginative historical venues that offer a more inclusive, accurate perspective and attract steady streams of tourists. Many of these, such as the Natchez Trails, are a result of multi-institutional collaboration with local residents. Led by the nonprofit organization Community Alliance of Natchez–Adams County that included the Natchez National Historical Park and the Historic Natchez Foundation, the trails project encompasses five walking trails in downtown Natchez, including one trail that meanders along the town's magnificent bluff overlooking the mighty Mississippi River. The St. Catherine Street Trail is of particular interest to those seeking to learn more about a robust late nineteenth- and early twentieth-century African American neighborhood (see chapter 4). On this trail thirty-two cultural panels beginning at the site of the Forks of the Road slave market site lead visitors to the location of the ACE (All Colored Entertainment) Theatre, the National Landmark home of Emile Angeletti, a prominent African American contractor, and the home of physician John Banks, the town's first black doctor. The Rhythm Night Club Onsite Memorial Museum marks the site of the tragic fire that killed 209 young African American men and women in 1940 and remains one of the deadliest fires in American history.[10] Nearby, stands the MLK Triangle, the command center of the Natchez Civil Rights Movement in the 1960s. The trail ends at the Zion Chapel AME Church where Hiram Revels, the nation's first black US Senator, served as a minister after the Civil War.

To ensure the St. Catherine Street project's success, the Community Alliance hosted a community meeting inviting locals to bring their personal collection of historic images of the neighborhood's buildings and residents. Many black residents came to the meeting armed with photos of persons who had been well known within the African American community.[11] Later, black and white Natchez residents joined forces to write and craft the panels that told a racially integrated story of Natchez's past. Bond notes that this was one of the first projects that brought black and white residents together. She found this achievement particularly refreshing because in her mind "it didn't make sense to segregate the community when the town's history was not segregated."

In the process of creating the Natchez Trails some new and surprising historical discoveries emerged. For example, researchers learned that black Union soldiers upon their arrival in Natchez in 1863 were ordered to dismantle the notorious Forks of the Road slave market. Additionally, according to HNF director Mimi Miller, the project revealed that "St. Catherine Street was historically the city's most ethnically diverse neighborhood with citizens of African, Irish, Italian, French, German, Polish, English, Jewish, and even Danish descent operating businesses and living along the street." Images gathered from Natchez residents along with many photographs of the streetscapes, commercial buildings, and residences taken by photographer Henry C. Norman have been reproduced on handsome stainless-steel plates and installed in strategic locations along all five Natchez Trails to provide a "then and now" picture of what that particular spot looked like in centuries past.[12]

The trail markers throughout Natchez are a major step forward in using public space to create a more inclusive and accurate historical narrative, but outside historians note that the markers do not always go far enough in presenting a *critically* accurate rendering. The St. Catherine Street trail markers are a case in point and suggest the challenges of sharing Natchez's complex history of achievement alongside the story of racism within the limited space of a single street marker. The busy street, currently projected as an ethnically diverse and thriving nineteenth-century neighborhood in markers along the trail, also was the site of a much darker and troubling history. Slave traders once marched their enslaved cargo to the waterfront on this road, passing a slave hospital. During Reconstruction, white men constructed houses for their black mistresses and their mixed-race children on this road. That story is not currently told. According to Ron Davis, "by highlighting St. Catherine Street's mixed ethnic character without noting its tragic history, the markers essentially whitewash history."[13] Likewise, a marker stationed at the intersection of North Union and Franklin Streets, shares a story of the city's business growth, including the once-thriving black-owned drugstore and theater that operated in this area, but offers only a single sentence about the town's civil rights past, noting, "Franklin Street became a hub for Civil Rights protest marches by African Americans in the 1960s." Markers devoted to Natchez's robust civil rights activism would create a more inclusive and critically accurate interpretation of the town's past, while also saluting the courageous historical actors who participated.

Situated between the seventy Natchez Trails markers scattered throughout Natchez are other beacons of institutional change that further contextualize African American history here but also suggest more can be done. In 2005, after extensive restoration, the National Park Service opened the home of William Johnson, a prominent antebellum free black barber. His fourteen leather-bound volumes of diary entries are the primary source for house museum tours and exhibits, which depict the life of a prosperous free black family during the antebellum era.[14]

Johnson held sixteen slaves at the time of his death, a story which complicates the town's slave narrative, says Bond. "People in Natchez don't know what to do with the story of Johnson. He owned slaves, his clients were from the planter class, he was the son of a mixed-race woman and a white father." Because of Mississippi's "one drop African American rule," Johnson was pushed into the "black box," says Bond, even though he was likely very light skinned.[15] "But he did not identify as an African American. The culture of 1951 (when his diary was published) put him into that box." By the 1970s, Johnson was elevated by some in the white community for his accomplishments as a successful business owner. Conversely, the black community today largely denigrates him because Johnson was a slaveholder "Morality plays get us in trouble, and we need to remember that race is a social construct that changes over time," cautions Bond.

Ron Davis, who spent considerable time researching William Johnson and wrote many of the text panels for the museum, once again sounds a cautionary note, challenging his colleague's perspective of the free black barber's privileged status in nineteenth-century Natchez. "Johnson was not almost white except in his dreams," says Davis bluntly. "No whites in town accepted him as white although many thought of him as the most that a black person might become." While some whites came to view him as a trusted and good black person due to his white blood, he was always regarded and respected as a black who knew his place. Davis adds, "He could not enter any place of amusement or a restaurant because he was black. As a free person he could do things and go places that no slave could go. But so could any free black no matter the dark or light color of his or her skin as long as they accepted the fact that they were not white." Davis cautions that interpreting Johnson as a man of privilege who enjoyed a sense of equality suggests that Natchez was not nearly as racist as research findings document.[16]

While Bond and Davis may disagree about how to interpret and tell the story of Johnson and his complicated life, both would agree that more work needs to be done on the unique history of free people of color. For instance, Bond hopes to address questions about Johnson's appearance. In the original exhibits created in 2005, Johnson was portrayed in his childhood as a very dark boy. Bond wonders how the town would respond if Johnson today were more accurately represented as a white male with black hair, which is probably what he looked like given that a photo of his daughter shows a very fair woman. "It's complicated and Natchez struggles with adapting to change gracefully," she adds.

African American historic activist Ser Sesh Ab Heter-Clifford Boxley acknowledges that while major institutional shifts in recent years have resulted in a more racially inclusive history in Natchez, progress often has been "creepingly" slow. He is particularly critical that black Civil War history has yet to be fully integrated into the institutionalized history of Natchez. Specifically, Boxley calls attention to the Black and Blue reenactment event dedicated to the memory of black freedom fighters (formerly enslaved men who joined the Union Army). Hosted at Jefferson College on the outskirts of Natchez each fall, the event is not adequately promoted by local tourism professionals, says Boxley, resulting in poor attendance by white residents.

In what promises to be one of the most significant institutional changes to the Natchez historical landscape, Forks of the Road, once the South's second largest slave market, was recently designated to become a Natchez National Historical Park site. A process that began in 2005, the journey has been complicated and has frequently run into bureaucratic roadblocks. Boxley played a major role in seeing the project through to completion along with Natchez city officials, the National Park Service, and the Historic Natchez Foundation. In similar fashion to other Natchezian activists and historians profiled in this chapter, Boxley was somewhat an outsider himself after leaving Natchez for

California for several decades before returning in the early 1990s. Inspired after reading Ronald Davis's *The Black Experience in Natchez*, Boxley became a leading agitator to set the historic record straight by properly memorializing the Forks of the Road site. The project marks a major milestone in the city's history, he says. "After twenty-two years of resurrecting and promoting the story of America's domestic 'slave' trade from the upper South to Natchez, the National Park Service and federal government will be presenting and interpreting the historical, culture, art, music, life, and community contributions of enslaved people. This is a major attainment." Boxley notes that the project is long overdue and justified because "the American slave trade is a national and international phenomenon and is much bigger than just a local story." Boxley takes pride in the grassroots efforts he led that "constantly agitated" on behalf of federal recognition of the site. "From a nonprofit citizens group with no real resources we have managed to get interpretive signage and landscaping done." The current exhibit based on slave narratives and slaveholder diaries includes signage listing the names of approximately five hundred enslaved people who were sold here.[17]

Once the land transfer for Forks of the Road is completed, Kathleen Bond and the NNHP will collaborate with the community to determine how best to expand the interpretation of the site and build on the exhibit panels already on display. Several steps will unfold. A brick bridge adjacent to the site being donated by the city will be cleared of the kudzu that currently covers it. The bridge is historically significant because it was crossed by the enslaved as they made their way into the slave marketplace. Another important step will be to conduct "listening sessions" hosted by the NNHP to hear what "people's dreams, visions, and concerns are regarding the site," says Bond.[18]

TRICENTENNIAL CELEBRATION

Dreams and visions of Natchez's past and future were an integral focus of the yearlong celebration in 2016 to commemorate Natchez's three-hundredth anniversary as the state's oldest city. At the helm of the tricentennial production was Jennifer Ogden Combs, a Natchez native and Emmy award-winning film and television producer who brought her considerable organizational and creative talents to bear on the complex effort. Prior to returning to Natchez to marry her childhood sweetheart in 2008, Combs—yet another outsider of sorts—found herself pondering what it would take to bring the many divisive interest groups in her hometown together. "Natchez would soon be turning three hundred years old in 2016. One day while running, a lightbulb went off inside my head. I thought Natchez doesn't belong to just one group; it belongs to everybody." In between traveling back and forth between Los Angeles and Natchez in early 2014, Combs was asked to direct Natchez's tricentennial and now serves as director of the city's tourism bureau, Visit Natchez. She agreed to take the job on condition that the city agree to change the original slogan chosen for the upcoming celebration: "A Party 300 Years in the Making." Combs told city officials that the tricentennial was about much more than just a party. Instead, she saw an opportunity to use the tricentennial to communicate a more substantive message that would bring people together in ways never experienced before. Fittingly, the city chose the slogan "Where the River Is Wide and the History Runs Deep" to inspire their anniversary campaign. Simultaneously, the plan Combs had in mind included economic development and attracting new visitors to Natchez. A key theme of the project was to commemorate Natchez's past and celebrate its present, while working to create a brighter future. Additionally, the plan called for bringing groups of racially diverse people together who traditionally had never joined forces before.

The tricentennial highlighted nearly every aspect of Natchez's three-hundred-year-old history. One of the more noteworthy projects was the "Natchez History Minutes," a collection of 366 short videos documenting Natchez's past, some stories well known, others not. Park service lead historian Jeff Mansell produced the daily videos using the voices of Natchez residents to tell the stories. Assisted by two African American graduate students who did much of the research, Mansell says he devoted eighteen months to a project he claims as the "most rewarding" of his career. "We never ran out of topics and people would tell me that they woke up and drank their coffee every morning while watching the videos." The most rewarding aspect of the venture was including 140 local school children from elementary age through high school as video participants. Many of the segments on slavery, Reconstruction, and the civil rights movement were recorded by African American children. To date, "Natchez History Minutes" has received more than two million views on Facebook and other social media platforms and has been viewed around the world.[19]

"Natchez Legends and Lore," another NNHP program, offered close to fifty history lectures during the tricentennial year. "We thought we'd be lucky to get thirty people to come out," recalls Bond. Instead, the popular weekly series averaged about 125 attendees and sometimes drew as many as 200. Once again calling upon the slew of both professional and amateur historians living in Natchez, the program covered a broad variety of topics, including historic gardens and landscapes, Natchez sports legends and lore, author and native son Richard Wright, local architecture, and the gothic tale of the 1932 "Goat Castle" murder case.[20]

The more recent history of the modern civil rights movement in Natchez also found its way into the tricentennial commemoration, bringing black and white Natchezians together to learn and discuss what happened here. Thanks to the efforts of Darrell White, director of the African American History Museum in Natchez, among others, an incident known as the "Parchman Ordeal" became part of the tricentennial narrative. When asked at an early tricentennial planning meeting what it would take to get the black community involved in the effort, White initially rebuffed the request because blacks had not been included in past city events in any significant way. When pressed about the matter, White told the committee that there were those within the black community who were still experiencing pain from past events. The example White gave was the "Parchman incident," an infamous weekend when an estimated five hundred or more local African American men, women, and youths were arrested in October 1965 while marching for voting rights on the grounds of parading without a permit (an ordinance later found to be unconstitutional). According to newspaper reports, approximately 264 people of the more than 500 arrested—men and women, most twenty-five years old or younger—were bussed from Natchez to the Parchman State Penitentiary, some four hours away. The group was held in the maximum-security section of the penitentiary without ever being formally charged and many were subjected to brutal and inhumane treatment over the course of a week or more.[21]

When some tricentennial committee members insisted that the Parchman affair never happened, White returned to the next meeting armed with a thick stack of papers from the Natchez Police Department documenting the individuals arrested over that weekend.[22] It was then that the tricentennial committee began to listen, he says. Not long after this revelation, the National Park Service took steps to acknowledge the Parchman ordeal, producing a briefing paper presented to the Natchez Board of Aldermen and Adams County Board of Supervisors that detailed the atrocities of the 1965 incident. This action ultimately led to a formal apology from the mayor and board to the victims. In 2016 White worked with documentary producers G. Mark LaFrancis and Robert Morgan to record hours of interviews with Parchman survivors, producing *The Parchman Ordeal: The Untold Story*, a documentary that aired on Mississippi Public Broadcasting Television in late 2017.²³ Elizabeth Boggess was one of those who saw the film. Although not living in Natchez at the time of the massive arrests in October 1965, she claims that few in the white community knew about the incident because local newspapers did not cover it. (While whites living in Natchez may not have remembered the media coverage of the event from more than half a century ago, the *Natchez Democrat* did in fact cover the event as front-page news for four consecutive days.) Boggess now understands that the incident "has been a root cause of ongoing hostility" within the black community for decades. This concept became somewhat easier to digest for Boggess and others after attending a racial reconciliation conference hosted by Natchez's Holy Family Catholic Church and the NNHP in 2016. The full-day seminar brought several hundred people—blacks and whites—together to discuss the fear and hatred that too often exists between members of both communities. Boggess says she came to understand that between the 1945 Rhythm Night Club fire that claimed more than two hundred lives and the Parchman ordeal, the Natchez black community lost nearly two generations of male leadership. "Many of the men brutalized at Parchman never returned to Natchez. No wonder the town still has divisions," she says. "Thankfully, in the last three years we've seen much more willingness to honor and tell a more inclusive version of our history here."²⁴

As conversations about the Parchman affair sought to bring about reconciliation, the tricentennial year also included moments to celebrate Natchez's founding. The city paid tribute to its official birthday on August 3, 2016, with the grand opening of Fort Rosalie, the official birthplace of Natchez perched on the bluffs overlooking the Mississippi River. For thirty years the site sat idle with few visitors. The grand opening brought together local, state, and federal leaders with residents to welcome the fort as Natchez National Historical Park's third national park site in Natchez. Addressing the crowd, park supervisor Kathleen Bond noted that the fort provided an opportunity not only to tell a military story but to discuss the cultural interactions between local Native American tribes, European colonists, and African slaves. "Natchez is not just a little town with a bunch of old houses," she stated in her remarks to the audience attending the opening of the fort. "With strong partners like the National Park Service, the Historic Natchez Foundation, and the Mississippi Department of Archives and History, Natchez is already a twenty-first century leader in tourism information. We are ... undertaking reinterpretation of our inherited stories to recognize multiple perspectives and untold aspects, ... bravely tackling difficult and tragic stories in a way that can bring reconciliation and healing to the community and demonstrate our integrity and respect for all persons to the outside world."²⁵

Bond's message, in partnership with other city leaders, resonated throughout the tricentennial year and led to a commitment to press forward with the idea of commemorating Natchez's past while looking boldly into the future. "Our goal is to tell all our stories here and to celebrate our diversity, while supporting people in any way we can," says Visit Natchez's Jennifer Combs. With more than 20 percent of Natchez residents employed in local tourism, the tourism bureau hosts summits several times a year to help local entrepreneurs identify new tourism opportunities and determine how to better target younger audiences, while also giving attendees a chance to meet with a national public relations firm hired to boost local tourism. Additionally, Visit Natchez allocates staff to work with local start-up ventures like the Miss-Lou black heritage tours organized by entrepreneur Jeremy Houston. "We worked with Jeremy to help him develop his business idea and encouraged him," notes Combs. "For me, ventures like this one are important to Natchez's future."

MEDDLING WITH A SACRED TRADITION

Shortly before the end of the busy tricentennial year, another vintage Natchez institution was reexamined and reimagined, offering a stinging reminder that changing a community's complex historical narrative is no easy feat. The town's annual spring pageant, long known as the "Confederate Pageant," which complements the Pilgrimage home tours, received a dramatic facelift beginning in late 2016. Natchez native Chesney Blankenstein Doyle—award-winning documentary filmmaker, civil rights and historic preservation activist, and member of the Natchez Garden Club—wrote and produced a new pageant entitled "Historic Natchez Tableaux," which debuted during the eighty-fifth annual Pilgrimage in spring 2017.

When Doyle agreed to take on the project, she did so with the understanding that the garden clubs, sponsors of the production, would allow her to "move the conversation forward" on Natchez's racial and Reconstruction history. Bestselling novelist Greg Iles, a Natchez native and high school classmate of Doyle's, initiated that conversation a few years earlier when he rewrote the pageant script to include information on the South's decisive and devastating defeat in the Civil War, a first for the Natchez production that until then had primarily featured genteel antebellum scenes focused on white planter elites—maypole dances, soirees, hunting parties, and the like, based on an entertainment format popular in the nineteenth century. Doyle wanted to extend the story beyond the Civil War. "If you end the story with the South's defeat that leaves you with no pathway to move forward," she says, noting that she wanted to avoid "too much emphasis on the victims and villains' aspect of Southern defeat that all too frequently are the mainstay of the Civil War narrative." Instead, Doyle expanded the production's timeline, reaching back ten thousand years ago to the history of the Mississippi River, and closed with a scene from the 1930s paying homage to the women who organized the first Pilgrimage and pageant.[26]

Doyle faced considerable challenges on several fronts. The very nature of historical pageantry—traditionally a one-dimensional, superficial amusement—renders such a vehicle nearly incapable of accurately commenting on dark and disturbing elements of the past. She was also tampering with a longstanding, sacred tradition among white residents. The essential pageant message had remained intact for decades because it served the social needs of the presenters and many in the audience, who for most of its history were nearly all white. Many of the pageant participants are descendants of the original garden club members or have ties to Natchez's planter elite. Local white residents who participate or come to watch their children and grandchildren perform in the pageant cherish the annual spring ritual that honors and connects them to their ancestral heritage. Doyle acknowledged this longstanding tradition by continuing to feature the children and family of garden club members alongside paid professional actors and musicians.

In between the opening and closing pageant scenes, Doyle changed the longstanding narrative, inserting fresh new tableaux vignettes documenting Natchez's most noteworthy historical milestones in the last three decades of the nineteenth century and first three decades of the 1900s. Of the several new scenes devoted to African American history, one of the most poignant was the dismantling of the Forks of the Road slave market in early 1864. Other new pageant scenes detailed the rise of notable black Natchez politicos during Reconstruction, such as Hiram Revels, the nation's first black senator, and former slave John Lynch, a US congressman. Another noteworthy scene creatively showcased the remarkable historic portraits of photographer Henry Norman shot in his downtown Natchez studio.[27] The tableaux also paid tribute to popular black jazz musician Bud Scott, who was born into slavery in Natchez and later entertained audiences in Mississippi, New Orleans, and beyond in the early years of the twentieth century. These and other scenes featuring black stories and actors made for a far more inclusive story than had ever been told in the production's history.

The closing scene of the revised pageant paid tribute to the Natchez Garden Club, who made Natchez in the words of a local newspaper reporter "a tourist town." In Doyle's mind, it was high time that the production honor the women who created the original tableaux and tour of homes. "Tourism drives our economy. Without those women, it's possible that Natchez would not have survived," says Doyle. She also credits the early garden clubwomen for taking stock of their audience and creating a product that responded to the market forces of their day. "Our foremothers were wise to do what they did. We need to be equally wise or we are doing a disservice to their efforts."[28]

As one who grew up in a household immersed in Pilgrimage and pageant lore—her mother and sister were both Pilgrimage queens, she and her brother both performed in the pageant as children, and her grandmother worked as executive secretary for the Natchez Garden Club—Doyle seemed to be the perfect storyteller to revise and update the pageant for modern audiences hungry for a more factual interpretation of the past. While some Natchezians say that the time had come to permanently retire the pageant, Doyle saw the tableaux as an opportunity to enhance residents' and tourists' understanding of Natchez's past. "The tableaux offers a way to tell these stories in a way that helps people understand them and be proud of their history," she notes. "And the more we dig into our past, the more we find new history." For Doyle, her work on the pageant was all about letting go of a selective white memory that long ruled Natchez and "documenting a more inclusive past."[29]

The optimism shared by Doyle and other progressives who endorsed the revamped pageant was short lived and came to an abrupt halt in early fall 2017, reflecting the contestations and challenges that often surface when attempts are made to revise and correct sacred historical memory and traditions. When the Natchez Garden Club announced a decision to return to their traditional pageant format and that Doyle's services were no longer needed, it became clear that Doyle's progressive efforts to create a more inclusive historical narrative prompted a white conservative backlash based on an unwillingness to change an entrenched community tradition. Simultaneously, the Pilgrimage Garden Club announced they were parting ways with the Natchez Garden Club and would no longer participate in a dated production that failed to embrace a racially inclusive narrative of their town's past.[30] In analyzing the decision made by the Natchez Garden Club of which she is a member, Doyle claims that for some people it is "unsettling to rethink things about the past that they thought were solid." She responds with a pragmatic message to those uncomfortable with such changes, noting, "There is a $50 billion African American travel industry, and only six percent of our tourists are black. Natchez is still a frontier waiting to be discovered by scholars and visitors."

While bruised by the NGC's decision to abandon her updated pageant production, Doyle's persistent optimism reflects that while one battle was lost, the war to create progressive change in Natchez's historic narrative and heritage tourism marketplace is far from over. She points to the 2016 election of Mayor Darryl Grennell, only the third black mayor to be elected in Natchez since Reconstruction. Grennell told a national magazine not long after his election, "Here in Natchez, we're all about inclusion and telling the whole multicultural and multiethnic story."[31] Grennell's words are borne out in a flurry of projects currently under development in Natchez. For example, not far from the Forks of the Road site, the nonprofit group Friends of Our Riverfront (F.O.R. Natchez!), which focuses on economic redevelopment, is raising funds to create an open-air African American history museum in what was once a gas station owned and operated by blacks, known as the Triangle Filling Station. The museum will focus on Reconstruction-era and civil rights history and will also serve as a trailhead for the St. Catherine Street Trail. In similar fashion to her work on revamping the Historic Natchez Tableaux, Doyle, who serves as president of F.O.R., is passionate about the work planned for Triangle Filling Station. Recognizing that the 1940s-era building was in danger of collapsing, Doyle and her group quickly moved into action and raised the money needed to stabilize the building. Doyle attributes her strong sense of place as the motivation behind saving old houses (like the one she renovated and lives in) and the old, decaying filling station with unique architectural details she envisions turning into a museum. "When you're tied to place as I am, it hurts to lose a good house or building; it's like losing a member of your family," she says. It's a good business decision as well, she adds. "It's all about creating a big package." Saving such treasures and repurposing them for modern use creates more reasons to come to Natchez, a place that she contends is a "miracle" waiting to happen.

WHEN HISTORY BECOMES PERSONAL

The ongoing battle to establish a more inclusive, accurate, and critical Natchez history within local institutions is also being waged at a personal and emotional level, sometimes digging up painful family memories in the process. During the Civil War sesquicentennial in 2011, historic archeologist Elizabeth Boggess, whose family dates back to Natchez's planter class in the 1700s, found herself in the vanguard of setting the historical record straight—and this time the record was extremely personal. At a September

2011 conference sponsored by the National Park Service entitled "No More Silence at Second Creek: Slave Resistance and the Onset of the Civil War," Boggess was among several scholars who presented papers in response to the infamous 1861 execution of forty or more Adams County slaves accused of plotting a conspiracy to overthrow their masters (see chapter 3). Boggess became intrigued with the subject after her mother told her in the 1980s that Elizabeth's great-grandfather James Surget had hung ten of the male victims at the family-owned Cherry Grove property. "I was absolutely shocked," Boggess recalls. Growing up, Boggess says she had never heard family members mention the incident. "I'm not really sure whether this was because it was suppressed or too dangerous to talk about."[32]

Boggess's desire to learn more about her family's history and their relationship to slavery was in large part motivated by the scholarship of academic outsider Winthrop Jordan's book, *Tumult and Silence at Second Creek* (greatly substantiated by Justin Behrend's research that followed) and the many student papers and scholar presentations at numerous Historic Natchez Conferences, which she and her sister Anne attended. Driven to learn more about their family's past, Beth and Anne studied maps, census records, land records, and the Surget's estate inventories, which listed the names of the family's enslaved property, enabling the sisters to piece the story together and come to a better understanding of their great-grandfather's role in the incident. According to Boggess, James Surget, owner of Cherry Grove, managed several nearby plantations for his uncle, Jacob Surget, a wealthy planter who lived in New York and managed the family's shipping firm. A twenty-five-year-old captain in the local home guard, James was ordered by his military superior to hang the accused slaves. Boggess surmises that the incident must have haunted James Surget for the rest of his life. "What would it have done to young Captain James to whip and hang people he had grown up with as older mentors or former playmates? To carry out these orders has to have been a life-changing event." The record of James Surget's later life offers some evidence of the impact of that fateful day. After the war, Surget gave away a generous amount of land to his family's former slaves. Boggess interprets these actions as her ancestor's intention "to make his own reparations."[33]

The one hundred people who attended the Second Creek conference included the descendants of the executioners and the black insurgents they tortured and executed. The response to her presentation was powerful and at times very quiet remembers Boggess. "With African Americans in the audience, I knew I had to make it personal. I was neither justifying nor excusing what took place on my family's property. But I was not keeping it a secret either." Her work on the project continues as she scours archives for family letters and more information on the home guard unit to which her great-grandfather belonged. As she stated in her conference presentation, "We are left with unanswered questions. We want to know who died at Cherry Grove so we can give them back their names."[34]

The 2011 symposium marked a turning point in ending the silence at Second Creek and laid the groundwork for more openly sharing Natchez's troubling past. Following the lead of her sister Elizabeth Boggess, Anne MacNeil is today far more forthcoming in speaking about the role of slavery in her family's past than she was a decade ago and commits herself to delivering as accurate a historical narrative as possible when she shares stories of her family's ancestral home Elms Court. With the exception of probate papers that listed the family's enslaved property, MacNeil says that "For years I lacked having any real documentation about the slave population at Elms Court" and as a result did not feel that she could accurately address the topic of slavery. No more. According to MacNeil, with the help of NNHP's Kathleen Bond, HNF's Mimi Miller, and African American activist Ser Sesh Boxley's persistent drive for equal and inclusive history, "we've made enormous progress over the past ten years," referring to those like herself who open their antebellum homes to strangers during Pilgrimage season and other times of the year. "We're not all the way where we need to be, but twenty years ago, we wouldn't have talked about the enslaved population and relations between black and whites."[35]

The research work of the park service, the foundation, and the students and scholars who collaborated with these institutions provided residents like MacNeil with the documentation needed to begin addressing the history of enslavement within their own homes. MacNeil recalls her own epiphany in confronting slavery at a personal level when she visited a slavery exhibit at Melrose, the grand antebellum home now managed by the NNHP. MacNeil discovered from the exhibit that her great-grandfather Samuel Sillman Boyd was involved in the slave trade, an occupation that many wealthy planters dabbled in. An exhibit panel in Melrose's slave cabin shared the story about an enslaved woman whom Boyd purchased. "He mistreated her so badly that his friends tried to buy her," she says. Further researching her infamous ancestor, MacNeil learned that Boyd had a black concubine who was mother to his children. He later shipped her off to slave markets in Texas. "The woman was literate and wrote letters about all of this." MacNeil says her response was "Oh wow. This is not an ancestor to be proud of. Once you learn something like that you have to learn how to deal with it on a kind of spiritual level." Anne and her sister decided to make that ancestor available as part of their home's historical narrative. "We tell tourists, 'this is the ancestor we've tried to disown.'" While they don't always share the Boyd story with visitors, they do make a conscious effort to talk about slavery. "You can't talk about nineteenth-century history without talking about enslavement," states MacNeil.[36]

Response to her willingness to share documented evidence about her ancestors and their enslaved laborers has been overwhelmingly positive, reports MacNeil. Following the guidelines of the National Trust for Historic Preservation, MacNeil has tried to steer away from traditional house museum tours of talking excessively about the porcelain, silver, and portraits as inanimate objects of the past, which she says fails to captivate the interest of today's tourists. Instead, she strives to talk about the furnishings in terms of how people used them. While she is open to most questions, she draws a line when visitors broach the question of how much it costs to maintain such a large and old home. "I just say a bundle," she says with a gentle smile.[37]

SLAVE HOME JOINS PILGRIMAGE

Concord Quarters, located on the old Concord estate first owned by Spanish don Manuel Gayosa and later by the prominent Stephen Minor family, is the newest addition in the stable of Pilgrimage tour homes open to visitors twice a year and is like no other. Concord's large planter estate burned to the ground in 1901, but one of the two-story, three-thousand-square-foot slave quarters built in 1820 survived, albeit leaking, water damaged, and covered in thick kudzu. Debbie Cosey, a black Natchez native who grew up in the hospitality industry, decided to purchase and restore the property with her husband Greg in 2012. Initially, Cosey was drawn to the property with the idea of creating a wedding venue for budget-conscious brides. She also admits that as a young girl she dreamed of one day owning her own antebellum home as she played on the gallery of Hawthorne, an antebellum Natchez home where her mother worked as a domestic. She eventually got her wish, but instead of a fine big house, she finds herself today the proud owner of a former slave quarter home that she says has its own unique architectural charms.[38]

With support from the Mississippi Department of Archives and History and advice from the Historic Natchez Foundation, the Coseys moved forward to save the quarters. The couple moved into the first floor of the quarters and turned the upstairs into rooms for a bed and breakfast. "It's not elaborate, notes Cosey, but the architecture is quite beautiful." In December 2016 the quarters were open for Christmas season tours, and in the fall of 2017 the Cosey's home joined the lineup of Pilgrimage home tours for the first time. Cosey reports that while the response to her B&B venture has been overwhelmingly positive, some members of the local African American community have criticized saving a home once occupied by the enslaved. Upon hearing remarks, such as 'I didn't know slaves had houses,' or 'Why did you restore slave quarters that should be burned down?' Cosey counters such criticisms by speculating about the daily life of enslaved persons. "When the enslaved went to work each day, they were eager to return home at the end of the day, no matter what it looked like. I know the people who lived here were enslaved, but they were glad to come home, probably poked fun at the old master, and sang songs after a long day of working in the fields or inside the big house."[39]

While some in the historic community applaud Cosey's efforts to save an architecturally significant structure, others question sugarcoating a space used to house enslaved human beings as an "Old Slave Quarters," similarly to how antebellum homes are mythologized in Natchez and across the South. Compounding this argument, research shows that such spaces were frequently the site or refuge of inhabitants who had been abused, raped, and physically and emotionally tortured. While there may have been moments of laughter and joy in the quarters, there was little that was good about them. The harsh realities of life in the quarters as documented in historic research exposes the challenges of Cosey's dilemma as both a historic preservationist and bed and breakfast owner. Presenting the restored quarter through the lens of a mythic "home-sweet-home" perspective is perhaps the easier approach to take, one that will appeal to paying guests, many of whom are white, while also satisfying an emotional desire to see something good and worthwhile about slavery. But this is not sound history. To not tell the real story of what went on in the quarters is to miss an opportunity to share the tragic truth of slavery from a critical perspective, and in the end, those like Cosey risk becoming part of the problem, despite their good intentions.

To Cosey's credit, she is working to uncover more of her property's slave history, even as she strives to build a successful business. She frequently googles the names of the enslaved recorded in Stephen Minor's inventory. Information on the white families who resided at Concord is plentiful, not so the enslaved, she reports. At some point, she plans to delve into the papers of Stephen Minor housed in the LSU archives and elsewhere to try to learn more about the African Americans who once made their home where she too now resides. Fortunately, the Natchez National Historical Park serves as a community resource that is working to make Natchez slave history available to historic property owners like Cosey. "Restoring this house was painstaking," Cosey recalls. "But one of my motivations was to get people to start chatting about slavery. I chose to live here and not let this place be destroyed, and I believe this restoration is helping to open a dialogue." Indeed, Cosey's decision to save the quarters offers a unique opportunity to create a venue to ask the tough, critical-minded questions about slavery that need to be addressed rather than to simply assume that they were "homes" in any sense of the word. From all indications, Cosey appears to be on the right path to balancing the need for an inclusive yet critical history with the demands of marketing a successful heritage tourism experience.[40]

A PILGRIM'S RECKONING

Based on recent developments in Natchez heritage tourism, this city has made significant and admirable strides in creating a more inclusive and critical rendering of that past that is beginning to honor all of its citizens—African American, white, and Native American. Through honest and courageous soul searching led by the Natchez National Historical Park, the Historic Natchez Foundation, scholars, churches, and individuals, this community is reexamining and coming to grips with a past that was marred by slavery, racism, and civil rights injustice, while debating how that past should be told.

To be sure, Natchez has more work to do in sharing its complex history. Serious economic and social problems need to be addressed if Natchez is to fully capitalize on the progress made to date. Ranking as one of the poorest states in the nation in 2016 with 20.8 percent of Mississippians living in poverty and 36 percent of black Mississippians below the poverty line—fourteen points higher than the black national average—poor black neighborhoods in Natchez stand in stark contrast to the grand antebellum estates located within walking distance. The papermill and industrial jobs that evaporated in the 1990s have yet to be replaced, making it all but impossible to eradicate the poverty that keeps many African Americans and members of the white working class mired within its grasp. Major new sources of employment are needed to reduce poverty, but factories and companies are reluctant to come to Natchez with its failing public school system ranked as one of the worst in the state.[41]

Following the pattern of white flight established in the early 1970s, most white families send their children to better quality private schools alongside a growing number of black kids from middle-class homes. Meanwhile, Natchez public school students, more than 90 percent of them black, are dealt a cruel blow: Their substandard education offers them little chance of succeeding in the job market or college (if they are admitted or can afford to attend). Sadly, the local schoolboard struggles over how to solve these problems amidst infighting and racial divisions.

Despite the advances made in recent years, Natchez still struggles to refashion its traditional lily-white heritage tourism narrative, as evidenced by the Natchez Garden Club's recent decision to return to their traditional pageant dominated by an elite white antebellum ideology that obliterates the town's African American history. The NGC adopted the new pageant for one season, but the leadership found they could not live with the legacy of radical change that brought their town's slave history to the forefront of the program. If the pageant survives—and there are many in the town who question its longevity in the twenty-first century—the battle for a more inclusive, accurate, and critical adaptation of the historic narrative will need to be waged by a younger generation of garden club warriors.

Likewise, conflicts are evident within the black community over who should tell their history and how. As noted earlier, some African Americans resist working with progressive whites who are willing and eager to partner with the black community in telling a more racially inclusive story from a critical perspective. For many years, black leaders have preached the idea that it was wrong to give whites, who symbolized their historic oppressors, the responsibility of determining how African American history would be told. Some within the black community now question this logic and want to collaborate with whites in the community despite the painfulness of the past. Debbie Cosey, owner of Concord Quarters, is one of those African Americans. People whom she characterizes as "intelligent and no longer bitter" want whites and blacks to work together to tell the story of Natchez's past, adding, "as my mother used to say, 'We need a healing here.'"[42] Such battles are yet another reminder that all history is contested terrain and particularly so when the historical memories, such as enslavement, are painful and personal.

Other thorny issues in Natchez's past also need to be remembered and made public. One wonders why there is no mention of the role of the Ku Klux Klan in the post-Reconstruction era as well as the recent past. Moreover, why isn't the character of Jim Crow racism acknowledged in Natchez's public spaces? Furthermore, how can a town with a black community as large as Natchez's tolerate and indeed ignore all that the Confederate Memorial represents? On yet another front, the time has come to name more of those who labored as enslaved house servants and artisans in Natchez and tell their stories as other American historic sites recently have begun to do, such as Montpelier, the home of James Madison, "father of the US Constitution." Abundant scholarship now exists to document and explore these topics with critical accuracy, and additional historic records housed in the Historic Natchez Foundation are waiting to speak their truths. Space can and should be made to tell these and other stories in the Natchez National Historical Park visitor center, in the African American History Museum, through trail markers in outdoor spaces, and in antebellum house tour scripts. A truly inclusive presentation of the past must grapple with the horrors of a place that destroyed so many lives. That is the challenge that lies ahead for this storied place.[43]

Even as Natchez moves steadily forward to carve out a more accurate, racially inclusive, and critical historical narrative for itself, there are puzzling developments that raise questions. In the aftermath of Charlottesville, as a deeply divided nation fiercely defends and contests symbolic markers of its historic memory, Natchez is taking a gentler path, perhaps in keeping with the well-mannered civility that has long characterized this place. In the many conversations I had with black and white Natchezians during my visit, no one supported the idea of removing the Confederate memorial as other places like New Orleans have done. Some view the monument as a tribute to the dead, which should be treated as a sacred memorial. Others favored the idea of keeping the existing monument and adding another nearby to honor the United States Colored Troops who fought here as freedom fighters. Surprisingly, even Ser Sesh Boxley, the modern-day freedom fighter who has "constantly agitated for equal history" for more than two decades, publicly supports this approach. Now well into his seventies, Boxley reflects that he has reached a point in life where he would rather "build up than tear down." How to explain this attitude by a man who has been on the forefront fighting for racial equality, inclusion, and historical accuracy for decades? For some, Boxley's lack of rage over the Confederate monument issue is akin to survivors of the Jewish holocaust saying that they want to have statues of Jews erected next to a statue of an SS officer. But is there more to what seems like an abdication of responsibility as a community leader than first meets the eye? Perhaps as an aging warrior, Boxley is tired of fighting for change. More likely, Boxley, the veteran activist, is savvy enough to know that he has a better chance of achieving his goal of preserving the Forks of the Road slave market if he avoids the Confederate Monument issue—at least for now. On more than one occasion Boxley has been heard to say that it is far easier to get "plaques for blacks" from the conservative white state legislature as long as you don't ask for money or upset the apple cart. Boxley, like others in the Natchez professional history and heritage tourism community, is going for the plaques—or the Forks of the Road—but staying away from truly controversial and costly issues. To be sure, blacks here have achieved greater parity in recent years and perhaps some are comfortable to rest on their laurels and not as willing to contest every inch of ground as they might once have done. That doesn't mean there is not a fight left to fight. Acquiescing to the presence of a Confederate statue might be a sign that some inclusive-minded blacks in Natchez are comfortable with the status quo and that they have gained enough. That would be a shame.[44]

What becomes apparent as I wrap up my pilgrimage into Natchez's past is that it is no easy matter for the people who reside in this community to contest Natchez's historical memories in the same way a critical outsider might do. Not to diminish the extraordinary and courageous work that Natchez history professionals and civic and institutional leaders have done in recent years, here as in other southern communities, those sharing stories of the past are sometimes willing to let some myths survive in order to avoid angry resistance from conservative whites entrenched in the past. Likewise, black history leaders are sometimes tempted to forfeit a true and critical historical telling of their community's past to avoid rocking the boat in exchange for a few plaques.

Does an accurate and equal rendering of the past necessarily mean a more critical rendering? The Confederacy and the horrors of slavery should not be presented as equals. That is the reality that must be confronted by all southern historic memory making and those entrusted to share these memories. It is not just an inclusive memory that must emerge but a critically accurate memory. As former New Orleans Mayor Mitch Landrieu so poignantly stated in a speech he gave following the removal of Confederate monuments in his city: "The Confederacy was on the wrong side of history and humanity. It sought to tear apart our nation and subjugate our fellow Americans to slavery. This is the history we should never forget and one that we should never again put on a pedestal to be revered."[45]

Any effort to commemorate a past that was at times as ugly and troubled as Natchez's is fraught with moral dilemmas. Yet, thanks to the coupling of strong and wise external and homegrown influences the healing of Natchez's past is well underway, resulting in a flurry of innovative heritage tourism developments that while not always embracing a critically accurate narrative are far more racially inclusive and historically accurate than ever before. In the capable hands of today's Natchez memory makers—many of them women who like the garden clubwomen of the 1930s dedicate themselves to making Natchez a "tourist town"—the people here are largely succeeding in their mission to share a more accurate and inclusive rendering of their town's past. Given that the city depends on attracting largely white tourists interested in paying to see "where the Old South still lives," the wisest course of action may be to take small steady steps. Hopefully over time, civic and institutional leaders in Natchez will use the wealth of scholarship available to present a more critical, truthful, and meaningful perspective. Indeed, the town they proudly call home is increasingly becoming "Natchez: Where *More* than the Old South Still Lives," a mantra well worth striving for here and across the nation.

"Airlie, Natchez, Adams County, Mississippi," 1938. Frances Benjamin Johnston, photographer. Adams County Mississippi Natchez. Retrieved from the Library of Congress, https://www.loc.gov/item/csas201207171/. (Accessed March 6, 2018.)

GUIDE TO HISTORIC NATCHEZ HOMES

THE FOLLOWING SKETCHES OFFER BRIEF DESCRIPTIONS OF NATCHEZ HOMES that were part of the first Pilgrimage tour of homes in 1932 and remain standing today, many of which remain open to the public during Pilgrimage season. The historic photographs that accompany this section depict how these homes appeared in the 1930s, often reflecting a somewhat shabby appearance, far different from the beautifully restored homes open to the public today. These photographs feature the work of Earl Norman, son of Henry Norman, Francis Benjamin Johnston, who was sponsored by the Carnegie Survey of the Architecture of the South, and the Historic Architectural Building Survey (HABS), a Works Progress Administration (WPA) project funded during the New Deal in the 1930s. The cast of Natchez Pilgrimage homes has changed over the years and additional homes are now shown. Information on homes currently open to the public is available at the Natchez Visitor Center.

AIRLIE, CA. 1800

This unpretentious home is considered to be one of Natchez's earliest residences, likely built in the early 1800s. It was originally constructed for planter Stephen Minor and later sold to John Steele, a Revolutionary War Colonel who became secretary of the Mississippi Territory. Originally known as Belvedere, the home's name was changed to Airlie when Aylette Buckner purchased the property in 1832. The Buckner family remodeled Airlie's interior in the Greek revival style. The home's location on a bluff and its wide front gallery make it one of the most charming of Natchez's earlier homes.

Airlie is a private residence.
Address: 9 Elm St.

"Auburn, Natchez, Adams County, Mississippi," 1938. Auburn's famous spiral staircase. Frances Benjamin Johnston, photographer. Retrieved from the Library of Congress, https://www.loc.gov/item/csas200907168/. (Accessed March 6, 2018.)

"The Briars, Natchez vic., Adams County, Mississippi," 1938. Frances Benjamin Johnston, photographer. Retrieved from the Library of Congress, https://www.loc.gov/item/csas200907153/. (Accessed March 6, 2018.)

AUBURN, 1812

This National Historic Landmark was constructed in 1812 by architect Levi Weeks for attorney and planter Lyman Harding. The home was purchased in 1827 by Pennsylvania native Dr. Stephen Duncan, regarded as one of the world's wealthiest cotton planters, whose assets included more than one thousand slaves. Dr. Duncan's first wife was Margaret Ellis, daughter of an affluent Natchez planter. After Margaret's death, Dr. Duncan married Catherine Bingham, a member of another prominent local family.

Auburn is known for being the first house in the Natchez District to showcase classic architectural features, including a wide two-storied portico with four large Ionic columns. The entrance to the home is enhanced by majestically carved fan lights. Inside, the home features a remarkable freestanding spiral staircase. Dr. Duncan returned to the North during the Civil War and never returned to his Natchez home. The abandoned home remained unoccupied after the war and fell into severe disrepair. In 1911 Duncan descendants donated the house and surrounding land to the city of Natchez, which today is used as a public park and golf course. The home has been beautifully restored and is open daily for tours.

Contact info: 601-442-5981
Address: 400 Duncan Ave.
Open year round.

THE BRIARS, CA. 1818

The Briars, built on a bluff overlooking the Mississippi River, is best remembered as the girlhood home of Varina Howell, who married Jefferson Davis, future president of the Confederacy in the front parlor in February 1845. The home is an example of an elaborate version of a planter's cottage and is believed to have been built about 1818. In addition to the front gallery's six elegant large windows, the Briars features fan lit doorways, ornate mantle pieces and an unusual circular Spanish ceiling in the central hallway. The basement of the home originally served as slave quarters. After the Civil War, the home fell into severe disrepair and was rescued in 1927 by Mr. and Mrs. William Winnans Wall, who restored the home with many furnishings typical of the 1840s. Today the home operates as a bed and breakfast inn.

Contact info: 601-653-0018
Address: 130B John R. Junkin Dr.

"D'Evereux" (Courtesy of McMurran/Conner/Martin Collection, #110, University of Louisiana, Monroe, Special Collections Department.)

"Dunleith, 84 Homochito Street, Natchez, Adams County, MS." Historic American Buildings Survey, Creator, 1933. Retrieved from the Library of Congress, https://www.loc.gov/item/ms0026/. (Accessed March 6, 2018.)

D'EVEREUX, CA. 1835

D'Evereux represents one of America's most outstanding examples of Greek revival architecture. The front portico features six twenty-four-feet-tall Doric columns, which support a low, hipped roof. D'Evereux was built about 1840 by wealthy planter William St. John Elliott and named after his mother's family. William and his wife, Anna Conner Elliott, frequently hosted lavish entertainments at their home. During the Civil War, Union troops occupied the property, destroying the gardens, but sparing the home. In 1925 Miss Myra Virginia Smith purchased D'Evereux and began extensive restorations. Many of the fine furnishings on display are original to the house. Visitors can also enjoy the home's terraced gardens planted with azaleas and camellias.

D'Evereux is a private residence.
Address: 170 D'Evereux Dr.

DUNLEITH, CA. 1850

Dunleith stands on land originally occupied by Routhland, a house built by Job Routh and his wife during the late eighteenth century. Their daughter, Mary, a young teenage widow, married her second husband Charles Dahlgren and inherited the home. In 1855 Routhland burned down when lightning struck the chimney. Dahlgren built a second home in 1856, the present Dunleith. The majestic Greek revival home is the only surviving antebellum mansion in Mississippi to be encircled by two-story columns. After Mary's death, Dahlgren sold the home to Alfred Vidal Davis. It was Davis, a grandson of Don Jose Vidal and related to many of Natchez's most elite families, who gave the home the name Dunleith.

In 1880 the property was sold to Joseph Neibert Carpenter for $22,000. Carpenter's father Nathaniel Loomis had migrated to Natchez in 1833 from Lancaster, New York. N. L. Carpenter engaged in a variety of businesses, including construction, lumber mills, cotton factoring, textile manufacturing, and a line of steamers. His son Joseph, born in Natchez in 1846, served in the Confederate Army and upon his return joined his father in business. During his life he served as president of the Natchez Oil Company, the Natchez and Vidalia Packet Company, and the Natchez Cotton Exchange. Joseph and his wife Zipporah Russell Carpenter of Louisiana were the parents of two daughters and a son. Their son Nathaniel donated land for the town's

Elgin (Courtesy of the Thomas H. and Joan W. Gandy Photograph Collection, Louisiana Lower Mississippi Valley Collections, Special Collections, Hill Memorial Library, Louisiana State University Libraries, Baton Rouge.)

The Elms (Courtesy of the Thomas H. and Joan W. Gandy Photograph Collection, Louisiana Lower Mississippi Valley Collections, Special Collections, Hill Memorial Library, Louisiana State University Libraries, Baton Rouge.)

first public school in 1909. Their daughter Agnes inherited Dunleith in 1921. The property remained in the Carpenter family for several more decades. Today the property operates as a historic bed and breakfast and is open for tours year-round.

Contact info: 601-446-8500
Address: 84 Homochitto St.
Open year round

ELGIN, CA. 1792–1855

Elgin, built in several phases, began as a modest one-story home built with low ceilings, five rooms across, but only one room deep. The original home reflected a federal design. In 1839 Dr. John Jenkins, a Pennsylvania native, purchased the home for his bride, Annie Dunbar, granddaughter of the official surveyor of the Natchez Province, Sir William Dunbar. The following year Dr. Jenkins began making Greek revival additions to Elgin, making it a more comfortable home. In the early 1850s a two-story brick kitchen was constructed at the rear of the main house. Noteworthy interior features include a high-ceilinged library and the dining room, which has a punkah fan once operated by slaves to keep diners cool. Tragically, Dr. Jenkins and his wife died during a yellow fever epidemic in 1855. Their four children survived and with their descendants remained at Elgin until 1914. The home remains beautifully furnished with many heirlooms of the Jenkins family on display and operates as a bed and breakfast inn.

Contact info: 601-446-6100
Elgin1@bellsouth.net
Address: 1 Elgin Rd.

THE ELMS, CA.1804

The Elms, located in walking distance of downtown Natchez, is a blend of three architectural styles, built over a half century to fit the needs of its various occupants. John Henderson, who wrote the first book printed in Natchez, was an early resident. Before the Civil War, David Stanton (brother of Frederick Stanton, who built Stanton Hall) lived here. In addition to adding a two-story Greek revival-style stuccoed wing to the house's front porch,

"Elms Court, Natchez, Adams County, Mississippi," 1938. Frances Benjamin Johnston, photographer. Retrieved from the Library of Congress, https://www.loc.gov/item/csas201207182/. (Accessed March 6, 2018.)

Stanton built a billiard hall in the side yard, among other changes. In 1878 Moseley J. P. Drake purchased The Elms and was succeeded by generations of the Drake/Kellogg/Carpenter family, who still own the property. Alma Kellogg was a founding member of the Natchez Garden Club before joining the Pilgrimage Garden Club and served as club treasurer for many years. Her daughter, Alma Kellogg Carpenter, was a pageant queen and played a significant role in preserving Natchez history. Today, the home is open for tours and operates as a bed and breakfast inn.

Contact info: 601-445-5979
Address: 801 Washington St.

ELMS COURT, 1836

Elms Court, one of Natchez's loveliest suburban villas, was owned by several of Natchez's most prominent planter families, each of whom left a mark on the home, which today resembles a Mediterranean villa. Surrounded by a green, wooded, and parklike setting, the center portion of this Greek revival estate was originally built in 1836 for sisters Catherine and Eliza Evans, daughters of a prominent contractor. In 1852 the house was purchased by one of Natchez's wealthiest planters Francis Surget, who gave the mansion as a wedding gift to his daughter Jane and her husband Ayres P. Merrill, a Natchez native. Shortly after acquiring the home, the Merrills added one-story side wings, and made the most noticeable change to the house by replacing the original portico with a double-tiered, ornate cast-iron gallery. Not unlike other Natchez planters, the Merrills opposed secession. President Ulysses S. Grant rewarded Mr. Merrill for his loyalty to the Union by appointing him ambassador to Belgium in 1876.

A few years later in 1895, Elms Court was once again presented as a wedding gift to Surget descendants when James Surget of Cherry Grove Plantation gave the home to his daughter Carlotta and her husband David McKittrick. The couple was known for hosting lavish parties and lighting the interior of Elms Court with candled chandeliers. In the early days of the Natchez Pilgrimage the McKittricks hosted an event known as "The Ball of a Thousand Candles," which attracted hundreds of enchanted tourists. Descendants of the Surget and McKittrick families continue to live in the home.

Elms Court is a private residence.
Address: 542 John R. Junkin Dr.

"Gloucester, Natchez, Adams County, Mississippi, 1938." Retrieved from the Library of Congress, https://www.loc.gov/item/csa200907160/. (Accessed March 7, 2018.)

"Green Leaves, 303 Rankin Street Natchez, Adams County, MS, 1933." Historic American Buildings Survey, Creator, and Jonathon Thompson. Retrieved from the Library of Congress, https://www.loc.gov/item/ms0031/. (Accessed March 6, 2018.)

GLOUCESTER, CA. 1800

Gloucester ranks as one of the oldest and most historically significant homes in Natchez. Winthrop Sargent, appointed by President John Adams as the first governor of the Mississippi Territory, bought the home in 1807, naming it after his hometown of Gloucester, Massachusetts. The stately red-brick home makes a dramatic impression with its four large Tuscan columns gracing the front portico. The entrance to Gloucester is quite unusual with two separate doors at each end of the portico. These doors open to a large U-shaped hallway, which extends the length of the house. The home's ornate crystal chandeliers and marble mantels remain intact along with many fine furnishings. Gloucester was sold after the death of Winthrop Sargent. Twenty-five years later, Winthrop's son, George Washington Sargent, repurchased the estate. During the Union occupation of Natchez, Sargent was reportedly killed by Yankee soldiers on the property.

Gloucester is a private residence.
Address: Lower Woodville Rd. in South Natchez

GREEN LEAVES, CIRCA 1812

On the corner of Washington and Rankin stands Green Leaves, one of the most detailed and beautifully executed examples of Greek revival architecture in Natchez. Doric columns and an elaborate doorway with a broad rectangular fanlight above greet guests entering the home. In 1849 George Washington Koontz, a Pennsylvania native, purchased the home. Koontz was the business partner of William and Audley Britton, who established Britton and Koontz Bank, still in operation today. (Audley was the father of Mary Britton Conner, the amateur photographer profiled in chapter 5.)

During the Civil War, Mr. Koontz served the South by going to Europe in search of loans for the Confederacy. Mr. Koontz's affiliation with bankers and the South's loss in the war made him unpopular after the war. A failed assassination attempt on Mr. Koontz left a bullet hole in the home's entrance fanlight, still visible today.

The courtyard garden in the rear of the home has been beautifully restored. The grounds include a large oak, known as the Council Oak, which according to family legend was used by the Natchez Indians to hold tribal meetings. Ruth Audley Koontz Beltzhoover, daughter of George Koontz, grew

"Hope Farm, Natchez, Adams County, Mississippi, 1938. Frances Benjamin Johnston, photographer. Retrieved from the Library of Congress, https://www.loc.gov/item/csas201207187/. (Accessed March 6, 2018.)

up in the home and became an early Pilgrimage organizer. Mrs. Beltzhoover, with the encouragement of her husband Melchoir, created a small business serving lunch to Pilgrimage guests in her garden. She also was a successful buyer for her family's department store Famous and Price (see chapter 5). Descendants of George Koontz still occupy the home, which features many original nineteenth-century furnishings.

Green Leaves is a private residence.
Address: 303 Rankin St.

HOPE FARM, 1775

Hope Farm, located on Homochitto Street, is one of the few remaining colonial structures in Natchez. Construction began on the home in 1775 during the British period and was believed to have been purchased in 1789 by Spaniard Don Carlos de Grand Pre, Commandant of the Natchez District. Don Carlos was responsible for laying out the town of Natchez. In 1805 George Overtaker, merchant and owner of the nearby White Horse Tavern, acquired the property. The Montgomery family purchased Hope Farm in 1835 and kept it until 1926 when Balfour and Katherine Miller took ownership of the home, which by that time had greatly deteriorated. Katherine Miller is credited as the founder of the Natchez Pilgrimage. The home features both Spanish provincial and Greek revival architectural styles. Mrs. Miller frequently posed in the home's L-shaped garden for Pilgrimage publicity photos. After restoring their home, the Millers collected numerous colonial-era furnishings, including a "punishing chair" used to discipline students who misbehaved. Although childless, Mrs. Miller enjoyed entertaining young visitors. She is remembered for having hosted "Katherine" parties at Hope Farm for young Natchez girls who shared her name. Today Hope Farm is a popular bed and breakfast inn and Pilgrimage tour destination.

Contact info: 601-445-4848
www.hopefarmbedandbreakfast.com
Address: 147 Homochitto St.

Publicity shot of House on Ellicott's Hill shortly after its renovation in 1937 by the Natchez Garden Club. (Courtesy of the Thomas H. and Joan W. Gandy Photograph Collection, Louisiana Lower Mississippi Valley Collections, Special Collections, Hill Memorial Library, Louisiana State University Libraries, Baton Rouge.)

HOUSE ON ELLICOTT'S HILL, CA. 1798

This West Indies–style house, a National Historic Landmark, also known as Connelly's Tavern, was built on the campsite of Andrew Ellicott, a major in the US Army sent to survey the Natchez District. Major Ellicott raised the American flag on the site in February 1797, considered the first time the flag was raised in the lower Mississippi Valley.

Natchez merchant James Moore purchased the land from the mother-in-law of the Spanish governor, Manuel Gayoso de Lemos. Moore built the House on Ellicott's Hill about 1798 for use as a tavern. Much of the materials used to build the two stories of the house were harvested from old shipping vessels and flatboats. The first floor was used as a tap room and kitchen, and the upstairs housed paying guests. The views of the Mississippi River from the house's upstairs gallery are some of the best in town. Today the House on Ellicott's Hill stands as the last remaining merchant's home on Canal Street. A number of other residents lived in the house over the years, including the first mayor of Natchez, Samuel Brooks, and Dr. Frederick Seip, an early physician in the Natchez Territory. Prior to the Civil War, the Natchez High School for Boys was housed in the building. Around 1878, the house served as living quarters for workers at a nearby cotton mill. Following the closure of the mills in the 1920s, the house stood empty until 1934.

The Natchez Garden Club purchased the House on Ellicott's Hill in 1934 for $2,000. Club members persuaded prominent New Orleans architect Richard Koch to oversee the restoration of the dilapidated house for $150 plus his travel expenses. The work was completed in 1937 and marked the first historic restoration project undertaken by a civic organization in Mississippi. Garden club member Roane Fleming Byrnes, who also played an influential role in the Natchez Trace project (see chapter 5), served as chairwoman of the project. Club members carefully researched the best means to preserve the house and sought authentic furnishings in keeping with the 1819 estate inventory of Dr. Seip. In 2006 a three-year project to rehabilitate the exterior and interior of the building was completed. The House on Ellicott's Hill is open to visitors during Pilgrimage season as well as the rest of the year.

Contact info: 601-442-2011
www.natchezpilgrimage.com
Address: 211 North Canal St.

"Lansdowne, Natchez, Adams County, Mississippi, 1938." Frances Benjamin Johnston, photographer. Retrieved from the Library of Congress, https://www.loc.gov/item/csas201207190. (Accessed March 6, 2018.)

"Linden, Natchez, Adams County, Mississippi, 1938." Frances Benjamin Johnston, photographer. Retrieved from the Library of Congress, https://www.loc.gov/item/csas201207190. (Accessed March 7, 2018.)

LANSDOWNE, 1853

Located about a mile from downtown Natchez, Lansdowne is a well-preserved and charming example of Georgian and Greek revival architecture situated in a parklike setting. The home has been carefully preserved by the descendants of Mr. and Mrs. George Marshall, who built the home in 1853. Mrs. Marshall's father, David Hunt, one of the wealthiest planters in Mississippi, bestowed the land on his daughter and son-in-law as a wedding gift. The Marshalls built a one-story home with a white-railed captain's walk on the roof. Although they originally planned to build a second story, the home remains as it was originally built.

Although Lansdowne's exterior is rather modest, once inside guests quickly discover a hall measuring fifteen feet by sixty-five feet surrounded by a large parlor and bedrooms. The rear of the house features a gallery leading to a courtyard and two-story service buildings. These buildings contained a commissary, a schoolroom, a bedroom for the governess, a billiard room, and even a gas plant. George Marshall spent a great deal of time and money acquiring fine furnishings, carpets, paintings, and china for his country estate. Many of these items are still on display, making this one of Natchez's finest house museums. Female descendants of the Marshall family were actively involved in the Natchez Garden Club and later the Pilgrimage Garden Club.

Contact info: 225-335-2888
info@lansdowneplantation.com
Address: 17 Marshall Rd.

LINDEN, CA. 1785

Work on this gracious home probably first began sometime between 1785 and 1792 by merchant James Moore, who also built the House on Ellicott's Hill. Senator Thomas Reed of Mississippi acquired the home in 1818. Senator Reed likely added the wings on both sides of the original structure, the ninety-eight-foot gallery that spans the front entrance and the front entrance doorway with a majestic fanlight above. The entranceway to Linden so captivated the filmmakers who produced *Gone with the Wind* that they copied it for the design used for Scarlett O'Hara's girlhood home Tara. After Senator Reed's death, Dr. John Ker, a close family friend, acquired the property. Ker named his new home Linden and is believed to have added the current dining room.

"Longwood, Natchez, Adams County, MS, 1933." Historic American Buildings Survey, Creator with James Butters, photographer. Retrieved from the Library of Congress, https://www.loc.gov/item/ms0123/. (Accessed March 6, 2018.)

In 1849 Mrs. Jane Gustine Conner, widow of planter William C. Conner, bought Linden. Mrs. Conner continued to make improvements to the home, adding a west wing and a lovely outdoor courtyard surrounded on three sides by galleries. Mrs. Conner was recognized as the "little war mother" because seven of her sons served in the Confederate Army. Linden was the boyhood home of amateur photographer and history buff Mary Britton Conner's husband Lemuel Conner Jr. (see chapter 4). Today the home serves as both a bed and breakfast and a popular Pilgrimage tour stop.

Contact info: 601-445-5472
www.lindenbandb.com
Address: 1 Conner Circle

LONGWOOD, 1861

Longwood, a National Historic Landmark, is one of the most unusual homes in Natchez and stands as a testament to the impact of the Civil War on Natchez's planter class. Construction on this octagonal house—the largest and most elaborate in the nation—began in 1860, shortly before the Civil War began. Dr. and Mrs. Haller Nutt chose architect Samuel Sloan from Philadelphia to build a home for themselves and their eight children. Dr. Nutt was a physician, scientist, landowner, and wealthy planter. His father, Dr. Rush Nutt, had gained an international reputation for making improvements to the machinery planters used to process cotton. Haller Nutt and his wife Julia proclaimed themselves to be loyal to the Union.

Sloan hired artisans and construction workers who specialized in octagonal designs from Philadelphia to complete the job. Work proceeded rapidly on the six-story high building with eight sides. Inside rooms encircled a central rotunda. Interior rooms opened to a balcony or verandah through large floor-to-ceiling arched windows, assuring comfortable ventilation. An onion-shaped "oriental" dome painted in a deep red completed the architectural curiosity.

The exterior of Longwood was nearly completed in the fall of 1861; however, when war broke out, construction came to a sudden halt. Costly furniture and artwork en route to Natchez was confiscated and never reached Longwood. Meanwhile, the northern builders working on Longwood deserted the job site, leaving equipment, tools, and open cans of paint behind. Those objects remain on view for tourists today.

An illustration of Melrose's dining room and punkah fan created by the Historic American Buildings Survey, 1933. "Melrose," 1 Melrose-Montebello Parkway, Natchez, Adams County, MS. Retrieved from the Library of Congress, https://www.loc.gov/item/ms0209/. (Accessed April 14, 2018.)

Turning to local builders, Dr. Nutt finished the basement of his home, enabling his family to move into the house. During the war, the Nutt family lost most of their fortune when federal troops claimed their land and cotton crop. Destitute and depressed, Dr. Nutt died in 1864, leaving his widow Julia to raise the family and manage their property (see chapter 1). Longwood was also the site of the festive July 4 celebration staged by Natchez blacks shortly after the Civil War (see chapter 2). Although Julia Nutt sought bids to complete her home, the work was never finished.

For more than a century, three generations of Nutt descendants continued to live in the basement of Longwood. In the late 1960s the home was purchased and donated to the Pilgrimage Garden Club, which preserves the house and keeps it open for daily tours.

Contact info: 601-446-6631
Address: 140 Lower Woodville Rd.
Open year round and during Pilgrimage

MELROSE, 1840

Melrose, the centerpiece of the Natchez National Historical Park, is one of the town's antebellum treasures and looks much as it did when it was built in the 1840s by attorney John T. McMurran, a northerner by birth, and his wife Mary Louisa Turner McMurran. Mr. McMurran was a close friend of Mississippi Governor John Quitman, the owner of Monmouth. The expansive 15,000 square foot mansion, located on fifty-six acres of parklike grounds, features both Georgian and Greek revival styles. A beautifully carved mahogany punkah fan hangs over the dining room table once operated by slaves to keep the air circulating on warm days.

The McMurrans, who at one time had owned or held interest in five plantations and retained more than three hundred slaves, held on to Melrose through the Civil War, but due to financial hardship were forced to sell their property in 1865 to Elizabeth and George Davis, whose townhome Choctaw was occupied by Union soldiers. Melrose was rarely used and remained unoccupied for nearly forty years. Former slaves Alice Sims and Jane Johnson are credited with caring for Melrose during this time. Johnson later participated as a Melrose Pilgrimage tour guide. Heirs of the Davis family lived in the house until 1976. Native New Yorker Ethel Moore Kelly, an early garden club member who moved into the home in 1900 shortly after her marriage to

"Monmouth House, East Franklin Street & Melrose Ave., Natchez, Adams County, MS, 1933." Historic American Buildings Survey, Creator. Retrieved from the Library of Congress, https://www.loc.gov/item/ms0206. (Accessed March 6, 2018.)

Davis descendant George Malin Kelly, remained loyal to the Natchez Garden Club during the "Battle of the Hoopskirts" (see chapters 6 and 7). In 1974 Melrose was recognized as a National Historic Landmark and is operated by the Natchez National Historical Park. Due to the relatively few number of owners, much of Melrose's original furnishings, lighting fixtures, and marble fireplaces remain intact.

Contact info: 601-446-5790
Address: 1 Melrose-Montebello Pkwy.
Open year round and during Pilgrimage

MONMOUTH, 1818

The strong, bold exterior of Monmouth is in keeping with this home's most famous owner, General John A. Quitman, a hero of the Mexican War, who later served as a Mississippi governor and US congressman. Born in New York, Quitman migrated first to Ohio and then to Natchez while in his early twenties. He established a law practice and a short time later married Eliza Turner, the daughter of a wealthy Adams County planter. The Quitmans purchased Monmouth in 1824 and eventually became one of the largest landowners in the state, with holdings of 15,000 acres and three hundred slaves. In 1836 Quitman led the Natchez Fencibles, a volunteer militia group, to fight Mexican forces in Texas. Upon his return he was promoted to major general and later appointed provisional governor of Mexico during the United States' brief occupation of that country. Quitman was elected governor of Mississippi in 1849 but was forced to resign one year later when indicted by a federal grand jury for violating neutrality laws when he supported Cuban independence. (The charges were eventually dropped.) In 1855 Quitman was elected to Congress. Quitman was also active in the Freemasons and served as grand master of the Mississippi Masons from 1826 to 1838 and in 1840 and 1845 (see chapter 3). During his tenure at Monmouth, Quitman entertained Jefferson Davis and over time became one of the South's most ardent secessionists. He died in 1858 at Monmouth after contracting what is believed to be Legionnaires' disease while in the nation's capital. His wife died one year later. Papers and letters left by Quitman's daughters provide insights into the post–Civil War era (see chapter 1).

Monmouth was inhabited by General Quitman's descendants for nearly fifty years after the Civil War ended. During this time, Monmouth like so

"Montaigne," Natchez, Adams County, Mississippi, 1938. Johnston, Frances Benjamin, photographer. Sometime after Johnston shot this photo the exterior stucco was painted pink, which remains today. Retrieved from the Library of Congress, https://www.loc.gov/item/2017892855/. (Accessed April 14, 2018.)

many of Natchez's finest antebellum homes, began to lose its splendor. During the 1870s, Monmouth's main house and grounds were rented out and the land was used to grow cotton. During the 1880s Quitman family members lived at the estate along with a number of former slaves, some of whom purchased small plots of land from the Quitman family. In 1919 the home was sold to an outside party, but remained empty for several years. In 1922 Natchez widow Annie Gwin purchased Monmouth. The home remained in Gwin's family for more than fifty years. When Gwin married Herbert Barnum, she moved to nearby Arlington. Monmouth was primarily used as a dairy farm during this time, and for several decades the estate's once-elegant twenty-six acres served as pastures for cattle. Mrs. Barnum also served as a president of the Pilgrimage Garden Club and played a prominent role in the "Battle of the Hoopskirts" (see chapter 6).

Monmouth has been restored to its former splendor and now operates as an upscale historic inn and is open daily for tours.

Contact info: 601-442-5852
Address: 1358 John A. Quitman Blvd.

MONTEIGNE, 1855

Monteigne is historically significant because it was the residence of William T. Martin, a Natchez attorney and one of Mississippi's highest-ranking Confederate generals. Martin was married to Margaret Conner Martin, profiled in chapter 1. Mrs. Martin wrote numerous letters to the general describing the hardships of civilian life during the Civil War. According to some historians, the home suffered damage from Union troops during the war, most likely because of Martin's high rank in the Confederate Army.

The home was originally built as an Italianate cottage with front and side galleries. In 1927 Monteigne was remodeled in a neoclassical style by New Orleans architects Weiss, Dreyfus, and Seiferth, who also designed Natchez's Eola Hotel. Although many interior alterations were made, Monteigne retains the original classic doorway woodwork and fireplace mantles. Sometime after 1938 the home was stuccoed in pink. The home is known for its lush gardens, which feature azaleas and more than one hundred varieties of camellias, planted by William Kendall. (Kendall was the subject of an article written by newspaper columnist Ernie Pyle in the 1930s and shared in chapter 5.) Mary Louise Kendall, one of the founding members of the Natchez Garden Club

"Richmond," Natchez, Adams County, Mississippi, 1938. Johnston, Frances Benjamin, photographer. Retrieved from the Library of Congress, https://www.loc.gov/item/2017892855/. (Accessed March 6, 2018)

and later the Pilgrimage Garden Club, lived here for many years before her death at the age of 109 in 2015.

Monteigne is a private residence.
Address: Liberty Rd.

RICHMOND, 1784, C. 1800–1810, 1832, 1860

This spacious 16,000-foot home was built in three stages, beginning in the 1780s, and features three distinctive architectural styles: French plantation, colonial, and Greek revival. New Yorker Levin R. Marshall bought the home in 1832 for $7,500, and his descendants have been living at Richmond ever since. Numerous pieces of furniture, shipped from New York and dating back to the 1830s, remain in the home.

Levin Marshall was extremely wealthy and his holdings included 24,000 acres of land in several states and more than eight hundred slaves. He served as president of the Commercial Bank in Natchez and as a partner in the Natchez Steam Packet Company. Although Levin was a large slaveholder he was sympathetic to the Union cause and suffered severe losses during the Civil War. After the war, he left his Natchez home and returned to New York, while his descendants remained in the home. Among his grandchildren, Theodora Britton Marshall (1896–1967), affectionately referred to as Aunt Pedoty, played a role in the early years of the Pilgrimage. One of ten children, nine of them girls, Theodora never married (nor did five other sisters or her brother). Theodora was the author of two Natchez guidebooks and ran an antique store from the basement of Richmond along with Catharine Dunbar Brown, another passionate local amateur historian (see chapter 5).

Richmond is a private residence.
Address: 31 Government Fleet Rd.

ROSALIE, 1820

Rosalie is named for a French fort built on the bluffs of Natchez. In 1820 Pennsylvania native Peter Little, the owner of a prosperous sawmill, purchased a portion of the fort's land to build his impressive home. He kept the name Rosalie in honor of the old fort and its settlers. Little married his

"Rosalie, Natchez, Adams County, Mississippi, 1938." Frances Benjamin Johnston, photographer. Retrieved from the Library of Congress, https://www.loc.gov/item/csas201207204/. (Accessed March 6, 2018.)

ward Eliza Lowe, the orphaned daughter of his friend Jacob Lowe, a ferryboat owner. Before joining her husband at Rosalie, Eliza, a teenager at the time, was sent to Baltimore to complete her education. The Littles never had children of their own, but Rosalie became home for a number of Natchez children. Eliza helped found the Natchez Children's Home and the couple raised Peter's niece after her mother died. The couple remained devoted to one another throughout forty-five years of marriage. In 1853 Eliza died of yellow fever at the age of sixty and Peter died three years later. Peter Little left no will, thus requiring that the property be sold at public auction. Andrew Wilson and his wife, close friends of the Littles, purchased the home.

In 1863 Rosalie became headquarters to the Union Army under General Walter Gresham. Mrs. Gresham and Mrs. Wilson became friends, and the home and its contents were preserved. The Wilsons never had children, and like the Littles, they welcomed orphaned children to Rosalie. They adopted Fannie McMurty, who later married steamboat captain Stephen Rumble in the Rosalie parlor in 1866. The Rumbles had six children at Rosalie. Faced with difficult financial circumstances, two of the Rumble's daughters, Annie and Rebecca, sold Rosalie to the Mississippi State Society, Daughters of the American Revolution, in 1938. This effort was led by Catharine Dunbar Brown, who led a group of DAR delegates before the Mississippi legislature to petition the state to fund the restoration of Rosalie. The legislature appropriated $10,000 for the preservation of the home and estate (see chapter 6). Today the property operates as a DAR house museum. The Rumble sisters continued to live at Rosalie and gave tours of the house up until Annie Rumble Marsh's death in 1958.

Contact info: 601-446-5676
www.rosaliemansion.com
Address: 100 Orleans St.
Open year round and during Pilgrimage season

STANTON HALL, 1858

Considered by many to be the most stunning antebellum home in Natchez, Stanton Hall, built by Irish immigrant Frederick Stanton, was completed in late 1858, just a short time before the beginning of the Civil War. The home occupies an entire city block and is beautifully positioned on a parklike knoll

"Stanton Hall, Natchez, Adams County, Mississippi, 1938." Frances Benjamin Johnston, photographer. Retrieved from the Library of Congress, https://www.loc.gov/item/csas200907170/. (Accessed March 6, 2018.)

in the center of the property. Stanton became a successful cotton broker and married Huldah Helm, daughter of a wealthy and elite Natchez family.

The Stantons originally lived at Cherokee, but Stanton longed for a larger estate that would compare to the property his family owned in Ireland. Stanton spent lavishly on his new home—originally named Belfast—acquiring many of his furnishings from Europe. Frederick Stanton died in 1859, only a few months after the home was finished. Stanton's family lived in the home throughout the war and into the 1890s when they leased their home for use as a private girl's school. Known as Stanton College, the property eventually was renamed Stanton Hall. After being sold numerous times, the Pilgrimage Garden Club under the leadership of Katherine Miller purchased the home in 1940 and began extensive repairs to restore the property to its former glory.

Stanton Hall blends Greek revival and Italianate architectural styles and is surrounded by an elegant iron fence. The spacious home features sixteen-foot-high ceilings on the first floor. Sliding doors connecting double parlors to the music room creates an elaborate ballroom with ornate French mirrors at both ends. Its Carriage House Restaurant (another of Mrs. Miller's inspirations) is a popular place to enjoy authentic southern cuisine.

Contact info: 601-446-6631
www.stantonhall.com
Address: 401 High Street
Open year round

NOTES

INTRODUCTION

1. Visitmississippi.org/wp-content/uploads/2017/09/Tourism-Economic-Report-030317.pdf. Accessed March 22, 2018.

2. Katherine Grafton Miller, *Natchez of Long Ago and the Pilgrimage* (Natchez, MS: Rellimak, 1938), 31.

3. David Lowenthal, *The Past Is a Foreign Country* (Cambridge: Cambridge University Press, 1999). The Christian pilgrimage tradition originated in the early years of the church as Christians traveled to the tombs of saints. Although Martin Luther banned pilgrimages because the tradition was increasingly abused, the idea of pilgrimage was not abandoned within the Protestant movement. Pilgrimages remained important with the idea that life was a pilgrimage with the goal of reaching heaven. The University of York defines *pilgrimage* as a way to "describe an individual's journey through life, sometimes as a general description of personal growth and exploration, sometimes, as in Christianity, outlining a particular spiritual focus or pathway which it is believed will lead to an encounter with God." https://www.york.ac.uk/project/pilgrimage/intro.html#origins. Accessed August 3, 2017. Modern-day pilgrims continue to seek spiritual pilgrimage journeys such as the path opened between Oslo and Trondheim, Norway, on July 29, 1997, paying homage to the medieval pilgrimage undertaken to St. Olav's shrine in Trondheim. See St. Olav Ways, "The Pilgrimage Paths to Trondheim," https://www.pilgrimsleden.no/en. Accessed August 3, 2017.

4. David W. Blight, *Race and Reunion: The Civil War in American Memory* (Cambridge, MA: Belknap Press of Harvard University, 2001), 255–99.

5. Gaines M. Foster, *Ghosts of the Confederacy: Defeat, the Lost Cause, and the Emergence of the New South, 1865 to 1913* (New York: Oxford University Press, 1987).

6. Historical memory is a term that has been bandied about for decades by historians, many of whom studied the American South, and can be defined as the process an individual or entity uses to remember and think about the past. When a community or group engages in historical memory, it is often referred to as collective memory. Collective historical memory often leads to historical traditions that may include commemorations, parades, festivals, monument building, and heritage tourism sites.

7. Kathleen Clark, "Celebrating Freedom: Emancipation Day Celebrations and African American Memory in the Early Reconstruction South," in *Where These Memories Grow:*

History, Memory, and Southern Identity, ed. W. Fitzhugh Brundage (Chapel Hill: University of North Carolina Press, 2000), 109. Also see Kathleen Clark, *Defining Moments: African American Commemoration and Political Culture in the South, 1863–1913* (Chapel Hill: University of North Carolina Press, 2005), 240; Blight, 27, 49; Mitchell A. Kachun, *Festivals of Freedom: Memory and Meaning in African American Emancipation Celebrations, 1808–1915* (Amherst: University of Massachusetts Press, 2003); Justin Behrend, *Reconstructing Democracy: Grassroots Black Politics in the Deep South after the Civil War* (Athens: University of Georgia Press, 2017), 88–91, 113.

8. William C. Harris, *Presidential Reconstruction in Mississippi* (Baton Rouge: Louisiana State University Press, 1967), 27.

9. The "Natchez District" was initially defined by the French in the 1770s as an area in the southwest corner of Mississippi along the Mississippi River that included Adams and Claiborne Counties as well as Tensas and Concordia Parishes in Louisiana. This study focuses primarily on Adams County and the town of Natchez. A number of historians have written about the importance of the Natchez District, including Behrend, *Reconstructing Democracy*; Michael Wayne, *The Reshaping of Plantation Society: The Natchez District, 1860–1880* (Baton Rouge: Louisiana State University Press, 1982); Ronald L. F. Davis, *Good and Faithful Labor: From Slavery to Sharecropping in the Natchez District, 1860–1890* (Westport, Connecticut: Greenwood Press, 1982); Anthony E. Kaye, *Joining Places: Slave Neighborhoods in the Old South* (Chapel Hill: University of North Carolina Press, 2007); D. Clayton James, *Antebellum Natchez* (Baton Rouge: Louisiana State University Press, 1968). On demographics of Adams County, see Historical Census Browser, http://fisher.lib.virginia.edu/collections/stats/histcensus/index.html.

10. My good friend and fellow historian Janet Bruce is credited with coming up with the petri dish analogy.

11. Here are a few of the authors and books that had great personal impact on this study and my thinking in general: David Blight, *Race and Reunion*; W. Fitzhugh Brundage, *Where These Memories Grow*; Jack Davis, *Race against Time: Culture and Separation in Natchez since 1930*; Ronald L. F. Davis, *The Black Experience in Natchez: 1720–1880*; William Faulkner, *Light in August*; Greg Isles, *The Quiet Game*; Neil McMillen, *Dark Journey: Black Mississippians in the Age of Jim Crow*; William Alexander Percy, *Lanterns on the Levee*; Eudora Welty, *Delta Wedding* and *The Collected Stories of Eudora Welty*; Richard Wright, *Black Boy*; Stark Young, *So Red the Rose*.

12. This idea is the product of numerous conversations I had with Ron Davis about the concept of "all history being contested history." I am also indebted to him for sharing a conference paper he delivered in October 2009 at the Eighth Historic Natchez Conference that elaborated on this idea.

CHAPTER 1: FORGING NEW IDENTITIES IN A WORLD GONE MAD

1. Testimony of Janc Dent, SCC No. 6616, NARA. Jane Dent's story is also recounted in Joyce Broussard, *Stepping Lively in Place: The Not-Married Free Women of Civil-War-Era Natchez, Mississippi* (Athens: University of Georgia Press, 2016), 161–62.

2. Broussard, *Stepping Lively*, 162.

3. SCC claim 6616. Dent filed a claim for $2,969 and was awarded $300. The Southern Claims Commission is explained in more detail later in this chapter.

4. Margarette Dunlop Conner Martin to William T. Martin, October 25, 1862. Quoted in *Early Romances of Historic Natchez* by Elizabeth Dunbar Murray (Natchez: Natchez Printing and Stationery, 1950), 74–78.

5. Margarette Conner Martin to William T. Martin, September 27, 1863. Quoted in Murray, *Early Romances*, 76–78. The Martins' household was likely targeted because of William T. Martin's high-ranking position with the Confederate Army. Additionally, there may have been some truth to Amelia's claims that slaves were treated poorly in the Martin household and perhaps were seeking revenge. Prior to the war William Martin organized a militia company of leading Adams County whites in 1860 in an effort to "disarm all the negroes in the county," according to Martin. Quoted in Justin Behrend, *Reconstructing Democracy: Grassroots Black Politics in the Deep South after the Civil War* (Athens: University of Georgia Press, 2017), 38.

6. Broussard, *Stepping Lively*, 162.

7. John K. Bettersworth, *Confederate Mississippi: The People and Policies of a Confederate State in Wartime* (Baton Rouge: Louisiana State University, 1943) 287–88, as quoted in Ronald L. F. Davis, *The Black Experience in Natchez, 1720–1880* (Denver: Eastern, 1994), 126.

8. US Census (1860, 1870), Manuscript Population Schedules, Adams County, Mississippi.

9. Quoted in Ronald Davis, *The Black Experience*, 128. From Brig. Gen. Thomas E. G. Ransom, US Army, to Lt. Col. W. T. Clark, Assistant to the Adjutant-General, July 16, 1863, *Official Records*, Ser. 1, Vol. 24: 680–81.

10. Ronald Davis, *The Black Experience*, 141. From Maj. C. T. Christenson, Assistant Adjutant General Division of West Mississippi, to Maj. Gen. N. J. T. Dana, July 20, 1864, *Official Records*, Ser. 1, Vol. 39: 185.

11. Ronald Davis, *The Black Experience*, 148.

12. Ronald Davis, *The Black Experience*, 150.

13. Ellen Shields unpublished memoir, MDAH. Not until after the war when Natchez's National Cemetery was established were the human and animal remains properly interred by government contractors. For more on burial practices during the Civil War see Drew Gilpin Faust, *This Republic of Suffering: Death and the American Civil War* (New York: Alfred A. Knopf, 2008).

14. J. P. Bardwell to Reverend M. E. Strieby, January 5, 1865, Miss. roll 1, #71719, AMA.

15. Harriet E. Gaylord to Rev. George Whipple, May 1, 1865, Miss. roll 1, #71762, AMA.

16. Hattie E. Stryker to Rev. J. R. Shipherd, Feb. 4, 1868, Miss. Roll 1, #72262, AMA.

17. More than 22,000 professed southern Unionists from across the South bombarded the Washington, DC, claims office before the filing deadline of March 1873. White male planters, their wives or widows, middling-class merchants as well as a surprising number of former male and female slaves and free men and women of color participated in the often lengthy claims process. Claimants who could prove both their unwavering loyalty to the Union and offer a credible account of the property and how it was taken often received some financial restitution for their losses. The majority of claims filed were for less than

$10,000 and often for as little as a few hundred dollars. In claims that exceeded $10,000, claimants and their witnesses were required to travel to Washington, DC, to present their cases before the three-man commission. Most claims were handled by traveling field agents and special claims commissioners who set up offices across the South before forwarding their findings and recommendations to the Commissioner of Claims office in Washington. Claims allowed by the commission were forwarded to the House of Representatives for final approval, and in most instances, legislators followed the lead of the commission. By March 3, 1873—the deadline for filing a claim—the commissioners reported 22,298 claims had been filed for approximately $60.3 million. Seven years later the commission's final report to Congress revealed that some 41 percent of the 16,991 cases reported to Congress were allowed in the amount of $4.6 million, about 7 percent of the total claimed amount. See Frank Klingberg, *The Southern Claims Commission* (Berkeley: University of California Press, 1955).

18. Dylan Penningroth is one of the first scholars to turn attention to the experiences of allowed claims of black SCC petitioners. In his provocative study he reveals that the property acquired by enslaved persons often came from an informal and illegal system of hiring a slave's time out to acquire horses, mules, wagons, and other personal property. Penningroth's argument that black claimants not only attached great value to their hard-earned property and that of fellow slaves, but that such property was a way of cementing kinfolk connections becomes apparent in the testimony of Natchez claimants. Penningroth, *The Claims of Kinfolk: African American Property and Community in the Nineteenth-Century South* (Chapel Hill: University of North Carolina Press, 2003).

19. Disallowed claim. Commission questioned the ability of a poor colored woman to own "such a fine pair of horses," Adams County, Congressional Jurisdiction Case Files, Records of RG 123, USCC.

20. SCC claim 22176, Adams County, Congressional Jurisdiction Case Files, Records of RG 123, USCC.

21. Quoted in Michael Wayne, *The Reshaping of Plantation Society: The Natchez District, 1860–1880* (Baton Rouge: Louisiana State University Press, 1983), 31. Charles B. Tompkins to Mollie Tompkins, May 6, 1863, in Charles Brown Tompkins Papers, Manuscript Dept., William R. Perkins Library, Duke University, Durham, NC.

22. Margarette Martin to William T. Martin, Jan. 10, 1864, Quoted in Murray, *Early Romances*, 81.

23. Jas. A. Gillespie to [?], May 29, 1865, quoted in Wayne, 34.

24. Joyce Broussard, "Female Solitaires: Women Alone in the Lifeworld of Mid-Century Natchez, Mississippi, 1850–1880 (PhD diss., University of Southern California, 1998), 101–2. For more on single women in antebellum and postwar Natchez see Broussard's *Stepping Lively*.

25. Fortunately, a large number of Adams County court cases have been archived as part of the Natchez Courthouse Records Project, which was initiated by Professor Ronald L. F. Davis in 1991. Nearly 100,000 manuscript legal cases (civil and criminal litigation) dating from the Spanish period through the 1940s, were moved from a damp basement room in the Adams County courthouse and relocated to the Historic Natchez Foundation, where

they are now safely stored. The bulk of the cases were debt related, but there were many other types of litigation dealing with life in antebellum and post–Civil War Natchez, including slave traders, runaway slaves, emancipation petitions, manumissions, prostitution, murder, rape, arson, divorce, larceny, and much more.

26. With both Union and Confederate soldiers the most literate of any military force up to this time an enormous amount of correspondence was generated during the war years. Fortunately, many families kept these letters and journals, resulting in a rich collection of primary source material that reveals detailed aspects of the war experience both on the battlefield and the home front.

27. A number of elite women openly socialized and entertained white Union officers in their homes, a breach of social conduct considered traitorous by some stalwart rebels, but a move that may have played an important role in protecting their valued property form military plunder. See Joyce Broussard, "Occupied Natchez, Elite Women, and the Feminization of the Civil War," *Journal of Mississippi History* 70, no. 2 (Summer 2008): 179–208.

28. Margarette Martin to William T. Martin, August 26, 1863. Quoted in Murray, *Early Romances*.

29. Matilda Gresham, *Life of Walter Quentin Gresham, 1832–1895* (Chicago: Rand McNally, 1919), 244. Mrs. Wilson's outrage may have been targeted toward her husband A. L. Wilson, a prominent planter and secessionist who fled to Texas with his slaves before the Yankees arrived in Natchez. He left his wife and daughter to take care of his property and face the enemy on their own.

30. Kate Foster Diary, Sept. 20, 1863, Duke University Library, Durham, NC.

31. Broussard, *Stepping Lively*, 6–7.

32. Antonia Quitman Lovell to Alice McMurran, February 10, 1866. McMurran-Austen Family papers, LSU.

33. See Quitman family letters, UNC. For example, by the late 1870s and 1880s the Quitman sisters frequently wrote of the pleasure they took in preparing holiday meals, particularly the labor-intensive annual fruitcake they cooked for family and friends each Christmas.

34. Mattie W. Childs to Rev. George Whipple, Sept. 16, 1864, Miss. Roll 1, #71681, AMA.

35. Journal of Annie Rose Quitman Duncan, June 28, 1863. Quitman Family Papers, UNC.

36. Mrs. Minor's words moved the commission in her favor, despite the efforts of a vigilant SCC field officer who had worked tirelessly for several years to disprove her claim. She was awarded $13,000 in government funds, about a quarter of the sum she had claimed. Katherine S. Minor, Case 7960, Adams County, Congressional Jurisdiction Case Files, Records of RG 123, USCC.

37. Haller Nutt, Julia Nutt's husband, had hired a crew of skilled Philadelphia craftsmen in 1859 to build an unusual oriental-style octagonal villa designed by architect Samuel Sloan of Philadelphia. With war on the horizon, the craftsmen left leaving only the outer structure and roof completed. Nutt used his slaves and local artisans to finish the first floor of the house. The house remains unfinished to this day.

38. Letters from Julia Nutt to Prentiss Nutt, March 23, 1878; March 29, 1878; February 9, 1878, The Elms Papers, MDAH.

39. Broussard, *Stepping Lively*, 215.

40. Ellen Shields Memoir, 1903, Surget Family Papers, MDAH.

41. Quoted in Penningroth, 62.

42. John Hebron Moore, *The Emergence of the Cotton Kingdom in the Old Southwest: Mississippi, 1770–1860* (Baton Rouge: Louisiana State University Press, 1988), 190.

43. D. Clayton James, *Antebellum Natchez* (Baton Rouge, Louisiana State University Press, 1968), 159–60, 183–84; *Natchez City Directory*, 1858, JGWAL. Aaron D. Anderson, *Builders of a New South: Merchants, Capital, and the Remaking of Natchez, 1865-1914* (Jackson: University Press of Mississippi, 2013), 44, 60.

44. Anderson, 51–52.

45. *Tri-Weekly Democrat*, May 28, 1867.

46. *Natchez Democrat*, Board of Supervisors reports, May 27, 1871; Nov. 1, 1871; Nov. 2, 1871; Nov. 4, 1871; Nov. 26, 1871.

47. Ronald Davis, *The Black Experience in Natchez*, 176.

48. Ronald Davis, *The Black Experience in Natchez*, 170.

49. Jeanett Carter, Case 21,053; Richard Dorsey, Case 4337, and Jane Dent, Case 6616, Adams County, Congressional Jurisdiction, RG 213, USCC.

50. Ronald Davis, *The Black Experience in Natchez*, 155. R. S. Hart, Assistant Special Agent, Treasury Department to William P. Mellen, March 7, 1864, records of the US Treasury Department, Record Group 366, NARA.

51. Reginald Washington, "Sealing the Sacred Bonds of Holy Matrimony: Freedmen's Bureau Marriage Records," http://www.archives.gov/publicatons/prologue/2005/spring/freedman_marriage-recs.html.

52. www.freedmensbureau.com/Mississippi/Mississippimarriages.html.

53. Walter L. Fleming, *The Freedmen's Savings Bank: A Chapter in the Economic History of the Negro Race* (Chapel Hill: University of North Carolina Press, 1927). Freedman's Bank Records, 2000 Intellectual Reserve, Inc.

54. Historical Census Browser, http://fisher.lib.virginia.edu/collections/stats/histcensus/.

55. Justin Behrend, "Freedpeople's Democracy: African American Politics and Community in the Postemancipation Natchez District" (PhD diss., Northwestern University, 2006), 21.

56. Sheryl Nomelli, "Jim Crow, Louis J. Winston, and the Survival of Black Politics in Postbellum Natchez, Mississippi" (Master's thesis, California State University, Northridge, 2004), 40.

57. Ronald Davis, *The Black Experience in Natchez*, 178–80.

58. Darcy Bieber, "Making the Most of Freedom: Female Black Teachers in Postbellum Natchez: 1865–1910" (Master's thesis, California State University Northridge, 2005).

59. Adams County, Folder: Negro, Box 10634, Mississippi Historical Records Survey, Series 447, Works Progress Administration (WPA) Records, MDAH; Revels A. Adams, *Cyclopedia of African Methodism in Mississippi* (Natchez, MS, 1902), 146–54.

60. Jacqueline Jones, *Soldiers of Light and Love: Northern Teachers and Georgia Blacks, 1865-1873* (Athens: University of Georgia Press, 1992), 76 (quotation). Leon Litwack, *Been in the Storm So Long: The Aftermath of Slavery* (New York: Vintage Books, 1979), 471.

61. Richard N. Tristano, "Holy Family Parish: The Genesis of an African American Community in Natchez, Mississippi," *Journal of Negro History* 83, no. 4 (1998): 274.

62. *Christian Recorder*, May 25, 1867.

63. Behrend, "Freedpeople's Democracy," 116.

64. *Christian Recorder*, April 6, 1867.

65. *Christian Recorder*, July 31, 1873.

66. *Christian Recorder*, Editorial Correspondence, Notes by the Wayside, December 2, 1865.

67. *Christian Recorder*, April 6, 1867.

68. *Christian Recorder*, December 25, 1873.

69. Heather Williams, *Self-Taught: African American Education in Slavery and Freedom* (Chapel Hill: University of North Carolina Press, 2005), 39.

70. Lizzie Welsh to Rev. George Whipple, January 25, 1864, Mississippi, roll 1, 71583. AMA.

71. Palmer Litts to Rev. George Whipple, June 24, 1864, Mississippi, roll 1, 71582, 71619, AMA.

72. Mississippi roll 1, 71842, AMA.

73. Rev. S. G. Wright to Rev. Henry Cowles, March 15, 1864, Mississippi roll 1, 71613, 71614, AMA.

74. Palmer Litts to Rev. George Whipple, July 1865, Mississippi roll 1, 71789, AMA.

75. Ann M. Keen to Rev. J. R. Shipherd, February 4, 1868, Mississippi roll 1, 72263, AMA.

76. Blanche Harris to Rev. George Whipple, January 23, 1866, Mississippi roll 1, 71885 and March 10, 1866, 71971, AMA.

77. Palmer Litts to Rev. S. G. Wright, July 1865, Mississippi roll 1, #71750, AMA.

78. Williams, 38.

79. Blanche Harris to Rev. George Whipple, March 10, 1866, Mississippi roll 71971, AMA.

80. *Natchez Democrat*, November 25, 1871.

81. *Natchez Democrat*, November 9, 1877.

82. Elizabeth Dunbar Murray, *My Mother Used to Say: A Natchez Belle of the Sixties* (Boston: Christopher Publishing House, 1959), 183.

83. Antonio Quitman Lovell to Alice McMurran, Oct. 18, 1865, McMurran-Austin family papers, LSU.

84. Antonia Quitman Lovell to Alice McMurran, Feb. 10, 1866, McMurran-Austin family papers, LSU.

85. Prentiss Nutt to Julia Nutt, January 28, 1878, Alma Carpenter Papers, HNF.

86. Prentiss Nutt to Julia Nutt, February 6, 1878, Alma Carpenter Papers, HNF.

87. It is unknown exactly how much influence Congressman Lynch had with the SCC, but Julia Nutt eventually recovered more than $1 million from the government, one of the largest settlements issued by the Claims Commission. In another matter Lynch told Prentiss Nutt that he would not support his bid to unseat black Robert Fitzhugh, Natchez's black postmaster.

88. *Natchez Daily Courier*, May 31, 1866.

89. Quoted in William C. Harris, *Presidential Reconstruction in Mississippi* (Baton Rouge: Louisiana State University Press, 1967), 81.

90. *Tri-Weekly Democrat*, May 25, 28, 1867.

91. "Negro Suffering and Suffrage in the South," *Christian Recorder*, July 1, 1865.

92. Justin Behrend, "Rebellious Talk and Conspiratorial Plots: The Making of a Slave Insurrection in Civil War Natchez," *Journal of Southern History* 77 no. 1 (February 2011), 17. Behrend's article builds on the work of Winthrop Jordan, *Tumult and Silence at Second Creed: An Inquiry into a Civil War Slave Conspiracy* (Baton Rouge: Louisiana State University Press, 1995). Also see Behrend, "Rumors of Revolt," *New York Times*, September 15, 2011.

93. Joseph Shields to Mary Conway Shields, November 8, 1866, Joseph D. Shields Papers, LSU.

94. Prentiss Nutt to Julia Nutt, March 5, 1878; March 26, 1878. Julia Nutt to Prentiss Nutt, March 29, 1878, Alma Carpenter Papers, HNF.

CHAPTER 2: MEMORY MAKING ON PARADE: AFRICAN AMERICAN
HISTORICAL IDENTITY IN RECONSTRUCTION-ERA NATCHEZ

1. Phyllis Woodward Seawright, "Natchez Theatre, 1852–1940: Yearning for Fame" (PhD diss: Florida State University, 1996).

2. *Natchez Democrat*, July 8, 1867.

3. Clifford Geertz, quoted in Mary Ryan, "The American Parade: Representations of the Nineteenth-Century Social Order," in *The New Cultural History*, edited by Lynn Hunt (Berkeley: University of California Press, 1989), 132.

4. Genevieve Fabre, "African American Commemorative Celebrations in the Nineteenth Century," in *History and Memory in African American Culture*, edited by Genevieve Fabre and Robert G. O'Meally (New York: Oxford University Press, 1994), 75. While Fabre specifically references postrevolutionary and antebellum black celebrations, her findings are also relevant to the early post–Civil War era.

5. Kathleen Clark, "Celebrating Freedom: Emancipation Day Celebrations and African American Memory in the Early Reconstruction South," in *Where These Memories Grow: History, Memory, and Southern Identity*, edited by W. Fitzhugh Brundage (Chapel Hill: University of North Carolina Press, 2000), 109.

6. David W. Blight, *Race and Reunion: The Civil War in American Memory* (Cambridge, MA: Belknap Press of Harvard University, 2001), 27.

7. Edna Greene Medford, "Imagined Promises, Bitter Realities: African Americans and the Meaning of the Emancipation Proclamation," in *The Emancipation Proclamation: Three Views*, by Harold Holzer, Edna Greene Medford, and Frank J. Williams (Baton Rouge: Louisiana State University Press, 2006), 30–31.

8. See Blight, *Race and Reunion*; William A. Blair, *Cities of the Dead: Contesting the Memory of the Civil War in the South, 1865–1914* (Chapel Hill: University of North Carolina Press, 2004); and Fitzhugh Brundage, *The Southern Past: A Clash of Race and Memory* (Cambridge, MA: Belknap Press of Harvard University Press, 2005); Kathleen Clark,

Defining Moments; and Mitchell A. Kachun, *Festivals of Freedom: Memory and Meaning in African American Emancipation Celebrations, 1808-1915* (Amherst: University of Massachusetts Press, 2003).

9. J. P. Bardwell to M. E. Strieby, January 5, 1865, #71719 , Mississippi, roll 1, AMA. Only a handful of newspaper references are made of Emancipation Day celebrations in Natchez: *Natchez Democrat*, January 1, 1872 and September 28, 1896. For more on Emancipation Day celebrations in Norfolk, Virginia; Charleston; the Sea Islands of South Carolina; St. Louis, Missouri; New Bern, North Carolina; Washington, DC; and other places, see Kachun, 111–20, and Kathleen Clark, *Defining Moments*.

10. Anthony E. Kaye, *Joining Places: Slave Neighborhoods in the Old South* (Chapel Hill: University of North Carolina Press, 2007), 206.

11. *Laws of the State of Mississippi, Passed at a Regular Session of the Mississippi Legislature, held in Jackson, October, November, and December, 1865* (Jackson, 1866), 82–93, 165–67. Accessed from http://chnm.gmu.edu/coursese/122/recon/code.html.

12. On the Military Reconstruction Acts, see Eric Foner, *Reconstruction: America's Unfinished Revolution* (New York: Perennial Classics, 2002), 271–80.

13. *New Orleans Republican*, May 28, 1867.

14. For more on the Union League see Michael W. Fitzgerald, *The Union League Movement in the Deep South: Politics and Agricultural Change during Reconstruction* (Baton Rouge: Louisiana State University Press, 1989).

15. Report of H. R. Williams, in "Copy of statement charging *1st Lieut. D. M. White*," May 6, 1867, Comr., Letters Received, roll 47, BRFAL. Quoted in Justin Behrend, "Freedpeople's Democracy: African American Politics and Community in the Postemancipation Natchez District" (PhD diss., Northwestern University, 2006), 210.

16. *Natchez Tri-Weekly Democrat*, November 2, 1871.

17. *Natchez Weekly Democrat*, November 2, 1867.

18. *Natchez Democrat*, June 17, 1867.

19. *New Orleans Republican*, June 1, 1867.

20. *Natchez Democrat*, June 10, 1867.

21. Mary Ryan, "The American Parade: Representations of the Nineteenth Century Social Order," in *The New Cultural History*. Edited by Lynn Hunt, 152 (Berkeley: University of California Press, 1989).

22. Allen may have been chosen to lead the parade rather than League president E. J. Castello who was embroiled in legal problems referred to earlier.

23. *New Orleans Republican*, July 10, 1867. To date, I have not found any mention of the 1867 parade in the correspondence of Julia Nutt, a prolific letter writer. Julia may have rented out her property to the Union League since she was in the throes of severe economic problems after the war. She may also have been predisposed to allowing the freedmen to celebrate on her property as a show of her Unionist sentiments. The paper's description of Nutt as a "liberal-minded lady" is curious given the frequent negative comments Julia and other Nutt family members made about African Americans after the war.

24. Richard L. Bushman, *The Refinement of America: Persons, Houses, Cities* (New York: Alfred A. Knopf, 1992), 437.

25. Not far from the parade procession the *Natchez Democrat* documented at least one incident of disorderly conduct. A Federal soldier accused of "being full of 4th of July and bad whiskey" assaulted a black draymen "striking him a severe blow on the head with a brick, endeavoring to cut him with a razor, and otherwise abusing him." The drayman kicked his assailant and wounded him with a knife *Natchez Democrat*, July 8, 1867.

26. John Mercer Langston, 1829–1897, was a prominent African American educator and Virginia Congressman. In addition to being the first black elected to the US House of Representatives from Virginia, he served as the president of the National Equal Rights League, the president of Howard University, a US minister to Haiti and the Dominican Republic, and the first president of Virginia State College—a Historic Black College. See William Cheek and Aimee Lee Cheek, *John Mercer Langston and the Fight for Black Freedom: 1829–65* (Urbana: University of Illinois Press, 1989), and Roger D. Cunningham, "'They Are As Proud of Their Uniform As Any Who Serve Virginia': African American Participation in the Virginia Volunteers, 1872–99," *Virginia Magazine of History and Biography* 110, no. 3 (2002), 301. Langston's brother was the second great-grandfather of acclaimed poet Langston Hughes.

27. *Natchez Democrat*, July 8, 1867.

28. *New Orleans Republican*, July 10, 1867.

29. *New Orleans Republican*, July 10, 1867.

30. *New Orleans Republican*, July 11, 1867.

31. "The 4th of July," *Tri-Weekly Democrat*, July 8, 1867.

32. Although it is unclear why such a detail was not mentioned in the parade coverage, it is possible that such an omission was intended as a way to diminish fears among whites wary of armed black men.

33. Quoted in Justin Behrend, *Reconstructing Democracy: Grassroots Politics in the Deep South After the Civil War* (Athens: University of Georgia Press, 2017). 89–90. Tri-Monthly Report, Dunford, 10 August 1867, BRFAL, Louisiana Assistant Commander, roll 14.

34. *New Orleans Republican*, July 10, 1867.

35. Clark, "Celebrating Freedom," 119.

36. Carla L. Peterson, *Doers of the Word: African American Women Speakers and Writers in the North, 1830–1880* (New York: Oxford University Press, 1995); William Blair, *Cities of the Dead*, 33. Although not specifically mentioned in newspaper reports, it is possible that female members of the Good Samaritans and others took part in the procession.

37. Originally published in the *Chicago Times*; reprinted in the *Natchez Democrat*, August 5, 1867. Quoted in Behrend, "Freedpeople's Democracy," 195.

38. Lawrence W. Levine, *Black Culture and Black Consciousness: Afro-American Folk Thought from Slavery to Freedom* (New York: Oxford University Press, 1977), 25. Black military bands during the Civil War were "out of all proportion to the total number of black troops," according to Christopher Small, *Music of the Common Tongue: Survival and Celebration in Afro-American Music* (London: J. Calder, 1987), 261.

39. Levine, *Black Culture*, 161. Also see Mary Ellison, "African American Music and Muskets in Civil War New Orleans," *Louisiana History: The Journal of the Louisiana Historical Association* 35, no. 3 (July 1994), 285.

40. *Songs of the Civil War*, compiled and edited by Irwin Silber and Jerry Silverman (New York: Columbia University Press, 1960), 18–19.

41. *The Song Book of the School Room* (New York: Mason Brothers, 1857), 35.

42. Sidney Bechet, *Treat It Gentle* (New York: Hill and Wang), 50. Bechet tape recorded his memoir in the early 1930s, which was transcribed more than twenty years later.

43. Bechet, 48.

44. *New Orleans Republican*, July 10, 1867.

45. *Natchez Democrat*, July 8, 1867.

46. "The Good Samaritan," *Natchez Democrat*, July 8, 1867.

47. For more on the caste and class divides within Natchez see Allison Davis, Burleigh B. Gardner, and Mary R. Gardner, *Deep South: A Social Anthropological Study of Caste and Class* (Chicago: The University of Chicago Press, 1941).

48. Darcy Bieber, "Making the Most of Freedom: Black Female Schoolteachers in Postbellum Natchez, Mississippi, 1865–1910" (Master's thesis, California State University, Northridge, 2005), and Richard N. Tristano, "Holy Family Parish: The Genesis of an African American Community in Natchez, Mississippi," *Journal of Negro History* 83, no. 4 (1998): 258–84.

49. Ronald Davis, *The Black Experience in Natchez*, 59.

50. Behrend, "Freedpeople's Democracy," 547–48. Wood's later posts included postmaster, sheriff, and county assessor.

51. *Daily Democrat*, July 15, 1891. Quoted in Sheryl Nomelli, "Jim Crow, Louis J. Winston, and the Survival of Black Politics in Postbellum Natchez, Mississippi" (Master's thesis, California State University, Northridge, 2004), 62.

52. *Christian Recorder*, January 3, 1889. Winston won his last election as circuit clerk in 1893 and never held an elected position after completing his term in 1896. He cast his last ballot in 1901 but continued to register until 1907. Nomelli, 40, 43.

53. *Natchez Tri-Weekly Democrat*, January 2, 1872; *Natchez Democrat*, July 3, 1872; William J. Davis to Ames, 16 July 1872, Folder 130, Box 15, Ames Family Papers. Quoted in Behrend, "Freedpeople's Democracy," 313.

54. Membership lists were published in the *Natchez Courier*, July 23, 1870; *Natchez Democrat*, September 20, 1871, November 27, 1872. Also see Behrend, "Freedpeople's Democracy," 312–13.

55. Of the cemetery's more than 6,000 graves, more than 3,000 are of black and white Union troops with 2,000 more of unknown soldiers, which included an undetermined number of Confederate soldiers. Original interments were brought from locations in Louisiana and Mississippi within a fifty-mile radius of Adams County. According to a US Army report dated June 30, 1866, many of the dead had been found buried in the levees near the western shore of the Mississippi River. See http://www.cem.va.gov/cems/nchp/natchez.asp.

56. *The National Memorial Day: A Record of Ceremonies Over the Graves of the Union Soldiers May 29 & 30, 1869* (Washington, Headquarters, Grand Army of the Republic, 1870).

57. Blight, 64–97.

58. At the close of the senator's remarks, white Natchez county clerk A. H. Foster noted that the decoration committee intended to place flowers upon the Confederate graves nearby in a "spirit of peace and amity, and a tribute to the bravery of the dead." Foster's suggestion to honor both the Union and Confederate dead is similar to a Confederate Decoration Day in Columbus, Mississippi, four years earlier. During what came to be considered the state's first Decoration Day, a group of Confederate women "strewed flowers alike on the graves of Confederate and Union dead," according to Dunbar Rowland, ed., *Encyclopedia of Mississippi History: Comprising Sketches of Counties, Towns, Events, Institutions and Persons*, Vol. II (Madison, WI: Selwyn A. Brant, 1907), 216

59. Undated letter from Fred J. V. Le Cand, Commander, Camp No. 20 United Confederate Veterans and Secretary of Natchez Memorial Association, published in "Confederate Cemeteries and Monuments in Mississippi" by R. W. Jones, in *Publications of the Mississippi Historical Society, Vol. 8*, Franklin L. Riley, editor (Oxford, MS: Mississippi Historical Society, 1904), 90–91.

60. As a member of the Board of Directors of the Natchez school district, Pollard had attended a white school exhibition where the teacher abruptly stopped the exercises and dismissed her class when he entered the room. In response Pollard and others held an "indignation meeting" that night at the courthouse. Pollard had also confronted segregation as a slave preacher at a local Baptist church before the war and then as the leader of the Rose Hill Church after emancipation. Quoted in Behrend, "Freedpeople's Democracy," 296.

61. *Natchez Courier*, May 24, 1871; June 1, 1871.

62. *New National Era*, November 24, 1870.

63. Frederick Douglass, "Address at the Grave of the Unknown Dead," Arlington, Va., May 30, 1871, Frederick Douglass Papers, LC, reel 14. Quoted in Blight, 106.

64. A fraternal bond soon developed between five of the white members of the planning committee as founders and officers of the local Natchez Pythian Lodge, a Masonic organization, established a few months later. A. H. Foster served as the "Venerable Patriarch" of the Natchez Lodge no. 3, which was instituted on August 7, 1872. Other officers included Charles C. Walden, M. A. C. Hussey, H. C. Griffin, L. N. Clapp, William D. Kennedy, all of whom served on the Decoration Day planning committee. John Van Valkenberg, *The Knights of Pythias Complete Manual and Textbook* (Canton, Ohio: Memento Publishing Company, 1885), 422.

65. Neil R. McMillen, *Dark Journey: Black Mississippians in the Age of Jim Crow* (Urbana: University of Illinois Press, 1989), 299.

66. The People's Party is not to be confused with the late nineteenth century Populism movement, which formed a party of the same name. The Natchez People's tickets referred to an opposition party. See Behrend, "Freedpeople's Democracy," 414–16.

67. An article published in the *Natchez Democrat*, November 11, 1874, reported on the cheering crowds after the election and listed several black and white Decoration Day organizers: John Peck (black), E. J. Castello, A. H. Foster and H. C. Griffin, who was elected mayor on the People's ticket. William T. Martin, the leading spokesperson for white elite Democrats and a friend to black elites over the years, also celebrated the victory of the People's Party. Behrend, *Reconstructing Democracy*, 237–38.

68. Quoted in John Roy Lynch, *Reminiscences of an Active Life: The Autobiography of John Roy Lynch*. John Hope Franklin, ed. (Chicago: University of Chicago Press, 1970), xvii–xviii.

69. Address to the Citizens of Adams County pamphlet, March 1871, Ames Family Papers, Box 25, Folder 4, Sophia Smith Collection, Smith College.

70. *Natchez Democrat*, December 7, 1870.

71. McMillen, 299.

72. *Natchez Democrat*, September 23, 1896.

73. Quoted in "Natchez-Vidalia's Oldest Memorial Day Observance" by Stanley Nelson, *Concordia Sentinel*, http://www.concordiasentinel.com/news.php?id=5174, May 27, 2010.

74. Quoted in "Natchez-Vidalia's Oldest Memorial Day Observance."

75. Address to the Citizens of Adams County pamphlet, March 1871.

CHAPTER 3: "A TASTE FOR ASSOCIATIONS": RECONSTRUCTING WHITE IDENTITIES IN POSTWAR NATCHEZ

1. *Proceedings of the Grand Commandery Knights Templar of the State of Mississippi, 1877* (Jackson, Miss: Clarion Steam Printing Establishment, 1877), MDAH, 1.

2. *Natchez Democrat*, November 18, 1871.

3. *Natchez Weekly Democrat*, March 28, 1872; March 20, 1883; April 15, 1883; January 27, 1886. *Natchez Democrat*, January 18, 1882; February 1, 1882; March 14, 1886.

4. Joan W. Gandy and Thomas H. Gandy, *Natchez: Landmarks, Lifestyles, and Leisure* (Charleston: Arcadia, 1999). Joseph B. Stratton Diary, Joseph B. Stratton Papers, LSU. In addition to the temple the other main white houses of worship included Jefferson Street Methodist Church, Trinity Episcopal Church, First Presbyterian Church, and St. Mary's Cathedral.

5. David W. Blight, *Race and Reunion: The Civil War in American Memory* (Cambridge, MA: Belknap Press of Harvard University, 2001), 156–65.

6. LeeAnn Whites, *The Civil War as a Crisis in Gender: Augusta, Georgia, 1860–1890* (Athens: University of Georgia Press, 1995). Also see Craig Thompson Friend and Lorri Glover, eds., *Southern Manhood: Perspectives on Masculinity in the Old South* (Athens: University of Georgia Press, 2004) for an insightful collection of essays on how the Civil War and the Reconstruction era impacted male identity. Drew Gilpin Faust's *Mothers of Invention: Women of the Slaveholding South in the American Civil War* details how the war changed the lives of southern women and impacted their relationship with men (Chapel Hill: University of North Carolina Press, 1996).

7. Nancy Bercaw, *Gendered Freedoms: Race, Rights and the Politics of Household in the Delta, 1861–1875* (Gainesville: University Press of Florida, 2003), 88–89.

8. Numerous studies have been written about traits associated with southern masculinity. Bertram Wyatt-Brown wrote extensively about Southern honor and mastery in *Southern Honor: Ethics and Behavior in the Old South* (New York: Oxford University Press, 1982). Also see W. J. Cash, *The Mind of the South* (New York: Alfred A. Knopf, 1941); John Hope Franklin, *The Militant South, 1800–1861* (Cambridge, MA: Harvard University Press, 1956).

9. Friend and Glover, xi–xii.

10. Franklin, 14–79. Also see Bertram Wyatt-Brown, *The Shaping of Southern Culture: Honor, Grace, and War, 1760s–1880s* (Chapel Hill: University of North Carolina Press, 2001).

11. William Ransom Hogan and Edwin Adams Davis, *William Johnson's Natchez: The Ante-bellum Diary of a Free Negro* (Port Washington, NY: Kennikat Press, 1968).

12. Unfortunately for Johnson, his weapons and vigilance ultimately failed him. He was shot and killed in 1851 by a local farmer over a land dispute. His son Bryan met the same fate two decades later.

13. D. Clayton James, *Antebellum Natchez* (Baton Rouge, Louisiana State University Press, 1968), 256.

14. Hogan and Davis, 409. Johnson's diary indicates that he often accompanied the Natchez Fencibles to military musters where he shaved members of the troop.

15. William C. Martin in his testimony before the SCC, December 12, 1877. Quoted in Winthrop Jordan, *Tumult and Silence at Second Creek: An Inquiry into a Civil War Slave Conspiracy* (Baton Rouge: Louisiana State University Press, 1995), 253.

16. Justin Behrend, "Rebellious Talk and Conspiratorial Plots: The Making of a Slave Insurrection in Civil War Natchez," *The Journal of Southern History*, 77, No. 1 (February 2011), 17.

17. Justin Behrend, "Freedpeople's Democracy: African American Politics and Community in the Postemancipation Natchez District" (PhD diss., Northwestern University, 2006), 424–25, 487.

18. *Testimony as to Denial of Elective Franchise in Mississippi at the Elections of 1875 and 1876*, 44th Congress, 2nd session. Senate Misc. Document 45, 137. Hardy's claim that ALI members were active members of the local Democratic Party is supported by the finding that of the twenty-five members of the Adams County Democratic Executive Committee led by General William T. Martin, twelve were ALI members and another seven were related to a militia member. The Adams County Democratic Executive Committee was organized in September 1871. A list of members was published in the Natchez *Democrat* on September 20, 1871.

19. *Testimony as to Denial of Elective Franchise in Mississippi*, 139, 146. Hardy indicated that some ALI members were part of the mob but also noted that ALI members James Lambert, George M. Brown, and George Green tried to calm the crowd of young men. The editor also made anonymous references to militia members or other white Natchez men who he claimed were involved in the lynching of black men in Adams and neighboring counties. There are no extant copies available of Hardy's newspaper, which may have published additional information on these incidents.

20. "Rolls of the Several Military Organizations Which Entered the Service of the Confederate States of America, from the City and Natchez and Adams County, Mississippi. Compiled from the Archives of their Successors The Adams Light Infantry" (Natchez: Natchez Democrat Print, 1890), UM.

21. The compromise refers to the disputed 1876 presidential election in which the Republican candidate Rutherford B. Hayes was awarded the victory in exchange for an agreement to remove federal troops from the South. The deal effectively ended Reconstruction and returned power to white southern Democrats.

22. The Mississippi legislature chartered ten militia companies in 1877, including the Adams Light Infantry. Dunbar Rowland, ed., *Encyclopedia of Mississippi History: Comprising Sketches of Counties, Towns, Events, Institutions and Persons*, Vol. II (Madison, WI: Selwyn A. Brant, 1907), 236. The founders of the group in addition to T. Otis Baker included John S. Holt, W. H. Wilson, E. J. Perrault, F. J. Arrighi, T. A. Henderson, C. W. Babbitt, W. G. Benbrook, S. A. Mason, G. J. Bahin, S. W. Stanton, Hugh McGinty, K. P. Lanneau and H. Steitenroth. Taken from "Rolls of the Several Military Organizations," UM.

23. Jordan, 367. Martin was unlikely present when the hearings were conducted in September 1861 because he was serving in the Confederate Army. He no doubt became aware of the incident during the war because his brother-in-law, Lemuel P. Conner, served as president of the group.

24. Jordan, 367. While Jordan's research has found a number of men associated with the Vigilance Committee and their inquisition of Second Creek suspects, the records are not complete, and not all members have been identified. The account of the executions at Cherry Grove comes from the great-granddaughter of James Surget, Elizabeth MacNeil Boggess. Boggess delivered a paper, "Second Creek in 1861: People and Places," at No More Silence at Second Creek: Slave Resistance and the Onset of the Civil War, a symposium sponsored by the National Park Service, September 24, 2011. Paper in author's hands.

25. US Census (1860, 1870, 1880), Manuscript population, Adams County, Mississippi; *Directory of the City of Natchez* (Natchez: Banner Publishing, 1892). Political party affiliation found in newspaper reports of Democratic Executive Committee and comments made in *Testimony as to Denial of Elective Franchise in Mississippi*.

26. "Rolls of the Several Military Organizations," UM.

27. Nathaniel S. Shaler, "The Summing Up of the Story," in *The United States of America*, vol. 2 (New York: D. Appleton, 1894), 622. Quoted in "'Another Branch of Manly Sport:' American Rifle Games, 1840–1900" by Russell S. Gilmore in *Hard at Play: Leisure in America, 1840–1940*, Kathryn Grover, editor (Amherst: University of Massachusetts Press, 1992).

28. Anthony Rotundo, *American Manhood: Transformations in Masculinity from the Revolution to the Modern Era* (New York: Basic Books, 1993), 222–46. Gail Bederman, *Manliness and Civilization: A Cultural History of Gender and Race in the United States, 1880–1917* (Chicago: University of Chicago Press, 1995), 15–16, 186.

29. Patrick Miller, "The Manly, the Moral, and the Proficient: College Sport in the New South," in *The Sporting World of the Modern South*, Patrick Miller, editor (Urbana: University of Illinois Press, 2002), 21.

30. *Natchez Democrat*, July 6, 1882; July 6, 1884; July 4, 1888; July 6, 1896; July 5, 1898.

31. Theodore Roosevelt, *The Strenuous Life: Essays and Addresses* (New York: Century, 1918), 8, 20–21.

32. Bederman, 78.

33. Bederman, 12.

34. "Address of the Rev. Joseph B. Stratton, D.D., Delivered July 23, 1875, Before the Trustees, Professors, and Students of Jefferson College, Washington, Adams County, Mississippi," MDAH. Jefferson College opened in January 1811 in Washington, Mississippi.

A number of prominent Mississippians attended the academy, including Jefferson Davis. The school closed in 1964.

35. *Natchez Democrat*, July 6, 1887.

36. *Natchez Democrat*, July 6, 1887.

37. "Rolls of the Several Military Organizations, Preface, UM.

38. Letter from William Hawksby to K. P. Lanneau, August 4, 1876, UM.

39. Mary Ann Clawson, "Fraternal Orders and Class Formation in the Nineteenth-Century United States," *Comparative Studies in Society and History*, 27 (October 1985), 672–95. Based on various late nineteenth-century Masonic convention reports that listed Adams County, Mississippi, members.

40. Dave Rafferty, *The City of Natchez* (Natchez: Privately printed, 1881), 34. These groups included four Masonic orders: Harmony Lodge No. 1, Andrew Jackson Lodge No. 2, both established while Mississippi was still a territory, Royal Arch, and Rosalie Commandery (Knights Templar). Other groups were Odd Fellows, Knights of Pythias and Knights of Honor. Various Masonic convention reports and *Natchez Democrat* newspaper articles have also been useful in learning about these groups. It is unknown exactly how many Natchez men belonged to a secret society in the nineteenth century as records are incomplete.

41. Quoted in Ariela Julie Gross, *Double Character: Slavery and Mastery in the Antebellum Southern Courtroom* (Princeton: Princeton University Press, 2000), 177. From John A. Quitman and Family papers, Box 1, Folder 2, LSU.

42. Quitman, a wealthy Natchez planter, ranks as one of Mississippi's most successful political and military figures. He served as a state representative and senator, was a major general in the Mexican War, led the state's secession movement, served as governor from 1850 to 1851, and was a US congressman up until his death in July 1858.

43. Michael A. Halleran, *The Better Angels of Our Nature: Freemasonry in the Civil War* (Tuscaloosa: University of Alabama Press, 2010) details the growth of Freemasonry during the Civil War, and how both Union and Confederate soldiers frequently relied on their Masonic ties in times of peril.

44. Halleran, xiii. Michael S. Kimmel, *Manhood in America: A Cultural History* (New York: Oxford University Press, 2006), 114–15.

45. Mark C. Carnes, *Secret Ritual and Manhood in Victorian America* (New Haven, CT: Yale University Press, 1989), 4–14.

46. Lynn Dumenil, *Freemasonry and American Culture, 1880–1930* (Princeton, NJ: Princeton University Press, 1984), xii.

47. Rafferty, *The City of Natchez*. Henry Norman was the town's most successful portrait photographer and was also a member of the Royal Arch Masons.

48. *Proceedings of the Seventeenth Annual Conclave of the Grand Commandery Knights Templar, of the State of Mississippi, Held at Natchez, Thursday and Friday, May 10th and 11th, 1877* (Jackson, Miss: Clarion Steam Printing Establishment, 1877), MDAH.

49. *Chicago Tribune*, November 7, 1890. Quoted in Dumenil, 16.

50. For more on the Jewish merchant class, see Aaron Anderson, *The Builders of a New South: Merchants, Capital, and the Remaking of Natchez, 1865–1914* (Jackson: University Press of Mississippi, 2013); Wendy Machlovitz, *Clara Lowenburg Moses, Memoir of a*

Southern Jewish Woman (Jackson, MS: Museum of the Southern Jewish Experience, 2000). Jewish merchants who belonged to the Royal Arch Masons of Natchez in 1894 included Simon Mayer, Abe Moses, and C. L. Tillman. Natchez Jewish men and women joined the Adams County Confederate Memorial Association. Jewish women were also members and officers of the Natchez Protestant Orphanage Association.

51. *Proceedings of the Grand Commandery Knights Templar of the State of Mississippi, 1877*, 70, MDAH.

52. *Proceedings of the Grand Commandery of Mississippi, 1884*, 4–8, MDAH.

53. *Proceedings of the Grand Commandery Knights Templar of the State of Mississippi, 1877*, 70, MDAH.

54. *Natchez Democrat*, n.d.

55. Quoted in Gandy and Gandy, *Natchez: Landmarks, Lifestyles, and Leisure*, 21.

56. Joyce Broussard, "Coping with the Deluge: The Elite, Not Married Women of Postbellum Natchez, Mississippi—and the 'Other Men' in their Lives," *Southern Studies*, 17 (Spring/Summer 2010), 39–74.

57. Katherine Minor's successful claim before the SCC is profiled in chapter 1. Also see Rebecca Dresser, "Kate and John Minor: Confederate Unionists of Natchez," *Journal of Mississippi History* 64, no. 3 (September 2002), 188–216.

58. *Proceedings of the M. W. Grand Lodge of Colorado, September 20 & 21, 1892*, 117–18. https://books.google.com/books?id=HvoDAAAAYAAJ&printsec=frontcover&source

59. *Natchez Democrat*, January 2, 1895. Charles M. Sawyer, a fifty-five-year-old gas fitter, served as an officer in all four lodges.

60. Mark Twain, *Life on the Mississippi* (New York: Harper and Brothers, 1901), 287.

61. Henry W. Grady, "The New South," *New England Magazine* 2 (March 1890), 86.

62. *Natchez, Mississippi on Top, Not "Under the Hill"* (Natchez, MS: Daily Democrat Steam Press, 1892), 6.

63. Anderson, 177–78.

64. Aaron Anderson, "The Builders of a New South: Merchants, Capital and the Remaking of Natchez, 1865–1914" (PhD diss., University of Southern Mississippi, 2009), 256.

65. Audley C. Britton to Mary Britton, November 6, 1881. Britton Family Papers, LSU.

66. *Natchez, Mississippi on Top*, 11.

67. *Natchez, Mississippi on Top*, 14.

68. *Natchez, Mississippi on Top*, 14.

69. *Natchez Democrat*, "The New Club House," March 9, 1892. State of Mississippi to Prentiss Club, Charter, July 3, 1903, Office of Records, Adams County, Natchez, Mississippi.

70. From 1870 to 1890 Freemasonry had declined in most southern states. Mississippi lost 24 percent, Kentucky, 21 percent; North Carolina and South Carolina, about 20 percent; Tennessee and Alabama, 12 percent. Georgia showed a gain of 3 percent, while Texas reported a 70 percent increase in membership. Figures compiled from Freemason convention reports, such as "Proceedings of the Grand Lodge of free and accepted Masons of New York" (New York: J. J. Little, 1891).

71. Adams County Confederate Memorial Association Minutes, HNF,

72. Kate Foster Diary, DU.

73. Adams County Confederate Memorial Association Minutes, April 24, 1890, HNF.

74. *Natchez Democrat*, April 25, 1890. Quoted in Melody Kubassek, "Ask Us Not To Forget: The Lost Cause in Natchez, Mississippi," *Southern Studies* 3 (Fall 1992), 161.

75. *Natchez Weekly Democrat*, May 4, 1892.

76. *Natchez Democrat*, April 27, 1899.

77. *Natchez Democrat*, April 25, 1912. Quoted in Kubassek, 165.

78. Quoted in Kubassek, 161.

79. "Memorial to the Confederate Dead of Adams County, Mississippi, Natchez, Mississippi, September 24th, 1923" *Adams County, Mississippi Genealogical and Historical Research*, http://www.natchezbelle.org/adams (March 11, 2011).

80. Neil R. McMillen, *Dark Journey: Black Mississippians in the Age of Jim Crow* (Urbana: University of Illinois Press, 1989), 5.

81. McMillen, 10.

82. Quoted in Joan W. Gandy and Thomas H. Gandy, *Norman's Natchez: An Early Photographer and His Town* (Jackson: University Press of Mississippi, 1978), 51.

CHAPTER 4: "PICTURE MAKERS": BLACK AND WHITE HISTORICAL MEMORY IN POSTBELLUM NATCHEZ

1. Richard L. Bushman, *Refinement in America: Persons, Houses, Cities* (New York: Alfred A. Knopf, 1992), 277, 410.

2. Natchez city directories and newspapers list several addresses for Norman's studio on Main St. between 1877 and 1892 (111, 513, 519 and 525). Norman may have moved, but Natchez's street addresses were also revised during this time period. In June 1897 Norman and his family moved to a new home at 506 Washington St., which included a "state-of-the-art" studio, according to the *Natchez Democrat*. I am indebted to Janet Bruce, the author of "Nineteenth-Century Natchez, Mississippi in Photographs. Two Perspectives" (Master's thesis, California State University, Northridge, 2012). Ms. Bruce graciously and generously shared a great deal of information about Norman and his photographs and made many helpful suggestions to this chapter.

3. Thomas Gandy and Joan Gandy authored a number of books showcasing the collection of Norman photographs restored and reprinted by Dr. Gandy. The publication that is most informative of Henry Norman's life and how Gandy acquired the photos and went about his work is *Norman's Natchez: An Early Photographer and His Town* (Jackson: University Press of Mississippi, 1978). The Gandy collection of Norman photographs and negatives is now housed at LSU.

4. My analysis is informed by the work of Anne Laura Stoler, *Carnal Knowledge and Imperial Power: Race and the Intimate in Colonial Rule* (Berkeley: University of California Press, 2002). Stoler used family photograph albums of Dutch colonials to examine imperialism and race relations in the West Indies during the late nineteenth- and early twentieth-century.

5. Alan Trachtenburg, *The American Image: Photographs from the National Archives, 1860–1960* (New York: Pantheon Books, 1979), introduction, xxx, xxii.

6. Gandy and Gandy, *Norman's Natchez*, 15.

7. Gandy and Gandy, *Norman's Natchez*, 19. Gem pictures were tintypes, a popular type of image produced in the 1860s.

8. A photograph of Norman's Century No. 7 camera outfit was published in the *Natchez Democrat* sometime in the 1980s. A description of the camera is found in an advertisement appearing in the *Photographic Review* 22 (October 1916), 13. The camera was priced at $74 in 1916. Norman used the camera to produce glass plate negatives for much of his career from the 1880s until the early 1900s. His son Earl continued to use the camera well into the twentieth century.

9. Quoted in Gandy and Gandy, *Norman's Natchez*, 9.

10. Much of Norman's work was published in a series of books authored by Thomas Gandy and Joan Gandy. In addition to *Norman's Natchez*, these include *Victorian Children of Natchez* (Charleston, SC: Arcadia, 1998); *Natchez: Landmarks, Lifestyles, and Leisure* (Charleston, SC: Arcadia, 1999; *Natchez: City Streets Revisited* (Charleston, SC: Arcadia, 1999).

11. Deborah Willis, *A Small Nation of People: W. E. B. Du Bois and African American Portraits of Progress* (New York: Library of Congress and Harper Collins, 2003), 55.

12. The Thomas C. and Joan W. Gandy Collection is archived at LSU. More than one hundred of the photographs have been digitized and are accessible on the library website.

13. John Stauffer, "Interspatialism in the Nineteenth-Century South: The Natchez of Henry Norman," *Slavery and Abolition* 29, no. 2 (June 2008), 249.

14. bell hooks, "In Our Glory," from *Picturing Us: African American Identity in Photography*, Deborah Willis, editor (New York: New Press, 1994), 48.

15. Richard N. Tristano, "Holy Family Parish: The Genesis of an African American Catholic Community in Natchez, Mississippi, *Journal of Negro History* 83, no. 4 (August 1998), 258–83.

16. *Natchez City Directory*, 1892, JGWAL. Other Natchez streets that housed a substantial number of black households included Pine Street (49), Union Street (40), Homochitto Street (36), and Cemetery Road (29). All of these streets with the exception of Cemetery Road were in close proximity to Saint Catherine Street.

17. US Manuscript Census, 1880.

18. *Natchez City Directory*, 1892, JGWAL.

19. US Manuscript Census, 1900.

20. G. F. Richings, *Evidences of Progress among Colored People* (Philadelphia: Geo. S. Ferguson, 1903), 524.

21. Richings, 532.

22. Revels A. Adams, *Cyclopedia of African Methodism in Mississippi* (Natchez, MS: 1902), 150. In the 1900 US Census, Taylor, a fifty-six-year-old widow, boarded three fellow Zion Chapel members. Her occupation is noted as a wet nurse.

23. Based on information found in the *Natchez City Directory*, 1892, JGWAL.

24. Bushman, 437.

25. hooks, 47, 53.

26. Today a number of these portraits can be viewed in a permanent exhibit at the town's First Presbyterian Church. Additional Norman portraits are displayed at the Natchez Museum of African American History and Culture.

27. Beth L. Savage, *African American Historic Places* (Washington, DC: Preservation Press, 1994), 297–98.

28. This photo was captioned as "Janitor John's boys" in Gandy and Gandy, *Victorian Children*, 105.

29. Douglass's portrait appeared in the frontispiece of his second autobiography, *My Bondage and My Freedom* (New York: Miller, Orton, and Mulligan, 1855.) John Stauffer analyzes the photo in *The Black Hearts of Men: Radical Abolitionists and the Transformation of Race* (Cambridge, MA: Harvard University Press, 2002), 46.

30. Stauffer, *The Black Hearts*, 51.

31. Stauffer, *The Black Hearts*, 50.

32. Stauffer, *The Black Hearts*, 54.

33. The New Negro era, centered in Harlem, New York, encompassed the years 1895 to 1925 and represented a rebirth of African American literary, visual, and musical culture. Henry Louis Gates Jr. discusses the evolution of black visual imagery from the Reconstruction period through the New Negro era in the introduction to *Facing History: The Black Image in American Art, 1710–1940* by Guy C. McElroy (Washington, DC: Corcoran Gallery of Art, 1990).

34. Gandy did not immediately discover that the collection of approximately 75,000 negatives he purchased from the widow of Earl Norman, Henry Norman's son, also contained black portrait images.

35. A. C. Britton to Mary Britton, December 18, 1881. In letters written to Mary and her sister Selah, Britton showered his daughters with words of affection. For example, in a letter dated November 6, 1881, Britton closed a letter to Mary with the words, "I am with an ocean of warm love Your affectionate father." Britton Family papers, LSU.

36. Britton likely used Henry Norman to create his portrait. A glass negative with the banker's likeness was among those rescued by Thomas Gandy. The portrait of Audley C. Britton appears in *Norman's Natchez*, 124.

37. A. C. Britton to Mary Britton, November 6, 1881, LSU.

38. Conner family papers, LSU.

39. A handful of letters written by Mary to her parents in the early 1900s are found in the Britton family collection, LSU. Unfortunately, most of these letters were written in pencil or so illegible that they are nearly impossible to read.

40. Mary M. Britton, *A Southern Character Sketch*, Natchez: M. M. Black's Job Print, 1882, MDAH.

41. Britton, *A Southern Character Sketch*. Susy Banks's sons would not have been permitted to enlist in the Confederate Army but could have accompanied their master as enslaved servants. This was a common notion shared by many white southerners as a means to promote the idea of black loyalty to slaveholders.

42. Britton, *A Southern Character Sketch*.

43. The Kirmess is believed to have originated in Belgium in the 1500s as an annual fair or festival. An American form of the tradition, usually staged for charitable causes, enjoyed widespread popularity in the US in the late nineteenth and early twentieth centuries. Tableaux vivants were a popular form of entertainment throughout much of the nineteenth century. Tableaux featured costumed figures with no speaking parts who posed as imitators of famous scenes from paintings, sculptures, literature, or history.

44. A Natchez newspaper account of the production claimed Britton created her ornate gold and silver gauze dress, embroidered with images of serpents, the sphinx, and other Egyptian icons. Mary may have had some assistance from a local seamstress, but it is probable that she initiated the design and worked on the visually stunning, although historically inaccurate concoction. Many elite young southern women like Britton were trained in sewing and fine needlework by their mothers from a young age and took pride in putting their skills to use, a tradition dating back to the early antebellum era. A Natchez contemporary of Britton's, wealthy Clara Lowenburg Moses, makes several references in her unpublished memoir of sewing numerous pieces of clothing for herself and other family members. Copy in author's hands. Mary may have first been introduced to the pleasures of portrait making when she visited Henry Norman's studio at about the age of seven or eight. At this time, Mary posed as a miniature woman from the colonial period dressed in a formal powdered wig, ornate dress and petticoats, earbobs, fan, and white gloves. The photo appears in the introduction of Gandy and Gandy, *Victorian Children*.

45. W. S. Harwood, "Amateur Photography of To-Day," *Cosmopolitan Magazine*, January 1896, 253.

46. Margaret Bisland, "Women and Their Cameras," *Outing, an Illustrated Magazine of Recreation*, October 1890, 38.

47. Frances Benjamin Johnston, "What a Woman Can Do with a Camera," *Ladies Home Journal*, September 1897, 6.

48. Fortunately, much of Johnston's work has been preserved by the Library of Congress, a project initiated by Johnston in the 1930s and financially supported by the Carnegie Corporation. Several of Johnston's photos of Natchez homes photographed during the 1930s are featured in the appendix's Guide to Pilgrimage Homes. For more on Johnston, see Sam Watters, *Gardens for a Beautiful America, 1895–1935: Photographs by Frances Benjamin Johnston* (New York: Acanthus Press, 2012), and Bettina Berch, *The Woman behind the Lens: The Life and Work of Frances Benjamin Johnston, 1864–1952* (Charlottesville: University Press of Virginia, 2000).

49. Kodak ad. *Ladies Home Journal*, May 1901, 39.

50. "Clover Nook with Quaint Relics of Past," *Natchez Democrat*, n.d.

51. Mary Britton Conner's photo album can be accessed at the LSU's website: http://www.louisianadigitallibrary.org. To place Mary's "Book," dated 1907, into greater context, her album bears strong similarities to the dozens of scrapbooks compiled by Mildred Lewis Rutherford, historian general of the United Daughters of the Confederacy from 1911 to 1915. Rutherford filled her albums with images, clippings, and stories of faithful slaves gathered by Daughters across the country in her energetic quest to promote Lost Cause ideology. One such scrapbook was titled "Tributes to Faithful Slaves." Rutherford's collection of

scrapbooks is archived at the Museum of the Confederacy in Richmond, Virginia. Conner's "Her Book" expressed a similar message and passion, but from an intensely personal, local perspective. Another album compiled by Conner labeled "Clovernook" offers similar perspectives.

52. Gretchen Murphy, *Shadowing the White Man's Burden: U.S. Imperialism and the Problem of the Color Line* (New York: New York University Press, 2010), 4.

53. Murphy, 41–42. Tillman's speech was delivered February 7, 1899.

54. From Louisa Poppenheim, "Woman's Work in the South," in *The South in the Building of the Nation*, vol. 10 (1909). Quoted in Micki McElya, *Clinging to Mammy: The Faithful Slave in Twentieth-Century America* (Cambridge, MA: Harvard University Press, 2007), 144.

55. Allison L. Sneider, *Suffragists in an Imperial Age: United States Expansion and the Woman Question, 1870–1929* (Oxford: Oxford University Press, 2008), 111.

56. Susan Sontag, *On Photography* (New York: Farrar, Straus & Giroux, 1977), 12.

57. Jackson Lears, *Rebirth of a Nation: The Making of Modern America, 1877–1920* (New York: Harper Collins, 2009), 288–89. According to the captions in Conner's album, the baptisms took place at numerous sites, including Dix's Pond, Elgin, "brick yard pond," "near saw mill" and Under-the-Hill, which would have been on the banks of the Mississippi River. Judging from the composition and quality of the various photographs, Mary may have taken some of the photos, but those shot from the water were likely taken by other photographers, images which Mary later appropriated for her album.

58. McElya, 24, 44, 72, 144. Nancy Green, dressed in a brightly colored long skirt and a bandana wrapped around her head, played the part of Aunt Jemima for thirty years, performing as both cook and narrator of Old South tales at every World's fair until her death in 1923. At her premiere performance in Chicago, she stood over a hot griddle cooking up pancakes for hungry visitors in a booth shaped like a gigantic flour barrel, while dishing out entertaining stories of life during slavery times. The crowds ate up Green's griddle cakes and stories, placing more than 50,000 orders for the popular product. For more on the racialized aspect of the Chicago World's Fair, see Robert Reed, "*All the World Is Here!" The Black Presence at White City* (Bloomington: Indiana University Press, 2000). Jo-Ann Morgan, "Mammy the Huckster: Selling the Old South for the New Century," *American Art* 9, no. 1 (Spring, 1995), 86–109; Patricia A. Turner, *Ceramic Uncles and Celluloid Mammies: Black Images and Their Influence on Culture* (New York: Anchor Books, 1994); M. M. Manring, *Slave in a Box: The Strange Career of Aunt Jemima* (Charlottesville: University Press of Virginia, 1998).

59. Robert C. Rydell, quoted in *Delivering Views: Distant Cultures in Early Postcards*, edited by Christraud M. Geary and Virginia-Lee Webb (Washington, DC: Smithsonian Institution Press, 1998), 9.

60. Conner Sr. was forced into bankruptcy in 1869 and never returned to the level of prosperity he enjoyed before the war. He barely stayed afloat by handling cases in Louisiana and Mississippi, working as a plantation manager, and functioning as the agent for a distilling business. Conner Jr. never achieved the level of wealth his family had reveled in during the antebellum era, but fared notably better than his father. In 1909 he was the recipient of

a generous bequest of nearly $100,000 from a female client whose legal affairs he managed and who had never married. See Joyce Broussard, "Coping with the Deluge: The Elite, Not Married Women of Post-Bellum Natchez, Mississippi—and the 'Other Men' in Their Lives," *Southern Studies* 17 no. 1 (Spring/Summer 2010), 39–74.

61. Marian Klamkin, *Picture Postcards* (New York: Dodd, Mead, 1974), 38.

62. Lemuel P. Conner Family Papers, LSU.

63. McElya, 142. For more on the complex relationship between enslaved women and their white mistresses, see Elizabeth Fox-Genovese, *Within the Plantation Household: Black and White Women of the Old South* (Chapel Hill: University of North Carolina Press, 1988).

64. Howell Raines, "Grady's Gift," *New York Times*, December 1, 1991. Quoted in Kathryn Stockett, *The Help* (New York: Amy Einhorn Books, 2009), 450.

65. Bercaw, *Gendered Freedoms*, 3, 15–16.

66. Conner identified the following individuals in her album, often noting who their parents or children were: Fred Banks, Peter Banks (Britton's coachman in 1880), Mandy Berlin Scott, Lucy Black, Richard Butler, Minor Campbell, Sally Carraway, Joseph Christmas, Mandy Clark, Monroe Dixon, Cornelia Dobbins, Alec Drake, Ruth Audley Foster, Stewart Foster, Russ Harris, Mary Jackson, Johnny Jenkins, Harrison Joseph, Nancy Logan, Robert Macrery, Dust Bee Martin, Alf Miller, Ello Miller, Shed Moore, Fanny Ramsey, John Rud, Bud Scott (well-known musician), Ed Shaw, William Singleton, Harriet Taylor (Britton cook), Peter White, Lucy Wilson, Robert Woodbridge (coachman).

67. James M. McPherson, *The Negro's War* (New York: Ballantine Books, 1965), 23–25.

68. Throughout her adult life Roane Fleming Byrnes never assumed the mundane labors of housework. As one friend later recalled, Roane "never fried an egg, never washed a cup or saucer in her life, never did anything that would classify her as a housewife." Quoted in Verbie Lovorn Prevost, "Roane Fleming Byrnes: A Critical Biography" (PhD diss., University of Mississippi, 1974), 10.

69. On the role of domestic space as sites of black community, see Fox-Genovese, *Within the Plantation Household*, and Anthony E. Kaye, *Joining Places: Slave Neighborhoods in the Old South* (Chapel Hill: University of North Carolina Press, 2007).

70. John Roy Lynch, *Reminiscences of an Active Life: The Autobiography of John Roy Lynch*, edited with an introduction by John Hope Franklin (Chicago: University of Chicago Press, 1970). Lynch lived in Chicago for the remainder of his life. An obituary published in the *Chicago Tribune* after his death in November 1939 is telling of the respect he had earned in his new home. Lynch was referred to as "the grand old man of Chicago's Negro citizenry."

71. Fox-Genovese, 188.

72. W. E. B. Du Bois, *The Souls of Black Folk* (Chicago: A. C. McClurg, 1903; reprint Radford, Virginia: Wilder Publications, 2008), 31, 42, 94.

73. During its peak years of usage from about 1780 until 1820 the trace was a series of foot trails about five hundred miles long, used primarily to connect Nashville, Tennessee, to Natchez. Native Americans, missionaries, military troops, and Andrew Jackson traveled these various trails as a means of transportation. Thousands of enslaved Africans and African Americans also marched the trails, chained together as they were herded from the upper South to the lower South where they were auctioned off at slave markets in Natchez.

74. Mississippi Territorial Census, 1830.

75. D. Clayton James, *Antebellum Natchez* (Baton Rouge, Louisiana State University Press, 1968), 163.

76. US Slave Census, 1860. Much can be learned about the Britton family's slaves by reviewing the letters between Audley Britton and his overseer James W. Melvin written during and after the Civil War. See Britton Family Papers, LSU.

77. Winthrop Jordan, *Tumult and Silence at Second Creek: An Inquiry into a Civil War Slave Conspiracy* (Baton Rouge: Louisiana State University Press, 1995), 85. Justin Behrend, *Reconstructing Democracy: Grassroots Black Politics in the Deep South after the Civil War* (Athens: University of Georgia Press, 2017), 20–23.

78. Ellen Douglas, *Truth: Four Stories I Am Finally Old Enough to Tell* (Chapel Hill, NC: Algonquin Books, 1998), 133–46. Douglas, who was related to Lemuel Conner and many of Natchez's antebellum families, interviewed Mary Conner's daughter, Eliza Conner Martin, shortly before her death. Eliza told Douglas the story of her grandfather's papers, noting that her mother instructed her children to never throw them away. These papers were discovered by Winthrop Jordan and became the basis for his book *Tumult and Silence at Second Creek*.

79. Sontag, *On Photography*, 4.

80. Cheryl Thurber, "The Development of the Mammy Image and Mythology," in Virginia Bernhard, Betty Brandon, Elizabeth Fox-Genovese, and Theda Purdue, eds. *Southern Women: Histories and Identities* (Columbia: University of Missouri Press, 1992), 99.

81. A national mammy memorial was proposed in Congress in 1922. Although the measure passed in the Senate, it never made it out of committee in the House of Representatives, marking the end of the campaign. See McElya, 146–47.

82. Young Lemuel Conner died at the age of thirteen in 1907 from typhoid fever. Perhaps this photo was too painful a reminder of her son's death to be included in Conner's photo album. US Manuscript Census, 1920.

83. Mary Britton Conner to Audley and Eliza Britton, August 19, 1892. Britton Family Papers, LSU.

84. Joan Gandy, "Portraits of Pride," *Natchez Democrat*, February 16, 1986.

85. The majority of identified Norman portraits are of white patrons. Many of the Norman negatives of Natchez blacks archived at LSU remain unidentified.

CHAPTER 5: SELLING HISTORIC NATCHEZ TO DEPRESSION-ERA PILGRIMS

1. Ernie Pyle, newspaper clipping, n.d., Natchez Garden Club scrapbook, HNF.

2. A forerunner to the Pilgrimage home tours was organized in March 1931 when the Natchez Garden Club hosted a convention for Mississippi Garden Club delegates. Rumors abound as to how the event, originally intended to showcase the city's gardens, became an informal tour of homes. According to some club members and later perpetuated in local histories and media accounts, a late freeze killed the spring flowers and forced event planners to offer their guests an alternative form of entertainment. Katherine Miller, who was serving as club president that year, disputes the idea that bad weather played a decisive

factor in the origins of the Pilgrimage. Weather records, newspaper accounts, and common sense seem to support Miller's claim that the idea of opening Natchez's old homes was no accident brought on by fickle weather but planned well in advance of the delegates' arrival. Miller stated she appointed a committee to help her select the most outstanding Natchez houses based on history, architecture, and interiors.

3. Morton Rothstein, "The Changing Social Networks and Investment Behavior of a Slaveholding Elite in the Ante-Bellum South: Some Natchez 'Nabobs,' 1800–1860," in *Entrepreneurs in Cultural Context*, edited by Sidney M. Greenfield, Arnold Strickon, and Robert Aubrey (Albuquerque: University of New Mexico Press, 1979), 69.

4. Stephanie E. Yuhl, *A Golden Haze of Memory: The Making of Historic Charleston* (Chapel Hill: University of North Carolina Press, 2005), 3–4.

5. Roger D. Tate Jr., "Easing the Burden: The Era of Depression and New Deal in Mississippi" (PhD diss., University of Tennessee, 1978), 4, 36–27. Richard A. McLemore, *History of Mississippi* 2 (Jackson: College and University Press of Mississippi, 1975), 90–94. Eudora Welty quoted in Susan Haltom and Jane Roy Brown, *One Writer's Garden: Eudora Welty's Home Place* (Jackson: University Press of Mississippi, 2011), 103. Interview with Hunter Cole and Seetha Srinivasan, *Eudora Welty: Photographs* (Jackson: University Press of Mississippi, 1989), xvii.

6. William Allen quoted in Mary Warren Miller and Ronald W. Miller, *The Great Houses of Natchez* (Jackson: University Press of Mississippi, 1986), vii, ix.

7. Ronald L. F. Davis, who has written extensively about Natchez, coined this term of comparison. See *The Black Experience in Natchez* and *Good and Faithful Labor: From Slavery to Sharecropping in the Natchez District, 1860–1890* (Westport, Connecticut: Greenwood Press, 1982). Natchez residents also frequently referred to Natchez's "magical spell of the past, a Utopia and a land of dreams come true." See Theodora Britton Marshall and Gladys Crail Evans, *They Found It in Natchez* (New Orleans: Pelican, 1939), 230.

8. The Federal Writers' Project of the Works Progress Administration, *Mississippi: A Guide to the Magnolia State* (New York: Viking, 1938), 237.

9. Ernie Pyle, "Touring with Ernie Pyle," newspaper clipping, n.d.; David Cohn, "Natchez Was a Lady," *Atlantic Monthly*, January 1940, 15.

10. Marshall and Evans, 181.

11. Quoted in Leslie Smithers, "The Pleasure Garden of Nineteenth-Century Natchez: Illusions of Grandeur," in *Natchez on the Mississippi: A Journey through Southern History, 1870–1920*. Edited by Ronald L. F. Davis and Joyce L. Broussard (Los Angeles: Norstel, 1995), 23.

12. Marshall and Evans, 223.

13. Ronald Davis, *The Black Experience in Natchez*, 43. Marshall and Evans, 179.

14. Ronald Davis, *The Black Experience in Natchez*, 43.

15. Phyllis Ten Elshof, "Memories Sweeten Pilgrimages Past," *Jackson Clarion-Ledger*, n.d.

16. Natchez Garden Club minutes, April 13, 1931, Natchez Garden Club Archives, MDAH. It may have been Henry who actually coined the name "Natchez Pilgrimage." Another possible source could have been a Wisconsin club delegate who made the suggestion to create

"an annual pilgrimage to Natchez and opening the old homes for inspection to the visitors" during a garden club convention attended by Katherine Miller. "Natchez Club Affairs," edited by Nancy O. Leeds, March 1935, vol. 1, no. 6, MDAH.

17. Mary Louise Kendall, a Pilgrimage founder, told an interviewer of Agnes Marshall's initial reaction to Miller's request. "She said, 'Indeed you are not going to bring strange people into my house to see it like it is. Indeed, I am not about to do it!' But Katherine said, 'We are going to be there.' Sure enough, we were there, and Mrs. Agnes opened her house and we took in all the strangers." Interview with Graham Hicks, January 27, 1982, NGCH.

18. Katherine Miller, "Natchez Is A Fairy Story," n.d., MDAH.

19. Karen L. Cox, *Dreaming of Dixie: How the South Was Created in American Popular Culture* (Chapel Hill: University of North Carolina Press, 2013), 37.

20. Suzannah Patterson, "Promoting Pilgrimage Was Hard," March 12, 1962, *Natchez Democrat*.

21. Joan Gandy, "Remembering Ladies behind Pilgrimage," *Natchez Democrat*, March 6, 2002.

22. Interview with Alma Carpenter by author, April 9, 2001.

23. "Katherine's Fantastic Imagination," April 26, 1942, *Young People*. Katherine Miller Scrapbook, HNF.

24. Lillian Meriwether, "Impressions of a Visitor to the Ante-Bellum Homes of the Pilgrimage Garden Club Tours," magazine clipping, n.d., Katherine Miller Scrapbook, HNF.

25. Press release written by Natchez Garden Club member Roane Fleming Byrnes, "Natchez Pilgrimage Week 1933 Project of the Natchez Garden Club," circa 1936, Natchez Garden Club records, MDAH.

26. Consumer Price Index values were calculated at US Department of Labor Bureau of Labor Statistics website (http://www.bls.gov/data/inflation_calculator.htm).

27. Katherine Boatner Blankenstein. "The Natchez Garden Club," report, n.d., Natchez Pilgrimages 1935–1950 subject file, MDAH.

28. Byrnes press release, MDAH.

29. Correspondence from George Malin Davis Kelly to Ethel Moore Kelly, March 22, 25, 1935, Davis/Kelly Archival Collection, NNHP, National Park Service, Natchez, MS. (Courtesy of Natchez National Historical Park.) Kelly's grandfather George Malin Davis purchased Melrose in 1865. The house remained vacant for more than twenty-five years before Kelly, raised in New York, and his wife took up residence in 1901. According to a National Register of Historic Places 1974 report, "Melrose is most remarkable for the quality of the preservation and maintenance of this house, outbuildings and grounds." The furnishings of Melrose were never dispersed. In addition to supporting the Natchez Garden Club and Pilgrimage, Kelly was well known for his vocal talents. He frequently sang during worship services at the First Presbyterian Church as well as other local churches and Temple B'Nai Israel, Natchez's Jewish Temple.

30. George Malin Davis Kelly to Ethel Moore Kelly, March 31, 1935.

31. George Malin Davis Kelly to Ethel Moore Kelly, April 1, 1935.

32. George Malin Davis Kelly to Ethel Moore Kelly, April 2, 1935.

33. According to George Kelly's granddaughter Julie Ferry Hale, who transcribed and annotated the letters, the head of a moose, shot by Ethel Kelly in 1902 in Alaska, hung at Melrose in the great hall between the doors to the library and the pink parlor. It was reputed to have been the second largest moose shot that year. There was an often-repeated story about a little boy during one Pilgrimage who went from room and room and finally asked, "but where's the rest of him?"

34. George Malin Davis Kelly to Ethel Moore Kelly, April 4, 1935.

35. George Malin Davis Kelly to Ethel Moore Kelly, April 6, 1935. www.dollartimes.com/inflation.

36. Pilgrimage Guest Book, Arlington, March 14, 1937, HNF. The home, built in 1816, was once considered one of the town's most beautiful antebellum treasures and for many years was owned by Hubert and Annie Barnum, an early president of the Pilgrimage Garden Club. Arlington suffered a devastating fire in 2002 that destroyed the main roof and much of the second floor. Vandals subsequently broke many windows and destroyed or defaced the home. http://en.wikipedia.org/wiki/Arlington(Natchez,_Mississippi)—cite_note-7#cite_note-7.

37. "Pilgrimage Week, March 31st through April 7th 1935," booklet published by the Natchez Garden Club. Subject file, JGWAL.

38. *New York Times*, March 17, 1935.

39. Jasper B. Shannon describes the new elite as the "banker-merchant-farmer-lawyer-doctor governing class," a shorthand term to designate the white elites, the more affluent and successful townspeople combined with the more influential and wealthy planters. From Earl Black and Merle Black, *Politics and Society in the South* (Cambridge, MA: Harvard University Press, 1987), 25, 57.

40. Richard L. Bushman, *The Refinement of America: Persons, Houses, Cities* (New York: Alfred A. Knopf, 1992), 127–31. The first garden club in America was founded in January 1891 by the Ladies Garden Club of Athens, Georgia. By May 1929 thirteen federated state clubs became charter members of Garden Clubs of America at an organizational meeting in Washington, DC. www.gardenclub.org.

41. Virginia Tuttle Clayton, ed. *The Once and Future Gardener: Garden Writing from the Golden Age of Magazines, 1900–1940* (Boston: David R. Godine, 1999), xxiii.

42. Haltom and Brown, 46.

43. The United Daughters of the Confederacy achieved its greatest following in the 1920s with more than 100,000 members nationally. Cameron Freeman Napier, in *Encyclopedia of Southern Culture*, ed. by Charles Reagan Wilson and William Ferris (Chapel Hill: University of North Carolina Press, 1989), 706.

44. *United Daughters of the Confederacy Minutes* (Richmond, Virginia: Richmond Press, Inc., 1918, 1936), MDAH.

45. "Birthday of Lee Quietly Observed," *Natchez Democrat*, January 20, 1929.

46. Suzanne Mettler, *Dividing Citizens: Gender and Federalism in New Deal Public Policy* (Ithaca: Cornell University Press, 1998), 42.

47. The majority of working club members worked in jobs traditionally held by women, including clerical workers, teachers, nurses, and a few as Works Progress Administration (WPA) employees. A handful of the clubwomen held managerial positions. One member

served as the president of the department store owned by her family, another as president of the Natchez Coca-Cola Bottling Company (founded by her husband), and another as supervisor of the Natchez Sanatorium. *Natchez City Directory*, 1939, JGWAL.

48. Few if any members of the early NGC were themselves members of the UDC. This is not to say that the two groups did not interact on occasion. For instance, the garden club was asked by local UDC president Beatrice Perrault in 1937 to financially support efforts to beautify Memorial Park, home of the town's Confederate monument. NGC president Kate Brandon responded that the club would be happy to "cooperate with you in the preservation and restoration of this spot which is sacred to all of us." Natchez Garden Club minutes and correspondence, MDAH.

49. Allison Davis, Burleigh B. Gardner, and Mary R. Gardner, *Deep South: A Social Anthropological Study of Caste and Class* (Chicago: The University of Chicago Press, 1941), 191–97.

50. D. Clayton James, *Antebellum Natchez* (Baton Rouge, Louisiana State University Press, 1968), 155. Also see Rebecca M. Dresser, "The Minor Family of Natchez: A Case of Southern Unionism" (Master's thesis, California State University, Northridge, 2000), 113.

51. Interview with Mary Louise Kendall Goodrich by author, December 28, 2001.

52. US Manuscript Census, 1840, Adams County, Mississippi. *Biographical and Historical Memoirs of Mississippi* (Chicago: Goodspeed, 1891; reprinted Spartanburg, SC: The Reprint Company, 1978), Vol. 1, Section II, 809–16. Reuben Collins was the father of Miller's paternal grandmother, Catherine Collins Grafton.

53. *Natchez, Mississippi: On Top, Not "Under the Hill."* (Natchez, MS: Daily Democrat Steam Press, 1892), 6.

54. Slave Schedule, 1860, Adams County, Mississippi, MDAH, Jackson, Mississippi; Mississippi Tax Records (1862), MDAH; various wills for Grafton family, CCAC.

55. Sarah Dunbar Smith, "Thomas Rose: A Nineteenth-Century Master Builder in Natchez, Mississippi." (Master's thesis, Tulane University, 1993).

56. US Census, 1900, Adams County, Miss.; *Natchez City Directory*, 1892, 1912, JGWAL.

57. Bette Barber, "Southern Personalities," magazine clipping, April 1936, Katherine Miller scrapbook, HNF.

58. J. Balfour Miller, who died in 1985, left an estate valued at $255,000 plus his home Hope Farm. Katherine Miller, who died two years earlier, left an estate valued at slightly more than one million dollars, Will book 42, 111, CCAC.

59. A deed dated December 14, 1926, records that Katherine and J. Balfour Miller purchased Hope Farm for one thousand dollars from Mary and Elizabeth Montgomery, unmarried sisters whose family had owned the property for nearly a century. Deed Record Book No. 4-L, 100, CCAC. The Montgomery family had at one time been prosperous and influential planters. Mary and Elizabeth's father, Eli, served as president of the Commercial Bank as well as the Mississippi Railroad, and figured prominently as a Natchez cotton broker. Eli and his wife Maria had ten children, but only three of the children married. After the death of their parents, Mary and Elizabeth and a brother lived at Hope Farm. The two sisters were remembered as "delightful and typical gentlewomen of the Old South." Edith Wyatt Moore, "Fondly I Roam," *Natchez Times*, May 29, 1949, newspaper clipping, Miller

family file, JGWAL; "J. Balfour and Wife: Rhymes and $10 Orchestra," *Natchez Democrat*, March 7, 1976, newspaper clipping, Miller family file, JGWAL.

60. Katherine Grafton Miller, *Natchez of Long Ago and the Pilgrimage* (Natchez, MS: Rellimak, 1938), 24.

61. Letter to Mayor and Aldermen, November 25, 1930, Katherine Miller Scrapbook, HNF.

62. Handwritten note in Katherine Miller scrapbook, n.d., HNF.

63. Martha H. Swain, *Ellen S. Woodward: New Deal Advocate for Women* (Jackson: University Press of Mississippi, 1995) 19, 23.

64. Harnett Kane, *Natchez on the Mississippi* (New York: William Morrow, 1947). Quoted in Jack Davis, *Race against Time: Culture and Segregation in Natchez since 1930* (Baton Rouge: Louisiana State University Press, 2001), 68–69.

65. "Touring with Ernie Pyle," newspaper clipping, n.d., NGC Scrapbooks, NGCH.

66. Interview with Virginia Morrison, by Graham Hicks, August 4, 1981, NGCH.

67. Newspaper clipping, n.d., Katherine Miller Scrapbook, HNF.

68. Interview with Dr. Thomas Gandy by author April 9, 2001; interview with Alma Carpenter by author April 9, 2001.

69. Lantern slides gained popularity from the late 1800s through 1940s. Lecturers who used lantern slides gained authority as cultural leaders. Images began as black and white photos and then were hand painted according to the instructions of the photographer. Interview with Mimi Miller by author, August 2017. Many of Katherine Miller's slides were tinted by local photographer Earl Norman. Copies of Miller's slides are archived at the HNF. People were rarely featured in the slides, which often focused on gardens and historic homes that portrayed a "perfect world." Photographer Frances Benjamin Johnston, who created some of her finest work in Natchez during the late 1930s (chapter 4), was known for her beautiful lantern slides and lectures of outstanding residential gardens owned by garden club members across the United States. Johnston's slides are archived at the Library of Congress.

70. Quoted in promotional brochure, n.d., Natchez Garden Club file, JGWAL.

71. Katherine Miller, "Natchez Is a Fairy Story," n.d., MDAH.

72. A year after Stanton Hall was completed in 1858, its owner died. The home changed hands in 1870 for seven thousand dollars, substantially less than its value. Later it was sold again for less than the cost of the wrought-iron fence which surrounded its grounds. Today the house serves as the headquarters of the Pilgrimage Garden Club. William H. Nicholas, "History Repeats in Old Natchez," *National Geographic*, February 1949, 205.

73. Interview with Alma Carpenter by author, April 9, 2001.

74. Thomas Rose enjoyed a prolific career as a master builder in Natchez and is linked with a number of the town's most architecturally prestigious homes, including Auburn, The Elms, Elms Court, Edgewood, and Stanton Hall. By 1860, however, Rose faced mounting debts and suffered a nervous breakdown. He committed suicide on April 28, 1861. Smith, "Thomas Rose: A Nineteenth-Century Master Builder."

75. Ruth Wheeler's union with Melchoir Beltzhoover is a prime example of the complex family kinship networks that developed in nineteenth-century Natchez. Ruth's mother was

descended from the Britton family, founders of Britton and Koontz, one of the state's most prominent banking institutions. Ruth Beltzhoover's husband, Melchoir, was descended from the Koontz family. Ruth and Melchoir's marriage united the two banking families. Murray, *Early Romances*, 61.

76. Interview with Ruth Beltzhoover, by Graham Hicks, August 4, 1981. NGCH. In the interview Beltzhoover noted that Katherine Miller and her mother also operated a tearoom during Pilgrimage season at the Millers' home, Hope Farm. In 1933 the NGC fought a resolution adopted by the Natchez Association of Commerce that reserved the right of serving paid meals to Pilgrimage guests to restaurant owners only, noting that "The Garden Club feels that the serving of attractive home prepared meals, at reasonable prices, for its Pilgrimage guests, would be an added attraction." Serving meals to Pilgrimage tourists not only offered tourists more options but provided another source of income to Pilgrimage homeowners.

77. Interview with Mary Louise Kendall Goodrich, by Graham Hicks, January 27, 1982, NGCH.

78. James, *Antebellum Natchez*, 154.

79. Chancery Court Dockets, cause number 6776, docket 9, CCAC. The Bennerscheidt home, a rambling wood-frame structure, had once been owned by F. A. W. Davis and stood at the intersection of Homochitto and South Martin Luther King Street. The site is now occupied by Braden School and the Malt Shop. Correspondence with Mimi Miller to author, February 20, 2003.

80. Phyllis Ten Elshof, "Memories Sweeten Pilgrimages Past," *Clarion-Ledger* (Jackson, MS), newspaper clipping, n.d.

81. Interview with Marion Kelly Ferry (Ethel Kelly's daughter), by Graham Hicks, November 17, 1981, NGCH.

82. Early twentieth-century Natchez female writers included Catharine Dunbar Brown, Roane Fleming Byrnes, Ethel L. Fleming, Pearl Guyton, Caroline Lovell, Theodora Britton Marshall, Katherine Grafton Miller, Edith Wyatt Moore, Elizabeth Dunbar Murray, Nola Nance Oliver, Amanda W. Phipps, Elizabeth Brandon Stanton, Catharine Van Court, and Zaida Marion Wells.

83. Roane Fleming Byrnes, press release, n.d., Natchez Garden Club papers, MDAH.

84. Drew Gilpin Faust, *Southern Stories: Slaveholders in Peace and War* (Columbia: University of Missouri Press, 1992), 2.

85. Katherine Miller, *Natchez of Long Ago*, 31.

86. Edith Wyatt Moore, *Natchez Under-the-Hill* (Natchez: Southern Historical Publications, 1958). An archive of Moore's notes, early drafts and correspondence are housed at Northwestern State University of Louisiana, Watson Memorial Library, Cammie G. Henry Research Center.

87. Marshall and Evans, *They Found It in Natchez*.

88. A group of DAR delegates led by Catherine Dunbar Brown (she married George Brown in the late 1930s) went before the Mississippi legislature in 1938 to petition the state to fund the restoration of Rosalie, a home occupied by Union General William Gresham during the Civil War. The legislature appropriated $10,000 for the preservation of the home

and the estate quickly became a DAR shrine and continues to be managed by the organization. Ker Family Papers, 1776–1996, UNC.

89. Letter to S. J. Brown from Catharine Dunbar, February 2, 1935. Ye Olde Booke Shoppe by early 1935 had relocated to 124 South Commerce Street. Ker Family Papers, UNC.

90. *Commercial Appeal* magazine, September 7, 1969, 10. Byrnes held the position of president of her state's Natchez Trace Association for thirty-five years until shortly before her death in 1970.

91. Quoted in Verbie Lovorn Prevost, "Roane Fleming Byrnes: A Critical Biography" (PhD diss., University of Mississippi, 1974), 8.

92. Prevost.

93. *Commercial Appeal* magazine, 10.

94. Pyle, newspaper clipping, n.d.; Gail Borden, *Chicago Tribune*, newspaper clipping, n.d., NGC Scrapbooks, NGCH.

95. Gail Borden, "Club Works Wonders," *Chicago Tribune*, April 4, 1938.

96. For more on southern white antebellum women see Anne Firor Scott, *The Southern Lady: From Pedestal to Politics, 1830–1930* (Chicago: University of Chicago Press, 1970); Drew Gilpin Faust, *Mothers of Invention: Women of the Slaveholding South in the American Civil War* (Chapel Hill: University of North Carolina Press, 1996); Elizabeth Fox-Genovese, *Within the Plantation Household: Black and White Women of the Old South* (Chapel Hill: University of North Carolina Press, 1988).

97. Barber, "Southern Personalities."

98. Karen Altman, "Consumer Ideology: The Better Homes in America Campaign," *Critical Studies in Mass Communication* 7, no. 3 (September 1990), 288. Also see Blanche Halbert, *The Better Homes Manual* (Chicago: University of Chicago Press, in cooperation with Better Homes in America, 1931).

99. Sara E. Morris, "'Down in Tupelo Everybody Seems to be Feeling Grand': Early Home Electrification Promotion in Northeast Mississippi," in *Mississippi Women: Their Histories, Their Lives*, vol. 2, ed. by Elizabeth Anne Payne, Martha H. Swain, and Marjorie Julian Spruill (Athens: University of Georgia Press, 2010), 196.

100. Swain, 22. Woodward left Mississippi in 1933 to join Franklin Roosevelt's administration as the President's second highest woman advisor, second only to Frances Perkins, Secretary of Labor. She served as the director of work relief programs for women during the New Deal in the 1930s.

101. Altman, 289.

102. Katherine Miller, *Natchez of Long Ago*, 31.

103. Barber, "Southern Personalities."

104. Pilgrimage Week April 2nd through April 8th 1934. NGC subject file, JGWAL.

105. Natchez Pilgrimage Tour No. 1, n.d. Natchez Garden Club Papers, MDAH.

106. David W. Blight, *Race and Reunion: The Civil War in American Memory* (Cambridge, MA: Belknap Press of Harvard University, 2001), 388, 391.

107. Georgie Willson Newell and Charles Cromartie Compton, *Natchez and the Pilgrimage* (Natchez, MS: Southern Publishers, Inc., 1935), 23.

108. Interview with Marion Kelly Ferry by Graham Hicks, November 17, 1981. In 1940 a law was passed by the Natchez Board of Aldermen that Natchez guides were required to

pass an exam developed by the garden clubs in local history, architecture, horticulture, and "cultural facts." Violators of the ordinance could be fined up to fifty dollars and jailed for ten days. *Code of the City of Natchez, Mississippi*, 1954.

109. Cohn, "Natchez Was a Lady," 18–19.

110. Tableaux, also known as "tableaux vivants" were a popular home entertainment in the late 1800s and early twentieth century that featured costumed actors standing in place, often imitating famous scenes from history, literature, and paintings. Over time the scenes were performed in public venues and gave women an opportunity to appear in public celebrations, seen but silent. See David Glassberg, *American Historical Pageantry: The Uses of Tradition in the Early Twentieth Century* (Chapel Hill: University of North Carolina Press, 1990), 16–18.

111. Murray also wrote books that frequently used family letters of prominent residents to create biographical sketches, such as *Early Romances of Historic Natchez* (Natchez: Natchez Printing and Stationery, 1938). "Natchez Club Affairs," 7, MDAH. Also see Katherine Miller, *Natchez of Long Ago*, 43.

112. Jack Temple Kirby, *Media-Made Dixie: The South in the American Imagination* (Baton Rouge: Louisiana State University Press, 1986), 75.

113. William A. Adams interview with Graham Hicks, August 4, 1981, NGCH.

114. Mary Louise Geddes interview with Graham Hicks, August 4, 1981, NGCH.

115. Cathy Cluck, "Pageant Costumes Result of Much Research," *Natchez Democrat*, n.d.

116. Natchez Pageant program, Pilgrimage Garden Club, 1938, JGWAL.

117. Blight, 4.

118. Elmer T. Peterson, "The Old South Lives Again!" *Better Homes and Gardens*, February 1938.

119. Natchez Confederate Pageant, 1948, JGWAL.

120. Tableau 15—Ball in Honor of Henry Clay, pageant program, Pilgrimage Garden Club, 1941, JGWAL.

121. Michael Berkowitz, "A 'New Deal' for Leisure: Making Mass Tourism during the Great Depression," in *Being Elsewhere: Tourism, Consumer Culture, and Identity in Modern Europe and North America*, Shelley Baranowski and Ellen Furlough, eds. (Ann Arbor, MI: University of Michigan Press, 2001), 187.

122. Berkowitz.

123. Dana Frank, *Buy American: The Untold Story of Economic Nationalism* (Boston: Beacon Press, 1999), 56–78.

124. Blight, 394.

125. Kirby, 67–70. Also see Ken Emerson, *Doo Dah! Stephen Foster and the Rise of American Popular Culture* (New York: Simon and Schuster, 1998).

126. *Old Natchez on the Mississippi*, MGM, 1939. A copy of the film is in the possession of NGC member Kathie Blankenstein.

127. Kirby, 75.

128. Lillie Boatner's daughter, Kathie Blankenstein, reports that the original Camellia pattern presented to club members was rejected because they desired something a bit more ornate. The Melrose design was enthusiastically accepted, and though a huge introduction was planned, World War II intervened. The pattern was finally introduced in 1946. "The

ladies had to keep a secret for five years. I don't know how they did it," says Blankenstein. Interview with Kathie Blankenstein by author, December 21, 2001.

129. Letter to Harriet Dixon from Charlie McCarthy, January 6, 1941, NGC Scrapbooks, NGCH.

130. Interview with Kathie Blankenstein by author, December 12, 2001. "27th Birthday of the Natchez Garden Club," prepared by Lillie Vidal Boatner, NGCH.

131. Blankenstein interview, December 12, 2001.

132. Of articles published on individual states, Mississippi ranked eighth in terms of coverage with 300 articles; Virginia, long considered the heart of the Old South, captured the most coverage with 1,471 articles. Natchez and the Pilgrimage received press coverage in twenty-one magazines during this period.

133. These articles included "The Old South Lives Again! (*Better Homes and Gardens*, February 1938); "Natchez Was a Lady" (*Atlantic Monthly*, January 1940); "So Red the Rose" (*Saturday Evening Post*, March 4, 1939); "The Deep South" (*House and Gardens*, November 1939); "Meet the Beltzhoovers" (*Ladies Home Journal*, January 1947); "History Repeats in Old Natchez" (*National Geographic Magazine*, February 1949); "The Mellow South" (*Chicago Tribune*, April 3, 1938); "The Charms of Old Natchez" (*New York Times*, December 11, 1938). Many more articles were published in smaller regional newspapers and magazines. By comparison other regions of the country received far less attention. Over the same period, the North received a meager 35 articles; the West, 105; and the Southwest, only 39.

134. Horace Mann Bond, "A Negro Looks at His South," *Harper's*, June 1931, 98–108.

135. *New York Times*, March 5, 1933.

136. ProQuest database. Mississippi recorded the most lynchings of African Americans of any state in the nation between 1882 and 1930, with 462 reported deaths, according to the digital archives at Tuskegee Institute.

137. Warren Susman, *Culture as History: The Transformation of American Society in the Twentieth Century* (New York: Pantheon Books, 1985), 159.

138. Alfred Haworth Jones, "The Search for a Usable American Past in the New Deal Era," *American Quarterly* 23, no. 5 (December 1971), 715.

139. Cox, *Dreaming of Dixie*, 149–53. For more on southern heritage tourism see Sidney R. Bland, *Preserving Charleston's Past, Shaping Its Future: The Life and Times of Susan Pringle Frost* (Columbia: University of South Carolina Press, 1999); Eric Gable, Richard Handler, and Anna Lawson, *The New History in an Old Museum* (Durham: Duke University Press, 1997); Patricia West, *Domesticating History: The Political Origins of America's House Museums* (Washington, DC: Smithsonian Institution Press, 1999); Stephanie E. Yuhl, *A Golden Haze of Memory: The Making of Historic Charleston* (Chapel Hill: University of North Carolina Press, 2005).

140. Cox, *Dreaming of Dixie*, 151.

141. Miller quoted in Elizabeth Mullener, "Springtime in Natchez," *Dixie*, May 30, 1982, x. Natchez is blessed with its collection of fine federal, Greek revival, and Italianate style homes primarily because Natchez was not considered a strategic military location during the Civil War due to its lack of railroad connections, unlike nearby Vicksburg, which suffered large scale destruction.

142. Pyle, newspaper clipping, n.d.

143. Peter Carmichael, "Mississippi Reconsidered: It Is Ante-Bellum Rather Than Neanderthal." *Baltimore Sun*, June 11, 1938.

144. Carmichael.

145. Lillian Meriwether, "Impressions of a Visitor," newspaper clipping, n.d. India Moffett, "Natchez—City that Still Is Living in Past," *Chicago Tribune*, clipping, 1940. Katherine Miller scrapbook, HNF.

146. Gail Borden, "The Mellow South," *Chicago Tribune*, April 3, 1936.

147. Meigs O. Frost, "Old South Lives Again in Fete and Pageantry," circa 1936. Clipping from NSUL.

148. Newell and Compton, 35.

149. Marshall and Evans, *They Found It in Natchez*, 220.

150. Nola Nance Oliver, *Natchez: Symbol of the Old South* (New York: Hastings House, 1940), 4. Her description of "Penny Day" included a photo of "Uncle Wash, a regular customer on Penny Day."

151. Such studies included Helen Merrell Lynd's *Middletown: A Study in Contemporary American Culture* (New York: Harcourt, Brace, 1929); John Dollard, *Caste and Class in a Southern Town* (New Haven: Yale University Press, 1937); and Hortense Powdermaker, *After Freedom: A Cultural Study in the Deep South* (New York: Viking, 1939).

152. For example, Burleigh Gardner was noted as the research team leader while in Natchez because many local whites would have questioned a white man working for a black. Additionally, the researchers could not live or socialize together and when conferring over their research findings often resorted to meeting clandestinely on isolated country roads. Davis, Gardner, and Gardner, xx.

153. Davis, Gardner, and Gardner.

154. Eleanor Roosevelt, "The Women Get the Credit," a "My Day" column, n.d., Katherine Miller scrapbook, HNF.

155. Interview with Ser Sesh Ab Heter-Clifford Boxley by author, April 4, 2009. Clifford Boxley changed his name to an African name in the 1990s.

156. Interview with Ralph Jennings by author, April 4, 2009.

157. Bushman, 19.

158. Robert McElvaine, *The Great Depression: America, 1929–1941* (New York: Times Books, 1984), 196–223.

159. Pyle, newspaper clipping, n.d. NGC Scrapbooks, NGCH.

160. Pyle.

161. Blight, 2–5, 173.

162. See Robin D. G. Kelley, *Hammer and Hoe: Alabama Communists During the Great Depression* (Chapel Hill: The University of North Carolina Press, 1990).

CHAPTER 6: THE BATTLE OF THE HOOPSKIRTS: THE LADIES GO TO COURT

1. The eight homes that remained loyal to the Natchez Garden Club were The Briars, Clover Nook, Elmscourt, Magnolia Vale, Melrose, Oakland, Ravenna, and Rosalie. Natchez Garden Club Minutes, August 26, 1935; June 8, 1936, Natchez Garden Club Papers, MDAH.

2. Minutes from joint negotiation session held by Natchez Garden Club and Pilgrimage Garden Club, November 16, 1937, MDAH.

3. Minutes, November 16, 1937, MDAH.

4. Minutes, November 16, 1937, MDAH. Annie Green Gwin Barnum was the granddaughter of planters who settled in the Mississippi territory around 1830. Her grandfather, Thomas K. Green, accumulated a sizeable amount of property, according to a biographical sketch, and the 1840 census recorded him as the owner of thirty-three slaves. Annie's father, T. K. Green, owned more than six thousand acres of land in Louisiana in the 1880s. Unlike some of the planter class, Annie Green's father was active in local politics and served as a Louisiana legislator and as sheriff of Concordia Parish, Louisiana. *Biographical and Historical Memoirs of Mississippi* (Chicago: Goodspeed, 1891; reprinted Spartanburg, SC: The Reprint Company, 1978), vol. 2, 813. Annie's second husband, Hubert F. Barnum, is remembered as a wealthy "yankee" who bought Arlington from the Boyd family when they fell on hard times. The home, which suffered a devastating fire in the 1990s, belong to a grandson of Annie Barnum. E-mail from Kathie Blankenstein to author March 11, 2003.

5. As news of the dispute between club members reached garden clubs outside of Natchez some sympathetic clubwomen wrote to express their viewpoints. Marian Price Scruggs, a member of a Virginia garden club, wrote suggesting that the Natchez Garden Club take on the mission of beautifying Natchez's gardens. "Your lack of beautifully kept grounds—all over the town, has been greatly commented on. Here is your chance to take the strength away from the importance now stressed on 'old houses and having your own place as restoring all the old plants, and walks and shrubs, used in those far away times." She added: "Mrs. Miller has had her glory—and publicity. You must take that into account— even if she has not always made friends or admirers. You can't but recognize facts." NGC Papers, MDAH.

6. Interview with Kathie Blankenstein by author December 27, 2001.

7. "To Continue Tours," *Natchez Democrat*, newspaper clipping, March 21, 1941, NGC Scrapbooks, NGCH.

8. "Fiddle-dee-dee—Natchez Ladies Fighting over Tourist Trade," *Atlanta Constitution*, March 26, 1941, newspaper clipping, NGC Scrapbooks, NGCH.

9. "More Fights Mean Better Pilgrimages for Natchez," Associated Press newspaper clipping, March 22, 1941, NGC Scrapbooks, NGCH.

10. "Natchez Club War Has Casualties," *Atlanta Journal*, newspaper clipping, March 29, 1941, NGC Scrapbooks, NGCH. Interview with Mary Louise Kendall Shields by author, December 28, 2001. Mrs. Shields died at the age of 109 in November 2015.

11. "Memories Sweeten Pilgrimage Past," *Jackson Clarion-Ledger*, newspaper clipping, n.d., NGC Scrapbooks, NGCH.

12. Interview with Kathie Blankenstein by author, December 27, 2001.

13. "Alternate Glares, Smiles," Associated Press newspaper clipping, March 23, 1941; "Fiddle-dee-dee.".

14. Writ of Injunction, Chancery Court, Adams County, Mississippi, March 25, 1941.

15. Supplemental Fiat, Case #8328, Box 242, Chancery Court, Adams County, Mississippi, March 26, 1941.

16. Writ of Injunction, Case #8328, Box 242, Chancery Court, Adams County, Mississippi, March 27, 1941.

17. "Natchez Club Defies Court, Extends Tour," *Jackson Daily News*, newspaper clipping, n.d., NGC Scrapbooks, NGCH.

18. "Natchez Club Defies Court."

19. "Civil War in Natchez," magazine clipping, n.d. Harriet Shields Dixon scrapbook, box 1, MDAH.

20. "Fiddle-dee-dee."

21. *Brewton (Alabama) Standard*, newspaper clipping, n.d., Katherine Miller scrapbook, HNF.

22. Quoted in Elizabeth Mullener, "Springtime in Natchez," *Dixie*, May 30, 1982.

23. "Injunction Is against Organized Tours of Pilgrimage Garden Club Says Judge," *Natchez Democrat*, newspaper clipping, March 29, 1941, NGC Scrapbooks, NGCH.

24. "'Hoop-Skirt War' Claims Heard in Natchez Court," *New Orleans Times-Picayune*, newspaper clipping, August 13, 1941, NGC Scrapbooks, NGCH.

25. Bill of Complaint, Case #8328, Box 242, Chancery Court, Adams County, Mississippi, March 24, 1941.

26. "Division of Tour Revenue Blamed in Natchez Dispute," Associated Press, newspaper clipping, n.d. NGC Scrapbooks, NGCH.

27. "Garden Club Suit Enters Second Day, Judge Asks Quiet," Associated Press, newspaper clipping, n.d., NGC Scrapbooks, NGCH.

28. "Garden Club Suit."

29. "Much Testimony Heard Yesterday before Cutrer," *Natchez Democrat*, newspaper clipping, n.d. Clipping given to author by Alma Carpenter, daughter of Alma Kellogg. www.dollartimes.com/calculators.

30. "Chancellor Gives Ruling in Case of Garden Clubs," *Natchez Democrat*, newspaper clipping, August 15, 1941, NGC Scrapbooks, NGCH.

31. "Petticoat Peace Quiets Quarreling Natchez," *American Weekly*, August 16, 1942.

32. "Petticoat Peace." Karen L. Cox, *Goat Castle: A True Story of Murder, Race, and the Gothic South* (Chapel Hill: University of North Carolina Press, 2017), 174.

33. Correspondence from George Malin Davis Kelly to Ethel Moore Kelly, October 8, 1935, Davis/Kelly Archival Collection, NNIIC, National Park Service, Natchez, MS. Kelly wrote numerous letters to his wife during this time describing the hostilities among club members. He staunchly supported his wife's club, the Natchez Garden Club. *Deep South*, the sociological study conducted in Natchez during the 1930s, also makes note of a segment of elite Natchez whites who frequently partied, drank heavily, and conducted extramarital affairs. Allison Davis, Burleigh B. Gardner, and Mary R. Gardner, *Deep South: A Social Anthropological Study of Caste and Class* (Chicago: University of Chicago Press, 1941), 139–41.

34. Natchez Garden Club Minutes, July 1, 1937, MDAH.

35. Mary I. Wood, *The History of the General Federation of Women's Clubs for the First Twenty-Two Years of Its Organization* (New York: History Dept., General Federation of Women's Clubs, 1912), 4. Kelly's letters to his wife indicated that he like other homeowners welcomed the extra income Pilgrimage tours generated. Kelly frequently noted in his letters his concerns about his family's tight finances, in one letter stating, "As long as we had money to throw away, I only mildly protested, but now it's different," March 30, 1935. Davis/Kelly Archival Collection.

36. Correspondence from George Malin Davis Kelly, the owner of Melrose, to Ethel Moore Kelly, October 6, 1935, Davis/Kelly Archival Collection. Kelly added that he believed Katherine Miller's husband Balfour was behind her demands "as it had all the earmarks. 'Rule or Ruin' is the motto of these grasping swindlers."

37. Letter from Katherine Miller to Joseph N. Carpenter, May 17, 1934, NGC Papers, MDAH. In addition to a request for an annual fee of eight hundred dollars, Miller asked that she be paid a monthly fee of fifty dollars to cover her expenses as Pilgrimage director, which included money for a "stenographer, stamps, buying new slides, having pictures taken, having my own folders made . . . and to take little extra trips for contact purposes." According to friend and fellow club member Mary Louise Kendall, Miller and her husband were struggling financially during the Depression and needed the money to fund the expenses, both for waging a tourism campaign and for repairing their dilapidated home, Hope Farm. Interview with author, December 28, 2001.

38. Natchez Garden Club Minutes, July 1, 1937, MDAH.

39. Natchez Garden Club Minutes, November 17, 1937, MDAH.

40. Interview with Alma Carpenter by author, April 9, 2001.

41. Interview with Mary Louise Kendall Goodrich by author, December 27, 2001.

42. Correspondence from George Malin Davis Kelly to Ethel Moore Kelly, April 6, 1935, Davis/Kelly Archival Collection.

43. Twain quoted in Robert Cooper, *Around the World with Mark Twain* (New York: Arcade), 247. Reprinted from a speech made to Newspaper Correspondents' Club, Washington, DC, January 11, 1868.

44. Quoted in Jack Davis, *Race against Time: Culture and Segregation in Natchez since 1930* (Baton Rouge: Louisiana State University Press, 2001), 59.

EPILOGUE: NATCHEZ TODAY: WHERE MORE THAN THE OLD SOUTH STILL LIVES

1. Natchez's Confederate monument was unveiled on April 25, 1890, by the town's Confederate Memorial Association (see chapter 3). One of the most provocative commentaries on the controversy surrounding the memory and meaning of Confederate statues was delivered in a speech by Mitch Landrieu, Mayor of New Orleans, on the occasion of removing New Orleans' four Confederate monuments from the city's public spaces (https://www.nytimes.com/2017/05/23/opinion/mitch-landrieu-speech-transcript.html). Landrieu explores this topic further in *In the Shadow of Statues: A White Southerner Confronts History* (New York: Viking, 2018). For a thoughtful essay on the Charlottesville incident see Lisa Richardson, "A Black Daughter of the Confederacy Corrects History," *Los Angeles Times*, August 27, 2017.

2. Excerpted from an essay written by Ronald Davis and delivered at the Historic Natchez Conference, Oct. 8, 2009. Paper in author's hands.

3. "Foundation Document Overview Natchez National Historical Park," National Park Service, U.S. Department of the Interior.

4. Ronald L. F. Davis, *The Black Experience in Natchez, 1720–1880* (Denver: Eastman, 1994).

5. Much of the recent research on Natchez reflects work done in the records preserved and carefully archived by the Natchez Courthouse Records project and stored at the Historic Natchez Foundation. In addition to California students, scholars from the University of Southern Mississippi, the archival department from the Center of American History at University of Texas at Austin, Louisiana State University, University of North Carolina at Chapel Hill, and the Mississippi Department of Archives and History have contributed to Natchez scholarship. Among the historians who have contributed noteworthy works about Natchez are Aaron Anderson, Jim Barnett, Justin Behrend, Darcy Bieber, Kathleen Jenkins Bond, Joyce Broussard, Janet Bruce, Emily Clark, Cita Cook, Karen Cox, Jack E. Davis, Ronald L. F. Davis, Arthur DeRosier, Rebecca Dresser, Jack Elliot, Patricia Galloway, Virginia Gould, Hershel Gower, Ariella Gross, Cai Hamilton, Winthrop Jordan, Anthony Kaye, Wendy Machlovitz, Robert May, Mary Warren Miller, Ronald Miller, Sheryl Nomelli, Cynthia Parker, Shane Peterson, Thom Rosenblum, William Scarborough, Cecie Shulman, Leslie Smithers, Randy Sparks, anthropologist Vincas Steponaitis, Connie Tripp, Kimberly Welch, and Rosanne Welch. Funding support for student interns who participated in the Courthouse Records project was awarded by the Department of the Interior in collaboration with the Natchez National Historical Park as well as California State University, Northridge. Additionally, the Historic Natchez Foundation and the Mississippi Department of Archives and History played an important role in training students, and a number of Natchez residents generously provided housing, meals, and hospitality to students in the program. Thanks to the recent financial support by Courthouse Records alum Daniel Shiells, the Historic Natchez Foundation has hired a professional archivist to manage and oversee the collection, a sorely needed addition to the foundation staff.

6. Shotgun houses are narrow, rectangular, domestic residences, usually no more than about twelve feet wide, with rooms arranged one behind the other and doors at each end of the house. Many newly freed slaves lived in these structures scattered throughout Natchez during and after the Civil War.

7. "Visitor's Center Changing Exhibits," *Natchez Democrat*, April 20, 2009. "Exhibit Tells Area's Slave Trade History," *Natchez Democrat*, March 29, 2018.

8. That concern becomes even more problematic when it comes to the tours delivered in privately owned antebellum homes, open to the public in the fall and spring as part of Natchez Pilgrimage Tours. Individual homeowners, while strongly encouraged to share accurate and a more inclusive historical narrative that addresses slavery, control the tour script for their homes. Fortunately, an increasing number of tour home owners have expressed interest in addressing slavery.

9. Bond and her colleagues also are tasked with determining how to find the resources within the community to make the kinds of offerings that twenty-first-century tourists demand and expect. Her community currently lacks that capacity, according to Bond. Most residents are not trained in tourism, nor do they have capital to start new businesses.

10. On April 23, 1940, as the famous Walter Barnes Orchestra from Chicago played in the dance hall, a fire broke out when decorative Spanish moss was accidentally ignited. Windows and entrances had been sealed off to keep nonpaying guests out. The museum,

which opened in 2010, offers accounts of survivors, eyewitness accounts, and newspaper clippings of the tragedy.

11. Hannah Mask, "St. Catherine Memories Bubble Up," *Natchez Democrat*, July 8, 2011.

12. Megan Fink Leoni, "St. Catherine Trails Project Ahead of Schedule," http://for-natchezorg/trails.html. Accessed March 30, 2016.

13. Email from Ronald Davis to author, October 15, 2017.

14. www.nps.gov/natc/historyculture/williamjohnson.htm. Accessed September 20, 2017. Also see William Ransom Hogan and Edwin Adams Davis, *William Johnson's Natchez: The Ante-bellum Diary of a Free Negro* (Port Washington, NY: Kennikat Press, 1968).

15. The "one drop rule" refers to a cultural definition unique to the United States that a single drop of "black blood" makes a person a black. This idea is also sometimes referred to as the "one black ancestor rule," reflecting the nation's long experience with slavery and later with Jim Crow segregation. "This American cultural definition of what makes a person black is taken for granted by judges, affirmative action officers, and black protesters as it is with the Ku Klux Klan." www.pbs.org/wgbh/pages/frontline/shows/jefferson/mixed/onedrop.html. Accessed September 28, 2017.

16. Email from Ronald Davis to author, October 15, 2017. In additional comments Davis questioned why Bond chooses to interpret Johnson's life as one of privilege. He speculates that Bond, among others, has perhaps fallen into the trap of wanting to somewhat whitewash the past because after living in Natchez for twenty-five years she may not be the outsider she once was.

17. The effort to establish Forks of the Road as a National Park Service site has been long and arduous. In June 2003 a grant issued by the State of Mississippi Department of Archives and History was used to purchase the land where the R. H. Elam slave market once stood that over time came to be better known as Forks of the Road. The state of Mississippi appropriated additional money to create interpretive signage for the site. In October 2011 a new traveling exhibit comprised of a dozen six-by-eight-foot panels depicting the history of the site was unveiled. Documentation is based on slave narratives and slaveholder diaries. One panel displays copies of bills of sale for the slaves purchased in Natchez. Another panel shows a distribution chart that traces buyers, sellers, the slaves sold, and their destinations. Retired director of the Mississippi Department of Archives and History's Historic Property Division Jim Barnett is also credited with doing important research on the history of Forks of the Road. See Barnett's article, "The Forks of the Road Slave Market at Natchez," coauthored with H. Clark Burkett at mshistorynow.mdah.state.ms.us/articles/47/the forks-of-the-road-slave-market-at-Natchez, February 2003. Accessed on Sept. 28, 2017.

18. Another sign of institutional change came in 2011 when the Natchez federal courthouse dedicated four new memorial plaques bearing the names of 592 black Natchez soldiers who had served in World War I. The names of these veterans were omitted when the original markers were mounted in 1924 during the height of Jim Crow. Thanks to the research of California graduate student Shane Peterson, these names have been recovered and publicly honored. Peterson, "Lost Cause to Lost Generation: World War I, and the African American Troops from Adams County, Mississippi" (Master's thesis, California State University, Northridge, 2008).

19. Natchez History Minutes can be found on YouTube at http://bit.ly/295p2qH. Mansell is currently working on creating a kiosk display for the Natchez Visitor's Center where visitors can view the video series. The project has received numerous honors, including the National Park Service Southeast Region's Achieving Relevance award among others. While some historians question whether the NNHP's History Minutes adequately do justice to the horrors of Natchez's slave past, the argument can be made that such a program was a valuable way to get the public interested in history, alert them to important topics in local history, including slavery, and encourage them to read scholarly books and articles to gain a deeper understanding.

20. For more on the murder case of Jennie Merrill in August 1932, see Karen L. Cox, *Goat Castle: A True Story of Murder, Race, and the Gothic South* (Chapel Hill: University of North Carolina Press, 2017.)

21. "Injunctions Issued against Picketing on City Streets," *Natchez Democrat*, October 1, 1965; "Arrest 19 Negroes for Blocking Street," *Natchez Democrat*, October 2, 1965; "271 Are Arrested Here for Blocking Sidewalk," *Natchez Democrat*, October 3, 1965; "115 Additional Negroes Arrested Here on Sunday for Parading," *Natchez Democrat*, October 4, 1965; "Arrest 107 in March Last Night," *Natchez Democrat*, October 5, 1965.

22. Ser Sesh Boxley, Jeremy Houston, and Cynthia Parker, an alum of the Natchez Courthouse Records project, are credited with procuring the jail records that led to the public exposure of the victims of the Parchman incident. Parker is currently working on a manuscript documenting the incident. Draft in author's hands. A week after the Parchman incident, approximately six hundred local blacks took to Natchez streets again under the leadership of Charles Evers. No one was arrested during this march.

23. "The Parchman Ordeal: The Untold Story." New Dawn Video Productions and Natchez Association for the Preservation of Afro-American History and Culture, 2016.

24. Work is underway in Natchez to create a monument remembering victims in the Parchman incident. Race and reconciliation gatherings continue to meet in Natchez and are sponsored by Mission Mississippi, a nondenominational Christian organization seeking to improve racial relations in Natchez and other Mississippi communities.

25. Quoted from "Natchez National Historical Park's Fort Rosalie Site Open," *Natchez Democrat*, August 4, 2016.

26. Interview with Chesney Blankenstein Doyle by author, August 21, 2017.

27. In one of the most inventive scenes of the new production, historical re-enactors played the gifted photographer's subjects while carrying oversized Norman portraits.

28. Doyle took pride in developing a script that was based on historical research and facts and gives credit to the work of Ann Paradise who combed through the wealth of articles, books, and papers produced by scholars over the years as well as the knowledge of local public history professionals. "Our goal was to tie every scene to factual history as best we can and try to highlight stories that tourists can actually experience in the community," Doyle noted. Phone interview with author February 7, 2017.

29. Doyle interview, February 7. 2017.

30. Ben Hillyer, "PGC Pulls out of Tableaux," *Natchez Democrat*, October 6, 2017.

31. Bill Rauch, "Can the South Make Room for Reconstruction?" *Atlantic Monthly*, September 17, 2016.

32. Interview with Elizabeth Boggess by author, November 14, 2011.

33. Elizabeth MacNeil Boggess, "Second Creek in 1861: People and Places," paper delivered at "No More Silence at Second Creek: Slave Resistance and the Onset of the Civil War" symposium sponsored by the National Park Service, September 24, 2011. Paper in author's hands.

34. Boggess interview, November 14, 2011.

35. Interview with Anne MacNeil by author, August 22, 2017. While an increasing number of tour homes are including information about slavery, individual homeowners who participate in the biannual Pilgrimage Home Tours control the narrative delivered to tourists. The NNHP provides historical information to homeowners, such as scripts on local Civil War history, but the quality and accuracy of the tour experience varies from home to home.

36. Interview with Anne MacNeil by author, August 17, 2017.

37. MacNeil interview, August 17 2017.

38. According to Cosey, the Concord mansion was well known in the Natchez community and by historians studying the Minor family, one of the wealthiest planter dynasties in the Natchez District. The slave quarters and kitchen survived the 1901 fire that destroyed the mansion, but were largely forgotten. For many years, the annual Natchez pageant included a tableaux that depicted picnics at Concord. Ironically, the old estate's slave quarter now tells the story of Manuel Gayosa and the golden age of Spanish-era Natchez, the white Minor family as well as the African Americans who called Concord home. Prior to buying the Concord Quarters Cosey worked in management for Monmouth and Dunlieth, two of Natchez's most prominent antebellum estates and bed and breakfast properties. Interview with Debbie Cosey by author, August 17, 2017.

39. Cosey interview, August 17, 2017.

40. Cosey interview, August 17, 2017.

41. https://mississippitoday.org/2017/09/14/mississippi-still-work-poverty-household-income-U.S./ https://www.kff.org/other/state-indicator/poverty-rate-by-race-ethnicity/. Accessed March 22, 2017.

42. Cosey interview, August 17, 2017.

43. For more on Montpelier's groundbreaking exhibit on James and Dolly Madison's connections to slavery, visit https://www.montpelier.org/resources/mere-distinction-of-colour. Accessed March 23, 2018. Also see Cynthia J. Parker, "Monmouth: The Survival of a Grand Mansion Estate in Natchez, Mississippi, from the Era of Slavery to the Present" (Master's thesis, California State University, Northridge, 2010) for an example of research done on Natchez house slaves. Parker's research is available to Monmouth guests in the form of a booklet and a plaque on the grounds acknowledges the estate's slave labor force.

44. Interview with Ser Sesh Ab Heter-Clifford Boxley by author, August 17, 2017. Special thanks to Ronald Davis for sharing his insights on this topic.

45. "Mitch Landrieu's Speech on the Removal of Confederate Monuments in New Orleans." *New York Times*, May 23, 2017.

BIBLIOGRAPHY

ABBREVIATIONS: *ARCHIVES AND PUBLIC RECORDS*

AMA	American Missionary Association Papers, Amistad Research Center, Tulane University, New Orleans
CCAH	Circuit Court Records for Adams County, Natchez, Mississippi
DU	Duke University, William R. Perkins Library, Durham, North Carolina
HNF	Historic Natchez Foundation, Natchez, Mississippi
JGWAL	Judge George W. Armstrong Library, Natchez, Mississippi
LOC	Library of Congress, Prints and Photographs Division, Washington, DC
LSU	Louisiana and Lower Mississippi Valley Collections, Louisiana State University, Baton Rouge
MDAH	Mississippi Department of Archives and History, Jackson, Mississippi
NARA	National Archives and Records Administration, Washington, DC
NGC	Natchez Garden Club
NSUL	Northwestern State University of Louisiana, Cammie G. Henry Research Center.
NNHP	Natchez National Historical Park, Natchez, Mississippi
PGC	Pilgrimage Garden Club
RG	Record Group
SCC	Records of the Southern Claims Commission, Records of the General Accounting Office, Department of the Treasury, Record Group 2017, NARA
UM	University of Mississippi, Special Collections, Oxford, Mississippi
UNC-CH	Southern Historical Collection, University of North Carolina, Chapel Hill
WPA	Works Progress Administration

MANUSCRIPT MATERIALS

Adams County Office of Records, Natchez, Mississippi

Chancery Court Records.
Circuit Court Records.
Deeds, Liens, and Mortgage Records.

Inventories of Estates.
Probate Records.
Records of Wills.

Amistad Research Center, Tulane University, New Orleans

American Missionary Association Records.

Duke University, Perkins Library, Durham, North Carolina

Foster, Kate D., Diary, Foster Family Papers.

Historic Natchez Foundation, Natchez, Mississippi

Chancery Court Records.
Circuit Court Case Records.
Miller, Katherine Grafton, Scrapbook.
Natchez Confederate Memorial Association Minutes and Ledger.
Natchez Trails Exhibit.
Probate Records.

Louisiana State University, Louisiana and Lower Mississippi Valley Collections, Baton Rouge

Britton Family Papers.
Conner, Lemuel P., Family Papers.
Gandy, Thomas H. and Joan W., Photograph Collection.
McMurran-Austin Family Papers
Minor, William J., Family Papers.
Quitman, John Anthony, Papers.
Shields, Joseph D., Papers.
Stratton, Joseph B. Papers.

Mississippi Department of Archives and History, Jackson, Mississippi

The Elms Papers
Jefferson College Military Papers.
Minor Family Papers.
Natchez Garden Club Papers, 1931–1945.
Pilgrimage Historical Association Collection: Nutt Family Papers.
Shields, Ellen, Genealogical Memoir (typescript).
Subject Files.
Surget Family Papers.
Surget-McKitrick-McNeil Family Papers.
United Daughters of the Confederacy Membership Papers.

WPA Records, Adams County.
Stewart Photograph Collection

Natchez Garden Club Headquarters, Natchez, Mississippi

NGC Club Scrapbooks, 1930–1950.

Natchez National Historical Park, Natchez, Mississippi

Davis/Kelly Archival Collection, Natchez National Historical Park, National Park Service, Natchez, Mississippi.

National Archives and Records Administration, Washington, DC and College Park, Maryland

Records of the Bureau of Refugees, Freedmen, and Abandoned Lands, RG 105.
Records of the US Court of Claims, RG 123.

US Census

Adams County, Mississippi. Manuscript Agricultural, Manufacturing, Population, and Slave Schedules, 1850, 1860, 1870, 1880, 1900, 1920, 1930.

University of Louisiana at Monroe, Special Collections

Conner Family Papers.

University of Mississippi, Department of Archives and Special Collections, J. D. Williams Library, Oxford

Byrnes, Roane Fleming, Collection.
"Rolls of the Several Military Organizations Which Entered the Service of the Confederate States of America, from the City of Natchez and Adams County, Mississippi, Compiled from the Archives of their Successors The Adams Light Infantry," 1890.

University of North Carolina at Chapel Hill, Southern Historical Collection

Ker, Mary Susan, Papers, 1785–1958.
Quitman Family Papers, 1784–1940.

NEWSPAPERS

Christian Recorder.
Natchez Courier.
Natchez Daily Courier.

Natchez Democrat.
Natchez Tri-Weekly Democrat.
Natchez Weekly Democrat.
New Orleans Republican.
New Orleans Times-Picayune.
New National Era.

PUBLISHED SOURCES, FEDERAL GOVERNMENT

The National Memorial Day: A Record of Ceremonies Over the Graves of the Union Soldiers May 29 & 30, 1869 (Washington, Headquarters, Grand Army of the Republic, 1870).
Testimony as to Denial of Elective Franchise in Mississippi at the Elections of 1875 and 1876, 44th Congress, 2nd session. Senate Misc. Document 45.
United States American Freedman's Inquiry Commission Report, 1863.

INTERVIEWS

Adams, William A. Interview by Graham Hicks, August 4, 1981, Natchez, NGC Headquarters.
Beltzhhoover, Ruth Audley Britton Wheeler. Interview by Graham Hicks, August 4, 1981, Natchez, NGC Headquarters.
Benoist, Rebecca Fauntleroy. Interview by Graham Hicks, August 26, 1981, Natchez, NGC Headquarters.
Blankenstein, Kathie. Interview by author, December 2001, Natchez; August 17, 2018, Natchez.
Boggess, Elizabeth MacNeil. Phone interview by author, November 14, 2011; August 17, 2018, Natchez.
Boxley, Ser Sesh Ab Heter-Clifford. Interview by author, April 4, 2009; August 18, 2018, Natchez.
Carpenter, Alma. Interview by author, April 9, 2001, Natchez.
Colson, Marsha. Interview by author, April 9, 2009, Natchez.
Dixon, Harriet and Joseph F. Interview by Graham Hicks, n.d., Natchez, NGC Headquarters.
Ferry, Marion Kelly. Interview by Graham Hicks, November 17, 1981, Natchez, NGC Headquarters.
Gandy, Dr. Thomas. Interview by author, April 9, 2001, Natchez.
Gardner, Agnes Marshall. Interview by Elliott Trimble, n.d., Natchez, NGC Headquarters.
Geddes, Mary. Interview by Graham Hicks, August 4, 1981, Natchez, NGC Headquarters.
Goodrich, Mary Louise Kendall. Interview by author, December 28, 2001, Natchez.
Jennings, Ralph. Interview by author, April 4, 2009.
Kellogg, Alma. Interview by Elliott Trimble, August 15, 1981. Natchez, NGC Headquarters.
MacIlroy, Margaret Percell Marshall. Interview by Elliott Trimble, n.d., Natchez, NGC Headquarters.
MacNeil, Grace. Interview by Graham Hicks, n.d., Natchez, NGC Headquarters.

CONTEMPORARY ACCOUNTS AND PUBLISHED DOCUMENTS

Adams, Revels A. *Cyclopedia of African Methodism in Mississippi.* Natchez, MS: 1902.
Biographical and Historical Memoirs of Mississippi. Chicago: Goodspeed, 1891; reprinted Spartanburg, SC: The Reprint Company, 1978.
Bisland, Margaret. "Women and Their Cameras." *Outing, an Illustrated Magazine of Recreation,* October 1890.
Bond, Horace Mann. "A Negro Looks at His South." *Harper's* (June 1931), 98–108.
Britton, Mary M. *A Southern Character Sketch.* Natchez: M. M. Black's Job Print, 1882.
Butler, Pierce, and Carol Howard Pforzheimer. *The Unhurried Years: Memories of the Old Natchez Region.* Baton Rouge: Louisiana State University Press, 1948.
"Bylaws and Rules of Order of Washington Lodge, No. 2: Revised and Adopted, 1866." Natchez, MS: *Natchez Democrat,* 1867.
Carmichael, Peter. "Mississippi Reconsidered: It Is Ante-Bellum Rather Than Neanderthal." *Baltimore Sun,* June 11, 1938.
Cohn, David. "Natchez Was a Lady." *Atlantic Monthly* (January 1940).
Croly, Mrs. J. C. *The History of the Woman's Club Movement in America.* New York: H. G. Allen, 1898.
Davis, Allison, Burleigh B. Gardner, and Mary R. Gardner. *Deep South: A Social Anthropological Study of Caste and Class.* Chicago: University of Chicago Press, 1941.
Deen, Jeannie Marie, editor. *Annie Harper's Journal: A Southern Mother's Legacy.* Hattiesburg, MS: University of Southern Mississippi, 1983.
Directory of the City of Natchez. Natchez, MS: Banner, 1892.
Douglass, Frederick. *My Bondage and My Freedom.* New York: Miller, Orton, and Mulligan, 1855.
Du Bois, W. E. B. *The Souls of Black Folk.* Chicago: A. C. McClurg, 1903. Reprint. Radford, VA: Wilder Publications, 2008.
Eickemeyer, Rudolf. *Down South.* New York: R. H. Russell, 1900.
"General Federation of Women's Clubs." *Ladies Home Journal.* November 1940, 4.
Grady, Henry W. "The New South," *New England Magazine.* March 1890.
Gresham, Martha. *Life of Walter Quintin Gresham, 1832–1895.* Vol. 1. Chicago: Rand McNally, 1919.
Guyton, Pearl Vivian. *The Story of Rosalie, Natchez, Mississippi: Historic Shrine, Mississippi Society of the National Society of the American Revolution.* Jackson, MS: Hederman Bros., 1941.
Guyton, Pearl Vivian. *The Story of Connelly's Tavern on Ellicott Hill: A National Shrine Owned by the Natchez Garden Club, Natchez, Mississippi.* Jackson, MS: Hederman Bros., 1942.
Halbert, Blanche. *The Better Homes Manual.* Chicago: University of Chicago Press, in cooperation with Better Homes in America, 1931.
Hammer, Bette Barber. *Natchez' First Ladies: Katherine Grafton Miller and the Pilgrimage.* New York: Kintner, 1955.
Harwood, W. S. "Amateur Photography of To-Day." *Cosmopolitan Magazine,* January 1896.

"How Federation Members Earn." *Independent Woman*, June 1940.

Johnston, Frances Benjamin. "What a Woman Can Do with a Camera." *Ladies Home Journal*, September 1897.

Kane, Harnett Thomas. *Natchez on the Mississippi*. New York: W. Morrow, 1947.

Lynch, John Roy. *Reminiscences of an Active Life: The Autobiography of John Roy Lynch*. Edited by John Hope Franklin. Chicago: University of Chicago Press, 1970.

Lynch, John Roy. *The Facts of Reconstruction*. New York: Arno Press and New York Times, 1968. Original edition, New York: Neale, 1913.

Marshall, Theodora Britton, and Gladys Crail Evans. *They Found It in Natchez*. New Orleans: Pelican, 1939.

Merrill, D. P. "Women on the March [growth of women's organizations in the past three quarters of a century]. *Independent Woman* (October 1940): 330–32.

Miller, Katherine Grafton. *Natchez of Long Ago and the Pilgrimage*. Natchez, MS: Relimak, 1938.

Mississippi: A Guide to the Magnolia State. Federal Writer's Project American Guide Series, New York: Viking Press, 1938.

Moore, Edith Wyatt. *Natchez Under-the-Hill*. Natchez, MS: Southern Historical Publications, 1958.

Murray, Elizabeth Dunbar. *My Mother Used to Say: A Natchez Belle of the Sixties*. Boston: Christopher Publishing House, 1959.

Murray, Elizabeth Dunbar. *Early Romances of Historic Natchez*. Natchez, MS: Natchez Print and Stationery, 1938.

Natchez, Mississippi on Top, Not "Under the Hill." Natchez, MS: Daily Democrat Steam Press, 1892.

Newell, Georgie Willson, and Charles Cromartie Compton. *Natchez and the Pilgrimage*. Natchez, MS: Southern Publishers, Inc., 1935.

Nicholas, William H. "History Repeats in Old Natchez." *National Geographic*, February 1949.

Odum, Howard W., and Guy B. Johnson. *The Negro and His Songs: A Study of Typical Negro Songs in the South*. New York: Negro Universities Press, 1968. Original edition, 1925.

Oliver, Nola Nance. *Natchez: Symbol of the Old South*. New York: Hastings House, 1940.

Peterson, Elmer T. "The Old South Lives Again!" *Better Homes and Gardens* (February 1938).

Power, John Logan. *Blue Lodge Text-book: Adapted to the Work, Lectures and Ceremonies of Ancient Craft Masonry in the Jurisdiction of the Grand Lodge of Mississippi*. 1899.

Proceedings of the Grand Commandery of the Knights Templar of the State of Mississippi. Jackson, MS: Clarion Steam Printing Establishment, 1877, 1884, 1887.

Rafferty, Dave. *The City of Natchez*. Natchez, MS: Privately printed, 1881.

Reber, Thomas. *"Proud Old Natchez": History and Romance*. Natchez, MS: Natchez Print and Stationery, 1909.

Richings, G. F. *Evidences of Progress among Colored People*. Philadelphia: Geo. S. Ferguson, 1903.

Riley, Franklin L., ed. *Publications of the Mississippi Historical Society*. Vol. 8. Oxford, MS: Mississippi Historical Society, 1904.

Roosevelt, Theodore. *The Strenuous Life: Essays and Addresses.* New York: Century, 1918.

Rowland, Dunbar, ed. *Encyclopedia of Mississippi History: Comprising Sketches of Counties, Towns, Events, Institutions and Persons.* Vols. 1 and 2. Madison, WI: Selwyn A. Brand, 1907.

Scouller, Mildred Marshall. *Women Who Man Our Clubs.* Philadelphia: John C. Winston, 1934.

Shields, Joseph D., and Elizabeth Dunbar Murray. *Natchez: Its Early History.* Louisville, KY: J. P. Morton, 1930.

The Song Book of the School Room. New York: Mason Brothers, 1857.

Stanton, Elizabeth Brandon. *Sidelights on the Picturesque and Romantic History of Ye Old Natchez Trace of the Mysterious Natchez.* Natchez, MS: 1934.

Twain, Mark. *Life on the Mississippi.* New York: Harper and Brothers, 1901.

Van Court, Catharine. *In Old Natchez.* Garden City, NY: Doubleday, 1937.

Van Valkenberg, John. *The Knights of Pythias Complete Manual and Textbook.* Canton, Ohio: Memento Publishing Company, 1885.

Wood, Mary I. *The History of the General Federation of Women's Clubs for the First Twenty-Two Years of Its Organization.* New York: History Dept., General Federation of Women's Clubs, 1912.

Yenser, Thomas, ed. *Who's Who in Colored America, 1933–1937.* Alexandria, VA: Chadwyck-Healey, 1987. Original edition, Brooklyn, NY: T. Yenser, 1937.

Young, Stark. *So Red the Rose.* New York: C. Scribner's Sons, 1934.

BOOKS

Aaron, Cindy Sondik. *Working at Play: A History of Vacations in the United States.* New York: Oxford University Press, 1999.

Anderson, Aaron D. *Builders of a New South: Merchants, Capital, and the Remaking of Natchez, 1865–1914.* Jackson: University Press of Mississippi, 2013.

Anderson, James D. *The Education of Blacks in the South, 1860–1935.* Chapel Hill: University of North Carolina Press, 1988.

Ausherman, Maria Elizabeth. *The Photographic Legacy of Frances Benjamin Johnston.* Gainesville: University Press of Florida, 2009.

Axelrod, Alan, ed. *The Colonial Revival in America.* New York: Norton, 1985.

Barnett, James F., Jr. *The Natchez Indians: A History to 1735.* Jackson: University Press of Mississippi, 2007.

Bayor, Ronald H. *Race and the Shaping of Twentieth-Century Atlanta.* Chapel Hill: University of North Carolina Press, 1996.

Bechet, Sidney. *Treat It Gentle.* New York: Hill and Wang, 1960.

Bederman, Gail. *Manliness and Civilization: A Cultural History of Gender and Race in the United States, 1880–1917.* Chicago: University of Chicago Press, 1995.

Behrend, Justin. *Reconstructing Democracy: Grassroots Black Politics in the Deep South after the Civil War.* Athens: University of Georgia Press, 2017.

Belasco, Warren James. *Americans on the Road.* Cambridge, MA: MIT Press, 1979.

Bercaw, Nancy. *Gendered Freedoms: Race, Rights, and the Politics of Household in the Delta, 1861–1875.* Gainesville: University Press of Florida, 2003.

Berch, Bettina. *The Woman behind the Lens: The Life and Work of Frances Benjamin Johnston, 1864–1952*. Charlottesville: University Press of Virginia, 2000.

Bethel, Elizabeth Rauh. *The Roots of African American Identity: Memory and History in Free Antebellum Communities*. New York: St. Martin's Press, 1997.

Bettersworth, John K. *Confederate Mississippi: The People and Policies of a Confederate State in Wartime*. Baton Rouge: Louisiana State University Press, 1943.

Black, Earl, and Merle Black, *Politics and Society in the South*. Cambridge, MA: Harvard University Press, 1987.

Blair, Karen. *The Clubwoman as Feminist: True Womanhood Redefined, 1868–1914*. New York: Holmes and Meier, 1980.

Blair, Karen. *The History of American Women's Voluntary Organizations, 1810–1960, A Guide to Sources*. Boston: G. K. Hall, 1989.

Blair, William A. *Cities of the Dead: Contesting the Memory of the Civil War in the South, 1865–1914*. Chapel Hill: University of North Carolina Press, 2004.

Bland, Sidney R. *Preserving Charleston's Past, Shaping Its Future: The Life and Times of Susan Pringle Frost*. Columbia: University of South Carolina Press, 1999.

Blight, David. *Race and Reunion: The Civil War in American Memory*. Cambridge, MA: Belknap Press of Harvard University Press, 2001.

Bodnar, John. *Remaking America: Public Memory, Commemoration, and Patriotism in the Twentieth Century*. Princeton, NJ: Princeton University Press, 1992.

Bold, Christine. *The WPA Guides: Mapping America*. Jackson: University Press of Mississippi, 1999.

Boskin, Joseph. *Sambo: The Rise and Demise of an American Jester*. New York: Oxford University Press, 1989.

Brear, Holly Beachley. *Inherit the Alamo: Myth and Ritual at an American Shrine*. Austin: University of Texas Press, 1995.

Broussard, Joyce. *Stepping Lively in Place: The Not-Married, Free Women of Civil-War-Era Natchez, Mississippi*. Athens: University of Georgia Press, 2016.

Brundage, W. Fitzhugh. *The Southern Past: A Clash of Race and Memory*. Cambridge, MA: Belknap Press of Harvard University Press, 2005.

Bushman, Richard L. *The Refinement of America: Persons, Houses, Cities*. New York: Alfred A. Knopf, 1992.

Butler, Pierce. *The Unhurried Years: Memories of the Old Natchez Region*. Baton Rouge: Louisiana State University Press, 1948.

Campbell, Edward D. C., Jr. *The Celluloid South: Hollywood and the Southern Myth*. Knoxville: University of Tennessee Press, 1981.

Carnes, Mark C. *Secret Ritual and Manhood in Victorian America*. New Haven, CT: Yale University Press, 1989.

Cash, Floris Barnett. *African American Women and Social Action: The Clubwomen and Volunteerism from Jim Crow to the New Deal, 1896–1936*. Westport, CT: Greenwood Press, 2001.

Cash, Wilbur J. *The Mind of the South*. New York: Alfred A. Knopf, 1941.

Censer, Jane Turner. *The Reconstruction of White Southern Womanhood, 1865–1895*. Baton Rouge: Louisiana State University, 2003.
Cheek, William, and Aimee Lee Cheek, *John Mercer Langston and the Fight for Black Freedom, 1829–65*. Urbana: University of Illinois Press, 1989.
Clark, Emily. *The New Orleans Ursulines and the Development of a New World Society, 1727–1834*. Chapel Hill: University of North Carolina Press, 2007.
Clark, Kathleen. *Defining Moments: African American Commemoration and Political Culture in the South, 1863–1913*. Chapel Hill: University of North Carolina Press, 2005.
Clayton, Virginia Tuttle, ed. *The Once and Future Gardener: Garden Writing from the Golden Age of Magazines, 1900–1940*. Boston: David R. Godine, 1999.
Clinton, Catherine. *Battle Scars: Gender and Sexuality in the Civil War*. New York: Oxford University Press, 2006.
Clinton, Catherine. *The Plantation Mistress: Woman's World in the Old South*. New York: Pantheon Press, 1983.
Clinton, Catherine. *Tara Revisited: Women, War, and the Plantation Legend*. New York: Abbeville Press, 1995.
Cobb, James C. *Away Down South: A History of Southern Identity*. New York: Oxford University Press, 2005.
Cobb, James C., ed. *The Mississippi Delta and the World: The Memoirs of David L. Cohn*. Baton Rouge: Louisiana State University Press, 1995.
Coleman, Gregory D. *We're Heaven Bound: A Portrait of a Black Sacred Drama*. Athens: University of Georgia Press, 1994.
Collum, Danny Duncan. *Black and Catholic in the Jim Crow South: The Stuff That Makes Community*. New York: Paulist Press, 2006.
Connerton, Paul. *How Societies Remember*. New York: Cambridge University Press, 1989.
Coryell, Janet L., Thomas H. Appleton Jr., Anastatia Sims, and Sandra Gioia Treadway, eds. *Negotiating Boundaries of Southern Womanhood: Dealing with the Powers That Be*. Columbia: University of Missouri Press, 2000.
Cox, Karen L. *Dixie's Daughters: The United Daughters of the Confederacy and the Preservation of Confederate Culture*. Gainesville: University Press of Florida, 2003.
Cox, Karen L. *Dreaming of Dixie: How the South Was Created in American Popular Culture*. Chapel Hill: University of North Carolina Press, 2013.
Cox, Karen L. *Goat Castle: A True Story of Murder, Race, and the Gothic South*. Chapel Hill: University of North Carolina Press, 2017.
Cullen, Jim. *The Civil War in Popular Culture: A Reusable Past*. Washington, DC: Smithsonian Press, 1995.
Culpepper, Marilyn Mayer. *All Things Altered: Women in the Wake of Civil War and Reconstruction*. Jefferson, NC: McFarland, 2002.
Davis, Jack. *Race against Time: Culture and Segregation in Natchez since 1930*. Baton Rouge: Louisiana State University Press, 2001.
Davis, Ronald L. F. *The Black Experience in Natchez, 1720–1880*. Denver: Eastman, 1994.
Davis, Ronald L. F. *Good and Faithful Labor: From Slavery to Sharecropping in the Natchez District, 1860–1890*. Westport, CT: Greenwood Press, 1982.

DeRosier, Arthur H., Jr. *William Dunbar: Scientific Pioneer of the Old Southwest.* Lexington: University Press of Kentucky, 2014.

Des Jardins, Julie. *Women and the Historical Enterprise in America: Gender, Race, and the Politics of Memory, 1880–1945.* Chapel Hill: University of North Carolina Press, 2003.

Douglas, Ellen. *Truth: Four Stories I Am Finally Old Enough to Tell.* Chapel Hill: Algonquin Books, 1998.

Doyle, Dan. *New Men, New Cities, New South: Atlanta, Nashville, Charleston, Mobile, 1860–1910.* Chapel Hill: University of North Carolina Press, 1990.

Dumenil, Lynn. *Freemasonry and American Culture, 1880–1930.* Princeton, NJ: Princeton University Press, 1984.

Eaton, Clement. *The Mind of the Old South.* Baton Rouge: Louisiana State University Press, 1967.

Edwards, Laura F. *Gendered Strife and Confusion: The Political Culture of Reconstruction.* Urbana: University of Illinois Press, 1997.

Edwards, Laura F. *Scarlett Doesn't Live Here Anymore: Southern Women in the Civil War Era.* Urbana: University of Illinois Press, 2000.

Eichstedt, Jennifer L., and Stephen Small. *Representations of Slavery: Race and Ideology in Southern Plantation Museums.* Washington, DC: Smithsonian Institution Press, 2002.

Emerson, Ken. *Doo Dah! Stephen Foster and the Rise of American Popular Culture.* New York: Simon and Schuster, 1998.

Fahs, Alice, and Joan Waugh, eds. *The Memory of the Civil War in American Culture.* Chapel Hill: University of North Carolina Press, 2004.

Faust, Drew Gilpin. *Mothers of Invention: Women of the Slaveholding South in the American Civil War.* Chapel Hill: University of North Carolina Press, 1996.

Faust, Drew Gilpin. *This Republic of Suffering: Death and the American Civil War.* New York: Alfred A. Knopf, 2008.

Faust, Drew Gilpin. *Southern Stories: Slaveholders in Peace and War.* Columbia: University of Missouri Press, 1992.

Fisher, Miles Mark. *Negro Slave Songs in the United States.* New York: Russell and Russell, 1953.

Fitzgerald, Michael. W. *The Union League Movement in the Deep South: Politics and Agricultural Change during Reconstruction.* Baton Rouge: Louisiana State University Press, 1989.

Fleming, Walter L. *The Freedmen's Savings Bank: A Chapter in the Economic History of the Negro Race.* Chapel Hill: University of North Carolina Press, 1927.

Flores, Richard R. *Remembering the Alamo: Memory, Modernity, and the Master Symbol.* Austin: University of Texas Press, 2002.

Foner, Eric. *Reconstruction: America's Unfinished Revolution.* New York: Perennial Classics, 2002.

Foster, Gaines M. *Ghosts of the Confederacy: Defeat, the Lost Cause, and the Emergence of the New South, 1865 to 1913.* New York: Oxford University Press, 1987.

Fox-Genovese, Elizabeth. *Within the Plantation Household: Black and White Women of the Old South.* Chapel Hill: University of North Carolina Press, 1988.

Fox-Genovese, Elizabeth, and Eugene Genovese. *The Mind of the Master Class: History and Faith in the Southern Slaveholder's Worldview.* Cambridge: Cambridge University Press, 2005.

Frank, Dan. *Buy American: The Untold Story of Economic Nationalism.* Boston: Beacon Press, 1999.

Frankel, Noralee. *Freedom's Women: Black Women and Families in Civil War-Era Mississippi.* Bloomington: University of Indiana Press, 1999.

Franklin, John Hope. *The Militant South, 1800-1861.* Cambridge, MA: Harvard University Press, 1956.

Frankenburg, Ruth. *White Women, Race Matters: The Social Construction of Whiteness.* London: Routledge, 1993.

Friend, Craig Thompson, and Lorri Glover, eds. *Southern Manhood: Perspectives on Masculinity in the Old South.* Athens: University of Georgia Press, 2004.

Gable, Eric, Richard Handler, and Anna Lawson. *The New History in an Old Museum.* Durham, NC: Duke University Press, 1997.

Gandy, Joan W. and Thomas H. Gandy. *Natchez: City Streets Revisited.* Charleston: Arcadia, 1999.

Gandy, Joan W., and Thomas H. Gandy. *Natchez: Landmarks, Lifestyles, and Leisure.* Charleston: Arcadia, 1999.

Gandy, Joan W., and Thomas H. Gandy. *Victorian Children of Natchez.* Charleston, SC: Arcadia, 1998. First published as *Natchez Victorian Children: Photographic Portraits, 1865-1915.* Natchez, MS: Myrtle Bank Press, 1981.

Gandy, Joan W. and Thomas H. Gandy. *Norman's Natchez: An Early Photographer and His Town.* Jackson: University Press of Mississippi, 1978.

Gaston, Paul M. *The New South Creed: A Study in Southern Mythmaking.* New York: Alfred A. Knopf, 1970.

Gatewood, Willard. *Aristocrats of Color: The Black Elite, 1880-1920.* Bloomington: Indiana University Press, 1990.

Geary, Christraud M., and Virginia-Lee Webb, eds. *Delivering Views: Distant Cultures in Early Postcards.* Washington, DC: Smithsonian Institution Press, 1998.

Gere, Anne Ruggles. *Intimate Practices: Literacy and Cultural Work in U.S. Women's Clubs, 1880-1920.* Urbana: University of Illinois Press, 1997.

Gillis, John R., ed. *Commemorations: The Politics of National Identity.* Princeton, NJ: Princeton University Press, 1994.

Gilmore, Glenda. *Gender and Jim Crow: Women and the Politics of White Supremacy in North Carolina, 1896-1920.* Chapel Hill: University of North Carolina Press, 1996.

Glassberg, David. *American Historical Pageantry: The Uses of Tradition in the Early Twentieth Century.* Chapel Hill: University of North Carolina Pres, 1990.

Glassberg, David. *Sense of History: The Place of the Past in American Life.* Amherst: University of Massachusetts Press, 2001.

Goings, Kenneth W. *Mammy and Uncle Mose: Black Collectibles and American Stereotyping.* Bloomington: University of Indiana Press, 1994.

Gould, Virginia Meacham. *Chained to the Rock of Adversity: To Be Free, Black, and Female in the Old South.* Athens: University of Georgia Press, 1998.

Gower, Herschel. *Charles Dahlgren of Natchez: The Civil War and Dynastic Decline*. Washington, DC: Brassey's, 2002.

Gross, Ariela Julie. *Double Character: Slavery and Mastery in the Antebellum Southern Courtroom*. Princeton, NJ: Princeton University Press, 2000.

Grover, Kathryn, ed. *Hard at Play: Leisure in America, 1840–1940*. Amherst: University of Massachusetts, 1992.

Grover, Kathryn. *Make a Way Somehow: African American Life in a Northern Community, 1790–1965*. Syracuse, NY: Syracuse University Press, 1994.

Gutman, Herbert G. *The Black Family in Slavery and Freedom, 1750–1925*. New York: Pantheon Books, 1976.

Halbwachs, Maurice. *The Collective Memory*. Translated by Francis J. Ditter Jr. and Vida Yazdi Ditter. New York: Harper and Row: 1980.

Hale, Grace Elizabeth. *Making Whiteness: The Culture of Segregation in the South*. New York: Pantheon Books, 1998.

Halleran, Michael A. *The Better Angels of Our Nature: Freemasonry in the Civil War*. Tuscaloosa: University of Alabama Press, 2010.

Haltom, Susan, and Jane Roy Brown. *One Writer's Garden: Eudora Welty's Home Place*. Jackson: University Press of Mississippi, 2011.

Harris, William C. *Presidential Reconstruction in Mississippi*. Baton Rouge: Louisiana State University Press, 1967.

Higginbotham, Evelyn Brooks. *Righteous Discontent: The Women's Movement in the Black Baptist Church, 1880–1920*. Cambridge, MA: Harvard University Press, 1993.

Hine, Darlene Clark, and Kathleen Thompson. *A Shining Thread of Hope: The History of Black Women in America*. New York: Broadway Books, 1998.

Hobson, Archie. *Remembering America: A Sampler of the WPA American Guide Series*. New York: Columbia University Press, 1985.

Hogan, William Ransom, and Edwin Adams Davis. *William Johnson's Natchez: The Antebellum Diary of a Free Negro*. Port Washington, NY: Kennikat Press, 1968.

Holzer, Harold, Edna Greene Medford, and Frank J. Williams. *The Emancipation Proclamation: Three Views*. Baton Rouge: Louisiana State University Press, 2006.

Horwitz, Tony. *Confederates in the Attic: Dispatches from the Unfinished Civil War*. New York: Pantheon Books, 1998.

Howard, Hugh. *Natchez: The Houses and History of the Jewel of the Mississippi*. New York: Rizzoli, 2003.

Howell, Benita J. *Cultural Heritage Conservation in the American South*. Athens: University of Georgia Press, 1990.

Hutchisson, James M., and Harlan Green, eds. *Renaissance in Charleston: Art and Life in the Carolina Low Country, 1900–1940*. Athens: University of Georgia Press, 2003.

Hunter, Tera W. *To 'Joy my Freedom': Southern Black Women's Lives and Labors after the Civil War*. Cambridge, MA: Harvard University Press, 1997.

Jakle, John A. *The Tourist: Travel in Twentieth-Century North America*. Lincoln: University of Nebraska Press, 1985.

James, Clayton D. *Antebellum Natchez*. Baton Rouge: Louisiana State University Press, 1968.

Janiewski, Dolores E. *Sisterhood Denied: Race, Gender, and Class in a New South Community*. Philadelphia: Temple University Press, 1985.
Janney, Caroline E. *Burying the Dead but Not the Past: Ladies' Memorial Associations and the Lost Cause*, Chapel Hill: University of North Carolina Press, 2008.
Johnson, Joan Marie. *Southern Ladies, New Women: Race, Region, and Clubwomen in South Carolina; 1890–1930*. Gainesville: University Press of Florida, 2004.
Jones, Jacqueline. *Labor of Love, Labor of Sorrow: Black Women, Work, and the Family from Slavery to the Present*. New York: Basic Books, 1985.
Jones, Jacqueline. *Soldiers of Light and Love: Northern Teachers and Georgia Blacks, 1865–1873*. Athens: University of Georgia Press, 1992.
Jordan, Winthrop. *Tumult and Silence at Second Creek: An Inquiry into a Civil War Slave Conspiracy*. Baton Rouge: Louisiana State University Press, 1993.
Kachun, Mitchell A. *Festivals of Freedom: Memory and Meaning in African American Emancipation Celebrations, 1808–1915*. Amherst: University of Massachusetts Press, 2003.
Kammen, Michael. *Mystic Chords of Memory: The Transformation of Tradition in American Culture*. New York: Alfred A. Knopf, 1991.
Kaye, Anthony E. *Joining Places: Slave Neighborhoods in the Old South*. Chapel Hill: University of North Carolina Press, 2007.
Kelley, Robin D. G. Kelley. *Hammer and Hoe: Alabama Communists during the Great Depression*. Chapel Hill: University of North Carolina Press, 1990.
Kessler-Harris, Alice. *Out to Work: A History of Wage-Earning Women in the United States*. New York: Oxford University Press, 1982.
Kimmel, Michael S. *Manhood in America: A Cultural History*. New York: Oxford University Press, 2006.
Kirby, Jack Temple. *Media-Made Dixie: The South in the American Imagination*. Baton Rouge: Louisiana State University Press, 1998.
Kirshenblatt-Gimblett, Barbara. *Destination Culture: Tourism, Museums, and Heritage*. Berkeley: University of California Press, 1998.
Klamkin, Marian. *Picture Postcards*. New York: Dodd, Mead, 1974.
Klingberg, Frank. *The Southern Claims Commission*. Berkeley: University of California Press, 1955.
Knupfer, Anne Meis. *Toward a Tenderer Humanity and a Nobler Womanhood: African American Women's Clubs in Turn-of-the-Century Chicago*. New York: New York University Press, 1996.
Landrieu, Mitch. *In the Shadow of Statues: A White Southerner Confronts History*. New York: Viking, 2018.
Lears, Jackson. *Rebirth of a Nation: The Making of Modern America, 1877–1920*. New York: Harper Collins, 2009.
Levine, Lawrence W. *Black Culture and Black Consciousness: Afro-American Folk Thought from Slavery to Freedom*. New York: Oxford University Press, 1977.
Levine, Lawrence W. *The Unpredictable Past: Explorations in American Cultural History*. New York: Oxford University Press, 1993.

Lindgren, James M. *Preserving Historic New England: Preservation, Progressivism, and the Remaking of Memory*. New York: Oxford University Press, 1995.

Lindgren, James M. *Preserving the Old Dominion: Historic Preservation and Virginia Traditionalism*. Charlottesville: University Press of Virginia, 1993.

Litwack, Leon F. *Been in the Storm So Long: The Aftermath of Slavery*. New York: Vintage Books, 1979.

Litwack, Leon F. *Trouble in Mind: Black Southerners in the Age of Jim Crow*. New York: Alfred A. Knopf, 1998.

Loewen, James W. *Lies across America: What Our Historic Sites Get Wrong*. New York: New Press, 1999.

Lowenthal, David. *The Past Is a Foreign Country*. New York: Cambridge University Press, 1990.

Lowenthal, David. *Possessed by the Past: The Heritage Crusade and the Spoils of History*. New York: Free Press, 1998.

Machlovitz, Wendy. *Clara Lowenburg Moses, Memoir of a Southern Jewish Woman*. Jackson, MS: Museum of the Southern Jewish Experience, 2000.

Manring, M. M. *Slave in a Box: The Strange Career of Aunt Jemima*. Charlottesville: University Press of Virginia, 1998.

May, Robert E. *John A. Quitman, Old South Crusader*. Baton Rouge: Louisiana State University Press, 1985.

McElroy, Guy C. *Facing History: The Black Image in American Art, 1710–1940*. Washington, DC: Corcoran Gallery of Art, 1990.

McElvaine, Robert. *The Great Depression: America, 1929–1941*. New York: Times Books, 1984.

McElya, Micki. *Clinging to Mammy: The Faithful Slave in Twentieth-Century America*. Cambridge, Massachusetts: Harvard University Press, 2007.

McLemore, Richard A. *History of Mississippi*. Jackson: College and University Press of Mississippi, 1975.

McMillen, Neil R. *Dark Journey: Black Mississippians in the Age of Jim Crow*. Urbana: University of Illinois Press, 1989.

McPherson, James M. *The Negro's War*. New York: Ballantine, 1965.

Mettler, Suzanne. *Dividing Citizens: Gender and Federalism in New Deal Public Policy*. Ithaca: Cornell University Press, 1998.

Miller, Mary Warren, and Ronald W. Miller. *The Great Houses of Natchez*. Jackson: University Press of Mississippi, 1986.

Mills, Cynthia, and Pamela H. Simpson, eds. *Monuments to the Lost Cause: Women, Art, and the Landscapes of Southern Memory*. Knoxville: University of Tennessee, 2003.

Moore, John Hebron. *The Emergence of the Cotton Kingdom in the Old Southwest: Mississippi, 1770–1860*. Baton Rouge: Louisiana State University Press, 1988.

Morgan, Francesca. *Women and Patriotism in Jim Crow America*. Chapel Hill: University of North Carolina Press, 2005.

Morris, Robert C. *Reading, 'Riting, and Reconstruction: The Education of Freedmen in the South*. Chicago: University of Chicago Press, 1976.

Murphy, Gretchen. *Shadowing the White Man's Burden: U.S. Imperialism and the Problem of the Color Line*. New York: New York University Press, 2010.

Neverdon-Morton, Cynthia. *Afro-American Women of the South and the Advancement of the Race, 1895-1925*. Knoxville: University of Tennessee Press, 1989.

Newman, Harvey K. *Southern Hospitality: Tourism and the Growth of Atlanta*. Tuscaloosa: University of Alabama Press, 1999.

Nolan, Charles E. *St. Mary's of Natchez: The History of a Southern Catholic Congregation, 1716-1988*. Vol. 1. Natchez: St. Mary's Parish, 1992.

O'Brien, Michael. *The Idea of the American South, 1920-1941*. Baltimore: Johns Hopkins University Press, 1979.

Ownby, Ted. *American Dreams in Mississippi: Consumers, Poverty, and Culture, 1830-1998*. Chapel Hill: University of North Carolina Press, 1999.

Panzer, Mary. *In My Studio: Rudolf Eickemeyer, Jr. and the Art of the Camera*. Yonkers, New York: Hudson River Museum, 1986.

Penningroth, Dylan. *The Claims of Kinfolk: African American Property and Community in the Nineteenth-Century South*. Chapel Hill: University of North Carolina Press, 2003.

Peterson, Carla L. *Doers of the Word: African American Women Speakers and Writers in the North, 1830-1880*. New York: Oxford University Press, 1995.

Pilkington, John, ed. *Stark Young: A Life in the Arts; Letters, 1900-1962*. Baton Rouge: Louisiana State University Press, 1975.

Preston, Howard Lawrence. *Dirt Roads to Dixie: Accessibility and Modernization in the South, 1885-1935*. Knoxville: University of Tennessee Press, 1991.

Rable, George. *Civil Wars: Women and the Crisis of Southern Nationalism*. Urbana: University of Illinois Press, 1989.

Reed, Robert. *"All the World Is Here!" The Black Presence at White City*. Bloomington: Indiana University Press, 2000.

Richardson, Joe M. *Christian Reconstruction: The American Missionary Association and Southern Blacks, 1861-1890*. Athens: University of Georgia Press, 1986.

Roediger, David R. *The Wages of Whiteness: Race and the Making of an American Working Class*. New York: Verso, 1994.

Rosenbaum, Tommye Hogue. *A History of the Mississippi Federation of Women's Clubs, 1898-1998*. Jackson: GFWC Mississippi Federation of Women's Clubs, 1998.

Roth, Darlene Rebecca. *Matronage: Patterns in Women's Organizations, Atlanta, Georgia, 1890-1940*. Brooklyn, NY: Carlson Pub., 1994.

Rotundo, Anthony. *American Manhood: Transformations in Masculinity from the Revolution to the Modern Era*. New York: Basic Books, 1993.

Rowland, Dunbar. *History of Mississippi: Heart of the South*. Vols. 1-2. Chicago: J. Clarke, 1925.

Savage, Beth L. *African American Historic Places*. Washington, DC: Preservation Press, 1994.

Savage, Kirk. *Standing Soldier, Kneeling Slaves: Race, War, and Monument in Nineteenth-Century America*. Princeton, NJ: Princeton University Press, 1997.

Scarborough, William K. *Masters of the Big House: Elite Slaveholders of the Mid-Nineteenth-Century South*. Baton Rouge: Louisiana State University Press, 2003.

Schaffer, Marguerite. *See America First: Tourism and National Identity, 1880–1940.* Washington, DC: Smithsonian Institution Press, 2001.

Scharf, Lois. *To Work and to Wed: Female Unemployment, Feminism, and the Great Depression.* Westport, CT: Greenwood Press, 1980.

Scott, Anne Firor. *Making the Invisible Woman Visible.* Urbana: University of Illinois Press, 1984.

Scott, Anne Firor. *Natural Allies: Women's Associations in American History.* Urbana: University of Illinois Press, 1991.

Scott, Anne Firor. *The Southern Lady: From Pedestal to Politics, 1830–1930.* Chicago: University of Chicago Press, 1970.

Sears, John F. *Sacred Places: American Tourist Attractions in the Nineteenth Century.* New York: Oxford University Press, 1989.

Shackel, Paul A. *Memory in Black and White: Race, Commemoration, and the Post-Bellum Landscape.* Walnut Creek, CA: Altamia Press, 2003.

Shaffer, Marguerite. *See America First: Tourism and National Identity, 1880–1940.* Washington, DC: Smithsonian Press, 2001.

Silber, Irwin, and Jerry Silverman, eds. *Songs of the Civil War.* New York: Columbia University Press, 1960.

Silber, Nina. *The Romance of Reunion: Northerners and the South, 1865–1900.* Chapel Hill: University of North Carolina Press, 1993.

Sims, Anastatia. *The Power of Femininity in the New South: Women's Organizations and Politics in North Carolina.* Columbia: University of South Carolina Press, 1997.

Small, Christopher. *Music of the Common Tongue: Survival and Celebration in Afro-American Music.* London: J. Calder, 1987.

Sneider, Allison L. *Suffragists in an Imperial Age: United States Expansion and the Woman Question, 1870–1929.* Oxford: Oxford University Press, 2008.

Sontag, Susan. *On Photography.* New York: Farrar, Straus and Giroux, 1977.

Sparks, Randy. *Religion in Mississippi.* Jackson: University Press of Mississippi, 2001.

Starnes, Richard D., ed. *Southern Journeys: Tourism, History, and Culture in the Modern South.* Tuscaloosa: University of Alabama Press, 2003.

Stauffer, John. *The Black Hearts of Men: Radical Abolitionists and the Transformation of Race.* Cambridge, MA: Harvard University Press, 2002.

Stegner, Wallace. *Where the Bluebird Sings to the Lemonade Springs: Living and Writing in the West.* New York: Random House, 1992.

Steponaitis, Vincas P. *Ceramics, Chronology, and Community Patterns: An Archaeological Study at Moundville.* Academic Press, 1993. Reprint. Tuscaloosa: University of Alabama Press 2009.

Stoler, Anne Laura. *Carnal Knowledge and Imperial Power: Race and the Intimate in Colonial Rule.* Berkeley: University of California Press, 2012.

Stott, William. *Documentary Expression and Thirties America.* New York: Oxford University Press, 1973.

Sussman, Warren. *Culture as History: The Transformation of American Society in the Twentieth Century.* New York: Pantheon Books, 1984.

Taylor, Arnold H. *Travail and Triumph: Black Life and Culture in the South since the Civil War*. Westport, CT: Greenwood Press, 1976.
Thompson, Julius Eric. *The Black Press in Mississippi, 1865-1985*. Gainesville: University Press of Florida, 1993.
Trachtenburg, Alan. *The American Image: Photographs from the National Archives, 1860-1960*. New York: Pantheon Books, 1979.
Tucker, Susan. *Telling Memories among Southern Women: Domestic Workers and Their Employers in the Segregated South*. Baton Rouge: Louisiana State University Press, 1988.
Turner, Patricia A. *Ceramic Uncles and Celluloid Mammies: Black Images and Their Influence on Culture*. New York: Anchor Books, 1994.
Urry, John. *The Tourist Gaze: Leisure and Travel in Contemporary Societies*. London: Sage Publications, 1990.
Van Deburg, William L. *Slavery and Race in American Popular Culture*. Madison: University of Wisconsin Press, 1984.
Wandersee, Winifred D. *Woman's Work and Family Values, 1920-1940*. Cambridge, MA: Harvard University Press, 1981.
Ware, Susan. *Holding Their Own: American Women in the 1930s*. Boston: Twayne, 1982.
Watters, Sam. *Gardens for a Beautiful America, 1895-1935: Photographs by Frances Benjamin Johnston*. New York: Acanthus Press, 2012.
Wayne, Michael. *Death of an Overseer: Reopening a Murder Investigation from the Plantation South*. Oxnard: Oxford University Press, 2001.
Wayne, Michael. *The Reshaping of Plantation Society: The Natchez District, 1860-1880*. Baton Rouge: Louisiana State University Press, 1983.
Webster, Anne L. *African Americans: A Mississippi Source Book*. Carrollton, MS: Pioneer, 2001.
Wedell, Marsha. *Elite Women and the Reform Impulse in Memphis, 1875-1915*. Knoxville: University of Tennessee Press, 1991.
Weisberger, Bernard A., ed. *The WPA Guide to America: The Best of 1930s America as Seen by the Federal Writer's Project*. New York: Pantheon, 1985.
Welch, Kimberly M. *Black Litigants in the Antebellum American South*. Chapel Hill: University of North Carolina Press, 2018.
Wells, Mildred White. *Unity in Diversity: The History of the General Federation of Women's Clubs*. Washington, DC: General Federation of Women's Clubs, 1953.
Welty, Eudora. *Eudora Welty: Photographs*. Jackson: University Press of Mississippi, 1989.
Wesley, Charles Harris. *The History of the National Association of Colored Women's Clubs: Legacy of Service*. Washington, DC: The Association, 1984.
West, Patricia. *Domesticating History: The Political Origins of America's House Museums*. Washington, DC: Smithsonian Institution Press, 1999.
Weyeneth, Robert R. *Historic Preservation for a Living City: Historic Charleston Foundation, 1947-1997*. Columbia: University of South Carolina Press, 2000.
Wharton, Vernon Lane. *The Negro in Mississippi, 1865-1890*. New York: Harper and Row, 1965. Original edition, Chapel Hill: University of North Carolina Press, 1947.
White, Shane, and Graham White. *The Sounds of Slavery: Discovering African American History through Songs, Sermons, and Speech*. Boston: Beacon Press, 2005.

Whites, LeeAnn. *The Civil War as a Crisis in Gender: Augusta, Georgia, 1860–1890*. Athens: University of Georgia Press, 1995.

Whites, LeeAnn, and Alecia P. Long, eds. *Occupied Women: Gender, Military Occupation, and the American Civil War*. Baton Rouge: Louisiana State University Press, 2009.

Wiggins, Jr., William. *O Freedom! Afro-American Emancipation Celebrations*. Knoxville: University of Tennessee Press, 1987.

Williams, Heather. *Self-Taught: African American Education in Slavery and Freedom*. Chapel Hill: University of North Carolina Press, 2005.

Williamson, Joel. *The Crucible of Race: Black-White Relations in the American South since Emancipation*. New York: Oxford University Press, 1984.

Willis, Deborah, ed. *Picturing Us: African American Identity in Photography*. New York: New Press, 1994.

Willis, Deborah. *A Small Nation of People: W. E. B. Du Bois and African American Portraits of Progress*. New York: Library of Congress and Harper Collins, 2003.

Wilson, Charles Reagan. *Baptized in Blood: The Religion of the Lost Cause, 1865–1920*. Athens: University of Georgia Press, 1980.

Wilson, Charles Reagan, and William Ferris, eds., *The Encyclopedia of Southern Culture*. Chapel Hill: University of North Carolina Press, 1989.

Woodward, C. Vann. *The Strange Career of Jim Crow*. New York: Oxford University Press, 1966.

Wyatt-Brown, Bertram. *The Shaping of Southern Culture: Honor, Grace, and War, 1760s–1880s*. Chapel Hill: University of North Carolina Press, 2001.

Wyatt-Brown, Bertram. *Southern Honor: Ethics and Behavior in the Old South*. New York: Oxford University Press, 1982.

Yuhl, Stephanie E. *A Golden Haze of Memory: The Making of Historic Charleston*. Chapel Hill: University of North Carolina Press, 2005.

ARTICLES AND ESSAYS

Altman, Karen. "Consumer Ideology: The Better Homes in America Campaign." *Critical Studies in Mass Communication* 7, no. 3 (September 1990): 286–307.

Bailery, Fred Arthur. "For Something beyond the Battlefield: Frederick Douglass and the Struggle for the Memory of the Civil War." *Journal of American History* 75 (March 1989): 1156–78.

Bailery, Fred Arthur. "Mildred Lewis Rutherford and the Patrician Cult of the Old South." *Georgia History Quarterly* 78 (Fall 1994): 509–35.

Bailery, Fred Arthur. "The Textbooks of the 'Lost Cause': Censorship and the Creation of Southern State Histories." *Georgia History Quarterly* 75 (Fall 1991): 507–33.

Barnett, Jim, and H. Clark Burkett. "The Forks of the Road Slave Market at Natchez." *Journal of Mississippi History* 63 (Fall 2001): 169–87.

Behrend, Justin. "Rebellious Talk and Conspiratorial Plots: The Making of a Slave Insurrection in Civil War Natchez." *Journal of Southern History* 77 no. 1 (February 2011): 17–52.

Behrend, Justin. "Rumors of Revolt." *New York Times*, September 15, 2011.
Berkowitz, Michael. "A 'New Deal' for Leisure: Making Mass Tourism during the Great Depression." In *Being Elsewhere: Tourism, Consumer Culture, and Identity in Modern Europe and North America*, edited by Shelly Baranowski and Ellen Furlough, 185–212. Ann Arbor: University of Michigan Press 2001.
Bishir, Catherine W. "Landmarks of Power: Building a Southern Past in Raleigh and Wilmington, North Carolina, 1885–1915." In *Where These Memories Grow: History, Memory, and Southern Identity*, edited by W. Fitzhugh Brundage, 139–68. Chapel Hill: University of North Carolina Press, 2000.
Bishir, Catherine W. "'A Strong Force of Ladies': Women, Politics, and Confederate Memorial Associations in Nineteenth-Century Raleigh." In *Monuments to the Lost Cause: Women, Art, and the Landscapes of Southern Memory*, edited by Cynthia Mills and Pamela H. Simpson, 3–26. Knoxville: University of Tennessee Press, 2003.
Broussard, Joyce. "Coping with the Deluge: The Elite, Not Married Women of Post-Bellum Natchez, Mississippi—and the 'Other Men' in Their Lives." *Southern Studies* 17, no. 1 (Spring/Summer 2010): 39–74.
Broussard, Joyce. "Occupied Natchez, Elite Women, and the Feminization of the Civil War." *Journal of Mississippi History* 70, no. 2 (Summer 2008): 179–208.
Broussard, Joyce. "Stepping Lively in Place: The Free Black Women of Antebellum Natchez." In *Mississippi Women: Their Histories, Their Lives*, vol. 2, edited by Elizabeth Anne Payne, Martha H. Swain, and Marjorie Julian Spruill, 23–38. Athens: University of Georgia Press, 2010.
Brown, Elsa Barkley, and Gregg B. Kimball. "Mapping the Terrain of Black Richmond." *Journal of Urban History* 21 (March 1995): 296–346.
Brundage, W. Fitzhugh. "White Women and Historical Memory." In *Jumpin' Jim Crow: Southern Politics from Civil War to Civil Rights*, edited by Jane Daily, Glenda Elizabeth Gilmore, and Bryant Simon. Princeton, NJ: Princeton University Press, 2000: 115–39.
Cameron, Ardis. "When Strangers Bring Cameras: The Poetics and Politics of Othered Places." *American Quarterly* 54, no. 3 (2002): 411–35.
Case, Sarah H. "The Historical Ideology of Mildred Lewis Rutherford: A Confederate Historian's New South Creed." *Journal of Southern History* 68 (August 2002): 599–628.
Carlson, Shirley J. "Black Ideals of Womanhood in the Late Victorian Era," *Journal of Negro History* 77, no. 2 (Spring 1992): 61–73.
Clark, Kathleen. "Celebrating Freedom: Emancipation Day Celebrations and African American Memory in the Reconstruction South." In *Where These Memories Grow: History, Memory, and Southern Identity*, edited by W. Fitzhugh Brundage. Chapel Hill: University of North Carolina Press, 2000: 107–32.
Clawson, Mary Ann. "Fraternal Orders and Class Formation in the Nineteenth-Century United States." *Comparative Studies in Society and History* 27 (October 1985): 672–95.
Cook, Cita. "The Practical Ladies of Occupied Natchez." In *Occupied Women: Gender, Military Occupation, and the American Civil War*, edited by LeeAnnWhites and Alecia P. Long, 117–34. Baton Rouge: Louisiana State University Press, 2009. Corkern, Wilton.

"Heritage Tourism: Where Public and History Don't Always Meet." *American Studies International* 42, no. 2/3 (2004): 7–16.

Davis, Jack. "A Struggle for Public History: Black and White Claims to Natchez's Past." *Public Historian* 22, no. 1 (Winter 2000): 45–63.

Davis, Ronald L. F. "The Plantation Lifeworld of the Old Natchez District, 1840–1880." In *Plantation Society and Race Relations: The Origins of Inequality*, edited by Thomas J. Durant Jr. and J. David Knottnerus, 165–81. Westport, CT: Praeger, 1999.

Davis, Ronald L. F. "The Southern Merchant: A Perennial Source of Discontent." In *The Southern Enigma: Essays on Race, Class, and Folk Culture*, edited by Walter J. Fraser Jr. and Winfred B. Moore Jr., 131–43. Westport, CT: Greenwood Press, 1983.

Dresser, Rebecca. "Kate and John Minor: Confederate Unionists of Natchez." *Journal of Mississippi History* 64, no. 3 (September 2002): 182–216.

Elliott, Jack D., Jr. "City and Empire: The Spanish Origins of Natchez." *Journal of Mississippi History* 59 (Winter 1997): 271–322.

Ellison, Mary. "African American Music and Muskets in Civil War New Orleans." *Louisiana History: The Journal of the Louisiana Historical Association* 35 no. 3 (July 1994): 285–319.

Fabre, Genevieve. "African American Commemorative Celebrations in the Nineteenth Century." In *History and Memory in African American Culture*, edited by Genevieve Fabre and Robert G. O'Meally, 72–91. New York: Oxford University Press, 1994.

Faust, Drew Gilpin, Thavolia Glymph, and George C. Rable. "A Women's War: Southern Women in the Civil War." In *A Woman's War: Southern Women, Civil War, and the Confederate Legacy*, edited by Edward D. C. Campbell Jr. and Kym S. Rice, 1–27. Richmond, VA: The Museum of the Confederacy; Charlottesville: University Press of Virginia, 1996.

Fox-Genovese, Elizabeth. "Scarlett O'Hara: The Southern Lady as New Woman." *American Quarterly* 33, no. 4 (Autumn 1981): 391–411.

Gilmore, Russell S. "'Another Branch of Manly Sport:' American Rifle Games, 1840–1900." In *Hard at Play: Leisure in America, 1840–1940*, edited by Kathryn Grover, 93–111. Amherst: University of Massachusetts Press, 1992.

Glassberg, David. "Public History and the Study of Memory." *Public Historian* 18, no. 2 (Spring 1996): 7–23.

Glazer, Lee, and Susan Key. "Carry Me Back: Nostalgia for the Old South in Nineteenth-Century Popular Culture." *Journal of American Studies* 30 (April 1996): 1–24.

Gross, Andrew S. "The American Guide Series: Patriotism as Brand-Name Identification." *Arizona Quarterly* 62, no. 1 (2006): 85–111.

Gulley, H. E. "Women and the Lost Cause: Preserving a Confederate Identity in the American Deep South." *Journal of Historical Geography* 19 (1993): 125–41.

Hale, Grace Elizabeth. "'Some Women Have Never Been Reconstructed': Mildred Lewis Rutherford, Lucy M. Stanton, and the Racial Politics of Southern White Womanhood, 1900–1930." In *Georgia in Black and White: Explorations in the Race Relations of a Southern State, 1865–1950*, edited by John Inscoe, 173–200. Athens: University of Georgia Press, 1994.

Hoelscher, Steven. "'Where the Old South Still Lives': Displaying Heritage in Natchez, Mississippi." In *Southern Heritage on Display: Public Ritual and Ethnic Diversity within*

Southern Regionalism, edited by Celeste R. Ray, 218–49. Tuscaloosa: University of Alabama Press, 2003.

hooks, bell. "In Our Glory." In *Picturing Us: African American Identity in Photography*, edited by Deborah Willis, 50. New York: New Press, 1994.

Howe, Barbara J., "Women in Historic Preservation: The Legacy of Ann Pamela Cunningham." *Public Historian* 12 (Winter 1990): 31–61.

Johnson, Joan Marie. "'Drill into us ... the Rebel tradition'": The Contest over Southern Identity in Black and White Women's Clubs, South Carolina, 1898–1930." *Journal of Southern History* 66, no. 3 (August 2000): 525–62.

Johnson, Joan Marie. "'Ye Gave Them a Stone': African American Women's Clubs, the Frederick Douglass Home, and the Black Mammy Monument." *Journal of Women's History* 17, no. 1 (Spring 2005): 62–86.

Jones, Alfred Haworth. "The Search for a Usable American Past in the New Deal Era." *American Quarterly* 23, no. 5 (December 1971): 710–24.

Keenan, Hugh T. "Heaven Bound at the Crossroads: A Sketch of a Religious Pageant." *Journal of American Culture* 11, no. 3 (Fall 1988): 39–45.

Kelley, Robin D. G. "We Are Not What We Seem: Rethinking Black Working-Class Opposition in the Jim Crow South." *Journal of American History* 80 (June 1993): 75–112.

Kubasek, Melody, "Ask Us Not to Forget: The Lost Cause in Natchez, Mississippi." *Southern Studies* 3 (Fall 1992): 155–70.

Lerner, Gerda. "Early Community Work of Black Club Women." *Journal of Negro History* 59 (1974): 158–67.

Levine, Lawrence W. "The Folklore of Industrial Society: Popular Culture and Its Audiences." *American Historical Review* 97, no. 5 (December 1992): 1369–99.

Maffly-Kipp, Laurie F. "Redeeming Southern Memory: The Negro Race History, 1874–1915." In *Where These Memories Grow: History, Memory, and Southern Identity*, edited by W. Fitzhugh Brundage, 169–89. Chapel Hill: University of North Carolina Press, 2000.

Medford, Edna Greene. "Imagined Promises, Bitter Realities: African Americans and the Meaning of the Emancipation Proclamation." In *The Emancipation Proclamation: Three Views* by Harold Holzer, Edna Greene Medford, and Frank J. Williams. Baton Rouge: Louisiana State University Press, 2006.

Miller, Patrick. "The Manly, the Moral, and the Proficient: College Sport in the New South." In *The Sporting World of the Modern South*, edited by Patrick Miller, 17–49. Urbana: University of Illinois Press, 2002.

Montgomery, Rebecca. "Lost Cause Mythology in New South Reform: Gender, Class, Race, and the Politics of Patriotic Citizenship." In *Negotiating Boundaries of Southern Womanhood: Dealing with the Powers That Be*, edited by Janet L. Croyell, 174–98. Columbia: University of Missouri Press, 2000.

Morgan, Jo-Ann. "Mammy the Huckster: Selling the Old South for the New Century." *American Art* 9, no. 1 (Spring 1995): 86–109.

Morris, Sara E. "'Down in Tupelo Everybody Seems to be Feeling Grand': Early Home Electrification Promotion in Northeast Mississippi." In *Mississippi Women: Their Histories, Their Lives*, vol. 2, edited by Elizabeth Anne Payne, Martha H. Swain, and Marjorie Julian Spruill, 192–210. Athens: University of Georgia Press, 2010.

Mullener, Elizabeth. "Springtime in Natchez." *Dixie*, May 30, 1982.

Peters, Marsha, and Bernard Mergen, "'Doing the Rest': The Uses of Photographs in American Studies." *American Quarterly* 29, no. 3 (1977): 280–81.

Raines, Howell. "Grady's Gift." *New York Times*, December 1, 1991.

Rosenblum, Thom. "Driving Out the Slave Traders: The Natchez Uprising of 1833." *Journal of Mississippi History* 67 (2005): 45–68.

Rothstein, Morton. "The Changing Social Networks and Investment Behavior of a Slaveholding Elite in the Ante-Bellum South: Some Natchez 'Nabobs,' 1800–1860." In *Entrepreneurs in Cultural Context*, edited by Sidney M. Greenfield, Arnold Strickon, and Robert Aubrey, 65–84. Albuquerque: University of New Mexico Press, 1979.

Rauch, Bill. "Can the South Make Room for Reconstruction?" *Atlantic Monthly*, September 17, 2016.

Ryan, Mary. "The American Parade: Representations of the Nineteenth-Century Social Order." In *The New Cultural History*, edited by Lynn Hunt, 131–54. Berkeley: University of California Press, 1989.

Salem, Dorothy C. *To Better Our World: Black Women in Organized Reform, 1890–1920*. Brooklyn, NY: Carlson, 1990.

Scarborough, Thomas. "Cotton Planters and Plantations in the Natchez District, 1760–1880." In *Natchez on the Mississippi: A Journey through Southern History, 1870–1920*, edited by Ronald L. F. Davis and Joyce L. Broussard, 14–15. Los Angeles: Norstel, 1995.

Schulman, Cecelia M. "Adam Lewis Bingaman: A Southern Aristocrat of a Different Kind." In *Natchez on the Mississippi: A Journey through Southern History, 1870–1920*, edited by Ronald L. F. Davis and Joyce L. Broussard, 25. Los Angeles: Norstel, 1995.

Smithers, Leslie. "The Pleasure Garden of Nineteenth-Century Natchez: Illusions of Grandeur." In *Natchez on the Mississippi: A Journey Through Southern History, 1870–1920*, edited by Ronald L. F. Davis and Joyce L. Broussard. Los Angeles: Norstel, 1995.

Smithers, Leslie. "Profit and Corruption in Civil War Natchez: A Case History of Union Occupation Government." *Journal of Mississippi History* 64 (Spring 2002): 17–33.

Sparks, Randy J. "The Good Sisters: White Protestant Women and Institution Building in Antebellum Mississippi." In *Mississippi Women: Their Histories, Their Lives*, vol. 2, edited by Elizabeth Anne Payne, Martha H. Swain, and Marjorie Julian Spruill, 39–56. Athens: University of Georgia Press, 2010.

Sparks, Randy J. "'The White People's Arms Are Longer Than Ours': Blacks, Education, and the American Missionary Association in Reconstruction Mississippi." *Journal of Mississippi History* 54, no. 1 (March 1992): 1–27.

Stauffer, John. "Interspatialism in the Nineteenth-Century South: The Natchez of Henry Norman." *Slavery and Abolition* 29, no. 2 (June 2008): 247–63.

Thelen, David. "Memory and American History." *Journal of American History* 75, no. 4 (March 1989): 1117–29.

Thurber, Cheryl. "The Development of the Mammy Image and Mythology." In *Southern Women: Histories and Identities*, edited by Virginia Bernhard, Betty Brandon, Elizabeth Fox-Genovese, and Theda Purdue, 87–107. Columbia: University of Missouri Press, 1992.

Tristano, Richard N. "Holy Family Parish: The Genesis of an African American Community in Natchez, Mississippi." *Journal of Negro History* 83, no. 4 (1998): 258–84.

Weyeneth, Robert R. "Ancestral Architecture: The Early Preservation Movement in Charleston." In *Giving Preservation a History: Histories of Historic Preservation in the United States*, edited by Max Page and Randall Mason, 257–82. New York: Routledge, 2004.

White, Deborah Gray. "The Cost of Club Work, the Price of Black Feminism." In *Visible Women: New Essays on American Activism*, edited by Nancy A. Hewitt and Suzanne Lebsock, 247–69. Urbana: University of Illinois Press, 1993.

White, Deborah Gray. "Mining the Forgotten Manuscript Sources for Black Women's History." *Journal of American History* 74, no. 1 (June 1987): 237–42.

White, Shane. "'It Was a Proud Day': African American Festivals and Parades in the North, 1741–1834." *Journal of American History* 81 (June 1994): 13–50.

Whitfield, Stephen J. "'Sacred in History and in Art': The Shaw Memorial," *New England Quarterly* 60 (March 1987): 3–27.

Wiggins, William Jr. "Pilgrims, Crosses, and Faith: The Folk Dimensions of Heaven Bound," *Black American Literature Forum* 25, no. 1 (Spring 1991): 93–100.

Zelm, Antoinette G. "Virginia Women as Public Citizens: Emancipation Day Celebrations and Lost Cause Commemorations, 1863–1890." In *Negotiating the Boundaries of Southern Womanhood: Dealing with the Powers That Be*, edited by Janet L. Croyell et al. Columbia: University of Missouri, 2000.

UNPUBLISHED DISSERTATIONS, THESES, AND CONFERENCE PAPERS

Aaron Anderson, "The Builders of a New South: Merchants, Capital and the Remaking of Natchez, 1865–1914." PhD diss., University of Southern Mississippi, 2009.

Behrend, Justin. "Freedpeople's Democracy: African American Politics and Community in the Postemancipation Natchez District." PhD diss., Northwestern University, 2006.

Bieber, Darcy. "Making the Most of Freedom: Black Female Schoolteachers in Postbellum Natchez, Mississippi, 1865–1910." Master's thesis, California State University, Northridge, 2005.

Boggess, Elizabeth MacNeil. "Second Creek in 1861: People and Places." Paper delivered at No More Silence at Second Creek: Slave Resistance and the Onset of the Civil War Symposium, sponsored by the National Park Service, September 24, 2011. Paper in author's hands.

Broussard, Joyce. "Female Solitaires: Women Alone in the Lifeworld of Mid-Century Natchez, Mississippi, 1850–1880." PhD diss., University of Southern California, 1998.

Brown, Elsa Barkley. "Uncle Ned's Children: Negotiating Community and Freedom in Postemancipation Richmond, Virginia," PhD diss., Kent State University, 1994.

Bruce, Janet. "Nineteenth-Century Natchez, Mississippi, in Photographs: Two Perspectives." Master's thesis, California State University, Northridge, 2012.

Cook, Cita. "Growing Up White, Genteel, and Female in a Changing South, 1865–1915." PhD diss., University of California, Berkeley, 1992.

Dresser, Rebecca. "The Minor Family of Natchez: A Case of Southern Unionism." Master's thesis, California State University, Northridge, 2000.

Falck, Susan T. "The Garden Club Women of Natchez: 'To Preserve the South We Love.'" Master's thesis, California State University, Northridge, 2003.

Falck, Susan T. "Black and White Memory Making in Postwar Natchez, Mississippi, 1865–1935." PhD diss., University of California, Santa Barbara, 2012.

Hamilton, Cai. "Illuminating Lydia Dowell: The Extraordinary Life of Lydia Dowell in Antebellum Natchez, Mississippi." Paper presented at the Eighth Biennial Historic Natchez Conference, Natchez, MS, 2009.

Jenkins, Kathleen. "Next of Kin—the Turners, Quitmans, McMurans, and Conners: An Intimate Glimpse into the Households of Four Historically Prominent Natchez Families." Paper presented at the First Biennial Historic Natchez Conference, Natchez, MS, 1994.

Lenowski, Jaime. "William T. Martin: A Pillar of Southern Honor." Paper presented at the Fifth Biennial Historic Natchez Conference, Natchez, MS, 2002.

McFadden, Margaret. "'Anything Goes': Gender and Knowledge in the Comic Popular Culture of the 1930s," PhD diss., Yale University, 1996.

Miller, Mary Warren. "History of St. Catherine Street." Unpublished manuscript. Natchez Trails Project, Historic Natchez Foundation, Natchez, MS.

Nomelli, Sheryl. "Jim Crow, Louis J. Winston, and the Survival of Black Politics in Postbellum Natchez, Mississippi." Master's thesis, California State University, Northridge, 2004.

Parker, Cynthia J. "Monmouth: The Survival of a Grand Mansion Estate in Natchez, Mississippi, from the Era of Slavery to the Present." Master's thesis, California State University, Northridge, 2010.

Peterson, Shane. "Lost Cause to Lost Generation: World War I and the African American Troops from Adams County, Mississippi." Master's thesis, California State University, Northridge, 2008.

Prevost, Verbie Lovorn. "Roane Fleming Byrnes: A Critical Biography." PhD diss., University of Mississippi, 1974.

Seawright, Phyllis Woodward. "Natchez Theatre, 1852–1940: Yearning for Fame." PhD diss., Florida State University, 1996.

Shiells, Dan. "The Orphanages of Ant-bellum Natchez." Paper presented at the Fifth Biennial Historic Natchez Conference, Natchez, MS, 2002.

Tate, Roger D., Jr. "Easing the Burden: The Era of Depression and New Deal in Mississippi." PhD diss., University of Tennessee, 1978.

Smith, Sarah Dunbar. "Thomas Rose: A Nineteenth-Century Master Builder in Natchez, Mississippi." Master's thesis, Tulane University, 1993.

Smithers, Leslie. "Fermes ornees of the Lower Mississippi River Valley: Examining the Social Language of Plantation Gardens in Relationship to Planter Elite Culture." PhD diss., Purdue University, 2001.

Tripp, Connie. "An Affair of the Heart: A Natchez Scandal in the Midst of War." Paper presented at the Fifth Biennial Historic Natchez Conference, Natchez, MS, 2002.

Welch, Rosanne. "A Family Affair: Emancipation and Slavery in the Old Natchez District, 1795–1860." Master's thesis, California State University, Northridge, 2004.

INDEX

Page numbers in **bold** refer to illustrations.

Adams, Lalie, **186**
Adams, Revel A., 113–14
Adams, William A., 161, 193
Adams County: elections, 42; Republican Party, 37, 41, 53; Union League, 37, 44, 49, 52–55, 58, 60–63, 66, 69, 73
Adams County Dragoons, 77
Adams Light Infantry, 5, 73–77, 79–86, 92–93, 95, 97, 98–100, 102, 169
African Americans. *See* blacks
Airlie (estate), **253**
Alexander, Anna, 217
Allen, L. D., 52–54
Allen, William, 154–55
American Missionary Association, 22, 39–41, 51
American Weekly, **219**
Angeletti, Emile, 231
aristocracy. *See* planter aristocracy
Arlington (estate), 165–66, 212, 310n36, 318n4
Atlanta Constitution, 213
Atlantic Monthly, 156, 242
Auburn, **254**, 255
Audubon, John, 195
Aunt Jemima, 197, 305n58

Baker, Livie J., 98
Baker, Thomas Otis, 80, 84
Ballou, Clara, **186**
Baltimore Sun, 203
Banks, John B., 112–13, 231
Banks, Susy, 122
Barnum, Annie, 212
Bechet, Sidney, 59–60
Beemis, Lydia, 113
Behrend, Justin, 45, 78, 243, 286n5
Beltzhoover, Melchoir, 265, 312n75
Beltzhoover, Ruth Audley Britton, 158, 176, 178–79, **186**, 189, 214, 263, 265, 312n75
Benbrook, William G., 73, 82, 94–95
Bennerscheidt, Eliza, 179–80
Benoist, Beck, **186**
Bercaw, Nancy, 76
Better Homes America, 187–88
Better Homes and Gardens, 8, 194
Black Codes, 51–52
black men: fraternal associations, 50, 52, 57, 60–62, 111; in government posts, 41; political organizations, 5, 41–42, 49, 52, 55, 57, 60–61; politicos, 65–68, 71, 142; servants, 136; soldiers, 21, 30, 42, 73; suffrage, 52–53, 68, 73. *See also* free people of color
black women: 17–18, 33, 57–58, 65, **115**, 122, 131, 138, 143, 190; mammies, 149; portraits, 115, 118; servants, 136, 167; teachers, 36. *See also* free people of color
blacks: as Confederate soldiers, 301n41; freedom songs, 59–60; lynching, 45, 316n130; "mammies," 149–50; "one-drop rule," 322n15; post-Reconstruction citizenship, 58; respectability, 54–57, 60–62, 115–17, 119; uplift, 56, 62, 175
blacks, in Natchez: baptisms, 131, **132**, 143–44, 305n57; businesses, 111–14; churches,

349

Index

13, 36–38, 41–42, 50–51, 53, 111–13, 160, 232; children, **115**, **117**; civil rights, 67, 232–33, 237–38; Civil War experiences, 6, 19, 21–23, 234; class tensions, 50, 60–61, 67–68, 71; community, 111–12, 226, 231; consumers, 30–32, 107, 111, 113–14, 119; contestation of white mastery, 143–46, 150–51, 238; disfranchisement, 68, 71, 74, 102; education, 248; Emancipation traditions, 6, 19, 48–50, 60, 63, 68–70; enslavement, 18–19, 131, 147–48, 156, 189, 226–27, 229–34, 238, 243–44, 246; entrepreneurs, 113; fire companies, 63, 66; Fourth of July, 49, 52–55, 58–61, 63, 65, 72, 85; freedmen, 9, 21–22, 30; freedom fighters, 234; gender roles, 58; heritage tours, 239; historic sites, 226; involvement with Pilgrimage, 190–91, 194, 207; laborers, 33; literacy, 39; marriages, 34; merchants, 113–14; ministers, 37; middle class, 32–33; militia companies, 44; music, 58–60; neighborhoods, 302n16; parades and commemorations, 49, 51, 54–55, 57–59, 63–64, 68–72; photography, 105–9, 114–18, 132–35, 138–51, 232; Pilgrimage portrayal of, 6–7; political organizations, 41, 44, 52–55, 57–58, 60–63, 66, 69, 73; portraits, 13, 105–11, 114–19; postwar community, 6, 61; postwar identity, 49–51, 55, 57–58, 70–71, 107, 111, 119; Republicans, 66; response to Pilgrimage, 206–7; schools, 39–42, 61, 111, 113; servants, 121–22, 135–41, 143–52, 167, 184, 188–89; sharecroppers, 12, 32–33; Southern Claims Commission claimants, 23, 33–34; spirituals, 194; stereotypes, 145–46, 150–51, 197; street vendors, 207; teachers, 36, 41, 45, 58; tourism, 226, 241; Tricentennial involvement, 237; Union troops, 21, 30, 34, 43, 57–58, 63–64, 68, 73, 232–34, 249; veterans, 58, 65, 68–69, **70**, 71–72; voting, 41–42, 53, 237; working class, 113–15, 141–42, 191; World War I veterans, 322n18

Blankenstein, Kathie Boatner, 13, 69, 214
Blight, David, 5–6, 49, 190, 194, 209
Boatner, Lillie Vidal, 197–99, **198**
Boggess, Elizabeth, 238, 242–44
Bond, Horace Mann, 200
Bond, Kathleen J., 229–33, 235–36, 238–39, 244
Bowie, Wynant W., 37, 111–12
Bowles, G. F., 37, 111–12
Boxley, Se Sesh Ab Heter-Clifford, 13, 207, 234–35, 249–50
Boyd, Samuel Sillman, 244–45
Brandon, Gerard, 214, 221
Brandon, Kate Don, **198**, 221–22
Briars, The, **254**, 255
Britton, Audley C., 81, 96, 120–21, 147, 303n35
Britton, Eliza Macrery, 120
Britton, William J., 147
Britton & Koontz Bank, 81, 147, 263
Broussard, Joyce, 17, 25, 285n1, 288n27, 305n60
Brown, Catharine Dunbar, 182–83, 279, 281, 313n88
Brown, Elise, 161
Brown, George M., 81
Brown's Garden, 157
Bruce, Janet, 301n2
Brumfield, George W., 113
Buckner, Aylette, 253
Bushman, Richard, 55, 208
Butler, Richard, 136, **137**
"Buy American" movement, 196
Byrne, William J., 215
Byrnes, Roane Fleming, 139, 162–63, 166, 181, 183–84, **186**, 267, 306n68

Carnegie Survey of the Architecture of the South, 253
Carpenter, Agnes, 120, 259
Carpenter, Alma Kellogg, 12–13, 177
Carpenter, Joseph N., 81, 257
Carpenter, N. L., 257, 259
Carpenter, Zipporah Russell, 257
Carr, Elizabeth, 23

Carriage House Restaurant, 283
Carter, Jeanett, 33
Castello, E. J., 52, 66–67
Charlottesville, VA, 225
Cherry Grove, 243–44
Chicago Tribune, on Knights Templar parade, 89–90, 185, 204
Christian Recorder, 37–38, 51; on Winston, 62
Civil Rights Bill (1874), 67, 119
Civil War, reunions, 75
Clayton, Virginia Tuttle, 168–69
Clover Nook, 126–27, 134, 136, 146, 151
Cohn, David, 191
Collins, Reuben, 172
Colonial Williamsburg, 201
Combs, Jennifer Ogden, 235–36, 239
Concord Quarters, 245–47
Confederate Army, 8–9, 17, 25; veterans, 5, 64, 80, 86, 90, 92, 98–99, 137, 169
Confederate Memorial Association, 5, 92, 98–101, 110, 121, 169, 171–72, 174
Confederate Memorial Day, 99–101
Confederate monuments, 5, 100, 121, 225, 249–50, 320n1
Confederate nationalism, 5
Connelly's Tavern, **266**, 267
Conner, Eliza, **130**
Conner, Jane Gustine, 271
Conner, Lemuel P., III, 149
Conner, Lemuel P., Jr., 122, 133, 148, 271, 305n60
Conner, Lemuel P., Sr., 81, 133, 147–48, 305n60, 307n78
Conner, Mary Britton, 107, 120–24, 126, 181; black baptisms, 305n58; photo album, 127–29, **130**, 131, 133–52, 304n51, 306n66; role in Kirmess, 304n44
Conner, Richard Ellis, 81
Conner, William C., 271
Cosey, Debbie, 245–48
Cosmopolitan Magazine, 124
Cox, Karen, 159, 202, 218–19
Cutrer, Richard Wiltz, 216, 218

Dahlgren, Charles, 257
Dana, Richard, 218
Daughters of the American Revolution, 104, 183, 281
Davis, Alfred V., 90, 257
Davis, Allison, 205
Davis, Carolyn, 161
Davis, George, 273
Davis, Jefferson, 161–62, 195, 255
Davis, Laura, 112
Davis, Minor, 111–12
Davis, Ronald L. F., 9–12, 33, 61, 227–29, 233–35, 287n25, 308n7
Davis, Thomas, 112
Davis, William M., 37
Decoration Day, 63–71, 295n58
Deep South, 205–6, 317n152, 319n33
DeLap, Enoch George, 91–93
Dent, Jane, 17–18, 33
D'Evereux (estate), **256**, 257
Dicks, John A., 82
Dixie, 202, 216
Dixon, Harriet, 197–98, 217, 222
Dobbins, Cornelia, 140, **141**
Dockery, Octavia, 218
Dorsey, Richard, 33
Douglass, Frederick, 65, 118–19
Doyle, Chesney Blankenstein, 13, 239–41, 323n28
Drake, Moseley J. P., 261
Du Bois, W. E. B., 36, 145
Dunbar, Annie, 259
Dunbar, Mary Conway, 42
Duncan, Annie Rose Quitman, 27, 42
Duncan, Stephen, 255
Dunleith (estate), 7, 35, 166, **256**, 257–59

Earl, Isaac N., 29
Eastman, George, 120
Eastman Kodak Company, 120, 125
Elgin (estate), 258–59
Ellicott, Andrew, 267
Elliott, William St. John, 257
Elms, The (estate), 158, 166, 258–59, 261

Elms Court (estate), 189, 208, 244, 260–61, 260
Emancipation celebrations, 48, 50–51, 63, 68–69, 292n9
Emancipation Proclamation, 51
Evans, Gladys Crail, 156–57

Fabre, Genevieve, 49
Faust, Drew Gilpin, 181–82
Ferry, Marion Kelly, 190–91
First Union Republican Club, 52
Fitzhugh, Agnes, 34, 36
Fitzhugh, Nelson, 34, 36–37, 46
Fitzhugh, Robert, 36, 46, 63, 66
Forks of the Road slave market, 21, 63, 122, 226, 229, 231–35, 240, 249–50, 322n17
Fort Rosalie, 227, 238
Foster, Allison H., 66, 93
Foster, Kate, 26, 99, 101
Fourth of July, 48–49, 58–61, 65, 72, 79, 82–85
Frank, Henry, 31, 96
Frank, Melanie, 98, 101
free people of color, 6–9, 32, 35–37, 39–40, 51, 56, 61–63, 65–68, 71, 78, 93, 117–18, 133, 142, 233–34
Freedman's Bureau, 34, 44, 52, 54, 55, 78
Freedman's Savings Bank, 34
Freemasonry, 73–75, 86, 87–95, 102, 299n40; decline of, 97, 103–4, 300n70
Friends of Our Riverfront, 242

garden clubs, 125, 169; origins of, 310n40
gardening: of the home, 168–69; popularity of, 169, 187; publications, 169
Gandy, Joan, 151, 229
Gandy, Thomas, 12, 106, 150–51, 176–77, 229
Gardner, Burleigh, 205
Gardner, Mary, 205–6
Gaylord, Harriet, 22
Geddes, Mary Louise, 193
Geisenberger, Wilfred, 214
Geisenberger, Wolfe, 31
General Federation of Women's Clubs, 220
Gibbs, William H., 64–65
Glenwood, 218

Gloucester, **155**, 262–63, **262**
"Goat Castle" murder, 218–19
Gone with the Wind, 196, 199, 201, 269
Good Samaritans, 52, 60–62
Grady, Henry, 95
Grafton, Elodie Rose, 174
Grafton, Jennie, 174
Grafton, Kirby W., 174
Grafton, Molly, 174
Grafton, Thomas, 172–74
Grand Army of the Republic, 64, 69–70, 70
Grand Pre, Don Carlos de, 265
Great Migration, 142
Green Leaves (estate), 158, 178–79, **262**, 263, 265
Grennell, Darryl, 242
Gresham, Matilda, 25–26
Gresham, Walter, 25, 281
Gurney, Henry, 108–9, 134
Gwin, Annie, 277, 318n4

HABS, 253
Harding, Lyman, 255
Hardy, A. M., 79, 297nn18–19
Harris, Blanche, 41
Harris, Charles, 37
Harris, Joel Chandler, 4, 121, 199
Haviland, Laura, 45
Hearts of Dixie, 196
"Heaven Bound," 194
Henderson, Ella, 113
Henderson, Ellen, 98
Henderson, John, 259
heritage tourism, 6, 15, 196
Historic Architectural Building Survey, 253
Historic Jefferson College, 83–84, 230, 234
Historic Natchez Conference, 243
Historic Natchez Foundation, 226, 228–31, 234, 238, 244–45, 247, 249, 321n5
Historic Natchez Tableaux, 239–42
historical memory: black contemporary, 68–69, 246–49; black women, 58, 65, 115, 246–47; Civil War, 23–24, 27, 85–86, 100, 107, 169; contested, 6–7, 223–24, 234, 241–42, 246, 248, 250; critical, 250–51;

definition of, 248n6; evolution of in Natchez, 4–6, 19, 46–47, 225–33 241–42, 246–51; free blacks, 35, 61, 233–34; post-emancipation black, 49–51, 53, 55–61, 63, 65, 70–72, 107, 115–16, 150; selective white, 23, 45–47, 85–86, 107, 123, 138, 140, 169, 189–91, 194, 209, 248; white postwar, 81, 123; white women, 5–6, 100, 123, 140, 169, 178, 181, 221, 223–24, 248, 251
Hoggatt, Anthony, 32, 111–12
Hoggatt, William, 111
Holy Family Parish, 36–37, 112
hooks, bell, 110, 116
Hope Farm (estate), 174, 188, **264**, 265, 311n59
House on Ellicott's Hill, **266**, 267
Houston, Jeremy, 226, 239
Howell, Varina, 162, 255
Hunt, David, 269
Hussey, George St. Clair, 52

Iles, Greg, 239
imperialism: advertising, 132–33; southern, 131; tourism, 133
Ingraham, Joseph Holt, 30

Jackson Clarion-Ledger, 158, 180
Jacobs, H. P., 52–54, 66
Jefferson College, 83–84, 230, 234, 298n34
Jenkins, John, 259
Jennings, Ralph, 13, 207
Jim Crow, 6, 16, 35, 102, 107, 119–20; laws, 103; practices, 167; rhetoric, 225
Johnson, Anna, 36
Johnson, Jane, 273
Johnson, William, 77–78, 82, 233–34, 297n12; House, 226–27, 233
Johnston, Frances Benjamin, 124–26, 134; lantern slides, 312n69; photographs, 253–54, 260, 264, 268, 276, 278, 280, 282; preservation of work, 304n48

Kane, Harnett, 176
Kastor, Louis, 111–13
Keen, Ann, 40
Kellogg, Alma, 177, 180, **186**, 189, 217–18, 261

Kelly, Ethel Moore, 163–65, 180, 217; "Battle of the Hoopskirts," 220, 223; Melrose 273
Kelly, George M., 163–65, 180; "Battle of the Hoopskirts," 220, 223; Melrose, 275, 309n29, 319n33, 319–20nn35–37
Kendall, Mary Louise, 15, 172, 179, 189, 277
Kendall, William, 208, 277
Ker, John, 239
Kimmel, Michael, 87–88
King's Tavern, 162, 166, 180
Kipling, Rudyard, 128–29
Knights of Pythias, 93, 295n64
Knights Templars, 73–74, 89–90, 92, 103
Koontz, George W., 81, 90, 96, 263, 265
Ku Klux Klan, 225

Ladies Home Journal, 124–25
Lamdin, Mary, **186**
Landrieu, Mitch, 250, 320n1
Langston, John, 54–56, 64, 293n26
Lanneau, Emmie Martin, 101
Lanneau, K. Palmer, 100
Lansdowne, **268**, 269
Lansdowne Park, 74
Laub, Harriet, 162
Learned, Rufus F., 96
LeCand, F. J. V., 100
Lind, Jenny, 74
Linden, **268**, 269
Little, Eliza, 280
Little, Peter, 279–80
Litts, Palmer, 40–41
Logan, John A., 64
Longwood, 29, 49, 54, 59–60, 165, 180, **270**, 271, 273
Lost Cause, 4–6, 75, 80, 83, 86, 119–21, 129; feminization of, 99, 101; ideology, 91, 102, 122, 151, 169, 191, 194; imagery, 181; memorialization of, 26, 100, 225
Lovell, Antonia Quitman, 42–43
Lowenburg, Isaac, 31, 96
Lynch, John R., 35–36, 43–44, 66–67, 142, 240; influence with SCC, 290n8; later years, 306n70
Lynch, William H., 35

MacNeil, Anne, 243–45
Macrery, Andrew, 147
Macrery, Milberry Dickinson, 147
Magnolia Vale, **156**, 157
Marks, Emma, **186**
Marsh, Annie Rumble, 281
Marshall, George M., 81, 269
Marshall, Levin R., 279
Marshall, Theodora Britton, 156–57, 182, 204, 279
Martin, Margaret Conner, 18–19, 24–26, 100, 179, 277
Martin, William T., 18–19, 24, 35, 62, 78–79, 81, 84, 96, 100, 166, 179, 277, 298n23
Mazique, Alexander, **116**, 117, 119
McCary, William, 63
McDowell, Jeanne Minor, 172
McKittrick, Carlotta, 261
McKittrick, David, 208, 261
McMillen, Neil, 66–68, 102–3
McMurran, John T., 273
Meloney, Marie Mattingly, 187
Melrose (estate), 163–66, 180, 190–91, 197–99, 202, 217, 220, 222, 226–27, 230–31, 244, **272**, 273, 309n29
Merrill, Ayres P., 261
Merrill, Jennie, 218
Military Reconstruction Acts, 51–52
Miller, J. Balfour, 174, 311n58
Miller, Katherine, 3, 15, 158–59, 161–62, 169, 172, **173**, 174–78, 184, **186**, 187, 210, 311n58; "Battle of the Hoopskirts," 212, 217, 220–21; Hope Farm, 265; *Natchez of Long Ago and the Pilgrimage*, 182, 188–89; Pilgrimage mission, 224; Stanton Hall preservation, 283
Miller, Mimi, 202, 228–29, 232, 244
Miller, Patrick, 83
Miller, Ron, 228
Minor, Katharine, 25, 27–28, 94, 98–100, 172, 288n36
Minor, Stephen, 245–46, 253
missionaries, 39–40, 51
Mississippi: economy, 154; garden clubs, 169

Mississippi Builder, 175
Mississippi Cooperative Benefit Association, 112
Mississippi Department of Archives and History, 230, 238, 245, 321n5
Mississippi State Board of Development, 175, 187
Mitchell, Margaret, 153
Monmouth (estate), 7, 42, 157, 166, 212, **274**, 275, 277
Monteigne (estate), 24, 158, 166, 179, 208, **276**, 277
Monticello, 201
Montieth, Laura, 98
Moore, Edith Wyatt, 182
Moritz, Hartman, 161
Morris, George, 66
Morrison, Virginia, 176
Moses, Clara Lowenburg, 304n44
Mount Vernon, 201
Murray, Elizabeth Dunbar, 191–92

Natchez, Community Alliance of, 231–32
Natchez, homes and gardens: antebellum era, 7, 154; antebellum homes, 14–15, 135, 154–56, 158, 188–89, 202, 209, 316n141; gardens, 15, 155–58, 161, 164, 167–68, 187–88, 209; homeowners, 153; lantern slides of, 312n69; photographs of, 252–82; tours, 226, 230–31, 244–46, 249, 314n108
Natchez, MS: amateur historians, 12, 182–84; athletic competitions, 83; "Battle of the Hoopskirts," 210–19, 221–24; Black and Blue Re-enactment, 234; blacks in (*see* blacks, in Natchez); business growth, 95–97; churches, 7, 37, 75, 113; city beautification, 175; civil rights movement, 232–33, 237–38; Civil War, 17–22, 26–27; Civil War burials, 286n13; Civil War sesquicentennial, 229, 242; commerce, 30–32; Confederate monuments, 225, 248–50; Confederate Pageant, 213, 239–40; consumer culture, 106; Democratic Party, 66–67, 71, 79, 82;

Index

economic decline, 172, 179–80, 208–9, 247; economy, 154–56, 172, 248; fire companies, 95; Fourth of July celebrations, 48–49, 58–61, 65, 72, 79, 82–84; fraternal associations, 73, 76, 86–87, 90, 94–96, 102, 104, 110; fusion politics, 66–68, 71; garden clubs, 5, 13–14, 158, 162, 164–65, 169, 174–77, 179–80, 182, 184–85, **186**, 187–88, 192–93, 204, 209, 214, 240–41, 248, 251; gardens (*see* Natchez, homes and gardens); gender relations, 94–95, 136; Great Depression, impact of, 7, 15, 153–55, 158, 163–64, 170, 172, 179, 182, 184, 196, 201, 208, 253; guidebooks, 204; heritage tourism, 6, 15, 195, 201–2, 205, 225–26, 229–31, 238, 241–42, 247–48, 250–51; historic preservation of, 121, 169, 178–79, 229, 242, 246–47; historical sketches, 181–84; house museums, 233, 245; ideal homes, 187–89, 205; industry, 95–96; Jews, 31, 90, 155, 299n50; kinship ties, 148, 183–84, 222; Kirmess, 74, 122–23, 304nn43–44; Ku Klux Klan, 248; legal records, 228; Mardi Gras celebrations, 104; martial culture, 73, 75–86, 89–90, 99–100, 102, 298n22; Masonic orders, 73–75, 86–95, 97, 102–4, 299n40, 299n50; Masonic Temple, **104**; May 30 parade, 69, 72; Pilgrimage (*see* Natchez Pilgrimage); memoirs, 121–22, 139; Memorial Day, 99–100, 169; merchants, 20, 30–32, 68, 90, 95–96, 155; monuments, 7, 100, 121; Native Americans, 227, 229, 238; pageants, 6, 122–23, 191–95, 213, 240–42; parades and commemorations, 6–7, 48–49, 64, 69; paramilitary groups, 5, 7, 74–80, 82–83, 85–86, 89, 92–93, 95, 97–98, 100, 104, 110, 297nn18–19, 298n22; popular amusements, 7, 74–75, 94–95, 97–98, 104, 106, 119, 121, 123, 125; poverty, 247; public spaces, 14, 18–19, 30, 48, 57, 136, 232, 249; race relations, 135–36, 141, 151, 204–5, 244; racial demographics, 9, 30; racial hierarchy, 111, 127–28, 248;

racial reconciliation conference, 238; racism, 234, 247–48; railroads, 95–96; Reconstruction (*see* Natchez post–Civil War); refugee camps, 7, 21–22, 30; Republican Party, 67, 79–80; scholarship, 321n5; schools, 7, 39, 113, 248; segregation, 102–3, 205, 227; shops, 31; social problems, 247; sociological study of, 205; teachers, 39–41; theater, 74–75, 120, 123, 130; tourism, 153, 157–58, 185, 198, 201, 226, 239, 242, 251, 321n9; tourists, 156, 162, 185, 208–9, 215, 226, 230–31, 245; travelogues, 197; Tricentennial celebration, 229, 235–39; Unionism, 23–28, 288n27; urban disorder, 54–55; Victorian homes, 155; vigilance committee, 78, 81; voting rights, 237

Natchez Association for the Preservation of Afro-American Culture, 230

Natchez Club, 97

Natchez Confederate Memorial Association, 92, 98–101, 110, 121, 169, 171, 172, 174

Natchez Cotton and Merchants Exchange, 97

Natchez Courthouse Records Project, 12, 226, 228, 287n25, 321n5

Natchez Daily Courier: on armed black men, 44; on black Good Will Fire Company, 63; on Decoration Day 1871, 65

Natchez Democrat, 53, 55, 61–62, 68, 83, 84–85, 93, 99; on "Battle of the Hoopskirts," 213, 216, 217–18; on black fire companies, 63; on black Fourth of July celebrations, 1887; on black jurors, 32; on civil rights movement, 237; on commemoration of Confederate monument, 99; on Decoration Day 1874, 66; on Decoration Day 1896, 68; on election of 1870, 67; on Emancipation celebrations, 63; on Fort Rosalie opening, 238; on Freemason members, 95; on Good Samaritans, 60; on Good Will Fire Company members, 63; on Historic Natchez Tableaux, 241;

on Independence Day, 85; on infantry competitions, 83; on July 4, 1867, celebration, 48, 293n25; on Langston's address, 55; on Memorial Day 1912, 101; on men's clubs, 97; on Natchez Trails, 232; on Pilgrimage's early years, 159–60; on popular amusements, 74–75; on "Portraits of Black Natchez," 150–51; on registered voters, 42; on Republicans, 53; on United Daughters of the Confederacy, 100, 169; on Visitor's Center, 229; on Winston, 62

Natchez District, 285n9

Natchez Fencibles, 82, 275

Natchez Garden Club, 3, 15, 153, 168–69, 175, 177–80, 199, 239, 241, 261; "Battle of the Hoopskirts," 211–19, 222, 241–42; beautification campaigns, 174; civic volunteerism ideals, 220; employment of members, 310n47; licensing deals, 13; members who remained loyal during split, 317n1; membership, 170–72, **186**, 187, 220, 269, 275, 277; mission, 220–23; pageant, 248; passion for history, 181; preservation projects, 266–67; sociological study, 205–6; United Daughters of the Confederacy, cooperation with, 321n48

"Natchez History Minutes," 236, 323n19

Natchez Indians historic site, 230

"Natchez Legends and Lore," 236, 237

Natchez Masonic Hall, 73

Natchez Museum of African American History and Culture, 13, 150, 230, 249

Natchez National Cemetery, 63, 69, 294n53

Natchez National Historical Park, 227, 229–31, 235–36, 238, 244, 247, 249

Natchez People's Party, 295n67

Natchez photography, 105–8, 110, 123, 126, 128, 131, 133, 136–37, 139, 146–47, 150, 151, 232; amateur, 120, 126–28, 134, 141; antebellum homes, 125, 157, 158; camera clubs, 126; exhibits, 150–51, 229; female, 120; former slaves, 148; outdoors, 109, 139–40; portraits, 109–10, 114–18, 121, 130; servants, 150; studios, 109, 111, 114–16, 119

Natchez Pilgrimage, 3–4, 6, 15, 153, 155, 227, 240–41; accommodations, 161–62; advertising, 159, 180, 197–98, 216–17, 222; audience reception, 202–3, 205–6, 209; "Battle of the Hoopskirts," 210–19, 221–24, 318n5; black involvement in, 194; celebrity guests, 198–99; challenge to modernity, 203–5; commercialization of, 180, 220, 222, 224; costumes, 166; early years, 161–62, 176–77, 191–92; expenses, 217, 222; founders, 172; Great Depression impact on, 170, 201, 208–9; guidebooks, 204; home improvement campaigns, 160, 168–69; home tours, 7, 168, 178–79, 185, 188–91, 206, 211–13, 215–16, 230–31, 253, 269, 321n8; homeowners, 163, 207–8, 211–12, 215, 218, 220–21, 223, 226; homes, 161–62, 165–67, 172, 175, 208, 222–23; hosts, 166, 207; journalists, 166–67, 176, 184–85, 202; lantern slides, 177, 312n69; litigation, 214–19; map from 1934, 160; media coverage, 202–4, 208, 211–18, **219**; message, 205, 220; mission, 224; Old South narrative, 205; origins of, 158–59, 307n2; origins of name, 308n16; pageants, 7, 13, 192–95; paid employment, 221; portrayals of blacks, 181, 190, 197, 209, 246; product licensing, 197–98, 315n128; publicity, 159, 161, 166, **167**, 177, 181–82, 184–85, 189, 191, 198–99, 204–5; racialized imagery, use of, 190–91; response of blacks, 206–7; revenues, 163, 210–12, 218–19, 223; souvenirs, 206; tearooms, 162, 178–79, 313n76; tour guides, 160; tourists, 161–67, 185, 191, 202–3, 208, 213–15; volunteers, 160–61; during World War II, 218

Natchez post–Civil War: Confederate veterans, 64, 80–82, 85–86, 90, 92, 98–99, 137; demographics, 20, 30; economy, 8, 24, 30; fusion politics, 66–68; national

reunification, 64, 70–71, 85, 93; poverty, 9, 27–28; racial tensions, 42–44, 46, 50, 62, 71, 78–79, 102–3; social climate, 9, 27, 30, 46, 120; teachers, 22–23, 39–41; Union occupation, 7, 9, 14, 17–22, 24–32, 42–43, 52, 73; vigilantes, 45, 78, 81; violence, 44–45, 56, 76–79, 85
Natchez Public School, 113
Natchez Rifle Corps, 77, 82
Natchez Rosalie Grand Commandery, 90–91
Natchez slavery, 18–19, 131, 147–48, 156, 189–91, 226–27, 229–35, 238, 243; executions, 78, 147–48, 243; history, 245–46, 249–50; market, 7, 21; narratives, 148; patrols, 78; portrayal of in home tours, 244–45; quarters, 245–47, 255; resistance to, 243; slaveholders, 147–48, 172, 180; traders, 233–44
Natchez Trace, 12; Association, 183; Parkway, 147, 162, 183–84, 196, 306n73
Natchez Trails, 231–32
Natchez Tri-Weekly Democrat: on L. D. Allen, 52; on black fire companies, 63; on black jurors, 32; on Emancipation celebrations, 63; on July 4, 1867, celebration, 56
Natchez Visitor Center, 229, 249
Natchez Weekly Democrat: on commemoration of Confederate monument, 100; on influence of black women, 58; on Jacobs, 53; on popular amusements, 74–75
Natchez Women's Club, 168
National Geographic, 177
National Park Service, 226–28, 230–31, 233–37, 243
New Deal, 209
New National Era, on Douglass speech, 295
New Negro movement, 119, 303n33
New Orleans Republican: on L. D. Allen, 53; on July 4, 1867, celebration, 55, 57, 60, 292n23; on Langston speech, 56; on Natchez Union League, 52, 54–60
New Orleans Times-Picayune, 216

New South, 93, 95–97, 129, 154, 175, 178
New York Times, 166–67, 200
Nomelli, Sheryl, 289n56
Norman, Earl, 134, 152, 157, 158, 217, 253
Norman, Henry, 12–13, 74, 105–11, 114–20, 123, 130–31, 134, 141–42, 150–52, 232, 240; camera, 302n8; studio, 301n2
Nutt, Haller, 25, 271, 273, 288n37
Nutt, Julia, 13, 25, 28–29, 43, 46, 49, 54, 94, 100, 271, 273; July 4, 1867, celebration, 292n23; Southern Claims Commission, 290n8
Nutt, Prentiss, 13, 28, 43–44, 46, 290n8

Oakland (estate), 25, 172
Old South, 3–4; imagery, 132–33, 181; narrative, 202, 205
Oliver, Nola Nance, 204–5
Outing, an Illustrated Magazine of Recreation, 124

Page, Thomas Nelson, 4, 121, 199
Paradise, Ann, 323n28
Parchman Ordeal, 237–38, 323n22
Parker, Cynthia, 323n22
Parker, Edna, **186**
Parsons, Frederick, 52, 54
Peck, John, 66
Peterson, Shane, 322n18
photography, 6, 105–6; advertisements, 125, **126**; albums, 121, 127–28, 133; amateur, 120–22, 124, 127, 141, 145, 150; antebellum homes, 125; appropriation of subject, 148; camera clubs, 124; cameras, 125–26; as democratizing experience, 118–19; exhibits, 150; former slaves, 148; garden, 125; as historical memory, 107–8; Kodak Girls, 124–25; as popular amusement, 125, 145; popularity of, 121, 124; portraits, 114, 150; postcards, 133–34, 145; post-Reconstruction era, 108; women, 124, 125, 127. *See also* Natchez photography
Pierce, Abner, 23
Pilgrimage, history of term, 284n3. *See also* Natchez Pilgrimage

Pilgrimage Garden Club, 15, 176–78, 180, 239, 241, 261; "Battle of the Hoopskirts," 211–19, 222; homeowner expenses, 222; membership, 220, 277; mission, 221, 223; preservation work, 283

Plantation School literature, 4, 121, 143

Planter aristocracy, 9, 226, 240, 244–45, 261; during 1930s, 166–67, 171–74, 182–83, 207–9; domestic relationships, 135, 139; impact of Civil War, 20, 23–29; interactions with black elites, 62, 233; kinship ties, 148; male gender crisis, 76; militia groups, 78, 81, 148; post–Civil War, 32, 151, 155–56, 171–74, 180; racial ideology, 151, 153; women, 23–29, 172–76, 182–83

Pollard, Randall, 64, 295n60

Poppenheim, Laura, 129

"Portraits of Black Natchez," 150–51

Prentiss Club, 97

Pyle, Ernie, 153, 155, 176, 184–85, 202, 206, 208, 216

Quitman, John, 42, 87, 157, 275, 299n42

Quitman, Rose, 27, 157

Raines, Howell, 135

Ramsey, Fanny, 137, **138**

Randall, Clarence, 69

Ransom, Thomas E. G., 21

Ravenna, 183–84

Reber, Thomas, 96

Republican Party, 37, 52–53

Revels, Hiram, 65–66, 232, 240

Rhythm Night Club fire, 238, 321n10

Rhythm Night Club Memorial Museum, 231

Richmond (estate), 182, **278**, 279

Robinson, Ibby, 194

Roosevelt, Eleanor, 206

Roosevelt, Franklin, 209

Roosevelt, Theodore, 83

Rosalie (estate), 26, 279, **280**, 313n88

Rose, Thomas, 178, 312n74

Rose Hill Baptist Church, 38, 51

Routh, Job, 257

Russell, Charles, 112–13

Rutherford, Mildred Lewis, 304n51

Ryan, Mary, 54

Saint Catherine Street, 111–14; Trail, 231–33, 242

Saragosa (estate), 12

Sargent, George Washington, 263

Sargent, Winthrop, 263

Schwartz, C. T., 81

Schwartz, John C., 31

Scott, Bud, 74–75, 139, **140**, 160, 240

Second Creek conference, 228, 243

Second Creek uprising, 56, 78, 81, 147, 244; Vigilance Committee, 298n24

"See America First" campaign, 196

segregation, 102–3

Sharpe, Lucinda, **140**, 149

Shaw, Ed, 139, **140**

Shields, Ellen, 21, 29

Shields, Gabriel Benoist, 29

Shields, Joseph, 45–46

Sims, Alice, 273

slavery. *See* blacks in Natchez; Natchez slavery

Sloan, Samuel, 271

Smith, Charles, 105, **106**

So Red the Rose, 201

South, southern: advertising themes, 197–98; black laborers, 191; booster campaigns, 175; female empowerment, 219; gardens, 157; gender roles, 185; heritage tourism, 202, 219; historic preservation, 178; households, 135–36, 139, 183–84; ideal home, 188–89; kinship ties, 135–36, 183; lynching, 203; "mammy" reverence, 149; media coverage, 199–200, 203–4, 316nn132–33; memorialization of, 170, 219; movies, 196–97; popular culture, 153; race relations, 135, 141, 200, 209; racialized humor, 144–45; racialized imagery, 153; railroads, 154; reunification with North, 170; sociological studies, 205; tourism, 159, 196, 199–200, 202; Unionism, 288n27; white mastery, 148

Southern Claims Commission: black claimants, 18, 22–23, 33–34, 52, 287n18; summary of claims, 286n17; white claimants, 28–29, 43–44, 98–99
Standard Literary and Social Club, 97
Stanton, Aaron, 81
Stanton, David, 259, 261
Stanton, Frederick, 81, 178, 281, 283
Stanton Hall, 7, 15, 177–78, 180, 202, 281, **282**, 283, 312n72
Stauffer, John, 110
Stewart, Robert Livingston, 70, 120
Stewart, Virginia, 217
Stewart, William, 120
Stratton, Joseph B., 75, 84
Stryker, Hattie, 22
Sullivan, Tima, 217
Surget, Frances, 261
Surget, Jacob, 243
Surget, James, 81, 243, 261
Sussman, Warren, 200

tableaux vivants, 122, 191–92, 304n43, 315n110
Taylor, A. Jane, 113–14
Trachtenburg, Alan, 108
Turner, Eliza, 275
Twain, Mark, 95, 223

Under-the-Hill, 31, 54, 77
Union League, 37, 44, 49, 52–55, 58, 60–63, 66, 69, 73
Unionism, 23–28, 288n27
United Confederate Veterans, 101
United Daughters of the Confederacy, 5, 100–101, 104, 129, 169, 170–72, 304n51

Wall Street Baptist Church, 41
Walworth, Douglas, 103
Wayne, Michael, 24
Weeks, Levi, 255
Welsh, Lizzie, 39
Welty, Eudora, 154
Whipple, George, 39
White, Darrell, 237

white churches, 75
white lower class, 25
white responses to Reconstruction, 42
white vigilantes, 45, 56
white men: Civil War experiences, 29; fraternal associations, 5, 7, 73, 75–76, 86–87, 90–91, 94–95, 97, 102, 104, 110; gender crisis, 27, 76; identity, 75, 83–84, 88; leisure, 75, 97, 104; social clubs, 97, 104. *See also* Natchez planters
white supremacy, 4, 6, 57, 76, 80, 82, 91–93, 102–3, 128–29, 133, 135, 149, 167
white women: as businesswomen, 185–86; civic volunteerism, 180–81, 183–84, 223; Civil War experiences, 25–29; clubs, 5, 7, 168–71, 177, 180–81, 183–85, **186**, 187–89, 191–93, 204–5, 209–10, 212–13, 216, 219, 220–24, 240–41, 251; elite, 134, 171; employment of, 182–83, 221; garden clubs, 14, 169, 177, 185, 193; gender roles, 185–86; as homemakers, 188–89; leisure activities, 98, 104, 181; patriotic organizations, 99–101, 104, 129, 169–72, 183, 281; racial relationships, 129; self-identities, 181–82; writers, 182–84, 204, 313n82. *See also* Natchez planters
Williams, Jeremiah M. P., 66–67, 71
Willis, Deborah, 110
Wilson, Andrew, 281
Wilson, Ann Eliza Bowman., 26, 288n29
Wilson, Woodrow, 151
Winston, Louis J., 35, 37, 62, 111–12, 294n52
Wood, Robert H., 36–37, 61–62, 111
Wood, Wilson, 52–53
Woodward, Ellen Sullivan, 175–76, 187
WPA: American Guide series, 182; Federal Writer's Project, 182; Historical Records project, 182; slave narratives project, 182
Wright, S. G., 40–41

Young, Stark, 153, 201
Yuhl, Stephanie, 154

Zion AME Baptist Chapel, 13, 36–38, 51, 112–13, 160, 232

Credit: Suzy VanDyke

ABOUT THE AUTHOR

Susan T. Falck is executive director of Rancho Camulos Museum, a National Historic Landmark in Ventura County, California. She taught US history at California State University, Northridge. As an alumnus of the Natchez Courthouse Records Project, she helped process hundreds of nineteenth-century Natchez legal records and contributed research and editorial content to PBS websites on the history of slavery and Jim Crow.

www.ingramcontent.com/pod-product-compliance
Lightning Source LLC
Chambersburg PA
CBHW030604230426
43661CB00053B/1831